From

D0373282

Beijing

Here's what the critics say about Frommer's:

"Amazingly easy to use. Very portable, very complete."
—Booklist

♦

"The only mainstream guide to list specific prices. The Walter Cronkite of guidebooks—with all that implies."
—Travel & Leisure

♦

"Complete, concise, and filled with useful information."
—New York Daily News

♦

"Hotel information is close to encyclopedic."
—Des Moines Sunday Register

Other Great Guides for Your Trip:

Frommer's China: The 50 Most Memorable Trips

Frommer's Hong Kong

Frommer's®

1st
Edition

Beijing

by J. D. Brown

IDG Books Worldwide, Inc.
An International Data Group Company
Foster City, CA • Chicago, IL • Indianapolis, IN • New York, NY

About the Author

J.D. Brown has lived and worked in China and has written about China as a literary traveler, a travel writer, and a guidebook author. His work has appeared in such diverse publications as the *New York Times,* the *Washington Post,* the *Michigan Quarterly Review, Islands,* and *Newsday.* He is also the author of *Frommer's China: The 50 Most Memorable Trips.* When he is not traveling in the Far East, he lives in Eugene, Oregon.

IDG Books Worldwide, Inc.

An International Data Group Company
919 E. Hillsdale Blvd.
Suite 400
Foster City, CA 94404

Find us online at **www.frommers.com**

ISBN 0-02-862960-4
ISSN 1520-5568

Editor: Suzanne Roe Jannetta
Production Editor: Mark Enochs
Design by Michele Laseau
Staff Cartographers: John DeCamillis, Roberta Stockwell
Photo Editor: Richard Fox
Page Creation by John Bitter, Ellen Considine & Pete Lippincott

Special Sales

For general information on IDG Books Worldwide's books in the U.S., please call our Consumer Customer Service department at 1-800-762-2974. For reseller information, including discounts, bulk sales, customized editions, and premium sales, please call our Reseller Customer Service department at 1-800-434-3422.

Manufactured in the United States of America

5 4 3 2 1

Contents

List of Maps

An Invitation to the Reader

In researching this book, we discovered many wonderful places—hotels, restaurants, shops, and more. We're sure you'll find others. Please tell us about them, so we can share the information with your fellow travelers in upcoming editions. If you were disappointed with a recommendation, we'd love to know that, too. Please write to:

Frommer's Beijing
IDG Travel
1633 Broadway
New York, NY 10019

An Additional Note

Please be advised that travel information is subject to change at any time—and this is especially true of prices. We therefore suggest that you write or call ahead for confirmation when making your travel plans. The authors, editors, and publisher cannot be held responsible for the experiences of readers while traveling. Your safety is important to us, however, so we encourage you to stay alert and be aware of your surroundings. Keep a close eye on cameras, purses, and wallets, all favorite targets of thieves and pickpockets.

What the Symbols Mean

✪ Frommer's Favorites

Our favorite places and experiences—outstanding for quality, value, or both.

The following abbreviations are used for credit cards:

AE	American Express	ER	EnRoute
BC	Bankcard	EU	Eurocard
CB	Carte Blanche	JCB	Japan Credit Bank
DC	Diners Club	MC	MasterCard
DISC	Discover	V	Visa

Find Frommer's Online

Arthur Frommer's Budget Travel Online (**www.frommers.com**) offers more than 6,000 pages of up-to-the-minute travel information—including the latest bargains and candid, personal articles updated daily by Arthur Frommer himself. No other Web site offers such comprehensive and timely coverage of the world of travel.

The Best of Beijing

Beijing is China's preeminent city, hosting more travelers than any other city in China—and for good reason, since no other city offers so many marvels, ancient and modern. Where else in China (or in the world, for that matter) can you gorge yourself on crispy Peking duck, walk the Great Wall like a modern sentinel, crisscross the haunting expanses of Tiananmen Square, and freely explore the splendors of the Forbidden City, all in a day or two?

While serving as the capital for imperial dynasties from the Ming to the Qing, Beijing has had its pick of the empire's glorious creations, many of which it has guarded over the centuries. Beijing was the capital in the 13th century, when Kublai Khan built his palace there and Marco Polo first paid a visit. It reigned supreme from the 15th century, when the Ming rulers built the Forbidden City, to the 18th century, when the Manchu rulers built the Summer Palace. Beijing continued as the capital up to 1923, when the last of China's emperors was evicted from the Forbidden City. It was reanointed as the city of China's rulers in 1949, when Mao Zedong declared the establishment of the People's Republic of China. No city is more important in recent Chinese history, and more of that history is on display here than anywhere else.

The Forbidden City still stands at the center of Beijing, its golden tiled roofs and vast white courtyards glittering in the sun like an ancient giant's crown. The Summer Palace has survived, too, at the northwest edge of the city, as has the Temple of Heaven to the south, along with dozens of delicate monuments, old temples, and the courtyard houses in little alleyways (called *hutongs*) that were once the hallmark of ordinary city life.

Add to this Beijing's and China's number-one attraction: the Great Wall, Asia's answer to the pyramids and China's paramount monument to its romantic and turbulent past. As the popular saying has it, "You haven't been to China if you haven't stood on the Great Wall."

Beijing's temples, parks, and historic sites all sing wonderfully and powerfully of the dream that was Old Cathay, but in the same hallowed space there's a new Beijing taking shape. Just outside the exquisite walls of Beijing's historic monuments, steel and concrete are steadily replacing silk and carved wood. This transition can be jarring. Beijing is transforming itself before our eyes—reborn as the capital of the most populous (and potentially most powerful) nation on Earth.

For some visitors, this reconstruction in the old capital is more a tragedy than a triumph, but the modern cityscape imparts to the city much of its energy. Construction projects tromp through this Beijing of the future like mechanical Godzillas, pounding antiquated neighborhoods into oblivion block by block. At dawn, the city parks are still filled with Beijingers sleepwalking through their old tai chi exercises, but the surrounding streets are now packed with millionaires as well as street sweepers, with Mercedes as well as bicycles, with enterprising touts as well as destitute beggars. Beijing today is two cities in one, a crazy scroll of skyscrapers and shacks, of Pizza Huts and teahouses, unwinding in a chaotic sprawl.

Beijing is in the midst of remaking itself on a scale that can scarcely be believed, and this rapid modernization against a backdrop of ancient treasures gives Beijing a wild East-West flavor that is exhilarating. It is a city with two faces, both of which are endlessly fascinating to the foreign traveler. With all its celebrated historical attractions, Beijing may well be the capital of China's past, but it is also the vibrant capital of China's future, and it is here that you can see in broad and determined strokes both what China has been and what it will become.

1 Frommer's Favorite Beijing Experiences

- **Walking Up and Down on the Great Wall.** The three most popular sections of the Great Wall (at Badaling, Mutianyu, and Simatai) make for spectacular treks and photo opportunities. All three were built during the Ming Dynasty (A.D. 1368–1644) and are located in beautiful mountain forests outside Beijing. Make time to walk beyond the crowds. The least-visited section, at Simatai, is the best, as it's the only one that remains largely untouched by modern restoration. See chapter 10, "The Great Wall & Other Side Trips from Beijing," for all the details on visiting the Wall.
- **Getting Lost in the Forbidden City.** The vast inner city of emperors and eunuchs for 500 years (A.D. 1423–1923), this is China's most impressive treasure house. It's best enjoyed on your own, rather than as part of a group tour, particularly at the small pavilions off the beaten path that house unusual royal treasures, from toys to clocks. See chapter 6, "Exploring Beijing," for details.
- **Crossing Tiananmen Square.** The very center of the People's Republic of China and the largest public square on Earth, Tiananmen reverberates with the ghosts of recent history—from the Great Hall of the People to the Monument to the People's Heroes, where students encamped before the TV cameras of the world in 1989. It's at its best at sunset, when the flag is lowered. See chapter 6 for details.
- **Meeting Chairman Mao.** At Chairman Mao's Mausoleum—located dead center in Tiananmen Square—visitors are allowed 60 seconds of uncanny silence in which to contemplate the last real emperor as he lies in state on a bed of granite, preserved for the ages. See chapter 6 for details.
- **Enjoying a Sunset at the Ancient Observatory.** This remnant of the city wall, an island in the busy downtown thoroughfare of Chang'an Avenue, houses 17th-century astronomical instruments on its roof. It's the perfect place from which to overlook the heart of the city and enjoy a sunset. See chapter 6 for details.
- **Lingering in the Temple of Heaven.** Explore the byways and whisper your name at Echo Wall. These and other nooks and paths are favored by locals for exercising, recreational sports, and family picnics. The park is an ideal place to see Beijingers at leisure. See chapter 6 for details.

- **Rowing Your Boat at the Summer Palace.** The most beautiful spot in Beijing has a Long Corridor painted with thousands of scenes of China and its mythology. After seeing the sights on land, you can rent a rowboat for a dreamy afternoon on Kunming Lake. See chapter 6 for details.
- **Picnicking at the Old Summer Palace.** Left in haunting ruins by Western armies in the 1860s, the Old Summer Palace is the perfect place for a picnic and a hike. The lakes, arched bridges, and crumbling pavilions recall the days of imperial majesty, when this park was reserved for the emperors and their courts. See chapter 6 for details.
- **Touring the Eastern Qing Tombs.** The Ming Tombs are still a major tourist stop on the way to the Great Wall, but at the Eastern Qing Tombs, a longer excursion, you'll find a more fascinating, less congested display that reveals how emperors and their concubines entered the afterlife in style. See chapter 10 for details on getting there and visiting the tombs.
- **Burning Incense in the Temples.** The Lama Temple is rated number one by tourists and foreign residents alike, and it has all the hallmarks of a typical large and active Buddhist temple, as well as some exotic (and erotic) aspects all its own. A livelier shrine more frequented by locals is the White Cloud Temple, where ancient beliefs and superstitions are alive and flourishing, the incense is always burning, and hundreds of Beijingers converge to kowtow and pray for a dozen different wishes (from good health to more wealth). See chapter 6 for details on Beijing's temples.
- **Attending Church with the Chinese.** Foreigners can now attend Christian services in the 19th- and early 20th-century churches and cathedrals of Beijing, where locals in increasing numbers pray and masses in Latin are still practiced. See chapter 6 for details.
- **Shadowboxing in the Parks.** Every morning before heading to work or school, thousands of Beijingers, ages 8 to 80, perform tai chi and other traditional, even more mysterious exercises—as well as Western ballroom dancing—in the city parks. It's a sight not to be missed. See chapter 6 for details on Beijing's parks.
- **Window Shopping on Wangfujing.** Beijing's top shopping street in the heart of the capital now offers everything from art galleries and scroll shops to wedding stores and chic boutiques. Aging department stores compete with state-of-the art shopping plazas. Plenty of McDonald's have sprung up (it's the new favorite with Chinese), but the best native fast food is served from stalls in the night market off Wangfujing (Donghuamen Yeshi). See chapter 8, "Shopping," for complete details on Beijing shopping.
- **Banqueting on Beijing Duck (Peking Duck).** It's worth sampling this signature dish of Northern China several times over, preferably with a group, to see what Beijing banqueting is all about. Plenty of restaurants serve it; a half-dozen specialize in it. See chapter 5, "Dining," for recommended places to try Beijing duck, and even tips on how to eat it.
- **Watching the Acrobats.** A night at the opera can become tedious, even if this is the best place in the world to experience the fabled Beijing Opera. More to Western tastes are the dazzling acrobatic shows in the capital, which feature juggling, contortionism, unicycling, chair-stacking, and plate-spinning. See chapter 9, "Beijing After Dark," for details.
- **Lingering in the Teahouses.** The teahouse tradition has staged a comeback in Beijing, with tea and snacks served in old teahouses to the accompaniment of singing, dancing, comedy, acrobatics, and magic. The best place to soak up Qing

China

KAZAKHSTAN

Lake Balkash

Karamay

Kulja

KYRGYZSTAN

r mqi

Kashgar

XINJIANG

Yumen

PAK.

Golmud

Xining

QINGHAI

Shiqunhe

XIZANG

SICHUAN

NEPAL

Lhasa

BHUTAN

INDIA

BANGLADESH

Kunming

YUNNAN

MYANMAR

Bay of Bengal

| 0 | | 500 Miles |
| 0 | | 500 Kilometers |

N

LAOS

THAILAND

RUSSIA

Lake Baikal

MONGOLIA

Hailar

HEILONGJIANG

Qiqihar

Harbin

NEI MONGOL

Changchun

JILIN

Shenyang

LIAONING

HEBEI

Hohhot

Beijing

NORTH
KOREA

Tianjin

Dalian

Yinchuan

Shijiazhuang

Yantai

SOUTH
KOREA

NINGXIA

Taiyuan

Jinan

Lanzhou

SHANXI

SHANDONG

Qingdao

GANSU

Xi'an

Zhengzhou

JIANGSU

Yellow
Sea

JAPAN

SHAANXI

HENAN

ANHUI

Nanjing

Chengdu

HUBEI

Hefei

Shanghai

Wuhan

Hangzhou

Chongqing

Nanchang

ZHEJIANG

East China
Sea

Changsha

JIANGXI

GUIZHOU

HUNAN

Fuzhou

Guiyang

FUJIAN

GUANGXI

GUANGDONG

Xiamen

TAIWAN

Nanning

Guangzhou

Hong Kong

VIETNAM

Haikou

South China
Sea

HAINAN

PHILIPPINES

Dynasty atmosphere is the Tian Qiao Happy Teahouse, where one's tea cup is always full and the intimate stage is filled with opera singers and acrobats. See chapter 9 for details.

- **Barhopping in Sanlitun.** The Sanlitun diplomatic district is home to more than 50 bars that cater equally to foreigners and locals. Many have live pop music running into the wee hours. See chapter 9 for the names of some recommended bars.
- **Going to Market.** Beijing's most famous street market, Silk Alley, is a tourist trap, but an interesting one, with a gauntlet of stalls offering the latest designer fashion knockoffs. The most fascinating market is held Sunday morning at dawn: the open-air Dirt Market (also called the Ghost Market), offering Beijing's wildest and most wide-ranging collection of collectibles, family heirlooms, Qing Dynasty furniture, and curios. See chapter 8 for the complete lowdown on Beijing's markets.
- **Exploring the Hutongs.** Don't miss a chance to explore the hutongs—the twisting alleyways in the courtyard neighborhoods of Old Beijing—whether on an organized tour by tricycle taxi or on your own by rented bicycle. See chapter 6 for details on joining an escorted tour of the hutongs.
- **Bicycling Through Old Beijing.** Although riding a bike in Beijing looks dangerous, with eight million riders in motion, it isn't difficult to get into the flow. This is a city meant for bike riding, the best means to explore the capital on one's own. See chapter 3, "Getting to Know Beijing," for tips on renting a bike and navigating Beijing on two wheels.

2 Best Hotel Bets

For complete hotel listings, see chapter 4, "Accommodations."

- **Best Hotel in China:** The honor goes to **China World Hotel,** 1 Jianguomenwai Dajie (☎ **800/942-5050,** or 010/6505-2266). No hotel in Beijing has perfect service, but China World comes closest, combining good help with excellent facilities, from its executive floors to its comprehensive nightly turndown service.
- **Best Hotel Business Center: China World** (see above) wins this one, too, keeping one step ahead of a competitive pack with a vast new full-service 24-hour business center, complete with a coffee station and a useful library.
- **Best Sister Hotel:** Stay at the highly efficient four-star **Traders Hotel Beijing,** 1 Jianguomenwai Dajie (☎ **800/942-5050,** or 010/6505-2277), and you can enjoy the five-star guest facilities at its sister hotel, the China World, located next door, at no extra charge. Traders Hotel is a favorite of foreign business travelers trying to save a nickel, all the while keeping the most prestigious address in town.
- **Best Resort Hotel:** Beijing has no resorts, but the one that comes closest is the **Movenpick Hotel Beijing,** Xiao Tianzhu Village, Capital Airport (☎ **800/ 344-6835** or 010/6456-5588). It's far enough from the city to have noticeably better air, more blue sky, and a resident camel, and it offers plenty of outdoor activities on its spacious grounds (including beach volleyball). This is where Beijing's resident foreigners come for summer barbecues and horseback riding.
- **Best Hotel Deal:** Once Beijing's best three-star hotel hands down, the **Holiday Inn Downtown,** 98 Beilishi Lu (☎ **800/465-4329** or 010/6833-8822), has been upgraded to four-star, but it's still a good deal. Although quite far from the true city center and located in a financial rather than a tourist center, this hotel is just a hop, skip, and jump from a subway entrance.

- **Best Hotel Lobby for Pretending You're a Foreign VIP:** With millions of dollars invested in its marble and its stately design, the **Beijing International Club Hotel,** 21 Jianguomenwai Dajie (☎ **800/325-3589** or 010/6460-6688), a new addition to the Luxury Collection by Sheraton, has the most spectacular lobby in Beijing. Celebs and VIPs settle in here for a casual drink, and the ballroom at the top of the winding marble staircase is a favorite for diplomatic receptions.
- **Best Hotel Lobby to People-Watch:** Any ex-pat who's worth watching or talking to will at some time or another pass through Beijing's liveliest reception area at the venerable **Jianguo Hotel,** 5 Jianguomenwai Dajie (☎ **800/223-5652** or 010/6500-2233). The lobby is a favorite gathering place for afternoon tea, and its Sunday buffets with classical music are a mainstay.
- **Best Hotel for Travelers with Disabilities:** More and more Beijing hotels have rooms equipped for travelers with disabilities, but the **Swissotel,** Hong Kong Macau Centre, Dong Si Shi Tiao Li Jiao Qiao (☎ **800/637-9477** or 010/6501-2288), devotes the entire fourth floor to such travelers with some of the best barrier-free architecture in Asia.
- **Best World Unto Itself:** This odd category fits to a tee the hotel city-state known as the **Holiday Inn Lido,** Jichang Lu, Jiangtai Lu (☎ **800/465-4329** or 010/6437-6688). As the largest Holiday Inn on earth, the Lido contains everything a foreign traveler or resident could desire in one vast complex, from shoe repair and a bowling alley to an international school and kindergarten.
- **Best Hotel Shuttle Bus:** The most frequent and wide-ranging free hotel bus service around sprawling Beijing is offered by the **Kempinski Hotel,** Lufthansa Centre, 50 Liangmaqiao Lu (☎ **010/6465-3388**), which is also the hotel most tailored to Germans and Europeans.
- **Best Hotel Room Decor:** Luxury hotel rooms around the world all begin to look alike, but the standout rooms at the **Radisson SAS Hotel,** 6A Beisanhuan Donglu (☎ **800/333-3333** or 010/6466-3388), come in no less than three sterling decors, all quite stylish: Chinese, art deco, and high-tech.
- **Best Hotel Art:** Beijing is drab, but the **Holiday Inn Crowne Plaza,** 48 Wangfujing Dajie (☎ **800/465-4329** or 010/6513-3388), with its nine-story atrium, is dedicated to contemporary Chinese artists with its own fine art gallery on the first floor and an art salon on the mezzanine.
- **Best Historic Hotel:** Beijing's only truly historic hotel, the **Beijing Hotel,** 33 Dongchangan Jie (☎ **010/6513-7766**), more than fits the bill. With cathedral ceilings and sweeping staircases, its three conjoined wings, built in 1917, 1954, and 1974, manage to keep alive some of the atmosphere of old Peking, despite recent renovations.
- **Best Views of the Forbidden City:** Boasting that fully half its rooms overlook the Forbidden City, the **Wangfujing Grand Hotel,** 57 Wangfujing Dajie (☎ **010/6522-1188**), is your best chance for a close-up view of the ancient palaces from the comfort of a five-star room.
- **Best Upscale Hotel Shopping Arcade:** The elegant **Palace Hotel,** 8 Jinyu Hutong, Wangfujing Dajie (☎ **800/262-9467** or 010/6512-8899), maintains several floors of exclusive designer-name shops (Armani, Cartier, Hermes)—it's a Beverly Hills outpost in the heart of the Chinese capital.
- **Best Hotel Garden:** Traditional gardens are seldom a feature of Beijing's modern hotels, but the **Shangri-La Beijing Hotel,** 29 Zizhuyuan Lu (☎ **800/942-5050** or 010/6841-2211), is a notable exception, with a romantic garden of arched bridges, pavilions, ponds, and resident rabbits and birds.

3 Best Dining Bets

For complete restaurant listings, see chapter 5, "Dining."

- **Best Beijing Duck:** The capital's most famous dish, roasted duck, is served up at a chain of duck restaurants. **Quanjude Kaoyadian,** nicknamed "Big Duck," at 32 Qianmen Dajie, Chongmen District (☎ 010/6511-2418), south of Tiananmen Square, is the largest and most elegant of the group.

- **Best Dim Sum:** For steamed buns and pastries in the Northern Chinese style, **Sihexuan,** Jinglun Hotel, 3 Jianguomenwai Dajie, Chaoyang District (☎ 010/6500-2266, ext. 8116), offers unsurpassed quality in a rustic but relaxed setting.

- **Best Imperial Cuisine:** Served in a courtyard compound in a hutong neighborhood, the imperial dishes at the **Li Family Restaurant,** 11 Yangfang, Deshēngmennei Dajie, Xicheng District (☎ 010/6618-0107), are so popular that reservations can be backed up for weeks.

- **Best Chinese Decor: Fangshan Restaurant,** Beihai Gongyuan Nei, Xicheng District (☎ 010/6401-1879), was the first restaurant opened by former cooks from the Forbidden City, and its setting is pure Old Cathay: a courtyard mansion with views of Beihai Lake.

- **Best Spot for a Romantic Dinner:** The cuisine is French, the dress code is formal, and the mood is set by candlelight and a string quartet at elegant **Justine's,** Jianguo Hotel, 5 Jianguomenwai Dajie, Chaoyang District (☎ 010/6500-2233, ext. 8039).

- **Best Location for a Business Lunch: Windows On the World,** CITIC Building, 19 Jianguomenwai Dajie, Chaoyang District (☎ 010/6500-2255, ext. 2828), has long been a favorite of foreign journalists and expatriate CEOs. Many a mover and shaker has enjoyed the fare from its Cantonese woks and Continental grill and the view of Chang'an Avenue from its 28th-floor perch. Trendsetters, however, have been trying the Continental set lunches at **Bleu Marine,** 5 Dongdaqiao Lu, Chaoyang District (☎ 010/6500-6704).

- **Best Hotel for Sunday Brunch:** The international hotels all have lavish Sunday spreads in their lobbies, but the most elegant and expensive is at the **Swissotel,** Hong Kong Macau Center, Dong Si Shi Tiao Li Jiao Qiao, Chaoyang District (☎ 010/6501-2288, ext. 2232), where guests feast on unrestricted portions of caviar and Moet & Chandon champagne.

- **Best View of the City:** All of Beijing far to the east slowly spins into view from the 26th floor of the **Carousel Revolving Restaurant,** Xiyuan Hotel, 1 Sanlihe Lu, Xicheng District (☎ 010/6831-3388), where the lunch and dinner buffets fuse Asian and Western cuisines.

- **Best View of City Center: The Courtyard,** 95 Donghuamen Lu, Dongcheng District (☎ 010/6526-8881), is one of Beijing's trendiest independent restaurants, with a French and fusion cuisine, a contemporary Chinese art gallery, a cigar divan, and upstairs some breathtaking views of the Forbidden City.

- **Best People-Watching:** A decidedly hip jazz bar deluxe with a top Continental grill room, **Aria,** China World Hotel, 1 Jianguomenwai Dajie, Chaoyang District (☎ 010/6505-2266), attracts the capital's VIPs East and West. On its second floor, there's a secret nook, like a private box at the opera, that hovers above the busy hotel lobby.

- **Best Wine List:** Home of New American cuisine with a Cajun flare, **Louisiana,** Beijing Hilton Hotel, 1 Dong Fang Lu, Third Ring Road North

(☎ **010/6466-2288,** ext. 7420), has the city's largest wine list, cited for its excellence by *Wine Spectator* magazine.

- **Best for Kids:** With free soft drink refills and plenty of sandwiches, burgers, and Tex-Mex on the menu, **American Chili's Grill,** Gateway Building, 10 Yabao Lu, Chaoyang District (☎ **010/6592-5184**), is more fun than McDonald's, and kids under 10 eat free on weekends.
- **Best Burgers:** A cheerful American-style bar and grill, **Henry J. Bean's,** China World Hotel, 1 Jianguomenwai Dajie, Chaoyang District (☎ **010/6505-2266,** ext. 6334), knows how to turn out a consistently savory bacon cheeseburger with all the trimmings.
- **Best Coffee Spot:** Starbuck's has launched its invasion of the Land of Tea, but Beijing's first international coffeehouse, **Johnny's Coffee,** Third Ring Road, Chaoyang District Northeast (☎ **010/6461-0827**), is still the capital's top purveyor of lattes and bagels.
- **Best Ice Cream: Haagen-Dazs,** Beijing International Club, Room 196, 21 Jianguomenwai Dajie, Chaoyang District (☎ **010/6532-6661**), has opened its own little cafe in the diplomatic zone and serves some of the richest ice creams and sauces in Beijing.
- **Best Cantonese:** There are plenty of excellent Southern Chinese restaurants in Beijing, but one that blends service, selection, and quality to near perfection is **Summer Palace,** China World Hotel, 1 Jianguomenwai Dajie, Chaoyang District (☎ **010/6505-2266,** ext. 34).
- **Best French:** Superb French restaurants in China are not an incongruity. Beijing has its own Maxim's, but for maintaining the old traditions with just a twist of Asian invention, head downtown to **Plaza Grill,** Holiday Inn Crowne Plaza, 48 Wangfujing, Dongcheng District (☎ **010/6513-3388,** ext. 1132).
- **Best Indian:** Beijing's first Indian restaurant with an Indian chef, **Shamiana,** Holiday Inn Downtown, 98 Beilishi Lu, Xicheng District (☎ **010/6833-8822, ext. 7107**), flies in fresh ingredients from India and knows how to produce top curries and samosas.
- **Best Italian:** There are plenty of top contenders, but few can equal the simple charms of the Naples-style dishes in the new **Danieli's,** Beijing International Club Hotel, 21 Jianguomenwai Dajie (☎ **010/6460-6688,** ext. 2355).
- **Best Japanese: Nishimura,** Shangri-La Beijing Hotel, 29 Zizhuyuan Lu, Haidian District (☎ **010/6841-2211,** ext. 2702), Beijing's first robatayaki restaurant, and **Nadaman,** China World Hotel, 1 Jianguomenwai Dajie (☎ **010/6505-2266,** ext. 39), are two Japan-based restaurants that have made successful transits to China.
- **Best Thai:** Long regarded as Beijing's top Thai restaurant, **Borom Piman,** Holiday Inn Lido, Jichang Lu, Jiangtai Lu, Chaoyang District Northeast (☎ **010/6437-6688,** ext. 2899), imports its spices and cooks from the Land of Smiles.
- **Best Vegetarian:** Nothing on the Chinese menu contains meat, despite appearances, and everything is fresh and tantalizing at **Green Tian Shi,** 57 Dengshikou Lu (off Wangfujing), Dongcheng District (☎ **010/6524-2349**).

2 Planning a Trip to Beijing

Here are the basics for designing a trip to Beijing and entering China with the right documents in hand, as well as tips on how to navigate smoothly through the airport and arrive in the capital with the fewest hassles.

1 Visitor Information

Foreign travel to the People's Republic of China is handled by an official government agency, **China International Travel Service,** referred to by the initials **CITS.** In Chinese, CITS is called *guoji luxingshe.* CITS can set up international and domestic air flights, train and bus reservations within China, and hotel reservations for Beijing. It can also provide English-speaking guides and group or individual sight-seeing tours through its Beijing branch offices, which are often located in hotels. **China Travel Service (CTS)** and a host of other government and private travel services also cater to foreign travelers.

CITS OVERSEAS CITS has opened a few **China National Tourist Offices (CNTO)** abroad to provide tourist information and services.

- In the **United States:** China National Tourist Office, 350 Fifth Ave., Suite 6413, New York, NY 10118 (☎ **212/760-9700;** fax 212/760-8809); and 333 W. Broadway, Suite 201, Glendale, CA 91204 (☎ **818/545-7504;** fax 818/545-7506).
- In the **United Kingdom:** China National Tourist Office, 4 Glentworth St., London N.W. 1 (☎ **020/7935-9427;** fax 020/7487-5842).
- In **Australia:** China National Tourist Office, 44 Market St., Sydney NSW 2000 (☎ **02/9299-4057;** fax 02/9290-1958).

For the locations of CITS offices in Beijing, see "Orientation," in chapter 3, "Getting to Know Beijing.

BEIJING ONLINE The best way to get fairly up-to-date information on Beijing before leaving home is on the Internet. **CITS** maintains a helpful planning and reservations site at www.citusa.com. The CITS e-mail address is info@citusa.com. The **International Community in China (ICIC)** has a biweekly newsletter at www.chinesebusinessworld.com, and the online edition of a local magazine, *Beijing This Month,* is available at www. chinesebusinessworld.com/btm/index.html. Two other useful Beijing Web sites are www.surfchina.com and www.beijingnow.com.

2 Entry Requirements & Customs

ENTRY REQUIREMENTS

All visitors to Beijing and the People's Republic of China are required to have a valid **passport** (one that does not expire for at least 6 months after your arrival date in China). A special **tourist or business visa** is also required. Tour groups are usually issued a group visa, with the paperwork handled by the travel agency (check with your agent). Visas for individual travelers and business people can be obtained in one of three ways: (1) upon arrival at the Beijing airport, (2) from certain travel agents overseas and in Hong Kong, and (3) from the Chinese embassy or consulate in your country. Unless you are entering China through Hong Kong, where securing a visa from the Hong Kong CTS or a local travel agent is quite easy, the safest way to get a China visa is to contact an overseas China embassy or consulate several months before your trip. Telephone, fax, or mail a request for a visa application to the Chinese embassy or consulate in your home country and follow the printed instructions. You will be required to mail a completed visa application form, your valid passport, and payment. Payment depends on the visa you select. A 30-day single-entry tourist visa is the most economical ($30 for U.S. passport holders); 60-day, 90-day, and 6-month visas, permitting single or multiple entries, are also available. In the United States, it takes about 10 days to get your visa once you mail your application, passport, and payment.

The visa office of the Embassy of the People's Republic of China is at Room 110, 2201 Wisconsin Ave., Washington, D.C. 20007 (☎ **202/338-6688;** fax 202/588-9760).

The Consulate-General of the People's Republic of China has offices in the following countries:

> **In the United States:** 1450 Laguna St., San Francisco, CA 94115 (☎ 415/674-2900; fax 415/563-0494); 443 Shatto Place, Los Angeles, CA 90020 (☎ 213/807-8088; fax 213/380-1961); 3417 Montrose Blvd., Houston, TX 77006 (☎ 713/524-4311; fax 713/524-7656); 520 12th Ave., New York, NY 10036 (☎ 212/868-7752; fax 212/502-0245); and 100 W. Erie St., Chicago, IL 60610 (☎ 312/803-0098; fax 312/803-0122).
>
> **In Canada:** 515 Patrick St., Ottawa, ON K1N 5H3 (☎ 613/789-9608; fax 613/789-1414); 240 St. George St., Toronto, ON M5R 2P4 (☎ 416/964-7260; fax 416/324-6468); and 3380 Granville St., Vancouver, BC V6H 3K3 (☎ 604/736-7492; fax 604/737-0154).
>
> **In the United Kingdom:** 31 Portland Place, London W1N 3AG (☎ 0171/631-1430; fax 0171/436-9178); Denison House, 49 Denison Rd., Rusholme, Manchester M14 5RX (☎ 0161/224-8672; fax 0161/257-2672); and 43 Station Rd., Edinburgh EH12 7AF (☎ 0131/316-4789; fax 0131/334-6954).

Visa Application Tip

Americans can download visa application forms and instructions from the Chinese embassy's Web page at www.China-embassy.org.

In Ireland: 40 Ailesbury Rd., Dublin 4, Ireland (☎ 3531/269-1707).
In Australia: 15 Coronation Dr., Yarralumla, ACT 2600 (☎ 02/6273-4780; fax 02/6273-4878).
In New Zealand: 2–6 Glenmore St., Wellington (☎ 04/472-1382).

GETTING A VISA IN HONG KONG   Many U.S., Canadian, Australian, New Zealand, Irish, and British citizens enter China through Hong Kong. Although Hong Kong is now part of China, residents of these nations are required to have only a valid passport to enter Hong Kong. Visas for the rest of China can be secured at countless travel agencies in Hong Kong, including the highly efficient branch of **China Travel Service (CTS)** at 27–33 Nathan Rd., Kowloon (☎ **852/2315-7149;** fax 852/2721-7757), second floor of the Alpha Building (entrance on Peking Road).

EXTENDED STAYS   The **Foreign Affairs Section** of the Public Security Bureau (the police), located at 85 Beichizi Dajie (☎ **010/6525-5486**) in downtown Beijing, has the power to extend visas. Those who overstay are fined about $50 per day.

CUSTOMS

Travelers are allowed to **bring into China** four bottles of alcoholic beverages and three cartons of cigarettes. There is no limit on the amount of foreign currency (although amounts above $10,000 must be declared on a customs form). Weapons, explosives, ammunition, dangerous drugs, explosives, live animals, fresh produce, and books, films, tapes, and so on, deemed "detrimental to China's politics, economy, culture, and ethics" (meaning religious and pornographic materials) cannot be brought into China. Diamonds and rare animals and plants cannot be taken from China. Upon departure, note that antiques purchased in China must have a red wax seal for export. Customs declaration slips must be filled out before arrival and departure.

No vaccinations or inoculations are currently required (although an AIDs test certificate is required for those planning on living in China for longer than 6 months).

Returning U.S. citizens who have been away for 48 hours or longer are allowed to bring back, once every 30 days, $400 worth of merchandise duty-free. You'll be charged a flat rate of 10% duty on the next $1,000 worth of purchases. Be sure to have your receipts handy. On gifts, the duty-free limit is $100. You cannot bring fresh foodstuffs into the United States; tinned foods, however, are allowed. For more information, contact the **U.S. Customs Service,** 1301 Constitution Ave. (P.O. Box 7407), Washington, DC 20044 (☎ **202/927-6724**) and request the free pamphlet *Know Before You Go.* It's also available on the Web at www.customsustreas. gov/travel/kbygo.htm.

U.K. citizens returning from a non-EC country have a customs allowance of 200 cigarettes; 50 cigars; 250 grams of smoking tobacco; 2 liters of still table wine; 1 liter of spirits or strong liqueurs (over 22% volume); 2 liters of fortified wine, sparkling wine, or other liqueurs; 60cc (ml) perfume; 250cc (ml) of toilet water; and £145 worth of all other goods, including gifts and souvenirs. People under 17 cannot have the tobacco or alcohol allowance. For more information, contact **HM Customs & Excise, Passenger Enquiry Point,** 2nd Floor Wayfarer House, Great South West Road, Feltham, Middlesex, TW14 8NP (☎ **020/8910-3744;** from outside the U.K., 44/181-910-3744), or consult the office's Web site at www. open.gov.uk.

Packing for Security

Pickpockets are the bane of many world capitals, including Beijing, so be sure to tuck traveler's checks, excess cash, airline tickets, and your ID, especially your passport, into a concealed pouch or money belt—not into a purse or backpack. Leave copies of your passport and traveler's check receipts at your hotel (in a safety-deposit box or room safe) and carry a copy with you.

For a clear summary of **Canadian** rules, write for the booklet *I Declare,* issued by **Revenue Canada,** 2265 St. Laurent Blvd., Ottawa, ON K1G 4KE (☎ **613/ 993-0534**). Canada allows its citizens a $500 exemption, and you're allowed to bring back duty-free 200 cigarettes, 2.2 pounds of tobacco, 40 imperial ounces of liquor, and 50 cigars. In addition, you're allowed to mail gifts to Canada from abroad at the rate of Can$60 a day, provided the gifts are unsolicited and don't contain alcohol or tobacco (write on the package "Unsolicited gift, under $60 value"). All valuables should be declared on the Y-38 form before departure from Canada, including serial numbers of valuables you already own, such as expensive foreign cameras. *Note:* The $500 exemption can be used only once a year and only after an absence of 7 days.

The duty-free allowance in **Australia** is A$400 or, for those under 18, A$200. Upon returning to Australia, citizens can bring in 250 cigarettes or 250 grams of loose tobacco, and 1.125 liters of alcohol. If you're returning with valuable goods you already own, such as foreign-made cameras, you should file form B263. A helpful brochure, available from Australian consulates or Customs offices, is *Know Before You Go.* For more information, contact **Australian Customs Services,** GPO Box 8, Sydney NSW 2001 (☎ **02/9213-2000**).

The duty-free allowance for citizens of **New Zealand** is NZ$700. Citizens over 17 can bring in 200 cigarettes or 50 cigars or 250 grams of tobacco (or a mixture of all three if their combined weight doesn't exceed 250 grams), plus 4.5 liters of wine and beer or 1.125 liters of liquor. New Zealand currency does not carry import or export restrictions. Fill out a certificate of export, listing the valuables you are taking out of the country; that way, you can bring them back without paying duty. Most questions are answered in a free pamphlet available at New Zealand consulates and Customs offices: *New Zealand Customs Guide for Travellers, Notice no. 4.* For more information, contact **New Zealand Customs,** 50 Anzac Ave., P.O. Box 29, Auckland (☎ **09/359-6655**).

3 Money

Chinese currency, the *yuan,* is called Renminbi (RMB). The most common denominations of bills are the 100 yuan, 50 yuan, 10 yuan, 5 yuan, 2 yuan, and 1 yuan. The current exchange rate is about 8.3 yuan to 1 U.S. dollar, making the yuan worth about 12¢. In addition, there are smaller bills worth less than 1 yuan in denominations of 5 jiao, 2 jiao, and 1 jiao (10 jiao = 1 yuan). There are even smaller bills and coins, with denominations in fen (100 fen = 10 jiao = 1 yuan). The yuan is commonly called *kwai,* and the jiao is commonly called *mao.* Beijing is still a cash society, so most of your ordinary transactions in shops and cafes require Chinese currency. It is useful to carry a quantity of 10, 2, and 1 yuan notes to pay for taxis, bottled water, admissions, and other small daily purchases. Prices in China are usually marked with "RMB" but can also be marked with a "Y."

The Chinese Yuan, the U.S. Dollar & the British Pound

For U.S. Readers   At this writing, U.S.$1 = approximately 8.3RMB (or 1RMB = 12¢). This was the rate of exchange used to calculate the U.S. dollar rates given in this book (rounded off). Exchange rates at hotels are usually 8.2RMB per U.S.$1.

For British Readers   The rate of exchange used to calculate the pound values in the accompanying table was £1 = 13RMB (or 1RMB = 8p).

Check the current exchange rates before you arrive and use the following table only as a guide:

RMB	U.S.$	U.K.£	RMB	U.S.$	U.K.£
0.10	0.01	0.01	100	12.00	8.00
0.50	0.06	0.03	150	18.00	11.30
1.00	0.12	0.08	200	24.00	15.10
2.00	0.24	0.15	250	30.00	18.90
3.00	0.36	0.23	300	36.00	22.70
4.00	0.48	0.30	400	48.00	30.25
5.00	0.60	0.38	500	60.00	37.80
6.00	0.72	0.45	600	72.00	45.40
7.00	0.84	0.53	700	84.00	52.90
8.00	0.96	0.60	800	96.00	60.50
9.00	1.08	0.68	900	108.00	68.00
10.00	1.20	0.76	1,000	120.00	75.60
15.00	1.80	1.13	2,000	240.00	151.20
20.00	2.40	1.50	3,000	360.00	226.80
25.00	3.00	1.90	4,000	480.00	302.40
30.00	3.60	2.27	5,000	600.00	378.00
35.00	4.20	2.65	6,000	720.00	453.60
40.00	4.80	3.03	7,000	840.00	529.20
45.00	5.40	3.40	8,000	960.00	604.80
50.00	6.00	3.80	9,000	1,080.00	680.40
75.00	9.00	5.70	10,000	1,200.00	756.00

TRAVELER'S CHECKS   Traveler's checks are the easiest and safest way to bring money into China. Traveler's checks, as well as foreign currency, can be converted to RMB at nearly all hotels, many banks, and some restaurants and stores (particularly the Friendship Store). Hotels and banks charge a small fee for conducting exchanges, but hotel desks offer convenience and don't charge too much more than the banks. Note that the exchange rate for traveler's checks is slightly better than for cash. It is not possible to get Chinese currency before you leave home.

You can get traveler's checks at almost any bank. **American Express** offers denominations of $10, $20, $50, $100, $500, and $1,000. You'll pay a service charge ranging from 1% to 4%. You can also get American Express traveler's checks

What Things Cost in Beijing	U.S.$	U.K.£
Taxi from airport to city center	12.00	7.60
Subway ride	25¢	.15
Local telephone call	5¢	.03
Double room at the China World Hotel (very expensive)	240.00	151.20
Double room at the Holiday Inn Lido (expensive)	190.00	119.70
Double room at the Song He Hotel (moderate)	90.00	56.70
Double room at the Qiaoyuan Hotel (inexpensive)	40.00	25.20
Lunch for one at Berena's (moderate)	8.00	5.00
Lunch for one at Gold Cat Jiaozi City (inexpensive)	5.00	3.15
Dinner for one, without drinks, at Li Family Restaurant (very expensive)	40.00	25.20
Dinner for one, without drinks, at Summer Palace (expensive)	30.00	18.90
Dinner for one, without drinks, at a Beijing Duck (Peking Duck) restaurant (moderate)	20.00	12.60
Dinner for one, without drinks, at Sihexuan (inexpensive)	12.00	7.60
Glass of beer	3.50	2.20
Coca-Cola	1.25	.80
Roll of 100 ASA Fujicolor film (36 exposures)	6.00	3.80
Admission to the Forbidden City	7.50	4.70
Admission to the Lama Temple	1.25	.80
Movie ticket	4.00	2.50
Theater ticket (good seat) to Peking Opera	20.00	12.60

over the phone by calling ☎ **800/221-7282;** by using this number, Amex gold and platinum cardholders are exempt from the 1% fee. AAA members can get checks without a fee at most AAA offices.

Visa offers traveler's checks at Citibank locations nationwide, as well as several other banks. The service charge ranges between 1.5% and 2%; checks come in denominations of $20, $50, $100, $500, and $1,000. **MasterCard** also offers traveler's checks. Call ☎ **800/223-9920** for a location near you.

CREDIT CARDS   In general, it is easiest to exchange traveler's checks for RMB at your hotel and to use a credit card to pay the hotel bill. Most fine restaurants and large stores in Beijing where tourists go now accept major credit cards, too, but the practice is not as common as in North America and Europe. You can also withdraw cash advances from your American Express, Visa, Mastercard, or Diner's Club card at most branches of the Bank of China and at a few select ATMs (although you'll start paying hefty interest on the advance the moment you receive the cash, and you won't get frequent-flyer miles on an airline credit card). You will need your PIN number at an ATM and your passport at the bank when using your credit card for cash withdrawals. If you've forgotten your credit card PIN or didn't even know you had one, call the phone number on the back of your credit card and ask the bank to send it to you. It usually takes 5 to 7 business days, although some banks will supply the number over the phone if you tell them your mother's maiden name or pass some other security clearance.

Many ATMs honor only Chinese-issued credit cards, but American Express has a 24-hour ATM at the China World Trade Center (1 Jianguomenwai Dajie). Visa cardholders can withdraw RMB from any ATM labeled Visa/Plus, as well as from many banks. Visa/Plus ATMs are located at the airport, the CITIC Building, the Palace Hotel, and Bank of China branches.

ATMS   Beijing's ATMs are linked to a network that most likely includes your bank at home. **Cirrus** (☎ 800/424-7787; www.mastercard.com/atm/) and **Plus** (☎ 800/843-7587; www.visa.com/atms) are the two most popular networks; check the back of your ATM card to see which network your bank belongs to. Before your trip, use the 800 numbers or Web sites to locate ATMs in your destination or ask your bank for a list of ATMs in China. Be sure to check the daily withdrawal limit before you depart, and ask whether you need a new personal ID number.

Personal checks are almost impossible to cash in Beijing. **Western Union** (Beijing hotline, ☎ 010/6318-4313) has branches at the International Post Office and the Asian Games Post Office.

THEFT   Almost every credit card company has an emergency toll-free number that you can call if your wallet or purse is stolen. They may be able to wire you a cash advance off your credit card immediately, and in many places, they can deliver an emergency credit card in a day or two. In China, MasterCard holders should call ☎ 10-800-110-7309; Visa cardholders should call ☎ 10-800-110-2911. American Express cardholders should visit one of the AMEX offices in Beijing; see "American Express" under "Fast Facts: Beijing" in chapter 3 for a list of locations.

If you opt to carry traveler's checks, be sure to keep a record of their serial numbers, separately from the checks of course, so you're ensured a refund in just such an emergency.

4 When to Go

Beijing's busiest tourist periods coincide with its mildest weather in the spring and autumn. To avoid the big crowds and still enjoy decent weather, try to visit in late March or early November. Except for the long winter months, Beijing is usually filled with tourists and business travelers from May and through October, but the crowds (largely of Chinese tourists coming to see the sights of their nation's capital) can be interesting, too. In the winter, the crowds diminish, but the natural beauty suffers, and the nearly empty tourist sights, shops, and cafes often look dreary. In the fall, from mid-October to mid-November, the leaves in the parks and along avenues change color. In the low season, from November to April, air fares decrease markedly and hotel prices take a plunge. Whenever you visit, it is best to sight-see on weekdays (the weekends are crowded) and, at popular sites, early in the morning or late in the afternoon.

CLIMATE   Beijing, located on the 40th parallel north, has four distinct seasons. **Spring,** from mid-March to mid-May, is mild, although sometimes subject to dust storms. **Summer,** from mid-May to mid-September, is both humid and quite hot, and subject to heavy rains in July and August. Beijing's **"Golden Autumn,"** from mid-September to mid-November, is quite dry, with mild days and chilly nights. The long **winter,** from mid-November to mid-March, can be bitterly cold with Siberian winds, ice, and increased air pollution (due to increased burning of coal for heating); however, there is little snowfall and there are some days when the skies clear and turn refreshingly blue.

Beijing's Average Temperatures & Rainfall

	Jan	Feb	Mar	Apr	May	June	July	Aug	Sept	Oct	Nov	Dec
Temp. °F	23.5	27.8	39.9	55.8	68.4	75.6	78.8	76.3	67.1	54.5	39.2	27.0
Temp. °C	-4.7	-2.3	4.4	13.2	20.2	24.2	26.0	24.6	19.5	12.5	4.0	-2.8
Days of Rain	2.1	3.1	4.5	5.1	6.4	9.7	14.5	14.1	6.9	5.0	3.6	1.6

HOLIDAYS   National holidays observed in Beijing are January 1 (New Year's Day), Spring Festival/Chinese New Year (first day of the lunar calendar: February 5, 2000; January 24, 2001; February 12, 2002), March 4 (Arbor Day), March 8 (International Working Women's Day), May 1 (International Labor Day), May 4 (Chinese Youth Day), June 1 (International Children's Day), August 1 (Army Day), September 10 (Teacher's Day), and October 1 (National Day, a 2-day holiday).

Spring Festival, the Chinese New Year, is the most important holiday. Spring Festival can last up to 15 days; the 15th day is marked by the Lantern Festival celebrations. Officially, it is a 3-day national holiday, meaning on the first 3 days, banks, offices, and many workplaces are closed. Temples and parks put on fairs. **National Day,** a 2-day observance of the founding of the People's Republic of China on October 1, 1949, is the second most important national holiday. National Day is particularly big in the capital, with celebrations held at Tiananmen Square, where fireworks and other special performances are staged. Offices, banks, and many shops are also closed on January 1 and May 1 holidays.

Beijing Calendar of Events

Festivals and celebrations are not numerous in Beijing, and many are family affairs, but there are some opportunities to mix with the locals at city parks and other locations at annual public events.

Winter

- **Spring Festival/Chinese New Year.** This is the time when Chinese decorate their homes with red paper (signifying health, wealth, and prosperity), visit friends, settle the year's debts, visit temples, and enjoy family get-togethers. Parks and temples hold outdoor celebrations and markets and are the best places for tourists to experience the festival. First day of the lunar calendar: February 5, 2000; January 24, 2001; and February 12, 2002.
- **Lantern Festival.** On the 15th day after Chinese New Year, on the first full moon, parks and temples display elaborate and fanciful lanterns, often accompanied by fireworks and folk dances. Beihai Park is worth visiting on this day. Locals mark the festival by consuming a sweet steamed dumpling called *xuanxiao.*

Western Holidays in Beijing

Christmas has become an increasingly popular holiday in Beijing, celebrated at hotels and restaurants with large dinner parties. Western **New Year's** has not caught on to this extent. **Halloween** is usually celebrated by a mix of locals and expatriates at the discos.

- **Guanyin's Birthday**. Held on the 19th day of the second lunar month, about 50 days after Chinese New Year, in honor of the Goddess of Mercy, Guanyin, this is a good opportunity to visit one of the Buddhist temples in Beijing and join in the celebrations. March 24, 2000, and March 13, 2001.

Spring
- **Qing Ming Festival.** Also known as Grave Sweeping Day, held on the 15th day of the third lunar month (usually in April), this event honors the dead, although in Beijing it usually means a mass run on the parks, where kite-flying goes into high gear. The holiday is locally known as the "Stepping on Greenery Festival," a rite of spring. April 4, 2000, and April 5, 2001.
- **International Labor Day.** Nearly everything is closed except hotels, cafes, and some shops, but May Day holds no special celebrations for the tourist. May 1.
- **Chinese Youth Day.** This is a colorful day to be in Beijing. The streets and parks are filled with flower displays to commemorate the May 4th Movement when students protested on Tiananmen Square, May 4, 1989.

Summer
- **International Children's Day.** This holiday holds nothing special for most tourists, but local school classes enjoy themselves on field trips on the first day of June.
- **Watermelon Festival.** On this festival day, which is unique to Beijing, the city government organizes eating tours in the melon fields of Daxing County. Call ☎ **010/6924-3711** to book a place. Late June.

Autumn
- **Mid-Autumn Festival.** Held on the 15th day of the 8th lunar month (late September/early October), the "Moon Festival" celebrates the harvest moon and the revolt against the Yuan Dynasty. Beijingers visit their ancestral homes and enjoy eating moon cakes (round biscuits stuffed with sweet, dense red bean paste and egg, or with preserved fruits). The cakes are distributed to friends during the festival, a custom dating back to the Yuan Dynasty (1279–1368). September 12, 2000, and October 1, 2001.
- **National Day.** Be at Tiananmen or be square—this is Beijing and China's biggest mass patriotic demonstration, held every October 1.
- **"Red Leaf Festival."** From late October through mid-November, whenever the autumn leaves turn, thousands of Beijingers throng the Fragrant Hills Park northwest of the city for this informal festival. It's the best time for tourists to enjoy the scenery, markets, and temples there.
- **China International Jazz Festival.** Although it may seem out of character, Beijing can swing; it's been the site of this international jazz fest since 1993. At recent festivals, Chinese jazz bands and international groups played everything from big band swing to fusion, with performers ranging from the Danish Radio Jazz Orchestra and Australia's Ten Part Invention to American drummer Paul Motian and his Electric Bebop Band. Best spots to get into the swing are the

nightly jam sessions at local bars and teahouses that regularly feature jazz performers such as CD Jazz, Keep in Touch, and the Sanwei Bookstore. Mid-November.

5 Health & Insurance

STAYING HEALTHY No **vaccinations** are required for entry to Beijing, but make sure your inoculations are up-to-date, particularly for tetanus. Check updated information for travelers to China as provided by your doctor or local or national health agencies.

Probably the two most **common ailments** upon arrival or shortly after are jet lag and colds. Colds can be picked up on the flight over and from exposure to Beijing and its citizenry. Since common remedies are not always easy to find, pack an ample supply of cold remedies (tablets and sprays) as well as your preferred pain reliever.

Upset stomach and diarrhea are the bane of travelers to third-world countries, which Beijing still is to some extent. Avoid tap water and street food, and carry the remedies you depend on at home. Such diseases as malaria and hepatitis do exist, but they are no longer considered serious health risks in China's major cities.

Since the flight to Beijing is long and crosses many time zones, **jet lag** is a problem (less so if you are flying westward). Take the usual precautions on the flight—avoid alcohol, drink plenty of non-carbonated fluids, and walk and exercise as much as space allows. Set your watch to Beijing time upon departure. Whether or not you can sleep on the way to Beijing, upon arrival try to coordinate your schedule with the new time zone, putting in a full day and sleeping (as much as possible) through the night. It can take several days to reset your biological clock.

Due to the large number of foreign nationals serving as diplomats and working in the capital, several Beijing hospitals and clinics have special facilities for treating travelers. The level of service and care is of international caliber. The doctors are expertly trained in Western medicine (although many foreigners try Chinese herbal medicines and other traditional remedies, sometimes with great success). It is recommended, however, that travelers carry sterile syringes, since the hygiene in most facilities is not always dependable. See "Doctors & Dentists" and "Hospitals" in the "Fast Facts: Beijing" section of chapter 3 for a list of facilities catering to foreign visitors.

TRAVEL INSURANCE Hospitals, clinics, and physicians charge rates nearly on par with those in the West, so check with your health-insurance carrier to see if treatment in China is included in your coverage. In China, be sure to carry your identification card in your wallet. If you are not covered, consider purchasing a short-term **medical insurance** policy to cover medical and dental emergencies. Most health-insurance companies offer special overseas coverage plans for travelers, as do a number of private insurers (see below).

Emergency medical evacuation is quite expensive ($20,000 or more from Beijing to the U.S.), so investing in a plan to cover this emergency is also wise. **International SOS Assistance,** P.O. Box 11568, Philadelphia PA 11916 (☎ **800/523-8930** or 215/244-1500) has ties to the International Medical Center (IMC) in Beijing.

Trip cancellation insurance is a good idea if you have paid a large portion of your vacation expenses upfront. Trip cancellation insurance costs approximately 6% to 8% percent of the total value of your vacation.

If you require additional insurance, try one of the companies listed below, but don't pay for more than you need. For example, if you need only trip cancellation insurance, don't purchase coverage for lost or stolen property. Rule number one:

Many **prescriptions** can be filled at hospitals that cater to foreigners, but since this is costly and time-consuming, it is best to bring all prescriptions with you. Pack prescription medications in your carry-on luggage. Carry written prescriptions in generic, not brand-name form, and dispense all prescription medications from their original labeled vials.

If you wear **contact lenses,** pack an extra pair in case you lose one.

Check your existing policies before you buy any additional coverage. Among the reputable issuers of travel insurance are **Access America,** 6600 W. Broad St., Richmond, VA 23230 (☎ **800/284-8300**); **Travel Guard International,** 1145 Clark St., Stevens Point, WI 54481 (☎ **800/826-1300**); **Travel Insured International, Inc.,** P.O. Box 280568, East Hartford, CT 06128 (☎ **800/243-3174**); and **Columbus Travel Insurance,** 279 High St., Croydon CR0 1QH (☎ **020/7375-0011** in London; www2.columbusdirect.com/columbusdirect).

A comprehensive travel insurance plan should provide emergency medical and dental benefits (up to $2,500), emergency medical transportation (evacuation), emergency cash transfers, travel document and ticket replacement assistance, 24-hour multilingual assistance by telephone, and compensation for lost, delayed, and damaged baggage. Additional coverage options include trip cancellation protection, cash for emergencies, legal coverage, and trip delay insurance. Trip policies vary widely in price, but fairly comprehensive plans cost from $100 to $200.

6 Tips for Travelers with Special Needs

FOR TRAVELERS WITH DISABILITIES   Despite China having more citizens with disabilities than any nation on Earth, facilities for travelers with disabilities in Beijing can best be described as sporadic. Nevertheless, the Chinese have made notable efforts in addressing the needs of people with disabilities. Many Beijingers get around via special motorized carts, sections of some major sidewalks are now equipped with "raised dots" to assist the blind, and modern buildings and some major tourist sites have elevators. But the bottom line is that Beijing is a city of long stairways (even in the subway) and crowded, crumbling sidewalks. Even so, travelers with disabilities frequently make their way through the Beijing obstacle course and enjoy its many sights.

Contact **Mobility International USA** (45 W. Broadway, Eugene, OR 97405; ☎ **541/343-1284,** voice and TDD; www.miusa.org) for more information about visiting Beijing, especially since this group has led several special tours to Beijing and China. Annual membership to Mobility International is $35, which includes its quarterly newsletter, *Over the Rainbow.* You can also join **The Society for the Advancement of Travel for the Handicapped (SATH),** 347 Fifth Ave. Suite 610, New York, NY 10016 (☎ **212/447-7284;** fax 212-725-8253; www.sath.org) for $45 annually, $30 for seniors and students, to gain access to a vast network of connections in the travel industry. This group provides information sheets on travel destinations and referrals to tour operators that specialize in tours for travelers with disabilities. Its quarterly magazine, *Open World for Disability and Mature Travel,* is full of good information and resources. A year's subscription is $13 ($21 outside the U.S.).

FOR SENIORS   The Chinese respect age far more than their Western counterparts, but don't expect to find a plethora of "senior discounts" at tourist attractions

Beijing for Business Travelers

Thousands of foreign businesspeople arrive in Beijing each year. Business travelers should try to book an international hotel with a large 24-hour business center located near the work site or relevant local offices. Take plenty of business cards, with one side printed in English, the other in Chinese. Some Beijing hotel business centers offer this service.

A special **business visa** (the "F" visa) is required for entry into China. A business visa application must be accompanied by a formal invitation or authorization letter from a Chinese authority or institution, along with a cover letter from your company. For more on visas, see "Entry Requirements & Customs," earlier in this chapter.

Keys to business success in Beijing include patience, flexibility, and the cultivation of strong, friendly connections (*guanxi*) with Chinese associates, so read up on China and Chinese business before arrival. Three books business travelers to Beijing would be well advised to read are *Beijing Jeep: A Case Study of Western Business in China* by Jim Mann (Westview Press, 1997), *The Business Guide to China* by Laurence Brahm (Butterworth-Heinemann, 1997), and *Managing in China: An Executive Survival Guide* by Stephanie Jones (Butterworth-Heinemann, 1997).

The **U.S. China Business Council,** 1818 N Street NW, Suite 200, Washington, D.C. 20036 (☎ **202/429-0340;** fax 202/775-2476) provides business information and consulting; its office in Beijing is in the CITIC Building, Room 26D, 19 Jianguomenwai Dajie (☎ **010/6500-2255;** fax 010/6512-5854).

or in stores. If you book a hotel from an international hotel chain overseas, inquire about senior discounts. In Beijing, brace yourself for tiresome stairways at museums and temples, long walks at all tourist sites, and impatient crowds everywhere at your elbows.

Golden Companions, P.O. Box 5249, Reno, NV 89513 (☎ **702/324-2227**), helps travelers 45-plus find compatible companions through a personal voicemail service. Contact them for more information.

The Mature Traveler, a monthly 12-page newsletter on senior citizen travel is a valuable resource. It is available by subscription ($30 a year) from GEM Publishing Group, Box 50400, Reno, NV 89513-0400. Another helpful publication is *101 Tips for the Mature Traveler,* available from Grand Circle Travel, 347 Congress St., Suite 3A, Boston, MA 02210 (☎ **800/221-2610** or 617/350-7500; fax 617/346-6700).

FOR SINGLE TRAVELERS   The most common difficulties that solo travelers, male or female, encounter in Beijing are their own feelings of loneliness and isolation and having to fend off a variety of touts met in the streets, at tourist sites, or even in hotel lobbies. These freelancing entrepreneurs have a variety of come-ons, usually involving the purchase of whatever they are really selling (art works, souvenirs). Sometimes, of course, the Chinese are simply trying to be friendly or practice their English. Sexual harassment cases involving foreign visitors are quite rare. Single travelers are an inviting target for "street merchants," however, and Beijing is less annoying and far more fun when traveling in a small group. Restaurants are more interesting when you dine with companions, too.

FOR FAMILIES   While many children are not delighted with museums, temples, and the architecture of the Forbidden City, there are plenty of sites to dazzle them in Beijing. Beijingers are family-oriented and friendly toward all children. For Western kids, there are hundreds of familiar fast-food and foreign-style restaurants, several amusement and theme parks, the ancient observatory, the zoo, indoor playgrounds and toy stores in shopping centers, a wax museum, a do-it-yourself craft center, a Beijing version of "Universal Studios," a natural history museum with dinosaur exhibits, and plenty of parks for rowing, kite-flying, and in-line skating. Many hotels in Beijing allow young children (usually under 12) to stay free with their parents, and some hotels provide baby-sitting service (usually at an hourly fee). Travelers with infants and small children may well find themselves the center of attention at times, as Beijingers are often quite open about talking to and even touching very young visitors from faraway places.

As a rule, there are no special discounts for children at museums and attractions. The exceptions to this are amusement parks, recreation facilities (such as public swimming pools), and the Beijing Zoo.

Several books on the market offer tips to help you travel with kids. Most concentrate on the U.S., but two, *Family Travel* (Lanier Publishing International) and *How to Take Great Trips with Your Kids* (The Harvard Common Press), are full of good general advice that can apply to travel anywhere. Another reliable tome, with a worldwide focus, is *Adventuring with Children* (Foghorn Press).

FOR GAYS & LESBIANS   Beijing is quite tolerant of gay and lesbian travelers, but dating or sexual involvement with locals of the same sex can be dangerous. In sexual matters, gay or straight, Chinese society is quite puritanical, although walking hand in hand with a same-sex partner won't raise any eyebrows because it's deemed a sign of friendship. Beijing has a homosexual community, but it is not organized or officially sanctioned in any way. Since foreigners are perceived as "different" from Chinese in the first place, gay and lesbian travelers should experience no discrimination at all in Beijing. Recently, several nightspots have even become identified with gay, lesbian, and transsexual clienteles.

The International Gay & Lesbian Travel Association (IGLTA), (☎ 800/448-8550 or 954/776-2626; fax 954/776-3303; www.iglta.org), links travelers up with the appropriate gay-friendly service organization or tour specialist. With around 1,200 members, it offers quarterly newsletters, marketing mailings, and a membership directory that's updated quarterly. Membership often includes gay or lesbian businesses, but is open to individuals for $150 yearly, plus a $100 administration fee for new members. Members are kept informed of gay and gay-friendly hoteliers, tour operators, and airline and cruise-line representatives. Contact the IGLTA for a list of its member agencies.

General gay and lesbian travel agencies include **Family Abroad** (☎ 800/999-5500 or 212/459-1800; gay and lesbian); **Above and Beyond Tours** (☎ 800/397-2681; mainly gay men); and **Yellowbrick Road** (☎ 800/642-2488; gay and lesbian).

FOR STUDENTS   Student travelers, like visiting seniors, should not expect special rates or other discounts in Beijing. For students who want to party or exercise, Beijing has an increasingly interesting nightlife (discos, bars, live music, cinema) and a variety of outdoor and athletic activities, which are supported by an equally active resident population of foreign students studying at Beijing's universities.

The best resource for students is the **Council on International Educational Exchange,** or CIEE (www.ciee.org/). They can set you up with an International

Student Identity Card (ISIC), and their travel branch, **Council Travel Service** (☎ 800/226-8624; www.counciltravel.com), is the biggest student travel agency operation in the world. It can get you discounts on plane tickets and the like. The CTS office in Beijing is located at 2–101 Shaoyuan, Beijing University, Beijing 100871 (☎ **010/6275-1287;** fax 010/6275-7001; e-mail: gkulacki@public.sta. net.cn).

7 Getting There

More than 30 international airlines, from Aeroflot to Yugoslav Airlines, serve Beijing. It's a long trip from just about anywhere (10 hours from London, 11 hours from San Francisco, 13 hours from Sydney, 15 hours from New York—longer with stopovers and connections). Leading airlines serving Beijing from North America, England, Australia, and New Zealand include:

- **Air China** (☎ **310/335-0088;** www.airchina.com.cn), China's largest airline, offers flights from 28 countries, including four nonstops from San Francisco and Los Angeles weekly. Beijing office: 15 Xi Chang'an Jie (☎ **010/6601-6667**).
- **All Nippon Airways** (☎ **800/235-9262;** www.ana.co.jp) flies nonstop daily from Tokyo (trip time: 3 hours). Beijing office: China World Trade Center, Room 1510, 1 Jianguomenwai Dajie (☎ **010/6505-3311**).
- **British Airways** (☎ **800/247-9297** in the U.S., 03/4522-2211 in England; www. British-airways.com) flies nonstop from London three times a week (trip time: 10 hours). Beijing office: CVIK Tower, Room 210, 22 Jianguomenwai Dajie (☎ **010/6512-4070**).
- **Canadian Airlines International** (☎ **800/665-1177** in Canada, or 800/ 363-7530 in French outside Quebec; 800/426-7000 in the U.S.; www.cdnair.ca) flies nonstop from Vancouver 6 days a week (trip time: 10 hours, 30 minutes). Beijing office: Lufthansa Center, Room 201, 50 Liangmaqiao (☎ **010/6463-7906**).
- **China Southern Airline** (☎ **888/338-8988;** www.cs-air.com), China-owned and managed, has branched out to offer international flights from the U.S. Beijing office: 227 Chaoyangmenwai Dajie (☎ **010/6553-3622**).
- **Dragonair** (☎ **800/223-2742;** www.dragonair.com), partly owned by Cathay Pacific Airlines, offers the best flight from Hong Kong (trip time: 3 hours). Beijing office: China World Trade Center, Room L107, 1 Jianguomenwai Dajie (☎ **010/6518-2533**).
- **Japan Airlines** (☎ **800/525-3663;** www.jal.co.jp) flies nonstop from Tokyo (trip time: 3 hours, 40 minutes) 5 days a week and from Nagoya and Osaka less frequently. Beijing office: Changfugong Office Building, 26A Jianguomenwai Dajie (☎ **010/6513-0888**).
- **Korean Air** (☎ **800/438-5000;** www.koreanair.com) flies nonstop from Seoul 6 days a week (trip time: 2 hours). Beijing office: China World Trade Center, Room C-401, 1 Jianguomenwai Dajie (☎ **010/6505-0088**).
- **Northwest Airlines** (☎ 800/447-4747; www.nwa.com) flies nonstop from the U.S. four times weekly from Detroit (trip time: 13 hours), with direct flights via Tokyo from other cities. Northwest code-shares some flights to Beijing with Air China. Beijing office: China World Trade Center, Room 2426, 1 Jianguomenwai Dajie (☎ **010/6505-3505**).
- **Qantas Airlines** (☎ **800/227-4500** in North America, 13 13 13 in Australia; www.qantas.com) flies nonstop from Sydney 4 days a week (trip time: 13 hours). Beijing office: Lufthansa Center, Room S120B, 50 Liangmaqiao Lu (☎ **010/ 6467-4794**).

- **SAS** (☎ 800/221-2350; www.sas.se) flies nonstop from Copenhagen five times a week. Beijing office: 1403 Henderson Centre, Office Tower 1, 18 Jianguomennei Dajie (☎ 010/6518-3738).
- **Singapore Airlines** (☎ 800/742-3333; www.singaporeair.com) flies nonstop daily from Singapore (trip time: 6 hours). Beijing office: China World Trade Center, Room L109, 1 Jianguomenwai Dajie (☎ 010/6505-2233).
- **Swiss Air** (☎ 800/221-4750; www.swissair.com) flies nonstop from Zurich 3 days a week. Beijing office: CVIK Tower, Room 201, 22 Jianguomenwai Dajie (☎ 010/6512-3555).
- **United Airlines** (☎ 800/538-2929; www.ual.com) has daily direct service from San Francisco, Los Angeles, Chicago, and New York City via Tokyo. Beijing office: Lufthansa Centre, 50 Liangmaqiao Lu (☎ 010/6463-8551).

TIPS FOR GETTING THE BEST AIRFARE   Full-fare, unrestricted air tickets to Beijing are expensive. Some of the finest, most luxurious cabin service in the world is conducted on this route, particularly in first-class and business-class sections; if travel comfort is a concern, it might be worth spending the extra money (or airline club miles) for an upgrade. Economy class is crowded on most flights and the seats are narrow (although the food and drink can be of reasonably good quality). The rub is that a first-class round-trip seat can cost over $5,000 and a business-class seat over $2,500. Full fare for economy class usually runs from $1,500 to $2,000.

There are several ways to save hundreds, even thousands, of dollars on a Beijing flight. First, plan ahead, so you can book a less expensive **APEX** (Advance Purchase Excursion Fare) ticket. APEX tickets have some restrictions, depending on the airline; they usually must be purchased several weeks or more in advance and are often nonrefundable. Prices are lower in the winter, and weekend flights cost more than weekday flights. Nevertheless, an advance purchase round-trip ticket in economy class on a major airline, such as United, can be $1,200 or less, depending on how competitive flights to Asia happen to be at the time.

To save even more, shop around. Check the travel sections of major newspapers, particularly those on the West Coast. Dozens of travel agents, consolidators, and so-called "bucket shops" advertise deeply discounted tickets, sometimes as low as $800. These tickets, which the consolidators usually purchase in blocks from the airlines, carry about every restriction imaginable and are normally valid only on a few specific dates, but they are great bargains. Their small boxed ads usually run in the Sunday travel section at the bottom of the page. Before you pay, however, ask for a confirmation number from the consolidator and then call the airline itself to confirm your seat. Be prepared to book your ticket with a different consolidator—there are many to choose from—if the airline can't confirm your reservation. Also be aware that bucket shop tickets are usually nonrefundable or rigged with stiff cancellation penalties, often as high as 50% to 75% of the ticket price.

Council Travel (☎ 800/226-8624; www.counciltravel.com) and **STA Travel** (☎ 800/781-4040; www.sta.travel.com) cater especially to young travelers, but their bargain-basement prices are available to people of all ages. **Travel Bargains** (☎ 800/AIR-FARE; www.1800airfare.com) was formerly owned by TWA but now offers the deepest discounts on many other airlines, with a 4-day advance purchase. Other reliable consolidators include **1-800-FLY-CHEAP** (www.1800flycheap.com) and **TFI Tours International** (☎ 800-745-8000 or 212/736-1140), which serves as a clearinghouse for unused seats. "Rebators" such as **Travel Avenue** (☎ 800/333-3335 or 312/876-1116) and the **Smart Traveller** (☎ 800/448-3338 in the U.S., or 305/448-3338) rebate part of their commissions to you.

Flight Facts

Remember that a nonstop flight is quickest. Direct flights require at least one stopover along the way; this can mean a change of planes, which will add hours to your trip. Itineraries that involve "code-sharing" (where airlines cooperate in ticketing) can mean that a passenger must change airlines en route as well. Nevertheless, roundabout routes can also be less expensive than nonstop service.

Certain airlines, especially those based in Asia, offer low fares from North America and Europe, but be aware that these airlines cannot fly nonstop to Beijing; a stopover in their home country is required on the way. Korean Air, for example, flies to Beijing from North America, but it must first stop in Seoul, lengthening the long trip by hours; in addition, foreign-based airlines depart only from a major gateway city, which can require adding an expensive, time-consuming connecting flight.

The newest way to shop for cheap fares is via the Internet. It is now possible to book an international flight entirely online. Many travel sites and the airlines themselves routinely advertise special Internet fares at their Web sites, so don't hesitate to browse for electronic bargains. (See the box "Cyber Deals for Net Surfers," later in this chapter)

8 Booking a Tour Versus Traveling on Your Own

Whether you decide to visit Beijing independently or on a group tour depends on your experience and goals. Seasoned travelers, especially those who have visited other third-world destinations, or travelers who want to experience Beijing in some depth, can comfortably explore Beijing on their own. Touring Beijing without a net requires time, energy, resourcefulness, and a sense of adventure. If time is short, however, and your intent is to sample Beijing's leading treasures in comfort, with a minimum of hassles, a group tour is the answer. Seeing the Forbidden City and the Great Wall, tasting Peking Duck at an organized banquet, and perhaps venturing out on the streets to shop at Silk Alley are memorable experiences that group tours can deliver effectively. The crucial difference lies in the depth of the experience. The busy dawn-to-twilight group tour simply cannot allow more than an hour or two at even the major sites, barely enough time to snap a picture and get a general sense of the place.

Dozens of tour operators in North America, Europe, Australia, New Zealand, and Hong Kong offer excellent group tours of Beijing. Some of the largest operators are **Globus** (☎ 800/221-0090), **Maupintour** (☎ 800/225-4266), **Pacific Delight Tours** (☎ 800/221-7179), **Travcoa** (☎ 800/992-2003), and **United Vacations** (☎ 800/328-6877). You can speak to the operators directly or use a travel agent.

Between traveling as part of a group tour and traveling completely independently there is a wide middle ground. Travel agents, including **China International Travel Service** (CITS) and **China Travel Service** (CTS) in Hong Kong, Beijing, and overseas (see "Visitor Information," above), can book the essentials for independent-minded travelers who want to customize their trips. Hotel reservations, car and driver hires, airport transfers, personalized day tours with English-speaking guides, and other matters can be set up long before your trip or upon arrival, although the price can exceed that of a group tour if too many pieces are ordered this way. **Personal guides** can be hired for the entire duration of a stay, which is a luxurious way

Cyber Deals for Net Surfers

It's possible to get some great deals on airfare, hotels, and car rentals via the Internet. Grab your mouse and surf before you take off—you could save a bundle on your trip. The Web sites highlighted below are worth checking out, especially since all services are free. Always check the lowest published fare, however, before you shop for flights online.

- **Arthur Frommer's Budget Travel** (www.frommers.com). Home of the Encyclopedia of Travel and *Arthur Frommer's Budget Travel* magazine and daily newsletter, this site offers detailed information on 200 cities and islands around the world, and up-to-the-minute ways to save dramatically on flights, hotels, car reservations, and cruises. Book an entire vacation online and research your destination before you leave. Consult the message board to set up "hospitality exchanges" in other countries, to talk with other travelers who have visited a hotel you're considering, or to direct travel questions to Arthur Frommer himself. The newsletter is updated daily to keep you abreast of the latest-breaking ways to save, publicize new hot spots and best buys, and give veteran readers fresh, ever-changing approaches to travel.

- **Microsoft Expedia** (www.expedia.com). The best part of this multipurpose travel site is the "Fare Tracker": You fill out a form on the screen indicating that you're interested in cheap flights from your hometown, and once a week they'll e-mail you the best airfare deals on up to three destinations. The site's "Travel Agent" will steer you to bargains on hotels and car rentals, and with the help of hotel and airline seat pinpointers, you can book everything right online. This site is even useful after your trip is booked. Before you depart, log on to Expedia for maps and up-to-date travel information, including weather reports and foreign exchange rates.

- **Travelocity** (www.travelocity.com). This is one of the best travel sites out there, especially for finding cheap airfare. In addition to its "Personal Fare Watcher," which notifies you via e-mail of the lowest airfares for up to five different destinations, Travelocity will track the three lowest fares for any routes on any dates in minutes. You can book a flight right then and there, and if you need a rental car or hotel, Travelocity will find you the best deal via the SABRE computer reservations system (another huge travel agent database). Click on "Last Minute Deals" for the latest travel bargains, including a link to "H.O.T. Coupons" (www.hotcoupons.com), where you can print out electronic coupons for travel in the U.S. and Canada.

- **The Trip** (www.thetrip.com). This site is really geared toward the business traveler, but vacationers-to-be can also use The Trip's exceptionally powerful fare-finding engine, which will e-mail you every week with the best city-to-city airfare deals for as many as 10 routes. The Trip uses the Internet Travel Network, another reputable travel agent database, to book hotels and restaurants.

to see the capital—and often a great way to gain an insider's view. Independent packages can be engineered by tour operators who specialize in China, such as **Asian Pacific Adventures** (☎ 213/935-3156), **Geographic Expeditions** (☎ 800/777-8183), and **Orient Flexi-Pax** (☎ 800/545-5540).

Another option is to come to Beijing on a group tour that focuses on a special theme. If you are especially interested in Chinese cooking, acupuncture, shopping, architecture, education, tai chi, traditional medicine, art, or another topic, search magazines, newspapers, and the Internet for a small overseas group tour that meets your interest. Such tours are usually one-time offerings, however, led by experts in the field, so finding them requires research and some luck. Not only do **thematic tours** provide an opportunity to explore an interest in some depth, but they open doors that remain closed to independent travelers. Some of these tours also include a day or two of general sight-seeing, taking in the Great Wall and the Forbidden City, for example.

Fully **independent travel** in Beijing, on the other hand, depends on your energy, resourcefulness, and ability to act as your own tour guide and travel agent. It is easy to book the basics (flight and hotel) on your own. Beyond that point, you can rely on information in this guidebook—which I've field-tested—to find a wide variety of major sites and hidden delights. The Chinese language will present occasional difficulties, of course, but a good hotel staff (the concierges and bellhops, foremost) can help foreign travelers get around. Beijing hotels also maintain tour desks, should you tire of being on your own or find that reaching a remote site stretches your tactical skills to the breaking point. One tactic I've often employed when arriving in a strange Chinese city for the first time alone is to book a group tour at my hotel, using it as an introduction. Then, if what I've seen is intriguing, I return to the site on my own, properly oriented and prepared to deepen the experience.

3 Getting to Know Beijing

The alien language and initial strangeness of China's vast capital can intimidate as well as exhilarate any foreign visitor. This chapter deals with the practical matters you'll need to know about the city, from the moment you arrive at the airport. Its facts, tips, and overviews are designed to help you demystify Beijing's layout, unlock its facilities, and decipher some of the mysterious signs in its streets.

1 Orientation

ARRIVING

BY PLANE

Beijing's only commercial airport and China's largest, the aging **Capital Airport** (☎ 010/6456-3604), built in 1980, is 17 miles (27km) northeast of the city center. A new terminal is planned that will help with congestion, but in the meantime, the airport is an undersized, chaotic facility. Passengers receive health and customs declaration forms on the plane. They should fill them out before arrival and have their passports in hand. It usually takes less than 20 minutes to pass through the checkpoints and to retrieve luggage at the carousels. Then confusion can set in. Everyone is funneled through a very narrow exit door into the Arrival Hall. Beyond this final gate is always a sea of faces, crushing waves of humanity that you must part as you push straight ahead for the glass windows and doors of the main airport entrance. Unless you are part of a group tour or are being met by a local, you will be the target of roving taxi drivers and their advance men who will try every verbal stratagem to suck you into an overpriced taxi. Ignore these touts, whatever they promise. Try to exchange a small amount of money at the **Bank of China** counter (☎ 010/6456-3987), near the Arrival Hall exit; it's open from 6am to midnight daily, and the exchange rates are good. Airport porters do not exist at present, so you'll have to haul your own luggage through the masses.

GETTING INTO TOWN   There are three options for reaching the city, ranked here by convenience:

Hotel Shuttles   Hotel buses and limousines have service desks along the wall near the main terminal entrance. Line up at your hotel desk for help. Someone will make sure you get on the right hotel bus when it arrives. (When you make your hotel reservations, be sure to include a request for shuttle service from the airport, if it is offered, in order for your name to appear on the list at the airport counter.) Some hotels charge a small fee (less than taxi fare to destination) for shuttle service; others do not.

Airport Taxis   The legitimate taxis are lined up in a long queue just outside the Arrival Hall, to the right at the curb. Join the line. Taxis should charge 90 to 120RMB (about $11–$15), which includes a 10RMB ($1.25) expressway toll. Be sure the meter is on; if not, shout "Da biao," and if that doesn't work, get out and select another taxi. The trip into town can take up to an hour, depending on traffic. If you haven't been able to change money at the bank counter in the airport, don't panic: Many taxi drivers accept foreign currency. If they don't, they'll wait while you change money at your hotel. A tip should consist of a small bit of change (no more than a few RMB).

Airport Buses   The **Air Bus** runs outside the terminal every 30 minutes from 8am to 10pm and costs just 16RMB ($2). Tell the Air Bus service counter inside the terminal your destination, buy the ticket, and head outside in search of the bus. Someone on the curb outside may have to read your ticket and point you in the right direction. Bus "A" goes to the Beijing Railway Station with stops near the Kunlun and Hilton hotels and three subway stations. Bus "B" goes to the northwestern districts of Beijing, with stops near the Friendship and Beijing Shangri-La hotels. You might need to hail a taxi in the city to reach your final destination.

BY TRAIN

If you arrive by train from a Chinese city, from Hong Kong via the new 29-hour deluxe super-train (Train No. 97), or from Moscow on the Trans-Siberian Railway, you will have completed your immigration and customs procedures before arrival in Beijing. Whether your terminal is the old **Beijing Railway Station** (☎ 010/6563-4432) or the new **Beijing West Station** (☎ 010/6321-6263), you'll have to hail a taxi at the queues outside to reach your hotel.

   Beijing's train stations are crowded and chaotic, not the kind of places where you'll want to linger. Foreigners holding soft berth and sleeping car tickets can use the special lounges set aside for these passengers. These lounges, equipped with stuffed chairs and sofas, are quiet, but there's nothing much to do in them. The train stations lack ATMs and currency exchange outlets, but they do have counters for buying snacks, sodas, and sundries.

VISITOR INFORMATION

Beijing's official tourist bureau for foreign visitors, the **China International Tourist Service (CITS),** does not have information centers at the airport or train stations, although its main office can be helpful. The main CITS office is located

Departing Beijing

When you return to the Beijing Capital Airport by hotel shuttle, taxi, or Air Bus, be sure you have enough RMB in hand to pay the **international departure tax.** The tax is currently 90RMB ($11). Credit cards and foreign currencies are not accepted. Go to one of the clearly marked departure tax counters just inside the International Departure Hall. Be sure to arrive at least 2 hours early since departures require more time than arrivals. There are several levels of security to clear, and the lines at airline check-in counters can be long. You'll need to fill out a departure form as well.

Beijing

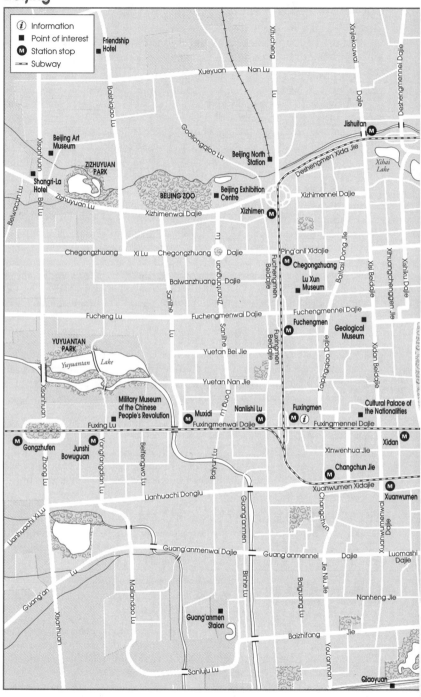

Legend:
- (i) Information
- ■ Point of interest
- (M) Station stop
- ⊨⊨ Subway

Friendship Hotel

Xueyuan Nan Lu

Xihucheng Lu

Xinjiekouwai Dajie

Deshengmennei Dajie

Baishiqiao Lu

Goaliongqiao Lu

Beijing North Station

Jishuitan (M)

Beijing Art Museum

Xisanhuan

ZIZHUYUAN PARK

Shangri-La Hotel

Beiwachn Lu

Bei Lu

Zizhuyuan Lu

BEIJING ZOO

Beijing Exhibition Centre

Deshengmen Xida Jie

Xihai Lake

Xizhimennei Dajie

Xizhimenwai Dajie

Xizhimen (M)

Chegongzhuang Xi Lu Chegongzhuang Dajie

Ping'anli Xidajie

Fuchengmen Beidajie

Chegongzhuang (M)

Baitasi Dong Jie

Xisi Beidajie

Xihuangchenggen Jie

Xishiku Dajie

Lu Xun Museum

Baiwanzhuang Dajie

Zhanlanguon Lu

Sanlihe

Fucheng Lu

Fuchengmenwai Dajie

Sanlihe Lu

Fuchengmennei Dajie

Fuchengmen (M)

Fuxingmen Beidajie

Geological Museum

Xidan Beidajie

Xiangiao Dajie

YUYUANTAN PARK

Yuyuantan Lake

Yuetan Bei Jie

Yuetan Nan Jie

Dong Lu

Xisanhuan

Military Museum of the Chinese People's Revolution

Muxidi (M)

Nanlishi Lu (M)

Fuxingmen (M) (i)

Cultural Palace of the Nationalities

Fuxing Lu

Fuxingmenwai Dajie

Fuxingmennei Dajie

Gongzhufen (M)

Junshi Bowuguan (M)

Yangfangdian Lu

Zhong Lu

Beifengwo Lu

Xinwenhua Jie

Xidan (M)

Changchun Jie (M)

Changchun Jie

Xuanwumen Xidajie

Xuanwumen (M)

Xuanwumennei Dajie

Lianhuachi XI Lu

Lianhuachi Donglu

Guang'anmen Lu

Guang'anmenwai Dajie

Guang'anmennei Dajie

Jie Niu Jie

Luomashi Dajie

Xisanhuan

Guang'an Lu

Malandao Lu

Binhe Lu

Baiguang Lu

Nanheng Jie

Guang'anmen Staion

Baizhifang Jie

You'anmen

Sanluju Lu

Qiaoyuan ■

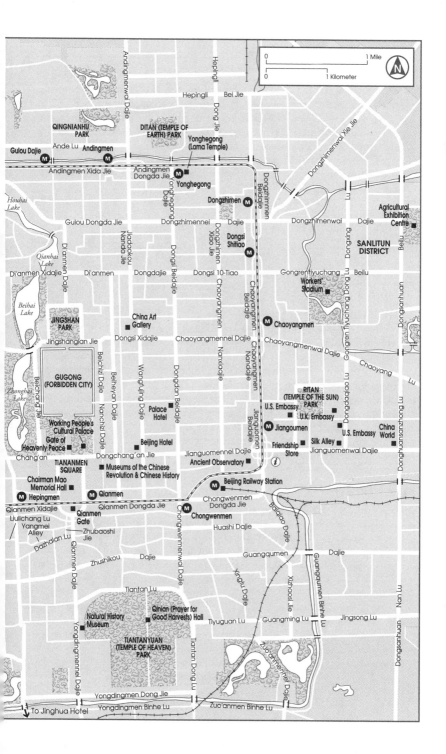

0 _____ 1 Mile
0 _____ 1 Kilometer

N

QINGNIANHU PARK

DITAN (TEMPLE OF EARTH) PARK

Yonghegong (Lama Temple)

Hepingli

Bei Jie

Hepingli

Dong Jie

Andingmenwai Dajie

Gulou Dajie

Ande Lu

Andingmen

Andingmen Xida Jie

Andingmen Dongda Jie

Yonghegong Dajie

Yonghegong

Dongzhimen Beidajie

Dongzhimenwai Xie Jie

Dongzhimen

Dongzhimennei Dajie

Dongzhimenwai Dajie

Agricultural Exhibition Centre

Houhai Lake

Gulou Dongda Jie

Jiaodaokou Nanda Jie

Dongsi Beidajie

Dongzhimen Xiao Jie

Chaoyangmen

Dongxing

SANLITUN DISTRICT

Beilu

Qianhai Lake

Di'anmen Dajie

Di'anmen Xidajie

Di'anmen

Dongdajie

Dongsi 10-Tiao

Dongsi Shitiao

Chaoyangmen Beidajie

Gongrentiyuchang Dong

Beilu

Gongrentiyuchang

Gongrentiyuchang

Beihai Lake

JINGSHAN PARK

Jingshanqian Jie

China Art Gallery

Dongsi Xidajie

Chaoyangmennei Dajie

Chaoyangmen Nandajie

Chaoyangmenwai Dajie

Workers' Stadium

Chaoyang Lu

Zhonghai Lake

Beichang Jie

Beichizi Dajie

Beiheyan Dajie

GUGONG (FORBIDDEN CITY)

Wangfujing Dajie

Nanchizi Dajie

Dongdan Beidajie

Nankidajie

Jianguomen Beidajie

RITAN (TEMPLE OF THE SUN) PARK

U.S. Embassy

U.K. Embassy

U.S. Embassy

China World

Palace Hotel

Working People's Cultural Palace

Gate of Heavenly Peace

Chang'an

Dongchang'an Jie

Beijing Hotel

Jianguomennei Dajie

Ancient Observatory

Jiangoumen

Friendship Store

Silk Alley

Jianguomenwai Dajie

TIANANMEN SQUARE

Museums of the Chinese Revolution & Chinese History

Beijing Railway Station

Chairman Mao Memorial Hall

Hepingmen

Qianmen

Qianmen Dongda Jie

Chongwenmen Dongda Jie

Chongwenmen

Qianmen Xidajie

Qianmen Gate

Chongwenmennai Dajie

Baihao Dajie

Liulichang Lu

Yangmei Alley

Zhubaoshi Jie

Huashi Dajie

Dazhalan Lu

Qianmen Dajie

Zhushikou

Dajie

Guangqumen

Dajie

Guangqumen Binhe Lu

Dongsanhuan Nan Lu

Tiantan Lu

Xingfu Dajie

Xizhaosi Jie

Jingsong Lu

Natural History Museum

Qinian (Prayer for Good Harvests) Hall

Tiyuguan Lu

Guangming Lu

Tiantan Dong Lu

TIANTANYUAN (TEMPLE OF HEAVEN) PARK

Yongdingmennei Dajie

Zuo'anmennei Dajie

To Jinghua Hotel

Yongdingmen Dong Jie

Yongdingmen Binhe Lu

Zuo'anmen Binhe Lu

31

at 28 Jianguomenwai Dajie (☎ **010/6515-8652;** fax 010/6515-8603), 3 miles due east of the Forbidden City on the main east/west avenue; it's open daily from 9am to 5pm. There's a Tourist Hotline as well (☎ **010/6513-0828**). A new office has opened in the CITS Building, Room 417, 103 Fuxingmennei Dajie (☎ **010/ 6607-1575** or 010/6608-7124), near the Nanlishilu subway stop. It is open Monday to Friday from 8:30am to 5:30pm.

For most visitors, their hotel and its tour desk are the initial source of information. The best source, particularly of current information about events, restaurants, and nightlife, consists of a number of free English-language newspapers and magazines that are distributed to hotels, shops, and cafes. *Beijing This Month* is a glossy magazine published by the Beijing Tourism Administration; it has feature stories, a city map, a monthly events calendar, and lots of useful ads. It is also available in an Internet edition (www.cbw.com/btm). Also keep an eye out for the monthly *Welcome To Beijing,* published in Hong Kong, which includes a good city map and an extensive updated listing of Beijing's markets, galleries, nightspots, bookshops, theaters, stores, businesses, and above all its restaurants. Three other free papers cover much the same ground, with a slant toward the expatriate community and the youth market: *Beijing Beat* (weekly), *Metro* (monthly), and *City Edition* (monthly).

CITY LAYOUT

Beijing is a flat, sprawling metropolis in northeast China; it's on roughly the same latitude as New York City (about 40°N). The **Beijing Municipality,** which has a status separate from any province, consists of four urban districts, six suburban districts, and eight counties. More than seven million inhabitants live in the city and suburbs. Steep mountain ranges, girded by the Great Wall, lie to the north. What will most concern the visitor is the center of this municipality, what was once the old city of Peking.

For 600 years, since the early days of the Ming Dynasty, the center of Beijing has been the **Forbidden City,** the grand imperial palace that faces **Tiananmen Square** to the south. The Forbidden City is still the central landmark for the traveler today. Now, picture a north-south axis through the Forbidden City and an east-west axis between palace and square. Surround this graph with two big ring roads. That's urban Beijing in a nutshell. Add orderly main streets and oblique lanes to complete the grid.

The east-west axis is Beijing's main thoroughfare, the wide and straight **Chang'an Avenue.** Chang'an, like most Beijing avenues, changes its name repeatedly, becoming Jianguomenwai Dajie in the east and Fuxingmenwai Dajie in the west. (*Dajie,* which is sometimes spelled *da jie,* means "avenue.") Running north from Chang'an Avenue, almost on the axis through the Forbidden City, is **Wang-fujing Avenue,** the city's main shopping street. Directly south of the Forbidden City and Tiananmen Square, again on the ancient axis, runs **Qianmen Avenue,** which leads to the Temple of Heaven.

This geometrically correct grid forms the outstretched arms and spine of Beijing past and present. Encircling central Beijing today are a First Ring Road, a Second Ring Road, and a Third Ring Road (and beyond that a Fourth and a Fifth Ring Road as well). The **First Ring Road** actually consists of no more than the streets encircling the Forbidden City. The **Second Ring Road** (which changes its name frequently as it completes its circle) traces the route of the old city walls. The **Third Ring Road** is largely an expressway, elevated at points. While the diameter of the Forbidden City is less than a mile, that of the Second Ring Road is more on the order of 4 miles, and of the Third Ring Road, 7 miles. The circle line of Beijing's subway lies under the Second Ring Road; its stops bear the names of the ancient city gates (some of which still stand). A crosstown subway line follows the east-west axis, running beneath Chang'an Avenue.

Beijing's **four inner districts** form four orderly quadrants inside the Second Ring Road. From the Forbidden City center point, Dongcheng District lies to the north-east, Xicheng to the northwest, Chongwen to the southeast, and Xuanwu to the southwest. Beijing's **four outer districts** (those outside the Second Ring Road) are Chaoyang to the east, Shijingshan to the west, Haidian to the northwest, and Fengtai to the southwest. Within these eight districts are many neighborhoods and subdistricts. District and area names are difficult to pronounce and to remember, but they can be useful. Most addresses bear not only the street name, but the district or neighborhood name, so knowing where an area lies can help in locating an attraction, shop, or cafe.

MAIN STREETS

Chang'an Avenue is the main east-west street, bisecting the north-south axis (as defined by the Forbidden City to the north and Tiananmen Square to the south). East of the Forbidden City, Chang'an Jie becomes Dongchang'an Jie (*dong* means "east" and *jie* means "street"), then Jianguomennei Dajie (*dajie* means "avenue"), and finally Jianguomenwai Dajie (*nei,* meaning "inner," has been changed to *wai,* which means "outer"). This eastern stretch of Chang'an Avenue contains many shops, hotels, and attractions (such as Silk Alley and the Friendship Store).

Parallel to and a few blocks south of Chang'an is another major street, **Qianmen Avenue,** which runs by the historic Qianmen Gate (*men* means "gate") at the southern end of Tiananmen Square. This street is called **Qianmen Dongdajie** to the east of the gate and **Qianmen Xidajie** to the west (*dong* means "east," and *xi* means "west").

North of Chang'an Avenue, there are several major east-west streets on the grid, all of which change names along the way, too. The first, **Jingshanqian Jie,** separates the north wall of the Forbidden City from the artificial hill that overlooks it (called

That Sinking Feeling

No matter how heavy the air pollution, the sky is not falling in Beijing, but the ground is. Scientists recently determined that the entire city of Beijing is sinking at an accelerating rate—now 20mm (nearly 1 inch) per year—due to increasing exploitation of underground water resources by industry.

Making Sense of Beijing Street Names

Unfortunately, Beijing's main streets, as well as the innumerable smaller streets and alleys that intersect them, are mouthfuls to pronounce and difficult to remember at first, but after a few trips through the city, they begin to sort themselves out. One reason that the street names in *pinyin* (see appendix B) seem so long is that they incorporate the characters for north or south, street or avenue, all running together in the street name. Pinyin is not English, so South Chizi Avenue is written as Nanchizi Dajie. Common items in street names and their English translations are as follows:

Bei = North	*Jie* = Street	*Wai* = Outer
Nan = South	*Dajie* = Avenue	*Nei* = Inner
Dong = East	*Lu* = Road	*Qiao* = Bridge
Xi = West	*Hutong* = Alley	*Men* = Gate

Jingshan Park or Coal Hill). As it runs east toward the Second Ring Road, Jing-shanqian Jie changes its name twice, becoming **Dongsi Xidajie,** and then **Chaoyangmen Neidajie.**

Farther north of the Forbidden City is another major east-west avenue, called **Di'anmen Xidajie** to the west and **Di'anmen Dongdajie** to the east of the main axis. When this street nears the Second Ring Road on the east, it changes its name yet again, to **Gongrentiyuchang Beilu.** Many cafes and Beijing's liveliest bar scene are located in this area, around the Sanlitun neighborhood, home of the diplomatic compounds.

The most important north-south street is **Wangfujing Dajie,** the capital's number-one shopping street, located 3 blocks east of the Forbidden City and running north from Chang'an Avenue. Other big north-south streets on the east side of the Forbidden City are **Nanchizi Dajie,** which runs along the palace moat; **Dongdan Beidajie,** a big shopping street 1 block east of Wangfujing; **Jianguomen Beidajie,** which is the name of the Second Ring Road north of Chang'an Avenue; and **Donghuansanzhong Lu,** which is the name of the Third Ring Road north of Chang'an Avenue. To the west of the Forbidden City, the most important north-south streets are **Xidan Beidajie** (a shopping street favored by locals) and **Fuxingmen Beidajie** (the name of the Second Ring Road north of Chang'an Avenue).

The **ring roads** are important streets in their own right, since many restaurants, hotels, shops, and attractions are located near them. This is especially true of the northeastern stretches of the Second and Third Ring Roads. At these points, the Second Ring Road is called **Chaoyangmen Beidajie** and the Third Ring Road is called **Dongsanhuan Beilu.**

FINDING AN ADDRESS

Even though the main streets are laid out in a checkerboard fashion on north-south and east-west axes, it is possible to get lost. The blocks, which appear short and simple on any map, are in reality extremely long. What looks like a 10-minute stroll can stretch to an hour on foot. Moreover, the main streets are constantly intersected by other, sometimes very substantial, streets that can be mistakenly identified. The trick is to locate a street sign. Nearly all of Beijing's big streets have signs on poles near intersections that give the names in Chinese characters and in pinyin, which is the alphabetical rendering of those characters (used on maps and throughout this book). The street signs can be obscured by the general chaos of the cityscape, by

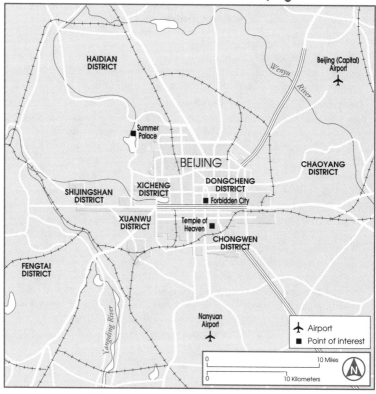

buses and traffic, and by their location, which may be as much as half a block from the actual intersection. Since one big block of buildings can be indistinguishable from the next, architectural landmarks are often few and far between. You have to be flexible and patient in navigating Beijing.

Actual street addresses can be even more difficult to discover, even on major buildings, and often don't exist at all. Part of the problem is caused by Beijing culture, which for centuries has not relied much on maps or numeric addresses, but on intimate familiarity with the neighborhood. Fortunately, most cafes and shops that cater to foreigners now post their addresses; parks, temples, and other large sites can usually be spotted by their traditional gates and the congregation of street vendors and taxis near their entrances.

MAPS

City maps (*ditu*) are indispensable, and are available from hotel desks. Street vendors sell maps as well, although they may be Chinese-only. The most useful maps are "trilingual," with street and place names in English, pinyin, and Chinese characters. The best city map, the Beijing China Regional Map, published by Periplus Editions, is available overseas as well as in Beijing. Streets and sights on this map are rendered in English, pinyin, and Chinese characters. While no map is perfect, and none can keep up with the daily onslaught of new construction (hotels, shops, restaurants) in this booming city, with this guidebook and a trilingual map in hand, you're set to explore the city.

Neighborhoods in Brief

As with any large metropolis, Beijing's main districts are subdivided into smaller districts and neighborhoods, but in the Chinese capital the main districts are also the main means of determining and describing locations. Of Beijing's eight main districts, the six of interest to the traveler are identified here.

Dongcheng   The sector north of Chang'an Avenue and from the Forbidden City east contains many of Beijing's top attractions, including Tiananmen Square and Wangfujing Dajie, the great shopping street. In its northern reaches, it encompasses Jingshan Park, the Lama Temple (Beijing's most popular), and the historic Bell and Drum Towers. Its northern and eastern borders are today enclosed by the Second Ring Road, which is where the city walls and gates once stood.

Chaoyang   Continuing east from Dongcheng District, you enter what was once the great suburb of Chaoyang. Chaoyang is now one of the city's wealthiest urban districts. In the area along Chang'an Avenue (here called Jianguomenwai Dajie) are Beijing's most famous open-air market (Silk Alley), the Friendship Store, the China World shopping center, and a row of grand international hotels. North of the Chang'an Avenue axis is Ritan Park and an adjacent, tree-lined embassy district. Farther north, near the large Workers' Stadium, is the Sanlitun diplomatic district, lined with scores of bars and small cafes. On the northeast arc of the Third Ring Road (here called Dongsanhuan Beilu), Chaoyang contains a number of international hotels, shopping plazas, and restaurants, including Beijing's Hard Rock Cafe.

Chongwen   Located south of Chang'an Avenue in the eastern quadrant of the great Beijing grid, Chongwen is home to the Natural History Museum, the old Qianmen neighborhood, and a stellar attraction, the Temple of Heaven (Tiantan Park).

Xuanwu   Also south of Chang'an Avenue, but in the western quadrant, Xuanwu contains the city's largest Moslem neighborhood (near the Ox Street Mosque) and, in the Dazhalan subdistrict, the historic street of Liulichang, Beijing's best strolling and antique shopping row.

Xicheng   The sector immediately west of the Forbidden City, Xicheng is the site of some of the most extensive old *hutong* (alleyway) neighborhoods left in Beijing. It is also the location of the city's most beautiful lakes: Beihai Lake, which Marco Polo praised, and the three "Back Lakes" of Xihai, Houhai, and Qianhai. The lakes are near some excellent temples and the lavish once-private grounds of Prince Gong's Mansion.

Haidian   Located far to the northwest on the way to the Summer Palace and the Western Hills, Haidian is best known as the capital's university district (site of China's Harvard, Beijing University). The zoo is its famous attraction, but Haidian is also the location of a new aquarium and an old temple that now houses the Beijing Art Museum.

Which Way Do I Go?

When finding an address proves impossible, ask a local. Even if they do not speak English, they might be able to locate the destination on your map and point you in the right direction. In moments of complete disorientation, you can also hail a cab to beam you back to your hotel. Becoming completely lost happens upon occasion even to experienced Beijing travelers.

2 Getting Around

Given the vastness of Beijing and the overcrowded conditions on its public buses, **taxis** and **the subway** become indispensable for any sight-seer. Fortunately, both are relatively inexpensive. An adventurous alternative is to travel as most Beijingers do, by bicycle.

BY SUBWAY

The Beijing subway (*ditie*) is the fastest way to cover longer distances, and it's incredibly inexpensive: 2RMB (25¢) per ride. The subway operates daily from 5am to 10:30pm. There are two lines: the circle line has 18 stops and girdles Beijing under the Second Ring Road; the crosstown line runs east-west along Chang'an Avenue. The two lines connect at Fuxingmen Station, where transfers are free (but passengers must walk upstairs or down to make the connection).

The **crosstown line,** which opened in 1969 and was China's first subway, has 13 stops, but most stations are far west of downtown and the city's attractions. The two exceptions are **Xidan Station,** which is near the shopping street of the same name (as well as the Sanwei Bookstore and the Beijing Concert Hall), and **Jianguomenwai Station,** located near the China World Hotel at the intersection of Jianguomenwai Dajie and the Third Ring Road. The latter is Beijing's newest subway station (opened October 1, 1999) and is the only stop in place on an 8-mile eastern extension of the crosstown line that's being developed. More stations are to be opened between China World and the Forbidden City in the near future along the crosstown line.

The 10-mile-long **circle line** is more useful. Many of its stations bear the names of the nine gates in the old city wall. (The wall itself was pulled down in the 1950s and replaced by the Second Ring Road and the subway loop.) Moving clockwise from the **Fuxingmen** stop (transfer point to the crosstown line), stops of interest to the sight-seer include **Xizhimen** (for the zoo, the aquarium, and the West Train Station), **Jishuitan** (for the Back Lakes and Soong Chingling's mansion), **Guluo Dajie** (for the Bell and Drum Tower area), **Yonghegong** (for the Lama Temple), **Jianguomen** (for Silk Alley and other sites along Jianguomenwai Dajie), **Beijing Zhan** (for the Beijing Train Station), **Qianmen** (for Tiananmen Square), and **Hepingmen** (for Dashalan and Liulichang Antique Street).

NAVIGATING THE SUBWAY   Using the subway is easy. Every platform looks the same, with trains running each direction on opposite sides. The station name in Chinese and pinyin is posted on pillars facing the tracks. Maps on tunnel walls indicate the next station on the route. Maps of the complete system are posted in each station and over each door inside the subway cars (always in Chinese characters and pinyin). In addition, a recording (usually quite audible), first in Chinese, then in

Finding the Subway

Finding a subway entrance can be tricky. First, study your map to see which intersection is nearest the station. There are usually at least four entrances, one on each side of the intersection (although not always on the corner). Look for a large sign with the letter D inside a circle. If you can't find the sign, look for a large bicycle park on the sidewalk. Subway entrances always have chain-link gates that are closed at night. Anywhere you see people entering and walking down a wide set of stairs is probably a subway entrance (except for a few street underpasses).

English, announces each upcoming stop. It's simple to navigate with all these aids, and should you find yourself going the wrong way, simply exit at the next station, cross the platform, and board the train running the opposite direction. The cars are a bit worn, but they're cleaner than the streets and most taxis. Subway cars lack air-conditioning, but they are seldom jam-packed except on Sundays and during rush hours (and even then you can get on). It takes from 3 to 4 minutes to travel between stations.

To enter a subway station, walk down the stairs. Subway entrances always have stairs; escalators—no elevators—are found at the exits, although they are often under repair. Walk through the tunnel until you come to the ticketing area. **Tickets** are sold at a ticket booth above the train platform. Push your cash through the ticket window and take your change and the paper ticket—there are no magnetic cards, passes, or tokens. Hand the paper ticket to the checker at the top of the final flight of stairs and hold onto the torn chit, which is sometimes checked again when you exit. Bilingual signs on platform posts can help direct you when you choose an exit. Your only problem upon exiting is determining what street you're standing on—not always easy until you locate a street sign or landmark.

BY TAXI

Beijing has some 70,000 taxis in the street, the most of any city in the world. Consequently, taxis are the most common means visitors use to get around the city. Expect to pay about 15RMB to 25RMB (about $2 to $3) for most excursions around town and up to 60RMB (up to $7.50) for a long crosstown trip. Credit cards aren't accepted. Tip 1RMB to 2RMB (10¢ to 25¢). To hail a taxi in the streets, stand on the edge of the sidewalk and stretch out your arm, raising an open palm. It's safest to ride in the backseat (especially for women traveling solo).

There are several levels of taxis. The cheapest are yellow minivans (*miandi*), which are being phased out by the government. They are seldom clean or comfortable, but they charge just 10RMB ($1.25) for the first 10 kilometers and 1.5RMB per additional kilometer. The best standard taxis, which congregate at leading hotels, are new cars (usually Japanese imports or Chinese-produced VW Santanas). They charge from 11.2RMB to 12RMB (about $1.50) for the first 4 kilometers and 1.8RMB to 2RMB (20¢ to 25¢) per additional kilometer. The smaller, older taxis (usually painted red) are less comfortable but are widely available. They charge 10.4RMB (about $1.30) for the first 4 kilometers plus 1.6RMB per additional kilometer. Note that taxis charge 20% more after 11pm and that the meters, which click every .5 kilometer, also click when the taxi is stopped in traffic (the meter clicks every 2½ minutes when car is motionless).

Always insist on using the taxi meter; any negotiated price is a rip-off. Be sure the meter is set at zero when you set off. If the meter is not on, say "*Qing da biao!*" If you want the taxi to stop, shout "*Ting che!*" Taxi complaints can be phoned in to

Taxi Tip: Breaking the Language Barrier

Most taxi drivers speak little or no English. If you speak little or no Chinese, get your hotel desk clerk or bellhop to write your destination (and your hotel name and address) on a slip of paper when you set out. Most hotels now provide printed cards for taxi travel; the card has the name of your hotel and a blank to fill in your destination. Many hotels also issue you a slip of paper with the taxi's ID number on it, in case you have a complaint later.

Yonghegong

Andingmen

Gulou Dajie

Jishuitan

Circle Line

Xizhimen

Dongzhimen

Chegongzhuang

Dongsi Shitiao

Pinggouyuan

Fuchengmen

Fuxingmen

Xidan

Chaoyangmen

East-West Line

Line Under Construction

Jianguomen

Gucheng Lu · Bajiaocun · Babaoshan · Yuquan Lu · Wukesong · Wanshou Lu · Gongzhufen · Junshi Bowuguan · Muxidi · Nanlishi Lu

Changchun Jie · Xuanwumen · Heplingmen · Qianmen · Chongwenmen · Beijing Zhan

the **Beijing Taxi Administration** (☎ **010/6601-2620**). Carry smaller bills to pay the driver (nothing over a 50RMB note). Receipts can be handwritten upon request (say "*Fa piao*").

BY BUS

Public buses (*gong gong qi che*) charge just .5RMB (6¢) for short trips (up to 2RMB, 25¢, for the longest trip), but they are more difficult to figure out and less comfortable than taxis and subways. Still, taking a bus in Beijing can be an inexpensive adventure. **Tickets** are sold on the bus; the conductor will want to know where you are going so he or she can figure the fare. Most conductors don't speak English, but most know the names of major attractions in English. Say your destination in English first, then attempt it in Chinese; if both attempts fall flat, point to your destination on a map. The red-and-white city buses service every bus stop. Electric trolleys cost the same as the buses. To figure out which bus number will get you to your destination, ask for help in your hotel. Buses 103 and 104, for example, run up and down the length of Chang'an Avenue. Be prepared to stand and be crammed during your expedition, and take care with backpacks and purses, as they can be inviting targets for thieves.

BY PEDICAB

These human-pedaled "tricycle taxis" or "rickshaws" appeal to tourists, but they can be expensive. You must haggle with the driver over the price, which usually starts in

Safety Tips for Pedestrians

A few things to keep in mind when navigating the capital on foot: Beijingers drive on the right side of the road, and they do not give pedestrians the right-of-way. At a red light, vehicles seldom stop when making a right turn, whether pedestrians are in the crosswalk or not. Walking in Beijing is rather like walking in downtown New York City, with the addition of millions of bicycles that don't always give way, either.

Renting a Car in Beijing

There are plenty of car rental outlets in Beijing, but don't plan on picking up a rental car at the airport or anywhere else. Tourists are forbidden to rent cars (or motorcycles or scooters) in China because a Chinese driver's license, which is available only to foreigners with an official residency permit, is required. Of course, major hotels are only too happy to rent chauffeured sedans to their foreign guests by the hour, day, or week, at rates that would make Mr. Avis or Mr. Hertz blush.

the 30RMB ($4) range but often ends up far higher. Ask the driver how much (*"Duo shou?"*) and then bargain from there; try to get the driver down to about half of his original asking price. Unless you are exploring the narrow and winding back alleys (*hutongs*) of old Beijing on your own, pedicabs aren't worth using. When bargaining, determine from the outset if the price is per person, one-way or round-trip, and in RMB or U.S.$.

BY BICYCLE

It may look intimidating and downright dangerous, but joining in with Beijing's millions of bike riders is not so difficult. The three main keys to success are riding at a leisurely pace, staying with the flow, and using the designated bike lanes on the big streets. A bicycle is the best way to see Beijing, especially its back streets, at your own pace. Most hotels rent good bicycles (usually newer mountain bikes) by the hour for 10RMB to 20RMB ($1.25 to $2.50), with better rates by the half or full day. Be sure the brakes are in good working order—you'll need them—and the tires fully inflated. Should you have a flat or need a repair, there are sidewalk bicycle mechanics in nearly every block, and they charge ridiculously low rates (1 to 2 *mao*, about 1 to 2¢). You'll also need a bicycle lock. Sometimes the lock is built into the back tire. When you reach your destination or need to stop and explore on foot, look for a forest of bikes parked at a major intersection or near a park, attraction, or major store. These are bike parks. Wheel your bike over, lock it next to others, and pay an attendant, who will give you a paper receipt. Parking costs are no more than a few *mao* (a few cents).

Fast Facts: Beijing

If you don't find what you're looking for in these listings, try the **Tourist Hotline** (☎ 010/6513-0828) or inquire at your hotel desk.

Airport   See "Arriving," under "Orientation" at the beginning of this chapter.

American Express   Holders of an American Express card can make inquiries about currency exchange, emergency card replacement, personal check cashing, and 24-hour access to an ATM at the China World Trade Center, Tower 1, Room 2101, 1 Jianguomenwai Dajie (☎ 010/6505-2888), but money exchange and other banking matters aren't handled here. Office hours are Monday to Friday from 9am to 5:30pm and Saturday from 9am to noon. American Express travel services are now handled at the new CITS office, Room 417, 4/F CITS Building, 103 Fuxingmennei Dajie (subway: Nanlishilu), which is open Monday to Friday from 8:30am to 5:30pm (☎ 010/6607-1575 or 101/6608-7124).

ATMs   See "Money" in chapter 2, "Planning a Trip to Beijing."

Baby-sitters   Most four- and five-star hotels can provide baby-sitting services, if you give them advance notice. Prices vary, but average about $5 per hour.

Banks   Convenient Bank of China locations for currency exchange and credit card cash withdrawals are **Bank of China Headquarters,** 410 Fuchengmenmei Dajie (☎ **010/6601-6688**), open Monday to Friday 9am to 4pm; **Bank of China Beijing Branch,** 8 Yaobao Lu (☎ **010/6519-9262**), open Monday to Friday 9am to noon and 1 to 5pm and Saturday and Sunday 9:30am to 3:30pm; **Bank of China Capital Airport Office** (☎ **010/6456-3987**), open daily 6am to midnight; **Bank of China Lufthansa Center Office** (☎ **010/6465-3388**), open Monday to Thursday 9am to 4pm and Friday 9am to 3:30pm. The **CITIC Industrial Bank** provides the same services at the CITIC Building, 19 Jianguomenwai Dajie (☎ **010/6501-3331**), open Monday to Friday 9am to noon and 1 to 4pm.

Bookstores   The **Foreign Language Bookstore,** 235 Wangfujing Dajie (☎ **010/6512-6922**), has the largest collection of English-language books in Beijing. The **Friendship Store,** 17 Jianguomenwai Dajie (☎ **010/6500-3311**), carries the next largest selection. Gift shops and kiosks in major hotels sometimes maintain a good collection of books about Beijing and China (as well as foreign newspapers). The gift shops at the Kempinski, the Kunlun, and the Traders hotel are worth browsing.

Business Hours   Since China adopted the 5-day work week in 1995, most banks and government offices are open Monday to Friday only, usually from 9am to 5pm, although some still close at the lunch hour (from noon to 2pm). Bank branches and CITS tour desks in hotels often keep longer hours and are usually open Saturday mornings. Shops and department stores are open every day, typically from 9am to 7pm or later. Most hotels keep their money exchange desks open 24 hours every day. Most temples and parks are open daily from sunrise to sunset. Other tourist sites are typically open daily from 9am to 5pm, although some, such as museums, may close for a day or two during the week (but are open on weekends). Restaurants outside hotels are generally open at least during these hours daily: 6am to 9am, 11:30am to 2pm, and 5pm to 9:30pm. Restaurants catering to foreigners may stay open later, and bars (which often have a cafe) don't close until the very wee hours.

Camera Repair/Film   Kodak, Fuji, and other imported camera films can be purchased all over Beijing, at hotel kiosks, mega-malls and shopping plazas, and camera stores. Prices are about on par with those in the West. There are 1-hour and next-day film processing outlets in hotels and shopping centers, too. For reliable camera repair and film developing, try **Beijing Photography,** 263 Wangfujing Dajie, Dongcheng District (☎ **010/6525-7301**), open daily 8:30am to 8pm.

Climate   See "When To Go" in chapter 2.

Computers & Laptops   Beijing lags behind Western capitals in installing data ports/modular plugs in hotel rooms, but it is quickly catching up. Most hotel business centers have computer (PC) rentals with up-to-date software, Internet access, and e-mail capabilities, and you may be able to plug in a laptop there. More hotels should be rewired for your laptop by the year 2000; at the moment, they really aren't.

Couriers   International parcel and courier services with offices in Beijing are **FedEx,** Golden Land Building, 32 Liangmaqiao Lu (☎ **010/6468-5566**), with four flights weekly to the U.S.; **DHL-Sinotrans,** with branches at China World Trade Center, Room 111, 1 Jianguomenwai Dajie (☎ **010/6505-2173**) and Lufthansa Center, 50 Liangmaqiao Lu (☎ **010/6465-1208**); and **UPS,** Kelun Building, Tower 2, 12A Guanghua Lu (☎ **010/6593-2932**).

Credit Cards   See "Money" in chapter 2 for details. American Express, Visa, MasterCard, and JCB are accepted at most hotels, hotel restaurants, and a growing number of stores and restaurants outside hotels. Diner's Club is accepted at many hotels, but the Eurocard is accepted at only a few of the top hotels. The Discover Card seems to be accepted almost nowhere in Beijing.

Currency   See "Money" in chapter 2 for an explanation of Renminbi (RMB) and conversion rates.

Currency Exchange   Certain branches of the Bank of China and other banks can convert your traveler's checks and national currencies to RMB. The rate is fixed by a government agency. Hotel desks also do currency exchanges, usually on a 24-hour basis, at rates nearly as good as the banks offer. A passport is required. There are no private offices or kiosks offering currency exchange services.

Customs   See "Entry Requirements & Customs" in chapter 2.

Doctors & Dentists   Hotels can refer foreign guests to dentists and doctors versed in Western medicine. Some hotels have in-house doctors and small clinics. The following medical clinics and hospitals specialize in treating foreigners and provide international-standard services: **Beijing United Family Hospital,** 2 Jiangti Lu (near the Hilton Hotel), is open 24 hours daily and has a pharmacy and in-patient and outpatient care (☎ **010/6433-3960**); **Beijing AEA International Clinic,** Building C, BITIC Leasing Center, 1 Xingfusancun Beijie, is open 24 hours daily and has a pharmacy, ambulance service, and three dentists (☎ **010/6462-9100**); **International Medical Center (IMC),** Beijing Lufthansa Center, Regus Office Building, Room 106, 50 Liangmaqiao Lu, is open 24 hours daily and has a pharmacy, ambulance service, dentists, and doctors speaking many foreign languages (☎ **010/6465-1561**). The **Hong Kong International Medical Clinic** at the Swissotel, Beijing Hong Kong Macau Center, 3rd Floor, Dongsishitiao, also provides doctors and dentists at its 24-hour clinic, which is closed Sundays (☎ **010/6501-2288,** ext. 2346). Medical charges at these facilities are on par with those in Western nations.

Documents Required   See "Entry Requirements & Customs" in chapter 2. Carry your passport and a copy of your passport at all times.

Drugstores   See "Pharmacies" below.

Earthquakes   Beijing is located in an earthquake-prone zone and is anticipating a San Francisco–style disaster, perhaps in the near (but unpredictable) future. In 1976, the nearby city of Tangshan was struck by a major quake that killed over 250,000 residents, the most fatal earthquake in history. China's earthquake experts are charged with making predictions and deciding upon ordering advance evacuations.

Electricity   The electricity in Beijing is 220 volts, alternating current (AC), 50 cycles. Outlets come in a variety of configurations. Be prepared to supply your own transformers and modem adapters. Hotels do supply a range of standard adapters. The most common adapters are the narrow round 2-pin, the slanted 2-prong, and the 3-prong types.

Embassies & Consulates   The embassies of most countries are located in Beijing in the Jianguomenwai and Sanlitun Embassy Compounds (Chaoyang District), several miles east and northeast of the city center. Visa and passport sections are open only at certain times of the day, so call in advance. Most embassies are open Monday to Friday only. The **U.S. Embassy** is at 3 Xiushui Beijie, Jianguomenwai Dajie (☎ 010/6532-3831/3431; fax 010/6532-3297). The **Canada Embassy** is at 19 Dongzhimenwai Dajie (☎ 010/6532-3536; fax 010/6532-4072). The **Ireland Embassy** is at 3 Ritan Donglu (☎ 010/6532-2914; fax 010/6532-2168). The **New Zealand Embassy** is at 1 Dong'erjie, Ritan Lu (☎ 010/6532-2731, fax 010/6532-4317). The **Australia Embassy** is at 21 Dongzhimenwai Dajie (☎ 010/6532-2331; fax 010/6532-4605). The **United Kingdom** of Great Britain and Northern Ireland Embassy is at 11 Guanghua Lu (☎ 010/6532-1961; fax 010/6532-1937).

Emergencies   The emergency phone numbers in Beijing are ☎ **110** for the police, ☎ **119** for the fire department, and ☎ **120** for an ambulance.

Holidays   See "When To Go" in chapter 2.

Hospitals   Consult the hospitals listed under "Doctors & Dentists" above; those hospitals cater to the expatriate community and foreign visitors. In addition, one Chinese hospital, the **Peking University Medical Hospital,** 53 Dongdanbei Dajie (☎ **010/6529-5284**), has a 24-hour emergency clinic for foreigners on its sixth floor.

Hotlines   The **Beijing Tourism Administration** maintains a 24-hour hotline for tourist inquiries and complaints in Chinese, Japanese, and English (☎ **010/ 6513-0828**).

Information   See "Visitor Information," above and in chapter 2.

Internet Access   While lagging well behind the West in Internet communications, the business centers at most large Beijing hotels now provide online access and e-mail services, including PC rentals that use familiar English-language software programs. Charges for computer rentals and e-mail can be put on your hotel bill and paid with a credit card. In-room Internet and e-mail access using your laptop is rarely available in Beijing at the present, but should become available by the year 2000. An alternative is to use the facilities at a growing number of independent Internet cafes around the city (see below).

Laundry & Dry Cleaning   Launderettes and Laundromats have not made a mark in Beijing. All hotels rated three stars and above provide full laundry and dry-cleaning services, often same-day service, with prices depending on the hotel's rating.

Internet Cafes

Since the first server was introduced in Beijing in 1994, Internet use in China has boomed, and Internet cafes are springing up everywhere. The most convenient outlets for travelers are provided by a Canadian joint-venture, **Unicom Sparkice Internet Cafes,** located across the capital (☎ **800-810-8100** in China; e-mail: csc@sparkice.co.cn; www.sparkice.co.cn). At the China World Trade Center branch (2nd Floor, 1 Jianguomenwai Dajie; ☎ **010/6505-0830**), there are two islands of Compaq PCs surrounded by counters and tables for coffee, cola, and snacks. There's a charge for sending and receiving e-mail, and each of the 20 workstations rent for 30RMB per hour ($3.60 per hour). Hours are daily from 10am to 10pm.

Liquor Laws   The drinking age in Beijing is 18. Bars keep irregular closing hours. Some bars don't close until 4am or later. Supermarkets and some hotel shops sell beer, wine, and spirits.

Beijingers don't drink much except on special occasions (birthdays, holidays, and family gatherings) and at banquets. Many Chinese have trouble tolerating alcohol, but some are also prodigious drinkers. Many Chinese believe that Westerners are big drinkers. At a banquet or dinner, follow your Chinese host's lead in drinking and toasting, but don't try to keep up if you're having too much.

Lost Property   First, contact the site where you think you lost an item. Then report the loss to your hotel staff for their suggestions and assistance in calling around town. Items lost in taxis are sometimes returned to your hotel.

Luggage Storage   The train stations have left-luggage counters, but the subway and airport do not. Hotels provide storage (often for a small daily fee) at their bell desks.

Mail   Most hotels sell postage stamps and can mail your letters and parcels. A few hotels even have small post offices. Overseas letters and postcards require 5 to 14 days for delivery. Rates are 3.20RMB (40¢) for an overseas postcard; 5.20RMB (60¢) for an aerogramme; and 5.40RMB (65¢) for a letter (up to 20g or 0.5 oz.). The main **International Post Office** (☎ 010/6512-8120) is on the Second Ring Road by the Jiangwai Diplomatic Compound, Jianguomen Beidajie, and is open Monday to Saturday from 8am to 6pm. There is also a post office branch located next to the Friendship Store on Jianguomenwai Dajie. For private couriers offering overseas express mail and parcel service, see "Couriers," above.

Money   See "Money" in chapter 2.

Newspapers & Magazines   The official *China Daily* English-language newspaper appears Monday to Friday, with a special edition on Saturdays. It's available free at hotel desks. It is a national newspaper, giving official views and China and world news and features, as well as a calendar of events and TV listings for Beijing. Monthly editions of English-language magazines and newspapers produced for travelers and expatriates in Beijing are also available at hotels and restaurants around town. Titles to look for include *Welcome to Beijing, Beijing This Month, Metro, Beijing Beat,* and *City Edition.* Foreign magazines and newspapers, including *USA Today, International Herald Tribune, South China Morning Post,* and Asian editions of the *Wall Street Journal* and *Newsweek* and *Time* magazines are available at the kiosks in all large international hotels.

Pharmacies   There are no 24-hour pharmacies in Beijing. Hotel kiosks, modern department stores, and supermarkets sometimes carry Western amenities and remedies (cough drops, toothpaste, shampoo, beauty aids), but bring your own pain and cold remedies. The best outlet for Westerners is **Watson's** at the Holiday Inn Lido, Jichang Lu, Jiangtai Lu (☎ 010/6437-6688, ext. 1277), open daily from 9am to 9pm, and at Full Link Plaza, 18 Chaoyangmenwai Dajie (☎ 010/6588-2145), open daily from 10am to 9pm. Prescriptions can be filled at the hospital pharmacies listed above under "Doctors & Dentists."

Police   The Beijing police force is known as the **Public Security Bureau (PSB).** The main office is at 85 Beichizi, near the Forbidden City. The emergency telephone number is ☎ 110.

Post Office   See "Mail," above.

Rest Rooms   For hygienic rest rooms, rely on the big hotels. Thousands of public rest rooms are located in parks, restaurants, and department stores; on the streets; and at the major tourist sites of Beijing. These public rest rooms are not clean and do not provide tissues or soap as a rule, although the rest rooms in the newest shopping plazas, fast-food outlets, and deluxe restaurants catering to foreigners often meet international standards. The more common public rest rooms often charge a small fee (usually .5RMB or less), but seldom provide Western-style facilities or private booths; instead, expect squat toilets (porcelain holes in the floor), open troughs, and rusty spigots. Look for WC signs at intersections pointing the way to these facilities. On the east side of the Forbidden City there is a large public rest room, with some Western toilets and booths; it charges a small fee, and its facilities are not particularly clean. Tourists often come armed with their own tissues and even a can of spray disinfectant. Be prepared to rough it if you are off the beaten track (meaning anywhere outside a major hotel).

Safety   Beijing is one of the safest capitals in the world for foreign travelers, but as the city modernizes and Westernizes, the usual precautions should be followed. Pickpockets and thieves do exist. At crowded public tourist sites, keep an eye on purses, wallets, and cameras. Always store valuables in a concealed safety pouch. Backpacks and fanny packs are targets on buses and the subway and in markets. Use hotel safety-deposit boxes or room safes, and do not open your door to strangers. Violent crimes and cases of sexual harassment against foreign visitors are quite rare, but do occur, so use common sense. Travel with others when possible, rebuff strangers in the streets, and avoid unlighted streets after dark. Beggars are common on Beijing streets, as are touts hawking merchandise. The touts often speak a little English and may pose as "friends"; they are not thieves, as a rule, but they should be rebuffed quickly. Don't give strangers the name or phone number of your hotel, unless you want to be bothered later.

Shoe Repair   There are streetside vendors who repair shoes and other leather goods for a small fee, but most hotels provide the same service.

Smoking   China has more smokers than any other nation, an estimated 350 million, accounting for one of every three cigarettes consumed worldwide. About 70% of the men smoke. Recent antismoking campaigns have led to laws banning smoking on all forms of public transport (including taxis) and in waiting rooms and terminals. The ban is spreading to some public buildings. Fines can be levied, but enforcement is sporadic. Hotels provide nonsmoking rooms and floors, and many restaurants have begun to set aside nonsmoking tables and sections. At present, expect to encounter more smoking in public places in China than in the West.

Taxes   Most hotels levy a 15% tax on rooms (including a city tax), and many restaurants and bars place a 15% service charge on bills. There is no sales tax. The other common tax tourists face is the international departure tax at the airport; it's currently 90RMB ($11) and is payable only in Chinese currency in the departure hall before checking in.

Taxis   See "Getting Around," above.

Telephone & Fax   The **country code** for China is 86. The **city code** for Beijing is 010. If you are calling a Beijing number from outside the capital but within China, dial the city code (010) and then the number. If you are calling Beijing from abroad, drop the first zero.

Kinko's in China

America's ubiquitous photocopy center opened its first branch in Beijing in 1998. Running 24 hours a day, it provides the same services in China as elsewhere, including copying, self-service copying (6 *mao* or 7¢ per page), scanning, and binding, along with PC rentals (65.60RMB/hr, $7.90/hr), conference room rentals (20RMB/hr, $2.40/hr), and free pickups and delivery (Monday through Friday 8am to 6:30pm). Fax rates are 4RMB (50¢) per page to receive, 6.20RMB (75¢) per page to send locally, 10RMB ($1.25) per page to send within China, and 20RMB ($2.50) per page plus phone charges to fax overseas. You can receive faxes free that are sent from any other Kinko's in the world. Kinko's Beijing is located 2 blocks north of the Jiangguang Centre on the Third Ring Road at A11 Xiangjun Beilu (☎ **010/ 6595-8020** or 010/6595-6388; fax 6595-8218; e-mail: kinkos@bj.col.com.cn).

Local calls in Beijing require no city code; just dial the 8-digit Beijing number (or the 3-digit emergency numbers for fire, police, and ambulance). Calls from Beijing to other locations in China require that you dial the full domestic city code (which always starts with **0**).

To call Beijing from the United States, dial 011 (the international access code) + 86 (the country code for China) + 10 (the city code for Beijing minus the initial zero) + the 8-digit Beijing number.

To make an international direct dial (IDD) call from Beijing (which you can now do from most Beijing hotel rooms), dial the international access code (**00**) + the country code for the country you are calling + the area code and the local phone number. The country code for the U.S. and Canada is **1,** for the United Kingdom **44,** for Australia **61,** and for New Zealand **64.** To call the U.S. from Beijing, for example, dial 00 + 1 + the U.S. area code + the U.S. phone number. If you have questions, speak with the hotel operator or an international operator (☎ **115**).

You can also use your **calling card** (AT&T, MCI, or Sprint, for example) to make international (but not domestic) calls from Beijing. The local access number for **AT&T** is ☎ **10-811;** for **MCI,** ☎ **10-812;** and for **Sprint,** ☎ **10-813.** Check with your hotel for the local access numbers for other companies. The directions for placing an international calling-card call vary from company to company, so check with your long-distance carrier before you leave home.

Most Beijing hotels provide **fax services.** Faxes are an efficient way to communicate overseas (and within Beijing and China). The charges for faxing overseas, however, can be two or three times those of faxing to Beijing from overseas, owing to hotel charges and the higher rates imposed on international communications by China.

Television   Chinese Central Television operates two stations (CCTV 1 and 2), and **Beijing Television** (BTV) has three stations. Nearly all programs (including amusing commercials, sports, and news) are in the Chinese language. Hotels, however, provide a spectrum of satellite stations and networks. Hong Kong–based Star TV has an English-language channel. Most hotels offer music video stations (such as MTV), CNN, and NHK (Japan), and some offer CNBC, BBC, ESPN, and other channels from the U.S., Europe, Australia, and even India. The most expensive hotels offer more than 20 Chinese and international channels. Most hotels provide either in-room movie channels or HBO (an Asian version); some hotels offer both.

Time Zone   Beijing (and all of China) is 8 hours ahead of Greenwich Mean Time (GMT + 8), meaning it is 13 hours ahead of New York, 14 hours ahead of Chicago, and 16 hours ahead of Los Angeles. Beijing does not use daylight savings time, so subtract 1 hour from the above times in the summer. Because China is on the other side of the international date line, you lose 1 day when traveling west from the U.S., but you gain it back upon return (across the Pacific). For the current time in Beijing, dial ☎ **117.**

Tipping   This practice is still officially forbidden in the People's Republic of China, and no tipping is necessary. In reality, however, Beijing hotel bellhops routinely receive 10RMB or $1 per bag; rest room attendants, 1RMB to 2RMB per visit; taxi drivers, the change from a bill (1RMB–5RMB); guides on day tours from hotels, 10RMB; and waiters (when no service charge is added), hairdressers, and other service personnel, 10% of the bill.

Water   Water from the tap is not safe for drinking (or for brushing teeth), even in the best hotels. The water available in hotel rooms in flasks or thermos has been boiled and is safe to drink. Clean bottled water can be purchased almost everywhere—even from street vendors and at tourist sites—for 10RMB to 40RMB ($1.25–$5) per liter. Western brands are sold at hotel kiosks, restaurants, and stores.

Weather   The *China Daily* newspaper, Chinese news programs, and some hotel bulletin boards furnish the next day's forecast. You can also dial Beijing's weather number, ☎ **121.**

4 Accommodations

Beijing offers more fine accommodations and international chain hotels than any other city in China (excepting Hong Kong), with higher prices to match. Even the budget hotels (there are no hostels, motels, or B&Bs in Beijing) charge more in Beijing than elsewhere in China. Rates are highest from May through October.

The first foreign joint venture (JV) hotel in China opened in Beijing in 1982. The Jianguo Hotel on Jianguomenwai Dajie introduced Western management and services to the capital. It became a favorite of expatriates and business travelers and paved the way for such foreign groups as Holiday Inn and Shangri-La (each with three Beijing hotels now). Foreign staff managed all these high-end ventures.

The Chinese government now ranks hotels on a star system. **Five-star hotels** have all the facilities and services of any international luxury hotel. The **four-star hotels** have many of the same facilities and services; they often lack only a few technical requirements (such as a large swimming pool or other amenities). Both four- and five-star accommodations have English-speaking staff and clean, luxurious rooms and are popular choices for Western travelers. **Three-star hotels** are usually Chinese-managed; the service at these hotels is less consistent, there are fewer amenities, and rooms are more basic, with a reduced dedication to upkeep and maintenance. Some three-star hotels are still adequate for the budget traveler who expects merely a decent place to spend the night. Few of the three-star hotels have experienced English-speaking staff, however, and most have limited facilities that can best be described as drab or run-down.

Acceptable **budget hotels** are almost nonexistent in Beijing. Most Western travelers (and tour groups) must select from more expensive four- and five-star accommodations. Hotels rated as two-star or below cater to the more rugged backpacking traveler who is not fussy; some offer dormitories and shared bathrooms. The government does not allow most of these lower-rated hotels to accept foreign travelers.

HOW TO CHOOSE THE LOCATION THAT'S RIGHT FOR YOU

The bulk of Beijing's international-level four- and five-star hotels are in one of three areas: (1) the **Dongcheng (City Center)** district near the Forbidden City, (2) the **Chaoyang East** district between the Second and Third Ring Roads along Jianguomenwai Dajie, and

For a complete rundown of Beijing's neighborhoods, see the "Neighborhoods in Brief" section in chapter 3, "Getting to Know Beijing."

(3) the **Chaoyang Northeast** district on the Third Ring Road North. The western and southern districts contain far fewer hotels.

On the face of it, you would think the most desirable location is in **Dongcheng**, nearest the Forbidden City, Tiananmen Square, and the Wangfujing shopping street. The only real drawback to staying in the city center is transportation. You can easily walk to some major sites and shops, but taxis have a hard time getting in and out of the heart of the capital, and it's a long walk to a subway entrance.

Some of China's best hotels are found east of the city center in the **Chaoyang East** district (those with Jianguomenwai Dajie addresses). It's up to a 45-minute walk to the city center and the Forbidden City from here, although a taxi can get you to the city center in about 10 minutes. When the subway extension is finished along Chang'an Avenue (see "Getting Around" in chapter 3), these hotels will be even closer to downtown. They are already closer to such attractions as Silk Alley and the Friendship Store than the city center hotels are.

Staying at one of the international hotels in the **Chaoyang Northeast** district on the Third Ring Road, about a 10- to 20-minute taxi ride from the city center, has its advantages, too. You can easily walk to the Sanlitun diplomatic district, for instance, which is Beijing's number-one neighborhood for international cafes, bars, and nightlife. Plenty of restaurants, markets, and shops surround these hotels, and guests out on the Third Ring Road North have a head start in reaching out-of-town destinations such as the airport (20 minutes by taxi) and the Great Wall.

None of these three main international hotel districts really has the upper hand in terms of convenience for the traveler. Even hotels in other districts are not necessarily undesirable, since the main tourist sites are scattered all over the sprawling city and therefore must be reached by taxi. The main drawback to choosing accommodations outside the three main hotel precincts is that other neighborhoods are less developed and more isolated. There are fewer shops, tourist attractions, and restaurants nearby.

HOW TO GET THE BEST ROOM FOR THE BEST RATE

The hotel rates listed in this guide are rack rates. The **rack rate** is the maximum rate a hotel charges for a room. You'd get that rate if you walked in off the street and asked for a room for the night. Hardly anybody pays these prices, however, and there are ways around them. Don't be afraid to bargain. Always ask politely whether a room less expensive than the first one mentioned is available. Rack rates change with the season (they're lowest from mid-November to mid-March) and are subject to competition within the industry.

Many four-star and five-star hotels in Beijing give travel agents discounts in exchange for steering business their way, so if you're shy about bargaining, an agent may be better equipped to negotiate discounts for you. Book your hotel overseas in advance when possible, through a travel agent, the hotel chain, or a reservation service.

Reservation services work as consolidators, buying up or reserving rooms in bulk, and then dealing them out to customers at a profit. Most of them offer online reservation services as well. A few of the more reputable providers are **Accommodations**

Last-Minute Deals

Independent travelers who haven't booked a hotel room before arrival can often get superb deals from the hotel desks in the Beijing Capital Airport. Last-minute rates offered here can sometimes translate into a stay at a four-star luxury hotel for the price of a no-star dump.

Express (☎ 800/950-4685; www.accommodationsxpress.com); **Hotel Reservations Network** (☎ 800/96HOTEL; www.180096HOTEL.com); **Quikbook** (☎ 800/789-9887, includes fax-on-demand service; www.quikbook.com); and **Room Exchange** (☎ 800/846-7000 in the U.S., 800/486-7000 in Canada). Online, try booking your hotel through **Arthur Frommer's Budget Travel** (www.frommers.com) and save up to 50% on the cost of your room. **Microsoft Expedia** (www.expedia.com) features a "Travel Agent" that can direct you to affordable lodgings.

Once in Beijing, keep your eye on the local city guides and monthly papers that are distributed free to hotels and restaurants. They frequently advertise tremendous hotel deals, with room rates far below published rack rates.

The hotel listings in this chapter are arranged first by price, then by location within the price category. Prices do not include a service charge of 15% per night and a city development tax of $1 to $2 per night. All rooms include private bathrooms, satellite television with foreign channels, and nonpotable (unless otherwise noted) tap water. Hotel names are rendered first in English, then in pinyin.

1 Dongcheng (City Center)

VERY EXPENSIVE

Grand Hotel (Guibinluo Fandian).

33 Dong Chang'an Jie (west side of Beijing Hotel), Beijing 100006. ☎ **800/223-6800,** or 010/6513-7788. Fax 010/6513-0048. 218 units. A/C MINIBAR TV TEL. $300 double. AE, DC, JCB, MC, V. No subway station nearby, but hotel is within walking distance of the Forbidden City.

This 10-story 1990 addition to the Beijing Hotel (see below) is the closest hotel to the Forbidden City. It's a true luxury hotel, although its staff and management are not quite as efficient as those of the other international five-star hotels in the city center. The facilities are first-rate and grand. The hotel's centerpiece is its seven-story atrium (beginning on the third floor) with marble floors, three glass elevators, cascading greenery, and fountains with figures of the zodiac. The atrium's east wall retains the facade and white marble archway of the original Peking Hotel (1917). The elegant guest rooms are of good size, with rosewood Chinese furniture and objets d'art, safes, hair dryers, and coffeemakers. The best rooms, on the west side of the tower, have fine views of the Forbidden City. Bathrooms feature separate tubs and showers, phones, and makeup mirrors. There is no hotel shuttle bus, but taxis are always at the front door.

Dining: The coffee shop on the second floor has good international dishes and buffets, the atrium offers snacks and ice cream, and the fourth-floor Cantonese restaurant (overlooking the atrium) serves bird's nest soup, shark's fin, abalone, and other pricey dishes ($40–$100 per person) in an elegant setting. In the summer, the rooftop terrace offers barbecues and a stunning view.

Amenities: Indoor swimming pool (under a skylight), health club with exercise machines, Jacuzzi, sauna, bicycle rental, small 24-hour business center (e-mail, PC rental), conference rooms, tour desk, beauty salon, shops (souvenirs, newsstand), 24-hour room service, same-day laundry and dry cleaning services, newspaper delivery, nightly turndown, baby-sitting, concierge, valet.

✪ Holiday Inn Crowne Plaza (Guoji Yiyuan Huangguan Jiari Fandian).

48 Wangfujing Dajie (corner of Dengshikou Dajie), Beijing 100006. ☎ **800/465-4329** in the U.S. and Canada, 1800/221-066 in Australia, 0800/442-222 in New Zealand, 1800/553-155 in Ireland, 0800/897-121 in the U.K., or 010/6513-3388. Fax 010/6513-2513. www.crowneplaza.com. E-mail: HICPB@public3.bta.net.cn. 385 units. A/C MINIBAR TV TEL. $220 double. Children under 19 stay free in parents' room. AE, DC, JCB, MC, V. No subway station nearby, but hotel is within walking distance of the Forbidden City.

This intimate Crowne Plaza—China's first—opened in 1991. It has a sky-lit atrium open to all nine floors and an art theme underlined by a sales gallery of contemporary Chinese work off the lobby and an art salon on the second-floor mezzanine. The service level is lifted by the presence of the most helpful bellhop staff in Beijing (ask them for sight-seeing, shopping, and restaurant tips). Every evening, live performances of classical music fill the atrium. Half of the guest rooms face into the high atrium, and the other half face the city's shopping streets. Standard rooms on floors 3 through 6 are exceedingly small for a five-star hotel, but are stuffed with lavish amenities (coffeemaker, hair dryer, robes). Counter space is minimal. Bathrooms (with phones) are clean and modern. There are two executive floors (7 and 8). The top floor (9) is nonsmoking and contains guest rooms, a swimming pool, and health facilities with a panoramic view of downtown. By Beijing standards, this is a tiny five-star hotel with tiny rooms, but the service and city-center location are excellent.

Dining/Diversions: The Atrium Coffee Shop serves buffets and well-prepared international dishes. There are two elegant restaurants on the second floor with mezzanine seating on the atrium: Pearl Garden specializes in Cantonese dishes and dim sum, and the Plaza Grill (see chapter 5, "Dining") has excellent continental fare. The Inn Bar on the mezzanine is a quiet place for a drink.

Amenities: Indoor swimming pool with views of the city, small health club with exercise machines, Jacuzzi, sauna, solarium, bicycle rental, small 24-hour business center (e-mail, PC rental), conference rooms, tour desk, beauty salon, shops (antiques, souvenirs, sundries), 24-hour room service, same-day laundry and dry cleaning services, newspaper delivery, nightly turndown, baby-sitting.

✪ The Palace Hotel (Wangfu Fandian).

8 Jingyu Hutong (1 block east off Wangfujing Dajie), Beijing 100006. ☎ **800/262-9467** or 010/6512-8899. Fax 010/6512-9050. E-mail: tph@peninsula.com. 530 units. A/C MINIBAR TV TEL. $300 double. AE, DC, JCB, MC, V. No subway station nearby, but hotel is within walking distance of the Forbidden City.

This is indeed a modern palace fit for China's modern capital. It's the most luxurious of Beijing's city-center hotels, with its own fleet of Rolls-Royces and a stunning red marble lobby with a waterfall. The services (presided over by the Hong Kong–based Peninsula Group) and the considerable facilities are at the top of the scale, too. This hotel pampers its guests in every way. The two basement floors contain China's most exclusive shops and boutiques, including the first Armani on the mainland. The gold-trimmed rooms are spacious. Robes, slippers, in-room safes, bedside control panels, two closed-circuit movie channels, and executive work desks are standard. The large marble bathrooms are equipped with safe drinking-water dispensers and mist-free bathroom mirrors. Westerners outnumber Asians among guests. The executive floors were renovated in 1998. Nonsmoking rooms are available by request.

Beijing Accommodations

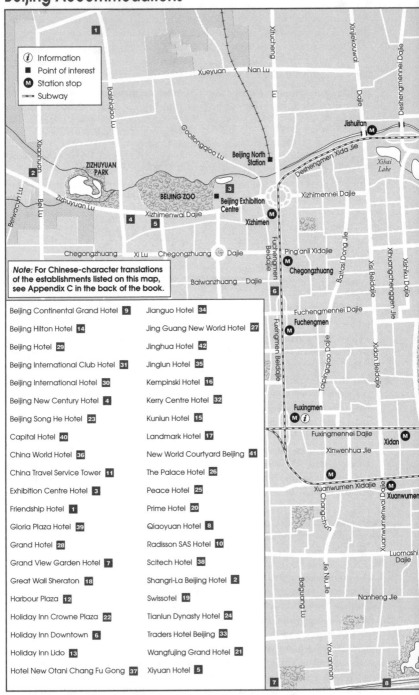

Legend:
- *ⓘ* Information
- ■ Point of interest
- Ⓜ Station stop
- Subway

Note: For Chinese-character translations of the establishments listed on this map, see Appendix C in the back of the book.

Beijing Continental Grand Hotel **9**	Jianguo Hotel **34**
Beijing Hilton Hotel **14**	Jing Guang New World Hotel **27**
Beijing Hotel **29**	Jinghua Hotel **42**
Beijing International Club Hotel **31**	Jinglun Hotel **35**
Beijing International Hotel **30**	Kempinski Hotel **16**
Beijing New Century Hotel **4**	Kerry Centre Hotel **32**
Beijing Song He Hotel **23**	Kunlun Hotel **15**
Capital Hotel **40**	Landmark Hotel **17**
China World Hotel **36**	New World Courtyard Beijing **41**
China Travel Service Tower **11**	The Palace Hotel **26**
Exhibition Centre Hotel **3**	Peace Hotel **25**
Friendship Hotel **1**	Prime Hotel **20**
Gloria Plaza Hotel **39**	Qiaoyuan Hotel **8**
Grand Hotel **28**	Radisson SAS Hotel **10**
Grand View Garden Hotel **7**	Scitech Hotel **38**
Great Wall Sheraton **18**	Shangri-La Beijing Hotel **2**
Harbour Plaza **12**	Swissotel **19**
Holiday Inn Crowne Plaza **22**	Tianlun Dynasty Hotel **24**
Holiday Inn Downtown **6**	Traders Hotel Beijing **33**
Holiday Inn Lido **13**	Wangfujing Grand Hotel **21**
Hotel New Otani Chang Fu Gong **37**	Xiyuan Hotel **5**

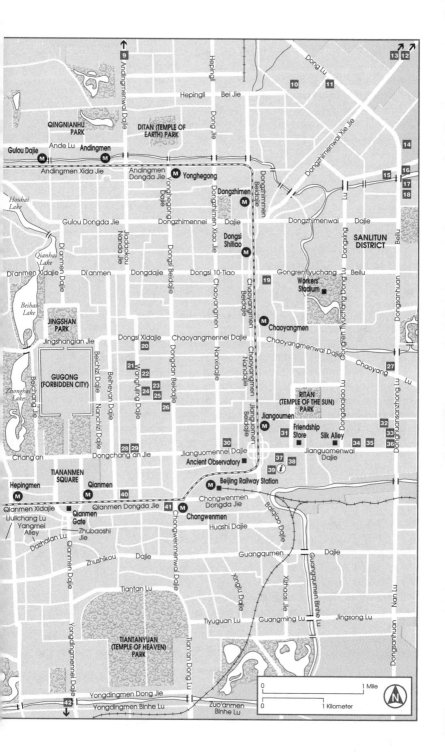

The health club and restaurants are top-flight. The only drawback (beyond the price) is that there's no airport shuttle bus (but airport transfer in a chauffeured Mercedes Benz can be booked for a mere $140 one-way).

Dining/Diversions: Four superb (and expensive) restaurants specialize in Italian, German, Cantonese, and Chaozhou (Southern Chinese) cuisines. The Palm Court Coffee House offers large buffets and international dishes. The Lobby Lounge has an afternoon tea. The Intermezzo Lounge serves cocktails, and the Point After has music, dancing, and karaoke.

Amenities: Indoor swimming pool, large health club with superb exercise machines and weights, Jacuzzi, sauna, solarium, large 24-hour business center (e-mail, PC rental), many conference rooms, tour desk, beauty salon (Clarins Beauty Institute, with French-trained staff), shopping arcade (the most exclusive boutiques in China), concierge, 24-hour room service, same-day laundry, same-day dry cleaning and pressing services, newspaper delivery, nightly turndown, massage, twice-daily maid service, baby-sitting, limousine fleet.

Prime Hotel (Huaqiao Dasha).
2 Wangfujing Dajie (on corner of Dongsi Xidajie), Beijing 100006. ☎ **800/223-5652** (Steigenberger Reservation Service) or 010/6513-6666. Fax 010/6513-4248. www. primehotel.com. E-mail: sales@phb.com.cn. 400 units. A/C MINIBAR TV TEL. $220 double. AE, DC, JCB, MC, V. No subway station nearby, but hotel is within walking distance of the Forbidden City.

Known as the Guangdong Regency when it opened in 1991, the nine-story Prime Hotel has been upgraded to five-star status, meaning its facilities are nominally on par with those of its nearest competitors, but it ranks no higher than fifth (behind The Palace, the Holiday Inn Crowne Plaza, the Grand Hotel, and the Wangfujing Grand, in that order). The Prime gets a lot of international tour groups these days, and even has a group check-in area off its spacious white marble lobby. Still, the hotel has splendid modern facilities. The rooms are fairly large, with hair dryers, bathrobes, safes, writing desks, and data plugs (for PCs) standard. There's an executive floor, some nonsmoking rooms, and a few rooms for travelers with disabilities. The four restaurants are good choices. No hotel shuttle is provided, but taxis come right to the door.

Dining: There are lots of choices in the hotel, which is a strong point. Alfred's is one of Beijing's few Mexican restaurants (although the Mexican chef departed recently). The Emperor Restaurant with its red-and-gold Forbidden City design has a tasty "Emperor Chicken" entree and Cantonese selections. La Dolce Vita serves Italian. Cafe Wangfujing offers buffets and international fare, including dim sum, pasta, and a salad bar. Off the lobby is a small international deli, and in the lobby lounge itself is an ice cream stand.

Amenities: Narrow indoor swimming pool, solarium, small health club with a few exercise machines, sauna, massage, business center (e-mail, PC rental), conference rooms, tour desk (extensive city tour options), beauty salon, shops (souvenirs, newsstand), 24-hour room service, nightly turndown, same-day laundry and dry cleaning services, newspaper delivery, small florist, concierge, valet, baby-sitting, bicycle rental.

EXPENSIVE

✪ Beijing Hotel (Beijing Fandian).
33 Dong Chang'an Jie (on corner of Wangfujing Dajie), Beijing 100004. ☎ **010/ 6513-7766.** Fax 010/6513-7703. 850 units. A/C MINIBAR TV TEL. $160 double. AE, DC, JCB, MC, V. No subway station nearby, but hotel is within walking distance of the Forbidden City.

Hotel Trivia

Until it was ordered to sell off its business investments in 1998 and 1999, the People's Liberation Army (PLA) was the behind-the-scenes owner of the ultra-chic **Palace Hotel**—with its fleet of Rolls-Royces rather than tanks.

This historic hotel consists of three parts: a seven-story middle section built in 1917 (known for decades as the Peking Hotel), a seven-story west wing added in 1954, and an 18-story east wing opened in 1974. In 1999, the two oldest sections were combined and extensively renovated, and the old French-style guest rooms with their brocade wallpapers were eliminated. Only a few reminders of the Peking Hotel's glory days remain, but the east wing still contains some older-style rooms with high ceilings and black Qing-style furniture. While these old rooms are a bit run-down, the bathrooms sparkle (with hair dryers and phone). The hotel has a five-star government rating, but this is a courtesy extended because of the hotel's history. In reality, the amenities and services rate just above three stars. There is no hotel shuttle service. The remodeling has brought about the addition of a swimming pool and tennis court; the televisions pick up CNN and in-house movies; and the shopping arcade is extensive. The hotel is still worth strolling through, even if you're not a guest, since it contains a massive old pre-revolutionary ballroom and in the east lobby a Bosendoufer grand piano that has been in Beijing since 1900. While services and amenities are better at other downtown hotels, the Beijing Hotel can't be equaled for its central location and links to the old Peking.

Dining: In addition to several large Chinese restaurants and banquet halls, there is the Mingyuan Tea House in the shopping arcade area serving tea and snacks, and a Japanese restaurant (Gonjin Byakusho) on the second floor. The Lucky Lounge off the lobby is a bright, new outlet serving Western buffet breakfast, lunch, and dinner and international snacks throughout the day.

Amenities: Indoor swimming pool, small health club with exercise machines, Jacuzzi, sauna, business center (e-mail, PC rental, from 8am to 11pm), conference rooms, tour desk (extensive city tour options), beauty salon, extensive shopping arcade (antiques, souvenirs, sundries, traditional medicines, wines, tobacco, newsstand), 24-hour room service, same-day laundry and dry cleaning services, newspaper delivery, post office, florist.

Capital Hotel (Shoudu Biguan).

3 Qianmen Dong Dajie (4 blocks east of Tiananmen Square), Beijing 100006. ☎ **010/6512-9988.** Fax 010/6512-0309. E-mail: cptlhtls@public3.bta.net.cn. 326 units. A/C MINIBAR TV TEL. $180 double. AE, DC, JCB, MC, V. Subway: Qianmen (15 minutes west).

Since a $10 million renovation in 1996, this four-star, 20-story hotel near the south entrance to Tiananmen Square has been leaning toward achieving five-star status in its facilities and services. It certainly has the facilities to qualify. The imposing red marble lobby is a bit dark, but the garden goldfish ponds and walkways outside are pleasant and bright. The rooms have adequate space and counters. Writing desks, safes, satellite TVs with CNN and HBO, coffeemakers, hair dryers, and separate showers and bathtubs are standard. There are two executive floors (14, 15), a non-smoking floor (12), and rooms for travelers with disabilities. The staff speaks English and is helpful. There is a hotel shuttle serving a few city locations (but not the airport). This is the best city-center hotel on the south side of Chang'an Avenue; it's within a 30-minute walk of downtown sites.

Dining/Diversions: The elegant Italian restaurant on the 20th floor, Ristorante Bologna, has superb views of the Forbidden City and reasonable prices. There are two Chinese restaurants and a fine Japanese restaurant (Kyotaru). The Chatterbox Cafe in the lobby serves international dishes 24 hours a day. The large outdoor garden features barbecues in the summer.

Amenities: Indoor swimming pool, small health club with exercise machines, Jacuzzi, sauna, bowling alley (four lanes), billiards, video games, massage, acupuncture, 24-hour business center (e-mail, PC rental), conference rooms, tour desk, air ticket office, beauty salon, shopping arcade (souvenirs, luggage, drugstore, newsstand), 24-hour room service, same-day laundry and dry cleaning services, nightly turndown, newspaper delivery, bicycles.

Peace Hotel (Heping Binguan).

3 Jinyu Hutong (1 block east of Wangfujing, opposite the Palace Hotel), Beijing 100004. ☎ **010/6512-8833.** Fax 010/6512-6863. 404 units. A/C MINIBAR TV TEL. $110 double (west wing); $150 double (east wing). AE, DC, JCB, MC, V. No subway station nearby, but hotel is within walking distance of the Forbidden City.

Built on the site of a Qing Dynasty garden in 1952, the Peace Hotel was rebuilt as a four-star, 22-story joint venture in 1984. Rooms in the east wing are larger and more modern, but the west wing is gradually being renovated and the lobby is being expanded. The hotel has a bustling, crowded feel. Enough Westerners stay here to give it an international feel. The staff speaks some English. Rooms in the east wing are of average size, with space for a writing desk, coffee table, and two chairs. Bathrooms are modern and clean. Rooms have hot-water thermoses, but no coffeemakers or hair dryers. There are two nonsmoking floors (10, 18) and three executive floors (16–18, $170) with their own business center and breakfast lounge. A wide range of facilities (post office, air ticket counter, disco) and downtown location make this a good choice for the price. There is no hotel shuttle bus, but taxis are readily available.

Dining/Diversions: The lobby bar serves snacks and dim sum. The Korean barbecue (Hanwoori) has lunch and dinner. American cuisine and seafood hotpots are available in the 24-hour Peppermint Park coffee shop. Two Chinese restaurants are open for lunch and dinner (Lu Chun Yuan for Shandong and Sichuan selections and Chaoi Ming Yuen for Cantonese cuisine). The hotel is connected to the House Discotheque.

Amenities: Small indoor swimming pool, small health club with exercise machines, Jacuzzi, sauna (Turkish style), massage, billiards and mahjong rooms, conference rooms, business center (without e-mail or PC rental), conference rooms, tour desk, beauty salon, shopping arcade (souvenirs, sundries, newsstand), 24-hour room service, same-day laundry and dry cleaning services, air ticket center, post office.

Tianlun Dynasty Hotel (Tianlun Wangchao Fandian).

50 Wangfujing Dajie (on the southeast corner of Dengshikou Dajie), Beijing 100006. ☎ **010/6513-8888.** Fax 010/6513-7866. www.tianlundynastyhotel.com. E-mail: tianlun@public.bta.net.cn. 408 units. A/C MINIBAR TV TEL. $186 double. AE, DC, JCB, MC, V. No subway station nearby, but hotel is within walking distance of the Forbidden City.

The Tianlun is a showy four-star hotel in downtown Beijing. It claims to have the largest hotel atrium in Asia: a miniature Tiananmen Square with copies of the Arc de Triumph and Roman and Greek palatial sculptures. There's a remodeled bowling alley in the basement and 13 new 3-D video games from Japan. Also in the basement is Timeless Medley, a new Asian snack emporium decorated with cinema memorabilia. Beyond the splash of big and trendy public spaces, however, are the rooms, which are of average size, just wide enough for a desk and a small sitting area. Rooms are modern, but don't have coffeemakers, hair dryers, or safes. The executive floor (10) has extra services. Tour groups (mainly Asian) make up most of the guests. There's no shuttle bus, but the hotel's central location on the big shopping street makes taxis easy to find. This hotel has had maintenance problems since its opening in 1991, but it appears to be pulling itself back into shape under the direction of a female general manager, one of the very few in China.

Dining/Diversions: In the lobby, the Courtyard serves international dishes and Western buffet breakfasts. On the second floor, Four Seasons, renovated in 1998, serves fine Sichuan and Cantonese dishes, accompanied by live traditional music. Downstairs, Timeless Medley, Beijing's first restaurant to combine movie and food cultures, is decorated to reflect scenes from famous Chinese films.

Amenities: Indoor swimming pool, small health club with exercise machines, Jacuzzi, sauna, billiards and mahjong rooms, outdoor tennis court, larger than average business center (e-mail, PC rental; open 7am to 10pm), conference rooms, tour desk, beauty salon, extensive shopping arcade (antiques, souvenirs, sundries, newsstand), 24-hour room service, same-day laundry and dry cleaning services, fresh pastry shop.

✪ Wangfujing Grand Hotel (Wangfujing Dafandian).

57 Wangfujing Dajie, Beijing 100006. ☎ **010/6522-1188.** Fax 010/6522-3816. 380 units. A/C MINIBAR TV TEL. $180 double. AE, DC, JCB, MC, V. No subway station nearby, but hotel is within walking distance of the Forbidden City.

With 14 stories, this grand five-star Chinese-managed hotel (opened in 1995) towers over the shops on the north end of Wangfujing and affords good views of the Forbidden City from half its rooms. The spacious lobby is grand as well, with inlaid marble, a fountain, and a hemispherical chandelier. The rooms are small (about the size of those at the nearby Holiday Inn Crowne Plaza), with just enough room for a coffee table and two chairs. They are freshly decorated with gold furnishings and warm bird's-eye maple trim; all have hair dryers and tea-making facilities (but no coffeemakers). The fourth floor is for nonsmoking guests. While the staff is not as efficient or as familiar with foreign travelers as that of the Crowne Plaza, some of the facilities here are larger, including several souvenir and clothing shops and the longest indoor swimming pool in the city center (25 meters). This is a luxurious place worth considering, especially if you can negotiate a good deal on the room rate. The hotel gets many large tour groups from Asia and Europe. There is no hotel airport shuttle.

Dining: The two Chinese restaurants are large, open, and glitzy. China Summit serves Sichuan dishes and has private rooms for karaoke; the smaller Chao Yue serves Chaozhou (southern Chinese) dishes. A Korean restaurant is to be added. The Rome Garden Coffee House in the lobby provides full buffets and an international menu. The wine bar has an extensive list of drinks and private rooms.

Amenities: Very large indoor swimming pool, hot tubs, good health club with new exercise machines, Jacuzzi, sauna, billiards, 24-hour business center (e-mail, PC rental), conference rooms, tour desk, beauty salon, shopping arcade (with crafts and clothing), concierge, 24-hour room service, same-day laundry and dry cleaning services, newspaper delivery, nightly turndown, massage.

MODERATE

Beijing International Hotel (Beijing Guoji Fandian).

9 Jianguomennai Dajie (on the northeast corner of Chaoyangmen Nanxiaojie), Beijing 100005. ☎ **010/6512-6688.** Fax 010/6512-9961. 1,008 units. A/C MINIBAR TV TEL. $110 double. AE, DC, JCB, MC, V. Subway: Jianguomen (½ mile northeast).

One of Beijing's largest hotel complexes, this 29-story, modern monolith (built in 1987 and renovated in 1996) is owned by the China National Tourism Administration and gets many Western and Asian tour groups. On the north side of Chang'an Avenue, it is over a mile east of the Forbidden City, but near some modern shopping complexes and less than half a mile from the railway station. The facilities are four-star, but the room rates are relatively low (with 67 standard rooms going for less than $80). The rooms are large and modern, and the bathrooms clean. The staff is familiar with international travelers. Satellite channels include CNN. Shops include a small supermarket stocked with some Western brands. There's no hotel shuttle, but catching taxis at the hotel entrance is easy.

Dining/Diversions: There are 16 restaurants in this complex, with outlets featuring Cantonese, Shanghai, and vegetarian Chinese dishes; Western buffets; and Japanese, Korean, and Swiss specialties. The revolving restaurant on top serves international dishes and gives an excellent view of downtown Beijing.

Amenities: Indoor swimming pool, health club with exercise machines, Jacuzzi, sauna, massage, one tennis court, bowling alley (10 lanes), small business center (e-mail, PC rental), conference rooms, tour desk (extensive options), beauty salon, large shopping arcade (souvenirs, clothing, newsstand), 24-hour room service, same-day laundry and dry cleaning services, florist, supermarket.

Beijing Song He Hotel (Songhe Da Jiudian).

88 Dengshikuo Jie (just off Wangfujing Dajie, south of the Holiday Inn Crowne Plaza), Beijing 100006. ☎ **010/6513-8822.** Fax 010/6513-9088. 310 units. A/C MINIBAR TV TEL. $90 double. AE, MC, V. No subway station nearby, but hotel is within walking distance of the Forbidden City.

A Novotel from 1992 to 1997, this three-star hotel is now flying under local management and trying hard to do a good job. From 1993 to 1995, it was rated by the city as the best hotel in its class. Its rooms are as large or larger than those across the street at the nearest five-star hotel (the Holiday Inn Crowne Plaza), but its amenities are simple and few (no hair dryer, no coffeemaker, no CNN), although there are safes. Bathrooms are modern and clean and even include a phone. The deluxe rooms are more spacious (worth the $10/night extra). The top floor (11) is for nonsmoking guests, and the executive floor (10) has extra amenities and services. Guests are mostly overseas Asian, but there are enough Westerners so you won't feel isolated. There are cheaper three-star hotels in Beijing, but given the fine location and adequate maintenance level of the Song He, it's one of the city's top in its class.

Dining/Diversions: The Sawasdee Restaurant has some of Beijing's best Thai buffets (lunch and dinner) and features a dancing troupe on weekends. The large Spring Garden restaurant, decorated in red and gold, specializes in fresh seafood. The Song He Coffee Shop serves inexpensive buffet breakfasts and à la carte lunch and dinner (Western and Asian cuisines). The hotel is a favorite of locals for parties and banquets, and there are two disco/karaoke bars.

Amenities: Small health club with exercise machines, sauna, massage, small business center (e-mail, PC rental; open 7:30am to 10:30pm), conference rooms, tour desk, beauty salon, shops (souvenirs, newsstand), 24-hour room service, same-day laundry and dry cleaning services.

2 Chaoyang East

VERY EXPENSIVE

✪ Beijing International Club Hotel (Guoji Julebu Fandian).

21 Jianguomenwai Dajie (entrance is 1 block north on west side of Xiushui Jie), Beijing 100020. ☎ **800/325-3589** in the U.S. and Canada, 1800/814-812 in Australia, 0800/ 44-5309 in New Zealand, 1800/597-000 in Ireland, 0800/973-119 in the U.K., or 010/ 6460-6688. Fax 010/6460-3299. www.sheraton.com. 287 units. A/C MINIBAR TV TEL. $390 double. AE, DC, JCB, MC, V. Subway: Jianguomen (3 blocks west).

Aiming at an unprecedented six-star rating, this new 19-story "boutique hotel" is a member of the ITT Sheraton Luxury Collection. The lobby and public areas, decorated in a sophisticated blend of Eastern and Western motifs, are the most spectacular in Beijing. The hotel currently shares health and athletic facilities with the neighboring historic Beijing International Club (built in 1911). (The hotel's own swimming pool and other facilities are to be constructed in the future.) The Great Hall banquet room at the top of the white marble lobby staircase caters to VIP functions and diplomatic receptions, and it sets the high-class image the hotel projects. Rooms are large with king or two double beds, writing desk, safe, fax machine, hair dryer, coffeemaker, slippers and robe, satellite TV with CNN and HBO, and data plugs for laptop PCs. Each bathroom comes with a separate bathtub and shower. There is 24-hour butler service on all floors. Guests come from both Asia and the West. This is a formal sort of place, where an average traveler might even feel a bit underdressed. There's no hotel shuttle bus, although the hotel does provide airport transport by hotel limousine (for a fee). The hotel is within walking distance to shops and cafes; it's a 30-minute stroll to the Forbidden City.

Dining: Stylish dining is offered in Danieli's (a southern Italian brasserie with an Italian chef), Tokyo Aoyama Mangetsu (sushi and teppanyaki), Celestial Court (Cantonese), and Garden Court (international buffets and a la carte meals). The palm tree–lined Garden Lounge has afternoon teas and evening cocktails and music. The Press Club Bar, decorated in 1950s style with mementos of diplomats and international correspondents, changes its snacks daily.

Amenities: Swimming pool and health club currently off-premises at nearby International Club, small fitness center with latest exercise machines, 24-hour business center (e-mail, PC rental), conference rooms, beauty salon, newsstand, concierge, 24-hour room service, same-day laundry and dry cleaning services, newspaper delivery, nightly turndown, twice-daily maid service, 24-hour personal butler service.

✪ China World Hotel (Zhongguo Da Fandian).

1 Jianguomenwai Dajie (on the northwest corner of the intersection with the Third Ring Road East), Beijing 100004. ☎ **800/942-5050** in the U.S. and Canada, 1800/222-448 in Australia, 0800/442-179 in New Zealand, 020/8747-8485 in London, or 010/6505-2266. Fax 010/6505-3167. www.shangri-la.com. 738 units. A/C MINIBAR TV TEL. $240 double. Children under 18 stay free in parents' room. AE, DC, JCB, MC, V. No subway station nearby (until completion of the cross-town line in 2000).

Frequently ranked by international business magazines as one of the top 100 hotels in the world and the best in Beijing, China World offers attentive service and deluxe facilities. While there are nearly a dozen five-star hotels in the capital, this one seems to have the most experience handling international guests. This is where CEOs and world leaders stay. The hotel is one unit in the China World Trade Center complex, which means it is directly attached (via escalators and elevators) to a large shopping center with restaurants and offices. The hotel's grand lobby has a comfortable lounge; the mezzanine serves as a contemporary art gallery; and the newly expanded business center is the best in Beijing. Rooms are quite spacious, with plenty of counter space, a writing desk, table and chairs, safes, bright lighting, coffeemaker, robes, slippers, and data ports for PCs. The bathrooms are also roomy and well appointed, with magnifying mirrors, phones, and hair dryers. There are 221 nonsmoking rooms. Rooms on the executive floors (18–21) are even larger, and executive-floor guests enjoy complimentary drinks and breakfast and their own business center and concierge. The hotel's restaurants are among the city's best, and the health and fitness facilities are first-rate. China World's only drawback (besides its high price) is perhaps its location, several miles from the Forbidden City, but Silk Alley and the Friendship Store are an easy walk and taxis reach the city center in 10 minutes. There's no hotel shuttle bus, but taxis are always at the front door.

Dining: The Summer Palace is one of the top Cantonese restaurants in Beijing, and Nadaman is one of the top Japanese restaurants (see chapter 5 for full reviews of both). The Coffee Garden in the main lobby serves international dishes and buffets 24 hours a day, with a classical orchestra performing at the Sunday brunch. Aria, with its jazz and wine bar, is one of the trendiest new dining spots. Henry J. Bean's, an American bar and grill, is across the street (see review in chapter 5), and China's first Starbucks coffee bar is in the shopping center basement.

Amenities: Large indoor swimming pool, extensive health and fitness club with new exercise machines, Jacuzzi, sauna, solarium, three indoor tennis courts, squash courts, aerobic dance studio, bowling alley, jogging routes, two driving ranges, putting green, two golf-simulator machines, 24-hour business center (Beijing's largest, with e-mail, PC rental, offices, library, business card printing, and coffee service), conference rooms, beauty salon, newsstand, crafts shop, concierge, valet, 24-hour room service, same-day laundry and dry cleaning services, newspaper delivery, nightly turndown, twice-daily maid service, 24-hour personal butler service.

Hotel New Otani Chang Fu Gong (Chang Fu Gong Fandian).

26 Jianguomenwai Dajie (south side of street, 1 block east of Second Ring Road overpass), Beijing 100022. ☎ **800/421-8795** or 010/6512-5555. Fax 010/6513-9830. 500 units. A/C MINIBAR TV TEL. $210 double. AE, DC, JCB, MC, V. Subway: Jianguomen (2 blocks north).

This neatly maintained 24-story, five-star hotel caters to Japanese visitors (70% of guests), but also hosts a considerable number of Europeans and Americans. A particularly attractive aspect is the large traditional Chinese garden in the rear, with its ponds, bridges, waterfall, and classical pavilion. The modern rooms are all equipped with coffeemakers, hair dryers, safes, satellite TV with CNN and in-house movies, bathrobes, and humidifiers (it's the only hotel in Beijing that offers them, despite the dry air). While the hotel is built with Japanese guests in mind (the four tour desks all have tours in Japanese), it is quite Westernized, and the staff is confident in English. There is no hotel shuttle bus, but taxis are plentiful and the subway is within walking distance.

Dining: Sakura is one of Beijing's finest Japanese restaurants (with chefs from Japan). The Grill has elegant continental dishes. The Orchid Terrace Coffee Shop provides Western buffets, with a view of the tranquil Chinese garden. Cantonese seafood is served at the Mudan Garden. The Silk Road Bar has evening drinks and Japanese-style karaoke.

Amenities: Large indoor swimming pool (with skylight), indoor jogging circuit, outdoor tennis court, aerobics classes, sauna, massage, health club with exercise machines, mahjong room, business center (with free Internet access), conference rooms, tour desks, beauty salon, large shopping arcade, newsstand, concierge, 24-hour room service, same-day laundry and dry cleaning services, newspaper delivery, nightly turndown.

Jing Guang New World Hotel (Jingguang Xinshijie Fandian).

Jingguang Centre, Hu Jia Lou (10-minute walk north of Jianguomenwai Dajie on Third Ring Road at Chaoyangmenwai Dajie), Beijing 100020. ☎ **800/228-9898** in the U.S. and Canada, 1800/222-431 in Australia, 0800/441-111 in New Zealand, 0800/181-737 in the U.K., or 010/6597-8888. Fax 010/6597-3333. www.newworld-intl.com. E-mail: jghef@ht.rol.cn.net. 446 units. A/C MINIBAR TV TEL. $200 double. Children under 12 stay free in parents' room. AE, DC, JCB, MC, V. No subway station nearby.

This 52-story, fan-shaped, blue glass tower, opened in 1990, is the tallest building in Beijing. Restaurants and other public facilities are on the first seven floors, the five-star hotel rooms are on floors 8 to 23, offices (180 tenants from 25 countries) are on floors 25 to 38, and 247 apartments occupy floors 40 to 52. Hotel guests have access to a wide range of services and facilities within a single tower, including a Bank of China office and a drugstore. The rooms are bright and clean, with considerable counter space and satellite TV (CNN, HBO). Coffeemakers and hair dryers are standard, but in-room safes and robes are available only on the executive floors (22, 23), which go for $240 a night. The hotel has good fitness facilities and a wide range of restaurants in many price ranges. Guests are Western and Asian; there are also many expatriates living in the apartments who use the hotel services. The efficient staff is conversant in English. There is currently no hotel shuttle bus, but there is a limousine fleet and taxis stop at the door.

Dining/Diversions: Choices include international buffets and weekday business lunches, fresh seafood Cantonese style, and Korean barbecues. The most fun (and least expensive) dining option is Food Street in the basement, where noodles and regional Chinese treats can be selected from stalls. There's also a Western-style deli with takeout in the basement. In the hall between the deli and Food Street, kids will find an array of video games. The Champagne Bar off the lobby has live music.

Amenities: Large indoor swimming pool (with skylights), health club with exercise machines and foot massage clinic, billiards, Jacuzzi, sauna, massage, large business center (e-mail, PC rental, offices), conference rooms, tour desk, beauty salon, shopping arcade, concierge, valet, baby-sitting (and free baby cots), 24-hour room service, same-day laundry and dry-cleaning services, newspaper delivery, nightly turndown, drugstore, bookstore, florist, Bank of China.

✪ Swissotel (Beijing Gang Ao Zhongxin).

Dongsishi Tiao Li Jiao Qiao, Hong Kong Macau-Centre (east side of the Second Ring Road overpass at Gongrentiyuchang Beilu), Beijing 100027. ☎ **800/637-9477** in U.S. and Canada, 1800/062-155 in Australia, 0800/614-145 in the U.K., or 010/6501-2288. Fax 010/6501-2501. www.swissotel.com. E-mail: swissotel@chinamail.com. 421 units. A/C MINIBAR TV TEL. $260 double. AE, DC, JCB, MC, V. Subway: Dongsishitiao.

Managed expertly by the Swissair Swissotel Management Group, this immaculate 16-story, five-star hotel has some of the best facilities in Beijing. The fourth floor, for example, has the best barrier-free architecture in the capital for travelers with disabilities. The International Medical Clinic is on the premises, as are an airline ticketing office and a courier service. There are three nonsmoking floors (6, 8, 13), and the executive floors (15, 16, 17) have butler services. The standard and larger deluxe rooms ($300) are brightly decorated with bleached oak trim and are equipped with coffeemaker, hair dryer, ample counter space, large desk, safe, bathrobes, and data ports for PCs. Swissotel has a European feel and among the highest levels of service and upkeep in Beijing. Limousine airport transfer is

295RMB ($35). There's no hotel shuttle. The location would be inconvenient were the subway station not so close.

Dining: The new Shanghai Restaurant is a romantic spot for lunch or dinner. Happy Valley serves Hong Kong dishes, dim sum, and Peking Duck. The 24-hour Cafe Suisse has international buffets as well as Swiss specialties; the Sunday champagne brunch at Cafe Suisse is superb. In the summer, the Sunset Terrace and Bar is open for outdoor Mongolian barbecues.

Amenities: Large indoor swimming pool (with glass walls); excellent workout facilities (FIRM Fitness Club) with latest exercise machines, aerobics studio, exercise classes; outdoor tennis court; Jacuzzi; sauna; massage; 24-hour business center (e-mail, PC rental, offices); conference rooms; tour desk; beauty salon; newsstand; concierge; valet; 24-hour room service; same-day laundry and dry cleaning services; newspaper delivery; nightly turndown.

EXPENSIVE

Gloria Plaza Hotel (Kailai Da Jiudian).
2 Jianguomenwai Nandajie (1 long block south of Jianguomenwai, east of the Second Ring Road overpass opposite the Ancient Observatory), Beijing 100022. ☎ **010/6515-8855.** Fax 010/6515-8533. www.gloriahl@hkstar.com. E-mail: gmgphbj@public.cn.net. 423 units. A/C MINIBAR TV TEL. $155 double. AE, DC, JCB, MC, V. Subway: Jianguomen (2 blocks north).

This 18-story, four-star, well-managed hotel, which was thoroughly renovated in 1997, has a good location and plenty of experience with international guests. The large lobby, decorated in red marble, is ostentatious, as are the facilities, capped by the biggest and brightest sports bar in Beijing, located on the mezzanine. Rooms are sparkling clean, of average size, with adequate counter space, safes, coffeemakers, and satellite TVs (CNN and in-house movies). Bathrooms are also well maintained, with phones but no hair dryers. Services and facilities are slightly better here than at the nearby Scitech Hotel (see below), and the views of downtown Beijing are excellent. There's no hotel shuttle bus, but it's a convenient walk to the subway, the Friendship Store, and the train station.

Dining/Diversions: The Sports City Cafe is immense, with such diversions as miniature golf, a half-court basketball hoop (which converts to a disco floor), Western sports displays, and a cigar room. The Sampan restaurant employs Cantonese chefs, the Golden Turtle serves Korean fare, and the Atrium coffee shop provides fairly inexpensive international buffets.

Amenities: Large indoor swimming pool (with wall-of-glass views of downtown Beijing), health club with exercise machines and city views, Jacuzzi, sauna, 24-hour business center (Internet connection 1RMB/12¢ per minute), tour desk, beauty salon, shops (newsstand, souvenirs), 24-hour room service, same-day laundry and dry cleaning services, nightly turndown, bicycle rental.

✪ Jianguo Hotel (Jianguo Fandian).
5 Jianguomenwai Dajie (north side of the street, 1 block east of Silk Alley), Beijing 100020. ☎ **800/223-5652** in the U.S. and Canada, 1800/553-549 in Australia, 0800/898-852 in the U.K., or 010/6500-2233. Fax 010/6500-2871. www.hoteljianguo.com. E-mail: exec@hoteljianguo.com. 399 units, including some suites with kitchenette. A/C MINIBAR TV TEL. $190 double (including breakfast); $115 in winter. AE, DISC, JCB, MC, V. No subway station nearby.

The landmark Jianguo—the first joint-venture hotel in China (1982)—was renovated in 1996. The bathrooms were upgraded and the rooms refurbished. For 2 decades it was the expatriate community's favorite meeting place in Beijing, and

---

ⓕ Family-Friendly Hotels

Beijing's hotels have plenty of amusements and amenities for adults, but what can they offer kids? These four hotels have special facilities designed for the young traveler:

Movenpick Hotel (*see p. 76*) runs organized children's programs all summer long using its excellent outdoor facilities, including a playground, tennis courts, and beach volleyball court. There's also an indoor/outdoor swimming pool and Beijing's only thermal hot springs pool, with horseback riding stables nearby.

Holiday Inn Lido (*see p. 75*) has plenty of foreign resident kids hanging about and a wider range of activities to keep children amused than any other hotel in Beijing, including an ice cream parlor, a 20-lane bowling alley, video games, a big swimming pool, and a large public park at its doorstep.

Kerry Centre Hotel (*see p. 64*) has a big new 25-meter pool, two indoor tennis courts, and on its fourth-floor roof garden a special splash pool and play area for kids, not to mention an outdoor track for in-line skating.

New World Courtyard Beijing (*see p. 70*) has a large swimming pool and rooftop garden area. It's also added a special playground just for kids and an amusement hall that houses an extensive collection of high-tech games.

---

the hotel still maintains a lively lobby under its golden chandelier. The hotel is divided into an East Wing (four stories) and a West Wing (nine stories), linked at ground level by a floor of restaurants and services. Some rooms have views of, or even open onto, a water garden and courtyard area; the rooms facing south onto Jianguomenwai have outdoor balconies (unusual in Beijing and nice in the summers). There is one executive floor in the East Wing. Rooms are of average size—although some appear a bit worn—with coffeemakers, hair dryers, a writing desk, and clean bathrooms. There is no newspaper delivery or nightly turndown. The balconies are a big plus. The hotel does have excellent facilities and some of the best restaurants and bars in Beijing, as well as an airport shuttle bus costing 40RMB ($5) one-way.

Dining/Diversions: The hotel restaurants are among Beijing's best and most popular. Justine's is a romantic spot for fine French and continental dishes (see review in chapter 5). Four Seasons presents Cantonese cuisine in elegant surroundings (see review in chapter 5). Charlie's American Bar is a mainstay for drinks. The lobby is the setting for buffets, afternoon tea, and an elaborate Sunday brunch with live classical music. The Galaxy bar offers karaoke.

Amenities: Indoor swimming pool, health club with a few exercise machines, Jacuzzi, sauna, acupuncture and massage parlor (full massage $25), conference rooms, 24-hour business center (e-mail, PC rental, offices), tour desk, beauty salon, shopping arcade (souvenirs, clothing), 24-hour room service, same-day laundry and dry cleaning services, bicycle rental (10RMB/$1.25 per hour).

Jinglun Hotel (Jinglun Fandian).

3 Jianguomenwai Dajie (next to Jianguo Hotel, north side of street), Beijing 100020. ☎ **800/645-5687** in the U.S. and Canada, 0800/282-502 in the U.K., or 010/6500-2266. Fax 010/6500-2022. www.jinglunhotel.com. E-mail: jinglun@public3.bta.net.cn. 558 units. A/C MINIBAR TV TEL. $180 double. AE, DISC, JCB, MC, V. No subway station nearby.

The former Beijing-Toronto Hotel (*Jinglun* means Toronto) is now managed by Nikko Hotels International, which maintains high levels of service and upkeep. This is a four-star hotel with many five-star facilities. It's a favorite of Western, Japanese, and Chinese guests, who stay here in equal numbers. Silk Alley and the Friendship Store are a few minutes' walk. Rooms are modern, clean, and fairly spacious, with adequate counter space, hot-water thermoses (no coffeemakers), and satellite TV with CNN and HBO. The compact bathrooms are equipped with hair dryers. The executive floor (8) has a new buffet lounge and free use of in-room fax machines. Deluxe rooms (floors 9–10) are just $10 more. Nonsmoking rooms are available. The hotel maintains an airport shuttle bus, with four runs a day (30RMB/$3.75).

Dining/Diversions: The hotel restaurants are quite good, particularly Sihexuan (see review in chapter 5). There's a Cantonese restaurant (Tao Li) with inexpensive business lunches and weekend dim sum, two Japanese restaurants (Sakura Ya and Gyoen Teppanyaki), and the 24-hour Cafe Serena serving continental cuisine. A French bistro will open soon in the lobby.

Amenities: Indoor swimming pool, health club with exercise machines, Jacuzzi, sauna, massage, conference rooms, business center (e-mail, PC rental, IDD phone booths; open 7:30am to 11:30pm), tour desk, air ticket counter, beauty salon, shops (souvenirs, sundries), 24-hour room service, same-day laundry and dry cleaning services, bicycle rental (50RMB/$6 per day).

Kerry Centre Hotel (Beijing Jiali Zhongxin Fandia).

1 Guanghua Lu (2 blocks north of China World, 1 block west of the Third Ring Road), Beijing 100004. ☎ **800/942-5050** in U.S. and Canada, 1800/222-448 in Australia, 0800/442-179 in New Zealand, 020/8747-8485 in London, or 010/8529-6999. Fax 010/8529-6333. www.shangri-la.com. 487 units. A/C MINIBAR TV TEL. $220 double. Children under 18 stay free in parents' room. AE, DC, JCB, MC, V. No subway station nearby (until the cross-town line is completed).

The Kerry, one of Beijing's newest (1999) hotels, is a four-star hotel with five-star facilities and service. It's the third sister in the Shangri-La hotel cluster on Jian-guomenwai Dajie. The hotel is in the 23-story west tower of the Beijing Kerry Centre, an office and apartment complex rising from a massive four-story platform. It's that four-story base that serves the hotel as a roof garden, encircled by jogging and in-line skating tracks. The roof garden also contains a children's play area and splash pool. The rooms (floors 5–21) are decorated in rich reds and golds with intri-cate geometric designs, but possess a high-tech edge, with steel trim and large, curving desktops. Safes, data plugs, coffeemakers, and hair dryers are standard. Bathrooms (each with a phone and a mirror de-mister) are designed so that there are no walls between the separate tubs and showers. Nonsmoking rooms are avail-able. The Kerry is an efficient hotel with a warm atmosphere; the staff is outgoing and responsive to Western travelers' demands.

Dining: The Kerry has three restaurants: a lobby lounge serving continental breakfast, light lunches, snacks, and dinners; a 24-hour coffee shop specializing in Western and Asian buffets; and a Chinese restaurant with Hong Kong chefs serving dim sum, Cantonese seafood, and local Beijing family fare.

Amenities: Beijing Kerry Centre Health Club and Spa (25-meter lap pool, Jacuzzi, sauna, latest exercise machines, locker rooms, two indoor tennis courts, one mixed-use court), sundeck, large 24-hour business center (e-mail, PC rental, offices), conference rooms, tour desk, newsstand, concierge, valet, 24-hour room service, same-day laundry and dry-cleaning services, nightly turndown, baby-sitting, express checkout.

Scitech Hotel (Saite Fandian).

22 Jianguomenwai Dajie (1 block south of Jianguomenwai Dajie on the south side of the Scitech Taohan Shopping Center), Beijing 100004. ☎ **010/6512-3388.** Fax 010/6512-3537.

E-mail: sthotel1@sun.sw.co.cn. 324 units. A/C MINIBAR TV TEL. $160 double. AE, JCB, MC, V. Subway: Jianguomen (5 blocks northwest).

Formerly the CVIK Hotel, this 15-floor, four-star hotel, situated behind the Scitech Plaza shopping center and office complex, caters to Asians but has Western guests, particularly business travelers. The rooms, last renovated in 1996, are bright and modern, with safes, hair dryers, hot-water thermoses, and satellite TV (CNN and in-house movies). Excellent health and fitness facilities are available free of charge for hotel guests at the health club in the attached Scitech Building. While the hotel's service level lags a bit behind that of the international hotels farther east along Jianguomenwai Dajie (such as the Jinglun and the Jianguo), it is closer to the city center and the subway and slightly more economical. There's no hotel shuttle bus.

Dining: Fortune Court has economical Cantonese-style set lunches and dinners (under $10). The 24-hour Lucky Corner coffee shop has international dishes and buffets. There is also a Korean restaurant and a lobby bar, Green Place.

Amenities: Superb indoor swimming pool, health club with exercise machines, Jacuzzi, sauna, massage, five-lane bowling alley, table tennis, indoor tennis court, business center (e-mail, PC rental; open 7am to 10:30pm), three tour desks, beauty salon, shopping arcade (souvenirs, sundries), 24-hour room service, same-day laundry and dry cleaning services, bicycle rental (in front of Scitech Plaza).

✪ Traders Hotel Beijing (Gumao Fandian).

1 Jianguomenwai Dajie (north side of China World, west of the Third Ring Road), Beijing 100004. ☎ **800/942-5050** in the U.S. and Canada, 1800/222-448 in Australia, 0800/442-179 in New Zealand, 020/8747-8485 in London, or 010/6505-2277. Fax 010/6505-0818. www.shangri-la.com. 564 units. A/C MINIBAR TV TEL. $140 double. Children under 18 stay free in parents' room. AE, DC, JCB, MC, V. No subway station nearby (until the cross-town line is completed).

A sister hotel to the China World (see above), to which it is now linked via a new underground shopping center complete with an ice-skating rink, Traders is one of the best four-star hotels in China, highly rated by foreign business travelers for its large rooms and efficient service. When you stay at Traders, you have full guest privileges at the adjoining five-star China World, including use of its superb fitness and health facilities. This hotel is in high demand most of the year. It opened with a west wing in 1990, added an east wing in 1996, and remodeled the west wing in 1999. Rooms in the west wing are the best, but all rooms are quite spacious, with writing desks, ample counter space, coffee table and chairs, firm beds, safes, bathrobe and slippers, satellite TV (CNN, HBO, ESPN), coffeemakers, hair dryers, and a desk drawer of office supplies. The marble bathrooms have phones and packets of detergent. It is a luxurious but practical hotel. Floors 5 through 7 (303 rooms in all) are for nonsmoking guests, and the west wing has added one new executive floor. The business center has one of the better-stocked English-language bookstores in Beijing. A free shuttle bus makes several downtown runs daily.

Dining: Traders Cafe is known for its international buffets and now has a view of the new garden above the underground shopping center. The Oriental Restaurant has an open kitchen where excellent Cantonese and Beijing dishes are prepared. Traders Bar has cocktails and live music nightly.

Amenities: Fitness center with sauna, Jacuzzi, exercise machines, locker rooms; guest access to China World swimming pool and tennis courts; large business center (e-mail, PC rental, offices; open 7am to 1am daily); conference rooms, tour desk; newsstand; souvenir shops; concierge; valet; 24-hour room service; same-day laundry and dry cleaning services; nightly turndown; baby-sitting; bicycle rental; bookstore.

3 Chaoyang Northeast

VERY EXPENSIVE

Beijing Hilton Hotel (Xierdun Fandian).

1 Dongfang Lu, Dongsanhuan Beilu (west side of Third Ring Road North, north of Xinyuan Nanlu), Beijing 100027. ☎ **800/445-8667** in U.S. and Canada, or 010/6466-2288. Fax 010/6465-3052. 363 units. A/C MINIBAR TV TEL. $200 double. AE, DC, JCB, MC, V. No subway station nearby.

This hotel is justifiably noted for its international atmosphere, efficient service, and fine restaurants. It's a favorite of many Western business travelers, perhaps because it is "a familiar name" as well as being a well-run establishment. The rooms are well kept and feature writing desks, safes, robes and slippers, umbrellas, coffeemakers, hair dryers, and Internet access (PC plugs). All bathrooms are equipped with separate showers and tubs. There are two rooms for travelers with disabilities, three executive floors (21–23), and three nonsmoking floors (10, 12, 16). The Health Club (managed by Clark Hatch) is a private membership club, but its facilities are open to hotel guests for a small daily fee. There's no hotel shuttle bus, but taxis are at the doorstep, and the immediate area is worth strolling for its small cafes.

Dining: A jazz theme is woven through the hotel's restaurants and bars. The Louisiana, with Cajun dishes and a fine wine list, is often cited as the best Western restaurant in Beijing. There are also restaurants specializing in Japanese, Cantonese, and international dishes. The Lobby Bar & Lounge, decorated in the style of Old Shanghai, presents live jazz nightly.

Amenities: Large indoor swimming pool, Clark Hatch fitness club ($6/day), exercise machines, massage, Jacuzzi, sauna, two squash courts, outdoor tennis court, bicycle rentals, small 24-hour business center (e-mail, PC rental), conference rooms, tour desk, beauty salon, newsstand, boutique, brandy shop, concierge, valet, 24-hour room service, same-day laundry and dry cleaning services, nightly turndown, newspaper delivery, baby-sitting, wheelchairs.

Great Wall Sheraton (Changcheng Fandian).

10 Dongsanhuan Beilu (east side of Third Ring Road North, south of Liangma River), Beijing 100026. ☎ **800/325-3535** in the U.S. and Canada, 1800/07-3535 in Australia, 0800/44-3535 in New Zealand, 1800/53-5353 in Ireland, 0800/353-535 in the U.K., or 010/6590-5566. Fax 010/6590-1938. 1,007 units. A/C MINIBAR TV TEL. $300 double. AE, DC, JCB, MC, V. No subway station nearby.

The Great Wall, the first five-star hotel to open (in 1984) on the Third Ring Road North, has set a high standard for the nearby hotels to match. This is a massive hotel with plenty of services and facilities. It is currently renovating its rooms floor by floor. The rooms are fairly spacious, with coffeemakers and hair dryers standard, and the furniture is rather stylish. There are plugs for PCs, with an in-room Internet charge of about $1 per 30 minutes. The bathrooms have marble floors, walls, and counters, but are small. There are two executive floors (17, 18), and the 14th floor is for nonsmoking guests. Public areas are elegant; guests are of a broad international mix; and the staff speaks good English and responds to requests. The Great Wall was the first Beijing hotel to initiate a hotel-wide express checkout system. There's no subway line out here, but there are many restaurants, shops and shopping plazas, other international hotels, and a growing strip of small cafes and bars within walking distance.

Dining: Le France hosts intimate European dinners and keeps its large wine cellar well stocked with French choices. Fortune Restaurant has Peking Duck and southern favorites (shark's fin). Yuen Tai, with a panoramic view from the 25th floor, serves fine Sichuan dishes, accompanied by traditional Chinese musicians. The Atrium in the lobby has a Sunday brunch. The Hard Rock Cafe is next door.

Amenities: Large indoor swimming pool, fitness club, exercise machines, aerobics studio, massage, two floodlit outdoor tennis courts, Jacuzzi, sauna, bicycle rental, 24-hour business center (e-mail, PC rental, business cards, offices), conference rooms, tour desk, beauty salon, newsstand, concierge, valet, 24-hour room service, same-day laundry and dry cleaning services, newspaper delivery, nightly turndown.

✪ Kempinski Hotel (Kaibinsiji Fandian).

50 Liangmaqiao Lu, Lufthansa Centre (1 block southwest of the Third Ring Road North), Beijing 100016. ☎ **800/426-3135** or 010/6465-3388. Fax 010/6465-3366. E-mail: khblc@public.east.cn.net. 529 units. A/C MINIBAR TV TEL. $270 double. Children 12 and under stay free in parents' room. AE, DC, ER, JCB, MC, V. No subway station nearby.

A favorite of Germans and other Europeans, this 18-story hotel, built in 1992, has extremely high levels of service and maintenance, meriting its five-star rating. The hotel is attached to the You Yi shopping center, which has modern shops and a department store. There's an efficient, high-tech atmosphere in the public spaces, which are covered in red marble. Rooms are of above average size, with coffee-makers, hair dryers, safes, and sufficient counter space, and the bathrooms sparkle. The Kempinski has considerable facilities, from its fitness center to its ten restaurants. It is one of the few hotels anywhere in Beijing with shuttle bus service to both the airport and downtown locations (on a frequent daily schedule).

Dining: The restaurants run the gamut from an excellent takeout deli and a German brewpub to the upscale Symphony Restaurant (gourmet European dishes) and Dragons Restaurant (Sichuan, Cantonese). The Decanter carries more than 300 international wines.

Amenities: Large indoor swimming pool, two health and fitness clubs, exercise machines, massage, outdoor tennis courts, squash courts, Jacuzzi, sauna, solarium, large 24-hour business center (e-mail, PC rental, offices), conference rooms, tour desk, airline reservations office, beauty salon, bookstore, concierge, valet, 24-hour room service, same-day laundry and dry cleaning services, nightly turndown, baby-sitting, photo shop, wine shop.

Kunlun Hotel (Kunlun Fandian).

2 Xinyuan Nanlu (1 block west of the Third Ring Road North), Beijing 100004. ☎ **010/6590-3388.** Fax 010/6590-3228. E-mail: kunlun@public.bta.net.cn. 900 units. A/C MINIBAR TV TEL. $270 double. Children 12 and under stay free in parents' room. AE, DC, JCB, MC, V. No subway station nearby.

This massive five-star, 28-story, Chinese-managed (Jinjiang Group) glass-and-steel tower has nearly every conceivable perk and facility under the sun, but the old joke still has some truth: It's a Chinese copy of the Great Wall Sheraton across the road. It's a good copy, but the atmosphere is cold rather than warm, and the service level, while good, is not great. Nevertheless, the Kunlun is popular with some Western travelers, and the facilities are impressive: CNN and in-house movies, safes, hair dryers, and Internet plugs standard in every room (although the rooms are cramped); a large, well-stocked bookstore (not to mention a Trinex Golf logo and golf club store); ten restaurants and bars, including karaoke and disco; and even a post office and a teaware shop. Despite all this, the nearby five-star competitors (Hilton, Sheraton) are more favored by Western travelers. There's no hotel shuttle bus or subway station, but plenty of taxis, and the Sanlitun bar and cafe district are within walking distance.

Dining: Ten hotel restaurants, cafes, and bars offer Shanghainese, Cantonese, Japanese, Vietnamese, and Western fare. The Four Seasons Coffee Shop serves international dishes 24 hours a day. The revolving restaurant on the 29th floor specializes in European entrees and is open for breakfast, lunch, and dinner. On the mezzanine is a plush lounge and billiards room.

Amenities: Indoor swimming pool, fitness club (from 6:30am to 11pm), exercise machines, massage ($35/hr.), outdoor tennis courts ($9/hr.), Jacuzzi, sauna, 24-hour business center (e-mail, PC rental, offices), conference rooms, tour desk (CITS), airline reservations office, beauty salon, bookstore, golf shop, photo developing, concierge, valet, 24-hour room service, same-day laundry and dry cleaning services, nightly turndown, baby-sitting.

✪ Radisson SAS Hotel (Huangjia Da Fandian).

6A Beisanhuan Donglu (at the China International Exhibition Centre, on the south side of the Third Ring Road East, 1 block from the Airport Expressway overpass), Beijing 100028. ☎ **800/333-3333** in the U.S. and Canada, 1800/333-333 in Australia, 0800/44-3333 in New Zealand, 1800/55-7474 in Ireland, 0800/374-411 in the U.K., or 010/6466-3388. Fax 010/6465-3186. www.radisson.com. 362 units. A/C MINIBAR TV TEL. $225 double. Children 12 and under stay free in parents' room. AE, DC, ER, JCB, MC, V. No subway station nearby.

This 15-story international hotel—the best four-star hotel in northeast Beijing, but also the most expensive—has the most stylish rooms in the capital. The three decor styles are Oriental (red carpets, carved wood trim, floors 3–6), high-tech (glass and chrome detailing, floors 7–9), and art deco (1920s touches, pastels, floors 10–12). All rooms are large, with coffeemakers, hair dryers, pressers, and satellite TV (CNN and HBO). The executive floors (13–15) are plush and modern. The hotel is spotless throughout and maintains a modern European atmosphere. The service is highly efficient, and the facilities are extensive. Built in 1993, the hotel began a comprehensive 5-year renovation plan in 1999. The SAS shuttle bus links the hotel and the airport (80RMB/$10 each way).

Dining: The LaxenOxen is the best Scandinavian grill in Beijing (see review in chapter 5), and the Chinese Brasserie uses its grill to prepare Sichuan and Cantonese dishes. The Royal Cafe, looking into a small garden, serves buffets and international dishes 24 hours a day. Rooftop barbecues are popular on summer evenings.

Amenities: Large indoor swimming pool, Jacuzzi, sauna, solarium, exercise machines, outdoor tennis court, two indoor squash courts, sundeck, business center (e-mail, PCs, mobile phone rental; open 7am to midnight), conference rooms, good tour desk (CTS), newsstand, shopping arcade (souvenirs, carpets), florist, concierge, valet, 24-hour room service, same-day laundry and dry-cleaning services, nightly turndown, newspaper delivery, free cribs, baby-sitting.

EXPENSIVE

China Travel Service Tower (Zhonglu Dasha).

2 Beisanhuan Donglu (at the intersection of the Third Ring Road East and the airport freeway), Beijing 100028. ☎ **010/6462-2288.** Fax 010/6461-2502. E-mail: ctstsale@public3. bta.net.cn. 185 units. A/C MINIBAR TV TEL. $150 double. AE, JCB, MC, V. No subway station nearby.

China Travel Service (CTS) opened its own hotel tower in 1995 with four-star facilities and an adequate service level. It has stiff competitors nearby, however, including the Radisson SAS Hotel (quite superior, but more expensive) and the Landmark (same quality, fewer services, but cheaper). Perhaps the main drawback is the tower's location on a difficult-to-reach island where freeways converge. Still, the staff is attentive, and the rooms are clean and modern. The CTS Travel Desk has excellent tours, but it is somewhat geared to Chinese-speaking clients. If you book this hotel through CTS, you can get a good room rate, especially in winter.

Dining: Dining options include a Western coffee shop and four regional Chinese restaurants (Chaozhou, Cantonese, Huaiyang, Sichuan). There's also the Cox Jazz Bar for a nightcap.

Amenities: Swimming pool, tennis courts, billiards room, mahjong room, business center, post office, tour desk.

Landmark Hotel (Liangmahe Dasha).

8 Dongsanhuan Beilu (east of the Third Ring Road North, across parking lot from Great Wall Sheraton), Beijing 100004. ☎ **010/6590-6688.** Fax 010/6590-6513. www.chinatour.com/lmt. E-mail: lmt@public.gb.com.net. 450 units. A/C MINIBAR TV TEL. $125 double. AE, JCB, MC, V. No subway station nearby.

This 15-story tower is lost among the other hotel towers along the northeast sector of the Third Ring Road, but it offers good value and fine four-star facilities. Rooms are modern, well maintained, bright, and average sized, with coffeemakers, hair dryers, and satellite TV (CNN and HBO) standard. There's a Chinese garden in the back and a children's playground off the mezzanine, as well as plenty of shops, two tour desks, a post office, and a branch of the Bank of China. There's even an entrance inside the hotel to the Hard Rock Cafe. If you want to stay in comfort in the vicinity of the Hilton, Kempinski, Kunlun, and Sheraton at a lower price, this is the place. There's no airport shuttle, but the hotel runs a free bus to downtown sites.

Dining: The Evergreen, with a view of the Chinese garden on the mezzanine, serves good international buffets. The Sorabol specializes in Korean hotpots, Lu Bolang in Shanghai dishes, Tao Ran Ju in Cantonese seafood, and the Food Court in Sichuan cuisine. The recently remodeled Pub has evening cocktails, and there's a tea lounge that serves Western breads and pastries.

Amenities: Swimming pool, fitness center with sauna, Jacuzzi, exercise machines, two outdoor tennis courts, children's playground, business center (e-mail, PC rental; open 7am to 10pm), tour desks (CITS, Panda Tours), shops (newsstand, souvenir, clothing), concierge, 24-hour room service, same-day laundry and dry cleaning services, nightly turndown, baby-sitting, Bank of China, post office, florist.

MODERATE

Beijing Continental Grand Hotel (Wuzhou Da Jiudian).

8 Beichen Dong Lu (on the north side of Third Ring Road North in the Asian Games Village), Beijing 100101. ☎ **010/6491-5588.** Fax 010/6491-0106. www.chinatour.com/bcgh. 1,259 units. A/C MINIBAR TV TEL. $120 double. AE, JCB, MC, V. Subway: Andingmen (2 miles south).

This immense double-winged complex, 5 miles north of the city center, opened in 1989, and had China won the bid for the 2000 Summer Olympics, it would have boomed, since it is attached to the International Olympic Sports Centre. These days, it is rather distant and forlorn. It has four-star rooms and facilities, but its staff is not terribly experienced with Western guests. Nevertheless, if you're willing to take long taxi rides into the city, this hotel delivers good value for the money. The rooms are clean, modern, and spacious. There are nearly two dozen restaurants and bars in the hotel complex, running the gamut from Cantonese to Japanese to Western fare, as well as a tour desk, air ticket office, beauty salon, fitness center, and an extensive shopping arcade. Given the service level, however, it might be worth waiting until the 2008 Olympics before checking in here.

4 Xuanwu (Southwest) & Chongwen (Southeast)

EXPENSIVE

Grand View Garden Hotel (Daguan Yuan Jiudian).

88 Nancaiyuan Jie (in the Xuanwu District, near the southwest corner of the lower loop of the Second Ring Road, west of Grand View Garden), Beijing 100054. ☎ 010/6353-8899. Fax 010/6353-9189. www.all-hotels.com/a/gvgh. E-mail: gvghotel@iuol.cn.net. 384 units. A/C MINIBAR TV TEL. $140 double. AE, DC, JCB, MC, V. No subway station nearby.

Many miles from the city center and even farther from most other attractions, the Grand View Garden Hotel does have its charms. The architecture is stunning: This is a four-story hotel that really looks Chinese, with its soaring tiled roofs and garden-pavilion layout fully in keeping with the famous Grand View classical garden nearby. On the inside, the hotel is a quiet, if distant, retreat, kept fresh and up to date. The average-sized rooms are bright, with a writing desk, chairs, safes, satellite TV (CNN and in-house movies), and coffeemakers standard. The hotel has three internal courtyard gardens of its own. The fine service and facilities are worthy of the hotel's four-star rating. More than half the guests are members of tour groups, many of them from Europe and the U.S. A taxi downtown takes about 30 minutes, and the hotel provides a free shuttle bus to city-center locations (but not to the airport).

Dining: Western buffets and European dishes are served at Les Continents, Cantonese cuisine at Rong Court, and hotpots at the Pavilion Restaurant. There are several cocktail lounges in the stunning lobby and a small disco where karaoke is popular.

Amenities: Indoor swimming pool, Jacuzzi, sauna, exercise machines, billiards, video arcade, eight-lane bowling alley, business center (e-mail, PCs; open 7am to 11:30pm), conference rooms, tour desk, newsstand, shopping arcade, 24-hour room service, same-day laundry and dry cleaning services, valet, nightly turndown, baby-sitting.

New World Courtyard Beijing (Beijing Xinshi Jie Wan Yi Jiudian).

3C Chongwenmenwai Dajie (in the Chongwen District, 1 block south of Qianmen Dong Dajie, 1 mile east of Tiananmen Square), Beijing 100062. ☎ 800/321-2211 in the U.S. and Canada, 1800/251-259 in Australia, 0800/441-035 in New Zealand, 0800/221-222 in the U.K., or 010/6718-1188. Fax 010/6708-1808. www.marriott.com. E-mail:nwcybj@ht.rol.cn. net. 293 units. A/C MINIBAR TV TEL. $148 double. Children under 17 stay free in parents' room. AE, DC, JCB, MC, V. Subway: Chongwenmen (1 block east).

This hotel, which opened in 1998, is a "Courtyard by Marriott," although the Marriott connection seems to be downplayed. The 15-story hotel tower is connected to a larger complex, the Beijing New World Centre, which includes office high-rises, apartments, a large shopping plaza, and the New World department store. The rooms are bright and spacious. Duvet, sofa, writing desk, hair dryer, coffeemaker, safe, satellite TV (CNN and HBO), and bathroom phone are standard. The 10th floor is for nonsmoking guests. There is an extensive children's play area with playground, video games, and a rooftop park. The hotel doesn't have a government star rating yet, but the facilities are four-star, and combined with Marriott management and its location, make this hotel a fine value. The location near Qianmen Avenue, midway between Tiananmen Square to the west and the Temple of Heaven to the east, puts both these sites within walking distance (about a mile to each). The subway station is a block away. Moreover, the hotel provides both a downtown shuttle and a twice-daily free airport bus (9:30am and 4pm to airport; noon and 7pm from airport).

Dining: Spices coffee shop serves Western and Asian buffets, and Hua Mei Garden specializes in Cantonese fare.

Amenities: Health and fitness facilities (indoor swimming pool, Jacuzzi, sauna, many exercise machines, billiards) are available to guests at private club in the apartment tower, business center (e-mail, PCs, air tickets), conference rooms, tour desk, newsstand, shopping center and department store attached via skybridge, 24-hour room service, same-day laundry and dry cleaning services, valet, nightly turndown, baby-sitting.

5 Xicheng (West) & Haidian (Northwest)

EXPENSIVE

Beijing New Century Hotel (Xin Shiji Fandian).

6 Shoudu Tiyuguan Nanlu (on the south side of Xizhimenwai Dajie, 4 blocks west of the Beijing Zoo), Beijing 100044. ☎ **010/6849-2001.** Fax 010/6849-1103. 738 units. A/C MINIBAR TV TEL. $170 double. AE, DC, JCB, MC, V. Subway: Xizhimen (20-minute walk east).

This 32-story white tower, connected by a skybridge to an 18-story office tower, is well managed by ANA, a Japanese hotel group. The majority of its guests are Japanese (40%), followed by Europeans, Americans, and Asians. The glittering lobby is worthy of its five-star status, with a waterfall in the lobby encircled by two mezzanines with gold railings. Each room has a window nook with good views of the zoo to the northeast, the Western Hills, and downtown in the distance. Safes, electric thermoses, CNN and HBO TV channels, and hair dryers are in every room. Although the hotel is far from the city center, a free shuttle bus operates three times a day.

Dining: A Japanese restaurant serves excellent but pricey fare all day. The Gold Coast on the top floor has reasonably priced Sichuan dishes for lunch and dinner and a splendid view; the Beijing Express on the third floor specializes in inexpensive noodles and Chinese fast food. The Cafe in the Park has international dishes and buffets. The lobby cocktail lounge, Captain Nemo's Bar, has a nautical decor.

Amenities: Large indoor swimming pool, fitness club (from 6:30am to midnight), many exercise machines, massage, two outdoor tennis courts, table tennis, billiards, mahjong, 12-lane bowling alley, golf driving range, Jacuzzi, sauna, business center (e-mail, PC rental, offices; open 7am to 11pm), conference rooms, tour desk (CITS), airline office (CAAC), beauty salon, florist, Bank of China and post office in attached office tower (weekday service), newsstand, photo developing, concierge, valet, 24-hour room service, same-day laundry and dry-cleaning services, nightly turndown, baby-sitting, silk and cashmere shop.

Friendship Hotel (Youyi Binguan).

3 Baishiqiao Lu (in the Haidian District, at the intersection of Haidian Lu and the Third Ring Road northwest), Beijing 100873. ☎ **010/6849-8888.** Fax 010/6849-8866. 800 units. A/C MINIBAR TV TEL. $160–$210 double. AE, DC, JCB, MC, V. No subway station nearby.

One of the largest garden-style hotels in Asia, the Friendship complex is immense, with more than 1,900 rooms, counting its apartments and offices. Since 1954, it has been the choice of many foreign delegations, experts, and academics. (Beijing University and other major universities are nearby to the north.) Over the years, the hotel has upgraded its rooms and facilities to four-star level. For the ordinary visitor, however, its location, near to the Summer Palace but quite distant from the city center, is a drawback. The various buildings are a bit bewildering, interlinked by walkways and large garden areas. The main lobby area with its red columns and gold filigree is surprisingly compact. Rooms are somewhat compact as well, but clean and modern, with electric hot pots and safes. The higher-priced rooms in Building 1 are larger, with more amenities. There are 26 restaurants and bars and a wide range of facilities, from a golf driving range and bowling alley to the hotel's own branch of the Friendship Store. Many of the restaurants are quite elegant. This is a self-contained home away from home for many foreigners who have taken up short-term residency in Beijing for teaching or business-related assignments, but ordinary visitors can use it as a base for exploring the capital as well. There is no shuttle bus service, but taxis are abundant (allow 40 to 60 minutes to reach major attractions).

Dining: Among the more than two dozen restaurants (mostly Chinese), there is a coffee shop, an ice cream stand, and a bakery in the lobby.

Amenities: Two indoor swimming pools, health club with exercise machines and weights, Jacuzzi, sauna, business center (e-mail, PC rental), golf driving range, bowling alley, outdoor tennis courts, billiards, conference rooms, tour desk, air ticket office, beauty salon, extensive shopping arcade and Friendship Store, 24-hour room service, same-day laundry and dry cleaning services, newspaper delivery, nightly turndown, baby-sitting.

○ Holiday Inn Downtown (Jindu Jiari Fandian).

98 Beilishi Lu (Xicheng District, northwest corner of Fuchengmenwai Dajie and Second Ring Road West), Beijing 100006. ☎ **800/465-4329** in the U.S. and Canada, 1800/221-066 in Australia, 0800/442-222 in New Zealand, 1800/55-3155 in Ireland, 0800/897-121 in the U.K., or 010/6833-8822. Fax 010/6834-0696. www.holiday-inn.com. 346 units. A/C MINIBAR TV TEL. $130 double. Children under 19 stay free in parents' room. AE, DC, JCB, MC, V. Subway: Fuchengmen (½ block south).

Formerly Beijing's best three-star international hotel, the Holiday Inn Downtown has been upgraded to four stars, which better describes its service level. The hotel is not really downtown (Tiananmen Square is miles to the east), but it is across the street from a major American-style shopping plaza (Vantone New World) and within an easy walk of Baita Temple and Temple of the Moon Park. Its location in a financial district brings many business travelers to its doors, nearly half from China itself (with a quarter from the West). The rooms are spacious, clean, and well equipped, with coffeemakers, hair dryers, satellite TV (CNN, CNBC, and free in-house movies), and king-sized beds. The bathrooms are small but spotless. This is an American-style hotel with good services, restaurants, and even a Holidome. There's no hotel shuttle bus, but the subway couldn't be much closer.

Dining: Beijing's first Indian restaurant, Shamiana, serves superb lunches and dinners (see review in chapter 5). Guan Yuan has a master chef from Hong Kong and good Cantonese dishes. The Oasis Coffee House has Western and Asian buffets and à la carte selections. Delicatessen Corner in the lobby is stocked with cakes, breads, and sandwiches. The Pavilion bar in the Holidome has a dartboard, and the Nightingale has five karaoke rooms.

Amenities: Small indoor swimming pool, health club with exercise machines and weights (from 7am to 11pm), Jacuzzi, sauna, business center (e-mail, PC rental; open 7am to midnight), conference rooms, tour desk (Panda city tours), air ticket office, beauty salon, shops (souvenirs, newsstand, sundries), 24-hour room service, same-day laundry and dry cleaning services, newspaper delivery, nightly turndown, baby-sitting ($2/hr.).

○ Shangri-La Beijing Hotel (Xiangge Lila Fandian).

29 Zizhuyuan Lu (on the northwest corner of the Third Ring Road), Beijing 100081. ☎ **800/942-5050** in the U.S. and Canada, 1800/222-448 in Australia, 0800/442-179 in

New Zealand, 020/8747-8485 in London, or 010/6841-2211. Fax 010/6841-8002. www.shangri-la.com. 640 units. A/C MINIBAR TV TEL. $190 double. Children under 18 stay free in parents' room. AE, DC, JCB, MC, V. No subway station nearby.

The number-one luxury hotel in northwest Beijing, this 24-story hotel has been noted for its high service levels and elegance since it opened in 1986. It's received *Condé Nast Traveler's* award as the "Best Hotel in China" three times and a nod from the Beijing Tourism Association in 1997 for the best doormen and best front office in the capital. The Shangri-La often hosts world dignitaries at its press center and provides catering for major events in the city. The large traditional garden is a serene focal point for its open lobby and the two-story wall of glass at the back of its lobby lounge. Rooms are also elegant and are among the largest in Beijing, with plenty of counter space and writing desks, satellite TV (with CNN, BBC, HBO, National Geographic, and the Cartoon Network), coffeemakers, hair dryers, safes, large closets, and marble bathrooms with phones. There are two executive floors (21, 22), nonsmoking rooms, and two guest rooms for travelers with disabilities. Fitness facilities are housed in a separate complex behind the courtyard garden. The service is worthy of the five-star rating, and the distant location is ameliorated by free shuttle service to downtown locations (although a taxi trip across town can take up to an hour).

Dining: Shang Palace, with chefs from Hong Kong, turns out excellent dim sum for lunch and fine Cantonese specialties for dinner, accompanied by performances of traditional Chinese music. Peppinos, with a resident Italian chef, has oven-baked pizzas and a strolling musician. Nishimura is an excellent Japanese restaurant with Beijing's first *robatayaki* (grill). The lobby Coffee Garden serves international fare and buffets 24 hours a day; it's attached to a takeout deli. The garden serves barbecue dinners in the summer.

Amenities: Health club with exercise machines, large swimming pool, sauna, solariums, massage (from 6am to 10:30pm); recreation center (from 9am to 11pm) with indoor tennis courts, squash courts, billiards, basketball court; 24-hour business center (e-mail, PC rental, offices, business card printing); conference rooms; tour desk; beauty salon; florist; newsstand; shopping arcade (antiques, crafts, clothing, jewelry); concierge; valet; 24-hour room service; same-day laundry and dry cleaning services; nightly turndown; baby-sitting.

Xiyuan Hotel (Xiyuan Fandian).
1 Sanlihe Lu (Xicheng District, south side of Xizhimenwai Dajie, across from Beijing Zoo), Beijing 100044. ☎ **800/821-0900** in the U.S. and Canada, 1800/655-147 in Australia, 0800/442-519 in New Zealand, 1800/55-3225 in Ireland, 0800/894-351 in the U.K., or 010/6831-3388. Fax 010/6831-4577. E-mail: xyhotel@public3.bta.net.cn. 707 units. A/C MINIBAR TV TEL. $150 double. Children under 12 stay free in parents' room. AE, JCB, MC, V. Subway: Xizhimen (1.25 miles east).

This towering 23-story hotel across from the Beijing Zoo epitomized the inefficiency of the large locally managed hotel in China during the 1980s, but with the dawn of the new century, the Xiyuan has taken on a new image. Extensive remodeling and upgrading of staff services (with the arrival of fresh international management) has put the Xiyuan firmly in the four-star category. Rooms are spacious, with sufficient counter space, writing desks, safes, satellite TV (CNN), and electric hot pots. Bathrooms are clean and equipped with phones and hair dryers. There are several rooms for travelers with disabilities, two new executive floors, and one floor dedicated to Islamic guests (no liquor, directions to Mecca). Most of the guests are Chinese and Asian, but the hotel is actively seeking Western visitors, and its staff is knowledgeable about the requirements of foreigners. With a large shopping arcade, a vast three-story lobby, and 11 restaurants and bars, the Xiyuan is a full service hotel, although guests must depend on taxis (or a long walk to the subway) to get downtown.

Dining: Headlining the dining choices is the Carousel Revolving Restaurant on the 26th floor with its excellent Asian buffets (see review in chapter 5). There are also restaurants specializing in Shandong and Sichuan fare, Xijiang dishes, Asian fast food, and Western buffets. For American food and excellent German microbrews made in the hotel, try the Kaiser Brewery.

Amenities: Indoor swimming pool, health club with exercise machines, Jacuzzi, sauna, billiard and mahjong room, table tennis, 24-hour business center (e-mail, PC rental), conference rooms, tour desk, beauty salon, shopping arcade (souvenirs, silks, sundries, cosmetics), large newsstand, 24-hour room service, valet, same-day laundry and dry cleaning services, newspaper delivery, baby-sitting.

INEXPENSIVE

Exhibition Centre Hotel (Zhanian Guan Binguan).

135 Xizhimenwai Dajie (on the east side of Exhibition Centre, 2 blocks north of Xizhimenwai Dajie), Beijing 100044. ☎ **010/6831-6633.** Fax 010/6834-7450. 250 units. A/C MINIBAR TV TEL. $60 double. AE, JCB, MC, V. Subway station: Xizhimen (about 6 blocks east).

This inexpensive three-star complex resembles the Russian-inspired Exhibition Centre next door. A KFC restaurant stands on Xizhimenwai Dajie, the main street, next to the entry lane. The marble lobby with mirrored ceiling is showing a bit of wear, as is the hotel, which bills itself as "the world's friendliest hotel." The staff does speak some English, but expect only basic help and service. Still, for the price, it's a reasonable choice in a pinch. The rooms are modern, compact, with brown carpets and brown Formica furniture, and small TVs (CNN and in-house movies) in the corner. Rooms have views of a courtyard garden fountain or a lake to the north. Westerners do stay here, some in tour groups, but most guests are Asian. There is no hotel shuttle bus, but the subway is within walking distance, as are restaurants along the main road west to the zoo.

Dining: Lu Wei Zhai serves Shandong provincial dishes and hotpots, while Chao Yang Fang offers good Chaozhou fare, including seafood dishes. Pete's Place (in a separate building east across the parking lot) is an American-style cafe and pub, serving buffets, hamburgers, steaks, and margaritas. There's a beer garden open in the summer.

Amenities: Exercise machines, sauna, massage, billiards, small business center, conference rooms, tour desk, beauty salon, shops (souvenirs), newsstand, 24-hour room service, next-day laundry and dry cleaning services.

6 Near the Airport

Harbour Plaza (Hai Yi Fandian).

8 Jiangtai Xi Lu (in the Chaoyang District, on the east side of Airport Expressway, 1 block southeast of the Holiday Inn Lido and 10.5 miles southwest of Capital Airport), Beijing 100004. ☎ **010/6436-2288.** Fax 010/6436-1818. 370 units. A/C MINIBAR TV TEL. $160 double. AE, DC, JCB, MC, V. No subway station nearby.

This newly remodeled (1998), 19-story, four-star hotel near the Holiday Inn Lido (see below; the hotels have a common owner) is close to the airport and offers good staff services and sparkling modern rooms. It is situated between Lido Park and a large, newly opened public park (once intended as a golf course). The spacious rooms have coffeemakers and satellite TV (CNN, HBO, and ESPN), but no hair dryers. When the Holiday Inn Lido is full (or too pricey), this is a nice alternative far from the urban center (although it's just 5 minutes by taxi from the Third Ring Road North area and 10 minutes from Sanlitun). The recreational facilities are spare, but the restaurants and other facilities are deluxe. There are plans to institute a hotel shuttle bus service to the airport and downtown sites. Taxis are readily available.

Dining/Diversions: Hoi Yat Heen serves Cantonese lunches and dinners, with an all-you-can-eat dim sum buffet. The Cafe California in the lobby has international buffets. There are also Japanese and Shanghainese restaurants. The Polo Bar is a plush, quiet, British-style pub. The Pit Stop is a bar and disco with live bands, American cuisine (including salads), and all-you-can-drink specials from 9pm to midnight.

Amenities: Health club with new exercise machines, Jacuzzi, sauna, massage, conference rooms, beauty salon, shops (souvenirs, crafts), newsstand, business center (e-mail, PCs; open 6am to 11pm), 24-hour room service, same-day laundry and dry cleaning services, newspaper delivery, nightly turndown.

✪ Holiday Inn Lido (Lidu Jiari Fandian).

Jichang Lu, Jiangtai Lu (in the Chaoyang District, on the east side of the Airport Expressway, 10.5 miles southwest of Capital Airport), Beijing 100004. ☎ **800/465-4329** in the U.S. and Canada, 1800/221-066 in Australia, 0800/442-222 in New Zealand, 1800/55-3155 in Ireland, 0800/897-121 in the U.K., or 010/6437-6688. Fax 010/6437-6237. www.holiday-inn.com. E-mail: lido@ht.rol.cn.net. 720 units. A/C MINIBAR TV TEL. $190 double. Children under 19 stay free in parents' room. AE, DC, JCB, MC, V. No subway station nearby.

The world's largest Holiday Inn hardly resembles the ones back home. This is a city within a city. Since it lies beyond the Fourth Ring Road on the expressway to the airport and offers airport shuttle bus service roughly every hour from 6am to 9:30pm (20RMB/$2.50 each way), business travelers find it handy. It is one of the best four-star hotels in China, and its facilities exceed those of most five-star hotels. The rooms are large, with writing desks, king-sized beds, chairs, coffee tables, coffeemakers, safes, robes, 44-channel satellite TV (CNN and BBC), modem links, and tidy bathrooms with hair dryers. There is an executive floor, and rooms for travelers with disabilities and nonsmoking rooms are available. The service level is quite high. Western travelers often outnumber Asian guests. The Lido's apartment complex, which includes a kindergarten and an international school, has a Clark Hatch–managed fitness club (with tennis, squash, golf range, aerobics classes) that hotel guests can use (for a fee) during off-hours (Monday to Friday from 7am to 5pm). In addition to the airport shuttle, the Lido provides a free downtown shuttle bus with four stops from 7:40am to 7:30pm daily.

Dining/Diversions: The Lido offers excellent Thai (Borom Piman), Mexican (Texan Bar & Grill), and Shanghainese (Lao Shanghai) restaurants (all reviewed in chapter 5). There are also Cantonese, Beijing fast food, German, and Italian restaurants. The Patio is a 24-hour lobby coffee shop with international buffets. Galateria was Beijing's first ice cream parlor. Nightlife outlets include the Pig and Whistle (an English-style pub with darts), the Grandstand Sports Bar, and the Freezer Disco.

Amenities: Indoor swimming pool, health club with exercise machines and weights (from 6am to 11pm), 20-lane Cosmic Bowling Centre, Jacuzzi, sauna, tennis courts, 24-hour business center (e-mail, PC rental), conference rooms, tour desk (CTS), United/Lufthansa air ticket office, beauty salon, large shopping arcade (souvenirs, clothing, sundries), newsstand, drugstore, supermarket, Bank of China, post office, film developing shop, medical clinic, shoe repair, florist, 24-hour room service, same-day laundry and dry cleaning services, newspaper delivery, nightly turndown, baby-sitting ($3/hr.), bicycle rental ($1.25/hr.).

✪ Movenpick Hotel Beijing (Guodu Da Fandian).

Xiao Tianzhu Village, Capital Airport (in Shunyi County, within 1.5 miles of airport), Beijing 100621. ☎ **800/344-6835** or 010/6456-5588. Fax 010/6456-5678. www.all-hotels.com. E-mail: bjmphtlc@iuol.cn.net. 408 units. A/C MINIBAR TV TEL. $140 double. Children under 16 stay free in parents' room. AE, DC, ER, JCB, MC, V. No subway station nearby.

This is a true airport hotel, about a 15-minute drive from the airport via the free Movenpick shuttle (but too far to walk). It's also Beijing's only hotel with a resort atmosphere and outdoor recreational facilities. The service is highly efficient, and the hotel is worthy of its four-star rating. Rooms (renovated in 1996) are spacious with generous counter space, two closets, writing desk with accessories, duvets, coffeemaker, and satellite TV (CNN, BBC, and in-house movies). Bathrooms have phones and hair dryers. For $10 more, the business superior rooms come with modem plugs, robes, express checkout, and a free breakfast. There's a comfortable, European atmosphere to this airport hotel/resort, and the resort facilities are special for Beijing, including the capital's only natural thermal hot springs pool, interconnected indoor and outdoor swimming pools, a courtyard chess board with resident master, children's programs all summer, beach volleyball with white sands, and even a resident camel. The free airport shuttle runs every half hour from 6am to 11pm (there's a Movenpick desk in the airport arrival hall), and the free downtown shuttle bus makes 10 runs daily from 8am to 10pm. (The trip downtown takes about an hour, depending on traffic.) This is the nearest international hotel with a four-star rating to the airport by far; it's located well beyond the urban smog belt.

Dining/Diversions: The Mongolian Gher, located in a yurt, serves steaming hotpots (see review in chapter 5). The Boulevard serves continental breakfast, ice cream, and sandwiches. There are also Chinese, Italian, and Japanese restaurants. Warp 8 and Cat's Tango are the hotel's bars.

Amenities: Indoor/outdoor swimming pool, hot springs pool (free for guests), health club with exercise machines, solarium, Jacuzzi, sauna, two outdoor tennis courts, indoor squash court, beach volleyball, children's summer programs, playground, horseback riding stables nearby, 24-hour business center (e-mail, PC rental), conference rooms, tour desk, beauty salon, large shopping arcade (souvenirs, clothing, sundries), newsstand, 24-hour room service, same-day laundry and dry cleaning services, baby-sitting, bicycle rental ($6 for 6 hrs., tandem bikes $7.25 for 6 hrs.).

Dining 5

In a nation with a history of famine and the largest of all populations, where to this day the most popular greeting heard in the streets translates as "Have you eaten?", it's little wonder that dining ranks as a chief concern, nearly as important as family or fortune. The average Beijinger spends more money on food than on housing. As incomes rose in the 1990s, the number of cafes in the capital mushroomed, from just over 10,000 in 1990 to nearly 40,000 in 1995; the number of cafes today may very well equal that of taxis (70,000). Foreign visitors have benefited from this dining explosion, too. A decade ago, travelers to Beijing had a choice between a few dozen rather expensive hotel restaurants and a few dozen cheaper but less appetizing private cafes. Now there are scores of fine restaurants for foreign guests located inside and outside the big hotels, covering a wide range of prices and cuisine.

Eating is almost reason enough to come to Beijing, because no other city in China offers such a range of Chinese dishes prepared at such a consistently high level. You can sample all of China's regional specialties in Beijing, from Cantonese to Sichuanese. The emphasis in Beijing, of course, is on Northern Chinese cuisine and the dishes for which Beijing is renowned. Beijing duck, also called Peking duck, is a must, and some restaurants serve little else. The capital is also celebrated for its version of dim sum (*jiaozi*), the steamed dumplings with meat or vegetable fillings. Unique to Beijing cuisine are the "Imperial dishes," which are derived from the lavish banquets enjoyed by the last emperors of the Qing Dynasty. Beijing has several restaurants that serve food of the imperial courts using the ingredients, style, and sometimes the actual recipes of the last chefs who worked in the Forbidden City. Recently, the dishes of the masses that were the hearty staples for millions during the Cultural Revolution (1966 to 1976) under Chairman Mao (mostly cabbage and steamed bread) have enjoyed a revival, spawning several popular, ever-so-humble eating places dedicated to Mao nostalgia.

The Mongolians from north of the Great Wall and the Muslim peoples from China's far northwest have supplied Beijing with excellent barbecues and hotpots, while the dishes of Canton, Sichuan, and lately Shanghai are particularly well represented in Beijing's restaurants. Visitors can spend weeks in Beijing these days eating nothing but the great regional cuisines of China. In reality, however, most foreigners quickly become homesick for home cooking—or for

Hotel Versus Non-Hotel Dining

For the visitor, the most pronounced division in Beijing dining is between the hotel and the street. Beijing's hotels boast many of the very best restaurants in China. The quality of the food, the skill of the chefs, the hygiene of the kitchen, and the service of the waiters is high caliber. Outside the hotels, these standards have generally taken a fierce beating—until recently, that is. Today, several dozen private restaurants rival those in the best hotels, and these upstarts consistently offer lower prices (as well as hygienic establishments, good service, and English-language menus). In addition, scores of smaller cafes outside the hotels offer tasty Western dishes at reasonable prices. The international hotels now find themselves quite literally surrounded by private competitors, so that even a gourmet visitor's dining experience in Beijing need no longer be confined to the hotel.

something other than another Chinese meal, no matter how tasty it is. The Beijing restaurant boom has brought with it a dramatic increase in foreign restaurants, particularly Western ones—American, French, German, Russian, Scandinavian, and even Mexican. There are also plenty of esteemed dining places serving Indian, Thai, Korean, and Japanese fare, too. It's possible, in other words, to visit the capital of China for 2 weeks and eat very well without once using chopsticks on a single Chinese dish.

Beijing is consistently ranked in the world's top five most costly cities in which to do business, but the average bill for dining in Beijing is remarkably lower than in Hong Kong, Tokyo, New York, or London. An inexpensive dinner without drinks can be had for less than 80RMB ($10) per person; a moderate dinner sets you back between 80 and 120RMB ($10 and $15); and an expensive dinner generally costs between 120 and 240RMB ($15 and $30). You can splurge at a very expensive place for about 240 to 400RMB ($30 to $50), but it's also easy to spend over $100 on a single entree at some Cantonese restaurants, even cheap and dingy ones. Lunches are considerably cheaper (often half the price). Hotels routinely add a 15% service charge to dining bills, although this practice is beginning to lessen as competition heats up with outside restaurants (many of which levy no service charges). Hotel restaurants accept major credit cards, as do a growing number of outside restaurants, but diners should always carry enough RMB to pay for a meal.

The restaurants listed below are arranged first by location, and then by price. The most popular locations for restaurants catering to visitors, regardless of cuisine, are in the city center (Dongcheng), east along Jianguomenwai Dajie (Chaoyang East), and in the Sanlitun and Third Ring Road areas northeast of downtown (Chaoyang Northeast)—in other words, in the neighborhoods where many international hotels are clustered.

1 Restaurants by Cuisine

CANTONESE/CONTINENTAL/AMERICAN

American Chili's Grill (Chaoyang East, *M*)

Annie's Cafe (Chaoyang Northeast, *I*)
Aria (Chaoyang East, *E*)
Cafe Renaissance (Chaoyang East, *E*)
Haagen-Dazs (Chaoyang East, *M*)

Key to abbreviations: *VE* = Very Expensive; *E* = Expensive; *M* = Moderate; *I* = Inexpensive

Henry J. Bean's (Chaoyang East, *M*)
Hollywood Star (Chaoyang
  Northeast, *I*)
Louisiana (Chaoyang Northeast, *VE*)
Schlotzsky's Deli (Chaoyang
  Northeast, *M*)
T.G.I. Fridays (Chaoyang
  Northeast, *M*)
Windows On the World (Chaoyang
  East, *E*)

ASIAN/THAI

Borom Piman (Chaoyang
  Northeast, *E*)
Carousel Revolving Restaurant
  (Xicheng, *E*)
Red Basil (Chaoyang Northeast, *M*)

BEIJING/SHANXI

Beijing Express (Xicheng, *I*)
Fangshan Restaurant (Xicheng, *E*)
Gold Cat Jiaozi City (Chaoyang
  Northeast, *I*)
Jinghua Shiyuan (Chongwen, *I*)
Jinyang Fanzhuang (Xuanwu, *M*)
Li Family Restaurant (Xicheng, *VE*)
Quanjude Hepingmen (Xuanwu, *M*)
Quanjude Kaoyadian (Chongwen, *E*)
Sihexuan (Chaoyang East, *M*)

BRITISH

John Bull (Chaoyang East, *M*)

CANTONESE

Fortune Garden (Dongcheng, *VE*)
Four Seasons (Chaoyang East, *E*)
Hong Kong Food City
  (Dongcheng, *E*)
Ritan Park (Chaoyang East, *M*)
Sampan (Chaoyang East, *M*)
Summer Palace (Chaoyang East, *E*)
Windows on the World (Chaoyang
  East, *E*)
Xihe Yaju (Chaoyang East, *M*)

FRENCH

Bleu Marine (Chaoyang East, *E*)
The Courtyard (Dongcheng, *VE*)
Justine's (Chaoyang East, *VE*)
Plaza Grill (Dongcheng, *VE*)

GERMAN

Bavaria Bierstube (Doncheng, *E*)
Kebab Kafe (Chaoyang
  Northeast, *M*)
Paulaner Brauhaus (Chaoyang
  Northeast, *E*)

INDIAN

Omar Khayyam (Chaoyang East, *M*)
Shamiana (Xicheng, *M*)

ITALIAN

Danieli's (Chaoyang East, *VE*)
Metro Cafe (Chaoyang Northeast, *E*)
Roma Ristorante Italiano
  (Dongcheng, *VE*)
Spageddie's (Chaoyang East, *M*)
Trattoria La Gondola (Chaoyang
  Northeast, *M*)

JAPANESE

Nadaman (Chaoyang East, *VE*)
Nishimura (Haidian, *VE*)
San Si Lang (Chaoyang
  Northeast, *M*)

MEXICAN

Mexican Wave (Chaoyang East, *M*)
Texan Bar & Grill (Chaoyang
  Northeast, *E*)

MONGOLIAN

Mongolian Gher (Chaoyang
  Northeast, *E*)

MUSLIM

Uncle Afanti (Dongcheng, *M*)

RUSSIAN

Baikal (Chaoyang Northeast, *E*)

SCANDINAVIAN

LaxenOxen (Chaoyang
  Northeast, *VE*)

SHANGHAI

Lao Shanghai (Chaoyang
  Northeast, *E*)
Shanghai Cuisine (Chaoyang
  Northeast, *E*)
Shanghai Moon (Chaoyang
  Northeast, *E*)

SICHUAN

Berena's Bistro (Chaoyang
Northeast, *M*)
Ritan Park (Chaoyang East, *M*)
Sichuan Fandian (Xicheng, *E*)
Xihe Yaju (Chaoyang East, *M*)

SPANISH

Ashanti Restaurant & Wine Bar
(Chaoyang Northeast, *E*)

VEGETARIAN

Gongdelin (Chongwen, *M*)
Green Tian Shi (Dongcheng, *E*)

2 Dongcheng (City Center)

VERY EXPENSIVE

✪ The Courtyard.

95 Donghuamen Lu (east side of Forbidden City Moat; look for lions and glass doors).
☎ **010/6526-8881.** Reservations recommended on weekends. Main courses 160–320RMB
($20–$40). AE, JCB, MC, V. Daily 6am–10:30pm. NOUVELLE FRENCH.

This is the hottest independent restaurant in town. Chef Ray Lin experiments with
East/West fusions. The fresh salads blend Western and Chinese ingredients. The
blackened salmon is a favorite entree (175RMB/$21), as are the Angus steak (from
the U.S.), the filet mignon, and an assortment of Chinese noodle dishes. Desserts
range from chocolate mousse to steamed dumplings stuffed with fruit. The decor is
contemporary bistro, with a gallery in the basement featuring contemporary Chinese artists and a cigar divan upstairs—with an exceptional view of the Forbidden
City. Although quite upscale, The Courtyard has an informal air.

Fortune Garden.

In the Palace Hotel, 8 Jinyu Hutong, Wangfujing Dajie (2 blocks east of Wangfujing).
☎ **010/6512-8899,** ext. 7900. Reservations recommended on weekends. Main courses
150–300RMB ($18–$38). AE, DC, JCB, MC, V. Daily 11:30am–2:30pm and 6–10pm.
CANTONESE.

The bright decor featuring Chinese motifs and the traditional music played by local
musicians in the evenings set the tone for enjoying fine southern Chinese dishes at
this elegant restaurant. Among the best Cantonese dishes (prepared by chefs from
Hong Kong) are the baked scallops in cheese sauce and the braised pigeon with
black mushroom. Fortune Garden also crosses regional lines and offers a Beijing
duck that is less greasy than those in most duck restaurants. The lunchtime specialty
is dim sum Cantonese style, well worth sampling. Service is attentive.

✪ Plaza Grill.

In the Holiday Inn Crowne Plaza, 48 Wangfujing Dajie. ☎ **010/6513-3388,** ext. 1132.
Reservations recommended on weekends. Main courses 160–320RMB ($20–$40). AE, DC,
JCB, MC, V. Mon–Sat noon–2pm and 6:30–10pm; Sun 6–10pm. FRENCH.

Reserve a table near the atrium railing on the mezzanine and prepare yourself for
good service, beautiful presentations, and chef Armin Wolfgang Lang's eclectic
"Cuisine Moderne." Traditional French cooking underlies many of the Asian-
flavored entrees. From the open kitchen to the white tablecloths, the setting is elegant but not formal, and the live music below (usually Western classical) makes for
a romantic evening. Start with a fresh salad (the Caesar is prepared tableside) or perhaps the borscht (with shredded duck and Harbin caviar), and then select from a
range of entrees (rainbow trout, Scottish salmon, tiger prawns). For the imported
sirloins and lamb chops from the grill, guests select their own sauce (herb butter,
mushroom, or béarnaise). Breast of duckling in a morel mango cream
(148RMB/$18) is one of the chef's best fusion inventions. To top off a gourmet

evening, try one of the ice cream creations, the cherries jubilée, a crêpe suzette flamed with brandy, or something from the dessert trolley.

Roma Ristorante Italiano.

In the Palace Hotel, 8 Jinyu Hutong, Wangfujing Dajie (2 blocks east of Wangfujing). ☎ **010/6512-8899**, ext. 7410. Reservations required. Main courses 160–240RMB ($20–$30). AE, DC, JCB, MC, V. Daily 11:30am–3pm and 6:30–11pm. NORTHERN ITALIAN.

This formal restaurant is a member of the Chaines des Rotisseurs, a group of international hotel gourmets, and the service and dishes here are of the highest standards. The top entrees are the veal médaillons, the pan-fried sea bass, and the rack of lamb with a black olive crust, topped off with a heavenly tiramisu for dessert. The selection of northern Italian choices includes fresh pastas, herbs, and seafood. The black olives and tomatoes with mozzarella is a superb appetizer, and the large European wine list complements stylish dining. Roma's bargain day is Sunday, when a big buffet featuring a wide range of Italian appetizers, main courses, and desserts goes for 165RMB ($20) per person.

EXPENSIVE

Bavaria Bierstube.

In the Palace Hotel, 8 Jinyu Hutong, Wangfujing Dajie (2 blocks east of Wangfujing). ☎ **010/6512-8899**, ext. 7410. Main courses 80–160RMB ($10–$20). AE, DC, JCB, MC, V. Daily 11:30am–3pm and 6:30–11pm. BAVARIAN.

Follow the lobby waterfall down the escalator, past the upscale boutiques in the basement, to this stunning German inn complete with polished floors and paneling, sculpted country chairs, and checkered tablecloths. This could be Bavaria—the menu certainly is. The sausages are made here, as is the apple strudel. Top entrees include the cheese fondue and the sliced veal tenderloin in a mushroom sauce. This is the monthly meeting place of the Beijing Wine and Cheese Club, and the cheeses are worth savoring. The Chinese staff, outfitted in Bavarian dress, is efficient and even versed in a bit of German (as well as English).

✪ Green Tian Shi.

57 Dengshi Xikou Lu (east of the Holiday Inn Crowne Plaza, 1 block off Wangfujing Dajie). ☎ **010/6524-2349**. Main courses 150–200RMB ($18–$25). AE, JCB, MC, V. Daily 11am–9pm (8am–midnight for drinks and snacks). VEGETARIAN.

There's a vegetarian grocery at the entrance and a gaudy dining room upstairs serving Beijing's tastiest and trendiest vegetarian fare. The menu (in English) is filled with Chinese dishes made entirely without meat or dairy products (although there are some egg and milk dishes available). The dishes use legumes, grains, and tuber stalks, along with artfully disguised chunks of *doufu* (bean curd) to achieve the appearance, texture, and sometimes the taste of fish, flesh, and fowl. There's a whole steamed "fish," a Gong Bao "chicken," an assortment of "lamb kebabs," and even the old Cantonese delicacy, "monkey brains." Perhaps the best treat on the menu is a faux braised eel (*hangshao shanyu*). Fruit juices and green teas are the drinks of choice here. This cafe has more of a New Age atmosphere than the bigger state-run vegetarian emporium, Gongdelin (see below), which uses a heavier hand (and more oil) in preparing its more extensive menu. Lunches are smaller and much more economical, costing less than 100RMB ($12.50) per person.

Hong Kong Food City.

18 Dong'anmen Dajie (on the southwest corner of Wangfujing Dajie). ☎ **010/6525-7349**. Main courses 120–200RMB ($15–$25). AE, JCB, MC, V. Daily 11am–2pm; 2:30–4pm; and 5–9pm. CANTONESE.

Beijing Dining

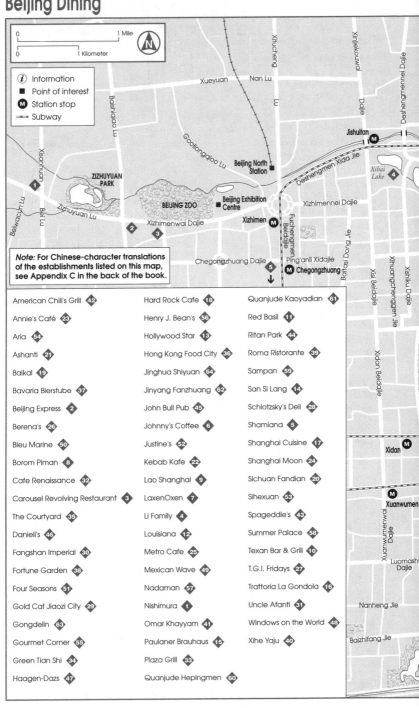

Map legend:
- (i) Information
- ■ Point of interest
- Ⓜ Station stop
- ▬▬ Subway

Note: For Chinese-character translations of the establishments listed on this map, see Appendix C in the back of the book.

American Chili's Grill 42
Annie's Café 23
Aria 54
Ashanti 21
Baikal 19
Bavaria Bierstube 37
Beijing Express 2
Berena's 26
Bleu Marine 50
Borom Piman 8
Cafe Renaissance 32
Carousel Revolving Restaurant 3
The Courtyard 35
Danieli's 46
Fangshan Imperial 30
Fortune Garden 38
Four Seasons 51
Gold Cat Jiaozi City 29
Gongdelin 63
Gourmet Corner 55
Green Tian Shi 34
Haagen-Dazs 47

Hard Rock Cafe 18
Henry J. Bean's 56
Hollywood Star 13
Hong Kong Food City 36
Jinghua Shiyuan 64
Jinyang Fanzhuang 62
John Bull Pub 45
Johnny's Coffee 6
Justine's 52
Kebab Kafe 22
Lao Shanghai 9
LaxenOxen 7
Li Family 4
Louisiana 12
Metro Cafe 25
Mexican Wave 49
Nadaman 57
Nishimura 1
Omar Khayyam 41
Paulaner Brauhaus 15
Plaza Grill 33
Quanjude Hepingmen 60

Quanjude Kaoyadian 61
Red Basil 11
Ritan Park 44
Roma Ristorante 39
Sampan 59
San Si Lang 14
Schlotzsky's Deli 28
Shamiana 5
Shanghai Cuisine 17
Shanghai Moon 24
Sichuan Fandian 20
Sihexuan 53
Spageddie's 43
Summer Palace 58
Texan Bar & Grill 10
T.G.I. Fridays 27
Trattoria La Gondola 16
Uncle Afanti 31
Windows on the World 48
Xihe Yaju 40

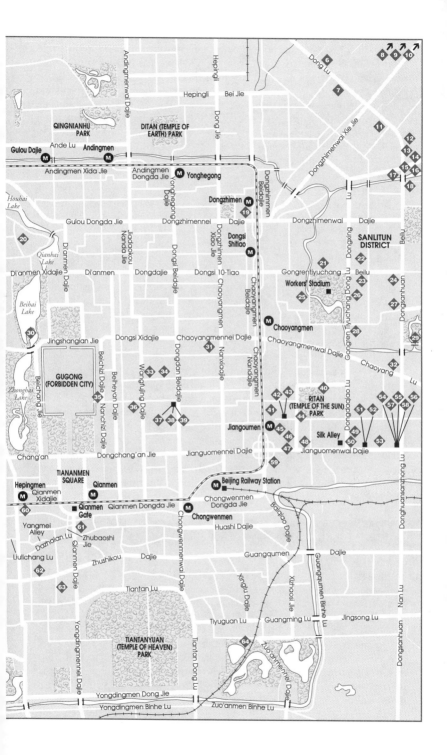

This bustling place was one of the first big independent restaurants to hit downtown Beijing. Its name says it all: This is a multilevel "hash house" with basic to extravagant Cantonese fare, from Hong Kong dim sum to shark's fin and bird's nest delicacies. The emphasis is on the business of eating, with large dining rooms and quick service. The seafood is fresh. Crab dishes cost from $8 to $35, depending on how elaborately they are prepared. Fortunately, there's an English menu to sort out all the possibilities, especially since the energetic staff seldom slows down enough to practice its English with customers.

MODERATE

Uncle Afanti.

2 Houguaibang Hutong, Chaoyangmennei Dajie (in an alley south off Chaoyangmennei, 2 long blocks east of Wangfujing Dajie) ☎ **010/6525-1071** or 010/6527-2288. Reservations recommended on weekends. Meals 70–100RMB ($8.75–$12.50). AE, JCB, MC, V. Daily 11am–2:30pm and 4:30–11:30pm. MUSLIM (XINJIANG).

The most rousing and popular of Beijing's Muslim restaurants, Uncle Afanti is as well known for its after-dinner performances as for its actual dinners. When it opened in 1996, Afanti was one of many dives specializing in cheap Uighur dishes. (The Uighurs are the minority Muslim people who constitute a near-majority in the far west Chinese province of Xinjiang.) Recently, it has gone upscale, with a large dining hall and a stage, although decorations are minimal (a few Arabic wall posters). The food is better than at most of the little Uighur cafes Afanti left behind, particularly the lamb and other meats, but of course the prices are much higher. Among traditional Uighur dishes not to miss are the *yang rou chuanr* (barbecued lamb skewers), *lamian* (long noodles with tomato sauce), and *nan* (flat bread with garlic). The *shala* (salad with tomato, onion, cucumber, and chilies) is just 8RMB ($1), and the roast lamb as a main dish is 75RMB ($9.25). The set dinners, which usually cost about 100RMB ($12.50), are an even better deal. If you're in the mood for a true Uighur celebration, order ahead for the all-from-one-sheep banquet (about $100 for the banquet, which feeds up to eight people). In the intervals between courses, resident Uighur women belly dance (inviting diners to join in), musicians pound on long-neck guitars and snakeskin drums, and Uighur dancers in their provincial dress kick up a storm.

3 Chaoyang East

VERY EXPENSIVE

✪ Danieli's.

In the Beijing International Club Hotel, 21 Jianguomenwai Dajie (1 block north of Jianguomenwai Dajie on the west side of Xiushui Jie; 2 blocks west of Jianguomen subway station). ☎ **010/6460-6688,** ext. 2355. Main courses 160–400RMB ($20–$50). AE, DC, JCB, MC, V. Daily 11:30am–2pm and 6:30–10pm. SOUTHERN ITALIAN.

The entrance is stylish—via a sweeping marble stairway from the grand lobby—and so is the restaurant, with windows on the tree-lined diplomatic compounds. The chef, a Naples native, creates superb, straightforward dishes from his region. There are also some surprises, perhaps the best of which is a lobster and saffron-flavored risotto with Australian yabbies (small crawfish). The pastas are fresh, many of the ingredients imported, and the European wine list is extensive. The leader on the dessert list is a cheesecake delicately flavored with nuts.

For All the Coffee in C

Beijing is still a city of tea drinkers, but Western vi... java withdrawal. Starbucks, America's number-one ... its invasion by opening a full-service coffee bar in F... Center on January 11, 1999. The prolific chain ha... capital with at least seven more outlets by the year 2000. ... blends on hand, as well as pastries, desserts, and brewing accessories, Starbucks may look like something new, but it isn't. Beijing already had several Western-style coffee bars of its own, including two in the same plaza where Starbucks began its belated campaign (which is why Starbucks promptly cut its prices to half what the competition was charging). Top choices for a premium coffee break include:

- **Johnny's Coffee** (*see p. 99*). From cappuccinos to bagels, Johnny's has been Beijing's top spot for slow sipping since 1996.
- **Gourmet Corner** (*see p. 91*). The basement competitor to Beijing's first Starbucks, located nearby, this is really more of a deli than a coffee center, but the lattes with lunch at the stand-up counter are good and cheap (15RMB/$1.90).
- **Regular Coffee,** in Full Link Plaza, east of the Second Ring Road on Chaoyangmenwai Dajie, is more of a cafe than a coffee bar, but the coffee is from Tully's, Starbucks top competitor in its own hometown (Seattle), and Tully's got to China first.
- **The Daily Grind,** Level 1 in the China World Trade Center, is a Starbucks look-alike with superb espresso and cappuccino. It slashed its prices to match the new kid on the block.
- **Lido Delicatessen,** near the supermarket in the Holiday Inn Lido, on the way to the airport, has plenty of cakes, pastries, and sandwiches to go with inexpensive American coffees and double espressos.

✪ Justine's.

In the Jianguo Hotel, 5 Jianguomenwai Dajie. ☎ **010/6500-2233,** ext. 8039. Reservations required. Main courses 200–600RMB ($25–$75). AE, DC, JCB, MC, V. Daily 6:30–10am; noon–3pm; and 6–11pm. FRENCH.

This is the perfect place for a romantic European evening in China's capital. With its dark, wood-trimmed decor, chandeliers, linen tablecloths, silverware and crystal, and a string quartet, Justine's continues its long tradition in fine Continental dining. The focus these days is dishes from Normandy—dishes featuring crustaceans and shellfish. The oysters are fresh, the goose liver the best in town, and the rack of lamb and the duck are hallmarks of Justine's, as is its excellent wine list.

✪ Nadaman.

In the China World Hotel, 1 Jianguomenwai Dajie (at the intersection with the Third Ring Road East). ☎ **010/6506-2266,** ext. 6127. Main courses 150–600RMB ($20–$75). AE, DC, JCB, MC, V. Daily 11:30am–2pm and 5:30–9:30pm. JAPANESE.

This is the first outlet in China of the Osaka family restaurant founded in Japan in 1830. Nadaman is celebrated for its Kansairyori cuisine, the regional cuisine of the

hat emphasizes grilled vegetables and meat. Ingredients are flown in
, and several of the chefs are Japanese. The teppan dishes, cooked at the
re a favorite, as is the fresh Nadaman salad. There are separate teppanyaki,
, and tatami rooms. The decor is modern Japanese and kept spotless. For a
riation on the Mongolian hotpots that are a feature of many Beijing restaurants,
Nadaman offers a shabu shabu hotpot along the same cook-it-yourself lines.

EXPENSIVE

✪ Aria.
In the China World Hotel, Levels 2–3, 1 Jianguomenwai Dajie (at the intersection with the
Third Ring Road East). ☎ 010/6505-2266. Main courses 80–200RMB ($10–$25). AE, DC,
JCB, MC, V. Daily 11am–midnight. AMERICAN/CONTINENTAL.

This plush but informal grill, with its open kitchen and rotisserie, where the chefs
love to put on a show, is Beijing's trendiest new nightspot. Jazz is the focus, especially at the piano bar, where featured performers play. The decor, with special
museum reproductions of European masterpieces, Chinese opera masks, and Thai
musical instruments, adds to the eclectic atmosphere. Beyond the long bar on the
first floor is the restaurant's stunning centerpiece, a massive spiral staircase of polished wood honeycombed with shelves for storing wines. The wine bar behind the
staircase serves up a special wine sampler—a row of tiny glasses for tasting what's
being featured. The manager and executive chef (both from America) have created
a snappy Western menu. Starters range from lobster potstickers to baked oysters
Rockefeller; entrees emphasize grilled fish and imported steaks; and desserts begin
with a ginger crème brûlée. Aria also has an extensive international wine list and
superb coffees. The most romantic seating in the joint is in the private nook on the
top floor, an intimate box for one or two couples overlooking the hotel lobby.

✪ Bleu Marine.
5 Dongdaqiao Lu (2 blocks north of Jianguomenwai Dajie). ☎ 010/6500-6704. Reservations recommended on weekends. Main courses 80–350RMB ($10–$44); 4-course set dinner
700RMB ($88) for two, including house wine. AE, JCB, MC, V. Mon–Sat 11:30am–3pm and
6:30–10:30pm. SOUTHERN FRENCH.

One of Beijing's trendiest cafes when it opened in 1998, Bleu Marine is run by two
Frenchmen, Chef Remy Filograno and Olivier Boudon, along with Chinese partner
Celine Shen. Sidewalk dining is available under the blue awning. Inside, the decor is
Mediterranean: bright and informal, with white canvas director's chairs comple-
menting the sea-blue and white interior. French melodies are piped in. The emphasis
is on seafood. The four-course set dinners change with the season and whatever fresh
ingredients are available at local markets. The menu might include a prosciutto ham
and melon salad, flamed tiger prawns with a cream sauce, Provençal-style frog legs,
grilled salmon with dill and sea urchin sauce, or grilled rumpsteak in a triple pepper
sauce. The white and dark chocolate mousse is a perfect dessert. The waiters keep the
supply of sliced baguette replenished throughout. Set lunches are far more modest:
80RMB ($10) per person, including one glass of wine or fruit juice. During the
summer, the patio is a fine place to enjoy a Mediterranean repast in Beijing.

Cafe Renaissance.
In the Jingguan New World Hotel, 7th floor, Hu Jia Lou (a 10-minute walk north of
Jianguomenwai Dajie on the Third Ring Road). ☎ 010/6597-8888, ext. 2513. Main courses
100–240RMB ($12–$30). AE, DC, JCB, MC, V. Daily 6:30am–midnight. AMERICAN.

This upscale American-style grill turns out excellent salmon and T-bone steaks from
its open kitchen, making it a solid choice for those nostalgic for the fine steakhouses

back home. The Wild West theme is emphasized by what's dubbed the "rodeo grill," where guests can watch their steaks roast in the barbecue pit. The best deals are on weekends. On Saturdays, the set curry lunches come with soup, a choice of grilled entree (fish or beef), dessert from the trolley, and coffee or tea, all for 68RMB ($8) per person. On Sundays, the set menu "Roast of the Day" includes soup, roast from the wagon, dessert from the trolley, and coffee or tea, all for 88RMB ($11), and a glass of the local Beijing beer or a soft drink is just 5RMB (60¢). This is a relaxed but pleasant place to be a lunchtime cowboy in Beijing.

Four Seasons.

In the Jianguo Hotel, 5 Jianguomenwai Dajie. ☎ 010/6500-2233, ext. 8041. Reservations required. Main courses 160–300RMB ($20–$37). AE, DC, JCB, MC, V. Daily 11am–2:30pm and 6–10pm. CANTONESE/BEIJING.

This is one of the most popular upscale Chinese restaurants in Beijing. The menu is varied, although most dishes are Cantonese, with fine versions of rice and seafood dishes, including the expensive shark's fin and bird's nest entrees. You'll also find a complete Beijing duck set menu for two people (320RMB/$40) as good as anything prepared at the specialty restaurants. The elegant setting is as much European as Chinese, with linen tablecloths and fine china settings. Evenings feature live performances of traditional Chinese music by local musicians. The Four Seasons is a top choice for a stylish evening celebration with Chinese cuisine. The best deals are had on the weekends, however, when an excellent set lunch of Cantonese dim sum (steamed pastries) is just 88RMB ($11).

✪ Summer Palace.

In the China World Hotel, Level 2, 1 Jianguomenwai Dajie (at the intersection of the Third Ring Road East). ☎ 010/6505-2266, ext. 34. Reservations recommended on weekends. Main courses 160–300RMB ($20–$37). AE, DC, JCB, MC, V. Daily 11:30am–2:30pm and 6–10:30pm. CANTONESE.

Sleekly decorated in the modern Chinese style, with tall wooden doors, marble walkways, and pale green and salmon walls trimmed in gold, the newly remodeled Summer Palace has service and southern Chinese cuisine second to none. Expect a gracious dining experience with generous portions prepared by Hong Kong chefs. About 70% of the menu is Cantonese, with some local Beijing favorites thrown in, including a delicious version of Beijing roast duck. Fresh seafood is a staple of Cantonese fare, and the Summer Palace has plenty of living specimens in its fish tanks from which you can select your catch of the day. The menu is copious, but several surefire choices are sautéed diced beef with black pepper sauce, sweet-and-sour pork, and deep-fried Mandarin fish with pine nuts. If you want to splurge, try the shark's fin. Traditional Chinese music performed by local musicians provides a serene background. The dim sum lunches aren't the cheapest in town ($10 to $15), but these Cantonese dumplings are among the best in the capital. The service level is extremely high, but the waiters are wise enough not to linger or rush things. This is a restaurant where you'll want to savor the evening.

✪ Windows on the World.

In the CITIC Building, 28th floor, 19 Jianguomenwai Dajie (1 block west of the Friendship Store). ☎ 010/6500-2255, ext. 2828. Reservations recommended on weekends. Main courses 160–300RMB ($20–$37). AE, DC, JCB, MC, V. Daily 11:30am–2:30pm and 5:30–10pm. CANTONESE/CONTINENTAL.

This bustling, modern, upscale favorite of businesspeople and expatriates gives you an East/West choice: Cantonese dishes expertly prepared by a Hong Kong chef or entrees from the Western grill. There's a good international wine list as well. The

Brunches by the Bunch

Every Sunday just before noon, it seems that half of Beijing's hotels have cleared out their lavish lobbies to make way for equally lavish all-you-can-eat brunches. Although these buffets have an international flare, Chinese families seem to turn out in as great a number as Western travelers and expatriates. Watch for Sunday specials when you're in Beijing. Meanwhile, here are a few samples to whet your appetite:

☼ The **Swissotel Champagne and Caviar Brunch** is the most lavish and expensive of the lobby bunches, at 280RMB ($35) plus a 15% service charge, but this includes all the Moet & Chandon you can sip, not to mention the sturgeon caviar and salmon roe from Harbin. Children up to 14 get a 50% discount. Each of the hotel's 64 chefs race into action for this Sunday feast (11:30am to 2:30pm), which takes 10 hours to set up. Buffet choices range from French pastries to dim sum, and there's even Beijing duck. The Swissotel is located at the Second Ring Road East next to the Dongsishitiao subway station; buffet reservations ☎ **010/6501-2288,** ext. 2232.

Holiday Inn Lido (☎ **010/6437-6688,** ext. 1971) puts on a full international Sunday champagne buffet from 11:30am to 3pm with live entertainment. This is a long-standing favorite of families, priced at 150RMB ($18), free for children under 10.

Roma Ristorante Italiano (*see p. 81*) puts out an elaborate Northern Italian spread in the plush Palace Hotel for 165RMB ($20) per person.

Sui Yuan, on the second floor of the Beijing Hilton (1 Dong Fang Lu, Third Ring Road North; ☎ **010/6465-3052**), serves a sumptuous Yum Cha (Cantonese dim sum) brunch Sundays from 11am to 2:45pm. Most items are 15 to 25RMB ($2 to $3).

---

dining room is long and narrow. The best tables are along the southern wall of windows overlooking Chang'an Avenue below. The service is quick and efficient. The grilled steaks (imported from the U.S. and Australia) are excellent, but pricey for Beijing (up to $40). Less elaborate Cantonese and Western dinners cost under $20, and lunches are even less. This is a popular choice for business lunches and dinners, and any foreign traveler will feel quite at home.

MODERATE

☼ American Chili's Grill.

In the Gateway Building, 2nd floor, Unit 03-01, 10 Ya Bao Lu (east side, ½ block north off Guanghua Lu, east of Second Ring Road). ☎ **010/6592-5317** or 010/6592-5184. Meals 60–100RMB ($7.50–$12.50). AE, JCB, MC, V. Mon–Fri 11am–2:30pm and 5:30–11pm; Sat–Sun 11am–11pm. SOUTHWEST AMERICAN.

This bright and airy modern restaurant, part of an American Tex-Mex chain, is a family place with a festive atmosphere. Some of the staff can even juggle. On weekends, children under 10 eat free. The pepper hamburger is a bit spicy (55RMB/$6.75), but the ice cream cake with Heath bar bits will cool things down. Set lunches vary in formula, but run about 80RMB ($10). The focus of the menu is on Mexican-American fare, with chicken quesadilla costing 75RMB ($9.25) and the filling "Guiltless Veggie Skewer with Chili-Lime Marinated

Where to Go for Ice Cream

✪ **Haagen-Dazs,** purveyor of premium ice cream, opened its first cafe in Beijing in 1998, aimed at the upscale local market and foreigners looking for a special treat. There are Western cakes, pastries, and snacks; specialty coffees and fruity summer drinks (some with alcohol); and even frozen yogurts, but the focus is on fancy ice cream desserts. A single scoop of Haagen-Dazs ice cream costs 25RMB ($3), but the larger desserts are pricey for Beijing. It's in the Beijing International Club complex (south from the hotel and 1 block north of Chang'an Ave. on Xiushui Lu; ☎ 010/6532-6661). Haagen-Dazs accepts American Express, Diner's Club, Japan Credit Bank, MasterCard, and Visa, and is open daily 11am to 11pm.

Corn" priced at 85RMB ($10.25). Adults might be tempted to savor a hand-shaken margarita, despite the 75RMB ($9.25) price tag. A good location for a family celebration, it's upstairs from another spot popular with foreign families, **Spageddie's** (see below).

✪ Henry J. Bean's.

West wing of the China World Trade Center, 1 Jianguomenwai Dajie (near the Third Ring Road East). ☎ **010/6505-2266,** ext. 6334. Main courses 58–120RMB ($7–$15). AE, DC, JCB, MC, V. Sun–Thurs 11:30am–1am; Fri–Sat 11:30am–2:30am. AMERICAN.

Beijing's best American bar and grill, at least for its food, Bean's will satisfy your craving for well-prepared American standards. The hamburger with all the trimmings (58RMB/$7) is about the best you'll taste in China. The chicken Caesar salad (60RMB/$7.50) and soups are delicious, too. The polished wood decor is more that of a spiffy family restaurant than of a bar, with kitschy American advertising posters and license plates on the walls, although there are enough TV monitors to give the place the feel of a sports bar. This is a good place to pull in at any hour to recharge your Western identity after it has been shredded a bit in China's capital.

John Bull Pub.

44 Guanghua Lu (1 block east of the Second Ring Road East). ☎ **010/6532-5906.** Main courses 80–160RMB ($10–$20). AE, JCB, MC, V. Daily 9am–midnight, until 1am Fri–Sat. BRITISH.

This is a fully English pub in decor and cuisine, classy down to its dark wood panels. There's a billiards rooms, dartboard, full bar with bitters on draught, and tables downstairs and upstairs in wood-paneled dining rooms. An American/British breakfast is served all day (65RMB/$8). This is the place to get Beijing's best bangers and mash, steak-and-kidney pie, and fish and chips with Scottish cod. There are always two Chinese dishes on the menu, as well as lasagna, grilled sirloin, and a fresh chef's salad. Food, service, and atmosphere are in the British mold, but not stuffy, making this a nice place in the diplomatic district to step out of Beijing and into London.

Mexican Wave.

On the east side of Dongdaqiao Lu, 1 block south of Guanghua Lu. ☎ **010/6506-3961.** Main courses 50–100RMB ($6–$12). Daily 11am–2pm. MEXICAN.

The fajitas and salads are good, but the burritos and enchiladas are unintentional fusion foods, as much Chinese as Mexican, and the pizzas are the frozen variety. Still, Mexican Wave is an institution, one of the first private restaurants outside the Beijing hotels that prepared something different at good prices for the expatriate crowd. It's still a favorite bar, with plenty of celebrating into the wee hours. In the summer, it's worth a stop for lunch on the patio with a beer and a Mexican burger (sesame seed bun, topped with a runny egg) and in the evenings for a delicious margarita. Next door is a bar/cafe called House that serves cheap set lunches (50RMB/$6), but the food is worse. If you have a yen for Mexican or Tex-Mex, try the Texan Bar & Grill in the Holiday Inn Lido Hotel (see below), but for a quick lunch or nighttime fun with bar food, catch the wave here.

Ritan Park Restaurant.
Inside the southwest gate of Ritan Park off Guanghau Lu. ☎ **010/6500-5939,** or 010/6500-5883. Main courses 50–150RMB ($6–$18). V. Daily 11am–1:30pm and 5–9pm. SICHUAN/CANTONESE.

This is almost a carbon copy of the Sihe Yaju restaurant at the opposite end of Ritan Park, set in a pretty imperial courtyard, but it tends to catch more tourists (and tour groups) and charge a bit more. Still, it is a good choice for Chinese food in an Imperial park setting when you want a break from shopping or a dinner with a garden atmosphere. The most fetching attraction, apart from the imperial decor inside the large dining hall, is the view from the courtyard of the park's pond and rock garden. The menu has meat and tofu dishes, but the restaurant is best known for its noodles and Beijing dim sum. The Zhongcha Duck is a bit greasy, but crispy enough to be authentic, and costs about 80RMB ($10) per person. Recently attached to the restaurant courtyard is a new cafe, Gaia, offering coffees and light snacks.

Sampan Restaurant.
In the Gloria Plaza Hotel, 2 Jianguomenwai Dajie (1 block south of Jianguomenwai Dajie on the Second Ring Road, a few blocks south of the Jianguomen subway stop). ☎ **010/6515-8855,** ext. 3155. Reservations accepted only for parties of 5 or more. Meals 50–100RMB ($6–$10). AE, DC, JCB, MC, V. Daily 11:30am–2pm and 5–10pm. CANTONESE/DIM SUM.

This is one of the best choices for Cantonese-style dim sum in Beijing, particularly on Sundays. The restaurant is sparkling bright and modern with Chinese touches: bamboo curtains, a model sampan boat as centerpiece, waitresses in costume serving from wicker market baskets. It's a place to have fun. Diners frequently leave their tables to watch the dishes and dim sum being prepared by the chefs at their cooking stations. The head chefs are from Hong Kong and know how to create fine standard Southern Chinese steamed pastries. Each little dumpling runs from 5 to 15RMB (under $2), but it's easy to pig out. Best treats: *char siu bao* (pork filled dumplings), *shao mai* (seafood in tofu wrapper), and *har gau* (shrimp dumpling).

Schlotzsky's Deli.
16 Gongrentiyuchang Dong Lu (across from the southeast corner of the Worker's Stadium near Baijiazhuang Lu). ☎ **010/6504-1246.** Menu items 50–100RMB ($6–$10). No credit cards. Daily 7am–1am. AMERICAN.

If you're ready for big sandwiches American-style at a modern new American-style deli, this international chain is a haven. Schlotzsky's has more than 700 outlets in 20 countries, but this is the first in Beijing. Besides being big on sandwiches ($4–$6), soups, and fresh salads, the deli has more than a dozen types of pizzas ($6–$8 each). The emphasis here is on low-fat, low-cholesterol foods. Whether this franchise can survive in its present off-the-tourist-path location is debatable—it's a long, dismal hike down a remarkably uninspiring series of blocks, southwest of the Sanlitun District, but it's a solid American lunch stop if you're in the vicinity.

✪ Sihexuan.
In the Jinglun Hotel, 4th floor, 3 Jianguomenwai Dajie. ☎ **010/6500-2266,** ext. 8116. Meals 50–120RMB ($6–$12.50). AE, JCB, MC, V. Daily 11:30am–2pm and 5:30–10pm. BEIJING.

This is the best place in town to sample Beijing specialties in a fine setting, complete with red lanterns, long-spout teapots, and photographs of old Beijing streets and pavilions. Many middle-class Beijingers come here for upscale versions of the authentic delicacies hawked at night markets. There's a fascinating open kitchen at the entrance where the dumplings and other treats are prepared. Trolley carts thread their way between tables; point at your choice or ask for help (and translations) from the waiters. Start with a cold dish or two, such as celery with shreds of tofu. Then order some traditional snacks off the bilingual menu. The spring roll is done in an almost Vietnamese style, and the pan-fried guan sausage is good. The main courses come from the Sihexuan house specials. Try the *wu si tong* (five shredded buckets), which consist of a thin egg pancake filled with duck, pork, celery, ginger, scallions, and plum sauce. The noodles Shaanxi style in a light soup is bracing. The showstopper is the Spring Pie (35RMB/$4.25), a roll-your-own pancake with onion strips and pork. After filling up here, you can say you've tried authentic Beijing cuisine in Beijing.

Spageddie's.

In the Gateway Building, 1st floor, Unit 03-01, 10 Ya Bao Lu (½ block north off Guanghua Lu, east of the Second Ring Road). ☎ 010/6592-5215. Main courses 60–120RMB ($7.50–$15). AE, JCB, MC, V. Sun–Thurs 11am–2pm and 5:30–11pm; Fri–Sat 11am–midnight. ITALIAN.

This is a spiffy, Western-style family restaurant famous for its pizza and generous portions of pasta. The facilities are spotless, and the staff seems to be having fun. Children love it, as does anyone in search of an authentic American-style pizza with plenty of cheese and a thick pan crust.

Xihe Yaju.

At the northeast gate of Ritan Park off Ritan Dong Lu. ☎ 010/6501-0385, or 010/6594-1915. Meals 50–100RMB ($6–$10). No credit cards. Daily 11am–2pm and 5–10pm. SICHUAN/CANTONESE.

Set in a beautifully reconstructed Qing Dynasty mansion with red doors, carved beams, columns decorated in gold leaf, and a sweeping tile roof, Xihe Yaju is an ideal courtyard retreat for a reasonably priced selection of Chinese dishes. In the summer, diners can sit outside on wire patio chairs and enjoy the park setting. There are two separate menus (both in English), one with Sichuan dishes (which foreigners favor), and the other with Cantonese dishes (which locals favor). The Sichuan dishes can be quite spicy. The *gong bao jiding* (chicken with peanuts) is a great buy at 18RMB ($2.25) and not too hot. The *tie ban niu rou*, a sizzling plate of sliced beef with onions is tangy, but the *shiu zhurou pianr* (pork with peppers) is red-hot. Cantonese choices range from steamed grass carp (starting at 28RMB/$2.50) to snake dishes at 120RMB ($15) and up. This is simply a nice place for a Chinese lunch or dinner, with an old imperial park at its doorstep where you can walk off the feast.

INEXPENSIVE

Gourmet Corner.

In the basement of the China World Trade Center, B124, 1 Jianguomenwai Dajie. ☎ 010/6505-2266, ext. 43. Menu items 20–60RMB ($2.50–$7.50). AE, DC, JCB, MC, V. Daily 8:30am–9pm. AMERICAN/CONTINENTAL.

For the best deli lunch, nosh, or light repast on the run, Gourmet Corner is the choice if you're on the east side of town. The counter spread is dazzling, with everything from fresh baguettes to a bottle of Veuve Clicquot champagne. The sausages, sliced meats, imported cheeses, and salads are fresh, and the pastries and cakes are done with a fairly light touch for China. But the real reason to come is for the soup of the day and a sandwich, prepared on the spot to your order, or a bagel and coffee. The bagels are actually quite close to North American standards, and the deli enjoys a steady stream of international and local regulars.

4　Chaoyang Northeast

VERY EXPENSIVE

LaxenOxen.

In the Radisson SAS Hotel, 6A Beisanhuan Dong Lu (on the south side of the Third Ring Road East, at the China International Exhibition Centre). ☎ **010/6466-3388,** ext. 3430. Reservations required at dinner. Main courses 200–500RMB ($25–$50). AE, DC, ER, JCB, MC, V. Daily 11:30am–2:30pm and 5:30–10pm. SCANDINAVIAN.

Beijing's premier Scandinavian restaurant is decidedly an elegant affair, although the decor is not ornate and formal attire is not required. Still, this is a place worth dressing up for to enjoy an evening of fine dining and quiet celebration. The European wine list is extensive, and the menu is strictly Scandinavian, headlined by Atlantic salmon, herring, lobster, and a superb blue mussel soup. The grilled steaks are a delight, as are the open-faced sandwiches at lunchtime. Even the hearty, chewy breads have a European flavor. No fewer than three chefs from the northern reaches of Europe have found their way here.

✪ Louisiana.

In the Beijing Hilton Hotel, 2nd floor, 1 Dongfang Lu (on the east side of the Third Ring Road East). ☎ **010/6466-2288,** ext. 7420. Reservations recommended on weekends. Main courses 200–500RMB ($25–$50). AE, DC, JCB, MC, V. Mon–Sat 11:30am–2:30pm and 6–10pm; Sun 6–10pm. AMERICAN/CAJUN.

Frequently named the best American restaurant in Beijing, Louisiana has a new head chef from New York City who has altered the once purely Cajun and Creole menu to incorporate some of the recent trends in new American cuisine and Pacific Rim fusions. The result is still at the top of the Beijing scale for Western cuisine, whatever its label. The wine list remains the city's best as well—quite extensive with a fine selection of cognacs (and a qualified sommelier at your service). Settle into the elegant decor, with soothing low lights, padded chairs, and posters of Louisiana, and choose from among such starters as the Creole salad (with tender scallops, balsamic vinegar, and extra-virgin olive oil) or the gumbo (thickened with okra). Main courses include smoked rack of lamb (a long-time favorite here), tuna steak in smoked tomato vinaigrette, and wood-oven roasted baby pork ribs encased in a brown-sugar glaze topped with mango relish on a bed of coconut mashed potatoes. This is a slightly new cuisine for Beijing and a tasty one. For dessert, try the chocolate terrine or the pecan pie, which is not too sweet.

EXPENSIVE

Ashanti Restaurant & Wine Bar.

168 Xing Zhong Jie (across from the north entrance of the Workers' Stadium). ☎ **010/6416-6231.** Main courses 65–130RMB ($8–$16). No credit cards. Daily 6pm–midnight. SPANISH.

Chef Carlos Chordi's native Spanish fare, heavy on tapas and raciones, has been influenced by where he lived, Pamplona, near the French border, and where he traveled, frequently in Portugal. The result is one of the most unusual dining choices in Beijing. The interior resembles a Mediterranean gallery, with white plaster walls and soft lights, and in fact it is a gallery for avant-garde Chinese artists. The furniture is

Night Market Nosh

Street food can be tempting, especially in the midst of a long stroll through the capital's packed streets, but the hygiene of vendors and their carts and stands is in no way regulated, meaning they are off-limits to visitors worried about the health consequences. Nevertheless, scores of foreigners can't resist sampling the culinary delights of the streets and alleyways.

Night markets, which are government-sanctioned but still far from safe on the stomach, line the streets after dark, stall by stall. The fried snacks and noodles are dirt cheap, costing from a few mao to a few kwai (2¢ to 25¢). There are popular night markets west of the Beijing Zoo (**Dongyuan Yeshi**) and near the north entrance to Beihai Park (called **Shichahai Yeshi,** the Lotus Bloom market). There's a **Tourist Snack Market,** set up by Beijing restaurants and monitored for hygiene by the hotels, that runs all summer across the street from the Palace Hotel (on Jinyu Hutong, 2 blocks east of Wangfujing Dajie). And the Muslim sections of Beijing always have sidewalk vendors hawking hot grilled lamb shish kebabs.

The biggest and the best night market for snacking, however, is **Donghuamen Yeshi,** which runs up and down Donganmen Dajie immediately west of Wangfujing toward the Forbidden City. The street food menu below describes the most common of the forbidden fruits cooked up nightly here.

Baozi   Steamed buns stuffed with anything from cabbage to pork

Huntun   Local version of wonton soup

Xianr bing   Tiny flat pancakes stuffed with vegetables and eggs

Jing bing guozi   A large crêpe the size of a pizza with egg, cilantro, and plum and hot sauces

Miantiao   Noodles in various forms, fried, boiled, or in soup

Youtiao   Deep-fried wands of dough, a breakfast favorite

Yams   Yes, there are sweet potatoes in those oil drums

Yang rou chuan   Lamb shish kebab roasted over an open flame

---

also Chinese (late Qing Dynasty designs). This is a dinner and late-night spot for many Beijing artists and musicians, as well as expatriates. The stuffed mushrooms (*champinones rellenos*) is a typical starter. A fine racione selection is the *ganbas al ajillo,* boiled shrimp in garlic and olive oil, served with French bread. Paellas are brought straight to the table still in the skillet where large chunks of seafood, game (such as rabbit), and beans and peas top a layer of saffron rice. Paellas are priced at 175RMB ($22) for two portions, up to 500RMB ($62) for six. In the late evenings, this becomes a cigar and sangria kind of place, with the South African sangria running 35RMB ($4.25) per glass, 175RMB ($22) per pitcher.

Baikal Cafe.

2 Beizhong Jie, Dongzhimennei Dajie (across the street from the Russian Embassy near the Second Ring Road East). ☎ **010/6405-4902,** or 010/6405-2380. Reservations recommended on weekends. Main courses 100–160RMB ($12.50–$20). V. Daily 11am–midnight. RUSSIAN.

More upscale than the old Moscow Restaurant, with better food and more entertainment, Baikal gets its name from Russia's deepest lake, which is also the source of the restaurant's fish and sturgeon caviar, flown in weekly from Siberia. The chef, the food, and the atmosphere are all Russian, albeit a stagy version of authentic Russian. A number of Russian diplomats are regulars here. The kebabs and the borscht are excellent, the fried and grilled fish fair, but the real emphasis is on the lounge show. There are strolling singers performing Russian folk songs during dinner, but come showtime, from 7:30 to 11:30pm every night, the stage and sometimes portions of the vodka-fueled audience explode with Russian bands, dancers, and singers who alternately belt out Western favorites and more northern pop melodies. This is the closest thing in Beijing to a Western supper show.

✪ Borom Piman.

In the Holiday Inn Lido, Jichang Lu, Jiangtai Lu (on the east side of the Airport Expressway). ☎ **010/6437-6688**, ext. 2899. Reservations recommended on weekends. Main courses 80–160RMB ($10–$20). AE, DC, JCB, MC, V. Daily 11am–2pm and 5–10pm. THAI.

Beijing's first major Thai restaurant, Borom Piman is still tops in the capital. Part of the reason is the cuisine, quite good indeed, and part is the setting. The interior is traditional and elegant, with silk cushions, wood paneling, and a section of recessed-in-the-floor tables (with upright chairs). A third ingredient is the prompt and unobtrusive service. Locals head here for the economical set lunches (well under $10) and set dinners, although the à la carte menu is extensive, too. Popular dishes are the spring prawn soup and the curry chicken. For a celebration or a fine dinner, Borom Piman does not disappoint.

✪ Lao Shanghai.

In the Holiday Inn Lido, Jichang Road, Jiangtai Road (on the east side of the Airport Expressway) ☎ **010/6437-6688**. Reservations recommended on weekends. Main courses 150–200RMB ($18–$25). AE, DC, JCB, MC, V. Daily 11:30am–2pm and 6–10pm. SHANGHAI.

Shanghai restaurants are all the rage in Beijing, and among the hotels that have introduced new venues, the Holiday Inn Lido has come up with the best new entry. The dinning room is upscale, with crystal and silver settings and photographs of old Shanghai on the walls, but the feeling is quite relaxed. This restaurant is a cooperative effort with the original Lao Shanghai, which was established in old Shanghai in 1875, and the cooks know how to prepare light, flavorful standards. An excellent starter is the clear soup with shredded pork, chicken, and bamboo shoots. The showstopper is the liquefied hairy crab, extremely flavorful here. This is a fine place for a long, quiet evening, with a good European wine list and in the evenings a three-piece jazz band recalling colonial days.

Metro Cafe.

6 Gongrentiyuchang Xi Lu (across from the west entrance of the Worker's Stadium). ☎ **010/6552-7828**. Main courses 80–160RMB ($10–$20). AE, JCB, MC, V. Sun–Thurs 11:30am–midnight; Fri–Sat 11:30am–2am; Sun 5:30pm–midnight. ITALIAN.

Within a relaxed, modern decor, with subdued light and soft music, the Metro serves up some of the finest fresh pasta dinners in town. You can create your own pasta and sauce combinations from the English-language menu. The spinach ravioli comes in large, delicious portions, and the marble cheesecake is a good choice for dessert. Lunch is served from 11:30am to 2:30pm, and the kitchen closes for dinner at about 10pm, when the Metro becomes a lively bar. In the summers, the outdoor courtyard is usually jammed with expats.

Mongolian Gher.

In the Movenpick Hotel at the Beijing Capital Airport, Xiao Tianzhu Village, Shunyi. ☎ **010/6456-5588**. Reservations required. Set dinners 158RMB and 188RMB ($19 and $22.50). AE, DC, EU, JCB, MC, V. Daily 6–11pm. MONGOLIAN.

The setting and the Mongolian food here make for quite an extraordinary evening, fully worth the extra journey back and forth from the airport. This is easily the best tent food in Beijing, as it is served in a traditional round fur tent, or yurt (called a *gher* in Mongolian). The yurts at the Movenpick, however, are far from basic itinerant affairs; instead, they are richly carpeted and decorated in northern and Muslim patterns. This is an adventurous dinner, but also an elegant one. The *gher* is spacious enough for exceptional after-dinner performances by Mongolian dancers in costume. Two Mongolian cooks do all the kitchen labors, specializing in barbecues in the summer and Mongolian hotpots in the winter, but you can try either here whatever the season. The two set menus vary slightly, but both consist of four starters, five hot dishes, and dessert.

Paulaner Brauhaus.
In the Kempinski Hotel, 50 Liangmaqiao (on the east side of Third Ring Road East). ☎ **010/ 6465-3388,** ext. 5732. Main courses 80–160RMB ($10–$20). AE, DC, EU, JCB, MC, V. Daily 11:30am–2am. GERMAN.

The best brewhouse in town, with the beer brewed right here in the tanks according to the pure "Paulaner" methods of Germany, the Paulaner also serves some of the finest German cuisine. The tile floors, black wood trim, and country tables are all polished to a shine (even the bathrooms are first-rate). The atmosphere is upscale, but casual and warm. If you like schnitzels, you've found their home in Beijing. One of the cheapest but most bracing choices on the menu is the country bacon potatoes with wild mushrooms (plenty of them) and a fried egg with melted cheese. This is a fine stop for lunch. Full German dinners are also available. Later in the evening thoughts turn to German microbrews and the German performers who dance and sing. The homemade beers are expensive, but quite tasty.

Shanghai Cuisine.
In the Kunlun Hotel, 2 Xinyuan Nanlu (2 blocks west of the Third Ring Road East). ☎ **010/ 6500-3388,** ext. 5394. Main courses 100–200RMB ($12.50–$25). AE, JCB, MC, V. Daily 11:30am–2:30pm and 5:30–9:30pm. SHANGHAI.

The Kunlun Hotel's Shanghai restaurant offers the most extensive and authentic Shanghai dishes in Beijing, not surprising since the hotel's management group is based in Shanghai. As a result, the chefs are not only Shanghai natives, but deeply experienced with preparing the dishes in a large setting. To enhance that setting within a great, rather garishly decorated hall, the wait staff is outfitted in 1930s Old Shanghai costumes. The staff knows the food it is serving, although service itself can be abrupt (also in character with the aggressive reputation of Shanghai). The Wuxi spareribs are among a raft of excellent dishes, as are the braised pork patties with oyster sauce and the shredded eel. The poached trout has become a signature dish.

Shanghai Moon.
4 Gongrentiyuchang Bei Lu (on the west side of the Third Ring Road East). ☎ **010/ 6506-9988,** ext. 203. Main courses 80–160RMB ($10–$20). AE, JCB, MC, V. Daily 11am– 2pm and 5–10pm. SHANGHAI.

A bit more modestly priced than Shanghai Cuisine (see above), and the current favorite of Beijing's foreign community for Shanghai dishes, Shanghai Moon is in a former jazz club. Here, too, the staff dresses up to evoke the notorious days of 1930s Shanghai, and the decor of polished dark woods underscores the nostalgia. Many of the ingredients are flown in from Shanghai, making any dish with vegetables and crab worth ordering. The third floor is given over to karaoke, snacks, and drinks in the evening, so the place does have a noisy, slightly notorious feel. The Shanghai food itself is good here, quite satisfying, but it is better at Shanghai Cuisine and Lao

Shanghai in the Holiday Inn Lido (see above). Shanghai Moon comes out ahead, however, on price and atmosphere.

Texan Bar & Grill.

In the Holiday Inn Lido, Jichang Lu, Jiangtai Lu (on the east side of the Airport Expressway). ☎ **010/6437-6688,** ext. 1849. Main courses 80–160RMB ($10–$20). AE, DC, JCB, MC, V. Daily 11am–2pm and 5–10pm. MEXICAN.

Despite its over-the-top Mexican decor (silly, tacky, but actually quite carefully done and utterly typical of the real Tex-Mex joints it emulates), the Texan delivers the best Mexican-American fare in Beijing. The Chinese staff in cowboy gear promenade from the grill to the tables toting genuine American steaks (rib-eye and T-bone) and solid Australian beef—never mind that neither has a whit to do with Mexico. What does come from Mexico are the sizzling fajitas, the enchiladas, the quesadillas, the tacos, and the margaritas, all rated passable to good (just don't expect the flare and spice of true Mexican cuisine). Worth a sombrero dance is the salad bar, a self-serve affair located in the chuck wagon.

MODERATE

Berena's Bistro.

6 Gongrentiyuchang Dong Lu (across from the east entrance of the Worker's Stadium). ☎ **010/6592-2628.** Main courses 80–120RMB ($10–$15). AE, JCB, MC, V. Daily 11:30am–2pm and 5–11:30pm. SICHUAN.

Long a favorite of the foreign community in Beijing, Berena's serves an extensive array of Sichuan dishes in a relaxed, romantic atmosphere. The lights are low, almost too low. The marble floors are dark as well, but there's enough candlelight to make out the Chinese and Western posters tacked to the walls. Most items on the menu are under $10. The Sichuan food is not as hot and spicy as in Sichuan, which pleases the mostly foreign crowd. The sweet and sour soup is too vinegary, but full of good red chilies. The chicken with almonds is a good safe choice, and the doufu dishes are pleasing. The *gong bao* chicken comes on a sizzling plate, and the sweet and sour pork is one of the most popular dishes, as is the Chengdu roast duck (80RMB/$10 per person), which some prefer to the greasy Beijing duck. As one of Beijing's top Sichuan restaurants, Berena's knows how to please foreign travelers looking for a good Chinese meal.

✪ Kebab Kafe.

On Sanlitun Bei Lu (near the bamboo market). ☎ **010/6415-5812.** Main courses 40–170RMB ($5–$21). AE, JCB, MC, V. Daily 11:30am–2:30pm and 6–10:30pm. GERMAN.

Not just another Sanlitun bar with a smattering of Western-style food, the Kebab is a serious restaurant serving some of the best German and Continental cuisine in Beijing. It's also the best cafe in this part of the city. The Chinese chef spent 20 years in Europe, training much of the time in German cooking, and the results show, from the humble kebabs that give the place its name (these are sandwich-style kebabs) to the salmon steak with dill cream. Each of the 34 main courses, which include chicken breast Cordon Bleu and Hungarian beef goulash, comes with fresh salads. Desserts include Italian ice cream, lemon tart, and apple strudel with vanilla sauce. Lunchtime favorites include the vegetarian pizza, ratatouille, and spaghetti with pesto, each under $8. In the winter, the Kebab comes up with excellent Swiss cheese fondues and rachettes. The interior is that of a run-down bistro, with red tablecloths and oil paintings on the wall. In the summer, the large patio opening onto Sanlitun fills with Europeans and other Westerners eating sandwiches and pastries and drinking the imported German beers.

⊕ Family-Friendly Restaurants

Almost any Beijing restaurant is used to serving children, but for foreign families there are several that stand out:

Xihe Yaju (*see p. 91*). This Cantonese courtyard restaurant is in a beautiful park and even has *ayis* (baby-sitting aunties) on hand to mind the younger children while dining outside.

Hard Rock Cafe (near the Sheraton Great Wall Hotel on the Third Ring Road, 8 Dongsanhuan Bei Lu; ☎ **010/6590-6688,** ext. 2571). The music, decor, and food (American hamburgers, fries, and fajitas—and it's actually quite good) should keep any Western teenager happy. It's open daily from 11:30am to 1am (100RMB/$12.50 cover charge after 10pm).

American Chili's Grill (*see p. 88*). Just the place for Tex-Mex, burgers, and ice cream desserts when the children start to drag during a shopping stroll.

Texan Bar & Grill (*see p. 96*). Chinese cowboys and cowgirls serve up the best Tex-Mex in town to foreign families (tourists and residents) in a hotel complex (Holiday Inn Lido) where Western children will feel right at home.

Cafe California (in the lobby of the new Harbour Plaza Hotel, 8 Jiang Tai Lu, in northeast Beijing; ☎ **010/6436-2288**). The inexpensive Sunday brunch here (from 11am to 2:30pm) is geared to children (under 12 eat for half price) with balloons, cartoon figures, and entertainers.

Omar Khayyam.
In the Asia Pacific Building, 8 Yabao Lu (1 block north of Guanghua Lu on east side of the Second Ring Road). ☎ **010/6513-9988,** ext. 20188. Reservations recommended on weekends. 70–100RMB ($8.75–$12.50). AE, JCB, MC, V. Daily 11:30am–2:30pm and 6–10:30pm. INDIAN.

Slightly cheaper than Beijing's best Indian restaurant—Shamiana, in the Holiday Inn Downtown (see section 6)—and boasting excellent dishes of its own, Omar Khayyam is a very popular lunch and dinner spot for foreigners living and working in the diplomatic district north of Chang'an Avenue east. Dishes are not too spicy, and portions are manageable. Of the literally scores of vegetarian choices here, the best reviews go to the *dahl* (with spinach, lentils, and cheese). The chicken, lamb, and fish dishes are roasted tandoori-style (over hot charcoals). An efficient, congenial staff and weekend set menu specials keep this one of Beijing's most popular and reliable Indian restaurants

Red Basil.
Building 8, Nanxiao Jie (on the south side of Third Ring Road opposite Jing Xin Plaza, northwest of the Hilton Hotel). ☎ **010/6460-2339,** or 010/6460-2342. Main courses 30–80RMB ($3.75–$10). AE, JCB, MC, V. Daily 11:30am–2pm and 5:30–10pm. THAI.

Opened in 1996 by a Thai businessman and employing chefs from his native land, Red Basil is an informal but stylish Asian restaurant noted for its efficient service and real Thai dishes (with some ingredients imported from Hong Kong). The decor includes floors of rich, polished wood and floor-to-ceiling mirrors; there's mezzanine dining as well. The menu has many of the Thai classics, from *phad thai* (rice noodles in peanut sauce) to a variety of curries, fine soups, beef salads, shrimp cakes, and delicate fish fillets. Most dishes are in the $4 to $7 range. The *tom yum koong* soup (using coconut milk) draws many raves. The food is hotly spiced, as it should be, but guests can ask the cook to hold back on the fiery chilies.

San Si Lang.
52 Liangmaqiao Lu (across the street from the Kempinski Hotel, east of the Third Ring Road). ☎ 010/6464-5030. 60–100RMB ($7.50–$12.50). AE, JCB, MC, V. Daily 11:30am–2pm and 5–11pm. JAPANESE.

Crowded at lunch and dinner, San Si Lang is the place to go for reasonably priced sushi and tempura. The first-floor dining room is neatly divided into comfortable booths separated by partitions. Upstairs are tatami rooms for groups. The multilingual menu is illustrated with pictures of each dish. Prices are several times lower than those in the leading Japanese restaurants in Beijing's hotels. The sushi bar has a variety of items, including an excellent shrimp sushi. The tuna or cucumber rolls, six to a plate, are just 15RMB (less than $2), the same price as the soba (cold noodles). At the "pricier" end are the tempura prawns (60RMB/$7.50), still a relative bargain. Sashimi is also a specialty here, although some items can cost up to 100RMB ($12.50). This is Beijing's best economy Japanese restaurant, a marvelous spot for a late lunch in graceful surroundings.

T.G.I. Fridays.
Huapeng Dasha, 19 Dongsanhuan Bei Lu (on the west side of the Third Ring Road, northwest of Tuanjiehu Park). ☎ 010/6595-1380. 60–100RMB ($7.50–$12.50). AE, JCB, MC, V. Daily 11am–midnight. AMERICAN.

This American chain does a fairly authentic imitation of American food, service, and atmosphere in Beijing, all with a menu quite close to the original, too. In addition to its burgers, fries, and stuffed potato skins, Beijing's T.G.I.F. branch has spicy Thai noodles, excellent fajitas, seafood pastas, and waiters and waitresses wearing big Chairman Mao buttons and grinning ear-to-ear, in caricature of the typical American teenager, it seems. The salads are generous and fresh. The interior is what you would expect—gaudy and dazzling, from its brass rails and Tiffany glass to the old (American) road signs. Lately it has become a favorite of younger Beijingers who want to hang out in a close copy of an American restaurant.

Trattoria La Gondola.
In the Kempinski Hotel, 50 Liangmaqiao Lu (in the southwest corner of the You Yi Shopping Center, east of the Third Ring Road). ☎ 010/6465-3388, ext. 5707. 70–160RMB ($8.75–$20). AE, DC, JCB, MC, V. Daily 11:30am–2:30pm and 5:30–11pm. ITALIAN.

This bright, open, upscale country-style Italian restaurant is both elegant and casual. It can be the scene of a fine, romantic dinner (complete with musical performers) or a relaxing, filling lunch. It's not as formal or as expensive as some of its hotel-based competitors (Danieli's, Roma Ristorante) nor as family-oriented as the more economical Spageddie's (see section 3). Lunch prices are lower, making that a good time to sample the cooking: You can choose your own pasta and sauce for 68RMB ($8.50), try a large pizza for 75RMB ($9), and select from among the antipastos, salads, and soups (from 40–80RMB/$5–$10).

INEXPENSIVE

Annie's Cafe.
At the intersection of Sanlitun Nan Lu and Gongrentiyuchang Bei Lu. ☎ 010/6594-2894. Main courses 40–130RMB ($5–$16). No credit cards. Daily 11am–2am. AMERICAN.

This red-and-chrome cafe/bar on the corner marks the beginning (or the end) of Beijing's premier cafe/bar district, Sanlitun. Annie's is a bar, but it also has a menu of American concoctions typical of the little cafes in the neighborhood. The best choices by far are the steaks, reasonably priced for Beijing (from 90–130RMB/ $11–$16), and the buffalo wings. Pizzas, on the other hand, are strictly heated-up-from-the-freezer affairs. Annie's is best enjoyed as a spot for sipping a beer and munching popcorn or French fries as you watch the world hurry by through the glass windows.

Gold Cat Jiaozi City.

At the east gate of Tuanjiehu Park on the Third Ring Road East. ☎ **010/6598-5011.** Snacks 40–130RMB ($5–$16). AE, JCB, MC, V. Daily 24 hrs. BEIJING.

For a cheap introduction to Beijing's famous *jiaozi* (steamed dumplings with meat or vegetable fillings), try this courtyard emporium, guarded by two stone lions. This is a no-frills restaurant dedicated to churning out from 20 to 40 separate varieties of the city's pastries, stuffed with pork, seafood, and the vegetables in season. Summertime sees dining in the open courtyard, the best time and the best seating (inside seating is serviceable but stark). Our favorite *jiaozi* is the standard *zhurou jiucai* (a steamed bun stuffed with shreds of pork and local chives). They are juicy and strongly flavored, and locals can eat them by the dozens. The Gold Cat jiaozi come four or five to a plate, each plate costing just 50¢ or so. An English menu helps narrow the choices. Avoid the late evenings and wee hours, when Gold Cat becomes a noisy karaoke palace.

Hollywood Star.

Midway in the new cafe/bar strip on the east side of the Third Ring Road between the Kempinski and Hilton hotels (no posted address). No telephone. Reservations not accepted. Meals 25–70RMB ($3–$8.75). No credit cards. Daily 11am–4am. AMERICAN.

Typical of the trend that swept the nearby Sanlitun District in the late 1990s, this cafe and a dozen more on either side of it now hug the main street connecting two of Beijing's larger international hotels, the Hilton and Kempinski. In the wee hours, they function strictly as friendly spots to drink and mix with the locals (at prices much lower than in the hotel bars and lounges). At lunchtime and through dinner, however, they function as intimate cafes turning out surprisingly good versions of foreign cuisine (most commonly American, Korean, and Japanese). Hollywood Star sprouted up seemingly out of nothing at a previously blank shopfront and promptly put out a sidewalk signboard with the day's specials chalked in English: sandwiches, subs, spaghetti, Caesar salad, pizzas, and steaks (not imported). They even had Starbucks coffee on the menu before Starbucks opened its own outlet. Inside, the Hollywood Star is hardly larger than a living room, with tables for about 20.

✪ Johnny's Coffee.

77 Xibahe Dongli (on the north side of the Third Ring Road North, across from the International Exhibition Centre). ☎ **010/6461-0827.** Snacks 10–30RMB ($1.25–$3.75). No credit cards. Daily 10am–11am. AMERICAN.

Beijing's first real coffee cafe has done everything so well that it qualifies as an institution, despite having been open only since April 1996. From the long coffee bar to the checkerboard floor to the round tables with bent-wire chairs, it has the look of what it is: the place to savor a latte, cappuccino, espresso, or freshly ground cup of coffee. It's possible to nosh here on muffins (10RMB/$1.25), egg and tuna sandwiches (30RMB/$3.75), or bagels and cream cheese (19RMB/$2.35). The coffees include decaffeinated versions and house blends as well as the straight Colombians and Sumatrans, with lattes and cappuccinos priced at 22 to 28RMB ($2.75 to

$3.50). Johnny's is a good place for snacks and coffees anytime you're in the neighborhood (which may not be often, since there are no major sights nearby). On many Friday evenings there's live jazz.

5 Xuanwu (Southwest) & Chongwen (Southeast)

EXPENSIVE

✪ Quanjude Kaoyadian (Roast Duck).

32 Qianmen Dajie, Chongwen District (a few blocks straight south of Tiananmen Square). ☎ 010/6511-2418. Main courses 110–200RMB ($13–$25). AE, JCB, MC, V. Daily 10:30am–1:30pm and 4:30–8:30pm. BEIJING DUCK.

The first Quanjude roast duck restaurant opened its doors during the Qing Dynasty in 1864 and has been the foremost purveyor of crispy duck ever since (even when it was taken over by the government for a period a few turbulent decades ago). Quanjude is now a chain. This particular restaurant is the most elegant (and expensive), and it enjoys the reputation as the best Beijing duck restaurant in the world. It may very well be, as outside the capital, few restaurants are so specialized. The interiors of this large restaurant, spread up and down several floors and including dining rooms and halls of various dimensions, are uniformly imperial, ornate, garish, and somewhat worn (as all truly royal halls are). You should go as a group here, reserving a private room if possible. Think of it as a small, relaxed banquet.

MODERATE

Gongdelin.

158 Qianmen Nan Dajie, Chongwen District (directly south of Tiananmen Square, about 2 blocks south of Zhushikuo Avenue on east side). ☎ 010/6511-2542. Main courses 40–120RMB ($5–$15). AE, JCB, MC, V. Daily 10am–8:30pm. VEGETARIAN.

Until Green Tian Shi Restaurant came along (see section 2), Gongdelin was by far Beijing's best place for vegetarian cuisine. It still has the most extensive menu, and some of its dishes are still the best. The institutional, run-down decor leaves a bit to be desired, but the staff is surprisingly efficient. This is a government-run restaurant—and well run—and your waiter or waitress can probably point out some things worth trying on the English-language menu. The central notion in Chinese vegetarian cooking is to create dishes that look, taste, and smell like what they are presumed to be replacing in the animal world: the flesh of the duck, chicken, fish, or pig so favored by most Chinese. Gongdelin, for example, has a faux jellyfish on its menu, but the *huase zijin* (many-colored gems) is better, with its use of almonds, tofu, and vegetables to suggest a duck-based appetizer. The *su yazi* resembles and even tastes vaguely like Beijing duck. Simple vegetable dishes here are superb. If you can get together a group of six or more, consider arranging a small banquet (usually about 100RMB/$12.50 per person).

Jinyang Fanzhuang.

241 Zhushikou Xi Dajie, Xuanwu District (on the north side of the street, 1 block east of Nanxinhua Jie, southwest of Tiananmen Square). ☎ 010/6303-1669. Main courses 80–120RMB ($10–$15). No credit cards. Daily 11am–2pm and 5–8:30pm. BEIJING/SHANXI (NORTHERN CHINESE).

Situated in the courtyard estate of an imperial scholar (Ji Xiaolan), who lived here 2 centuries ago during the reign of the great Qing Emperor Qianlong, the Jinyang broadcasts an ideal, if fading, image of Old Cathay. It actually opened its doors in this scholar's house a bit more recently, in 1956, but that makes it old in the new

How to Eat Beijing Duck

Beijing duck is roasted in such a way that the skin is terribly crispy and the meat is quite juicy—some would say fat and oily. But true Beijing Duck is on the greasy side. The ducks are carved at your table. Smear a thin pancake with plum sauce, sprinkle it with spring onion shreds, add bits of the carved duck, and then roll up the whole package and eat it with your hands.

China. The food here is that of the rough-and-tough north of China, the hard-scrabble Shanxi Province, where *dao xiao mian* (long noodles in vinegar) is the staple. Another regional noodle found here is known as *mao er duo,* meaning "cat's ear noodle," shaped and given the texture to go with vegetables and vinegary meats. The twice-fried pork with black fungus mushroom and vinegar (*guo you rou*) is yet another standard, here made an appetizer. Perhaps the most popular Shanxi dish served here is the *xiang suya,* the crispy duck that's less greasy than the Beijing duck, priced at 80RMB ($10) per person.

Quanjude Hepingmen (Roast Duck).

14 Qianmen Xi Dajie, Xuanwu District (on the southeast corner of the intersection with Nanxinhua Jie, near the Hepingmen subway station). ☎ **010/6301-8833.** Main courses 75–120RMB ($9–$15). AE, JCB, MC, V. Daily 10:30am–1:30pm and 4:30–8:30pm. BEIJING DUCK.

A more modern (still rather garish) member of the venerable Quanjude roast duck restaurant chain, the Hepingmen branch serves the same side dishes and roasted duck as the more elegant Kaoyadian outlet (see above), but at a lower price. The Hepingmen opened in 1979 (115 years after the chain got its start in the Qing Dynasty), and it still looks like a big hotel, marble lobby and all. It includes seven floors and more than 40 dining rooms, all pretty much dedicated to duck. When you walk in, you'll be seated in the bright and fairly uninspired main dining room. The side dishes are kept in the freezer section up front, supermarket style, and you can eyeball them before placing an order. For two or three people, one duck is enough, but for four or five diners, split two ducks. Each roasted duck costs 180RMB ($21.75). The duck is expertly carved at your table, and the pieces are incorporated as the final ingredient in the pancake you're about to roll. (The pancake, in turn, you coat with plum sauce and sprinkle with onion slices.) This is one of the few big Chinese dishes where chopsticks do not come into play. What this modern cavern of a roast duck restaurant lacks in charm, it makes up for with its main course—China's ultimate finger food.

INEXPENSIVE

Jinghua Shiyuan.

8 Longtan Lu, Chongwen District (at the big teapot sign beside the north entrance to the Beijing Amusement Park). ☎ **010/6711-5331.** Snacks 10–30RMB ($1.25–$3.75). No credit cards. Daily 8am–7pm. BEIJING DIM SUM.

The ambience is that of old Beijing, the setting is an ornate courtyard compound on the shores of Longtan Lake, and the food dishes are the simple snacks (*xiao chi*) native to the capital and North China, including *jiaozi,* the steamed dumpling with a meat or vegetable filling. In Beijing's *hutongs* (alleyways), the most common snack consists of a deep-fried bread stick (*you tiao*) and soy milk (*dou jiang*), which Jinghua provides in a traditional, more hygienic setting. Jinghua is known for its basic little cakes (*bing*), filled with meat or tofu (*doufu*), and its bean soup (*dou zhi*)

Fast-Food Invaders

One of the last of world's major capitals to experience it, Beijing is now in the throes of a full-scale "McAttack," with American fast-food chains slithering across this ancient Chinese city like a dragon run amok in French fries and milk shakes. At last count, there were more than 55 McDonald's in Beijing alone, one every few blocks or so in the main shopping districts and some setting up shop where few foreign tourists ever venture. These McDonald's are fairly faithful copies of the American model, with prices about on par and picture menus for non-Chinese speakers. Beijing yuppies, well-to-do teens, middle-class families, and anyone else able to scrape together the money for a truly American experience are slowly making burgers as popular as Beijing's own steamed dumplings.

Ordering by pointing is usually no problem for foreigners, but here are the essential translations:

Hamburger   *Han bao-bao*
French fries   *Shu Tiao*
Coffee   *Kafei*
Sprite   *Xuebi*
Coca-Cola   *Kekou-Kele*
Diet cola   *Jianyi kele*
McDonald's   *MaiDanglao*
Big Mac   *Juwuba*
McChicken   *Maixiang Ji*
Do you take credit cards?   *Ni shuo xinyongka ma?*

---

made from fermented ming berries. Most foreigners stick with the *jiaozi* and tea, enjoy the lake views in summer from the outdoor round wooden tables and benches, and watch the tea ceremonies performed at Jinghua's own teahouse. Jinghua's shop sign is a 9-foot-tall dragon-mouthed teapot on a pedestal, cocked to pour into an enormous tea bowl; it's the largest copper teapot in the world.

6 Xicheng (West) & Haidian (Northwest)

VERY EXPENSIVE

✪ Li Family Restaurant (Li Jia Cai).

11 Yangfang Hutong, Deshengmennei Dajie, Xicheng District (south of Xihai and Houhai lakes). ☎ **010/6618-0107.** Reservations required. Set menus 200–560RMB ($25–$70). No credit cards. Daily 6–10pm. IMPERIAL BEIJING.

Located in a traditional *hutong* courtyard complex near the historic Back Lakes, the Li Family Restaurant has taken Beijing by storm. Here you can enjoy the very recipes created for the Qing Dynasty Empress Dowager herself during the twilight of the Forbidden City. The restaurant owner's great-grandfather commanded the Palace Guard before the fall of the last dynasty, and he was able to walk away with a number of the royal recipes. Today's family patriarch, Li Shan Lin, beguiles diners with explanations of the ingredients and healthful benefits of the imperial cuisine. With all this going for it, Li Family is one of the most difficult restaurants to book in Beijing, with a waiting list stretching to 3 and 4 weeks. It is an experience not to be missed, but don't expect an "imperial" evening. Imperial cuisine is decidedly plain, rustic stuff, with interesting but hardly delicate flavors, served here in appropriate surroundings, a humble courtyard house in an old, curving *hutong*. Within are four cramped dining rooms with three or four tables each. While the Li Family Restaurant gets raves from all quarters and is surely a top Beijing experience, you may come away wondering what all the fuss is about. At a recent meal here, my two dining companions, a Chinese couple from Malaysia, scratched their heads at the exorbitant price, plain decor, and rough cuisine, declaring the place a monumental tourist rip-off.

✪ Nishimura.

In the Shangri-La Beijing Hotel, Level 2, 29 Zizhuyuan Lu, Haidian District (on the northwest corner of the Third Ring Road). ☎ **010/6841-2211.** Main courses 90–350RMB ($11–$42.50). AE, DC, JCB, MC, V. Daily 6–10pm. JAPANESE.

Beijing's first *robatayaki* (grill) opened in May 1998 and has been turning out delectable fare ever since. This clean, spacious restaurant consists of a standard dining room, two tatami mat rooms, a takeout counter, a large and small teppanyaki grill, and the long robatayaki grill. Go for the robatayaki, where the chef behind the counter grills whatever you point out. There are two Japanese chefs here and a manager also from Japan, with everyone trained at one of the many Nishimura restaurants overseas. The food is presented on a show-grill, then slow-cooked on the spot and served by the chef with large wooden paddles. A typical robatayaki meal might consist of miso soup, chicken, a bacon roll with asparagus, a potato section with butter, and a giant prawn. The prawn is heavenly and the potato is superb, simply prepared and delectably sweetened. Depending on your selections, this can serve as a modestly priced lunch or a very expensive and satisfying dinner.

EXPENSIVE

✪ Carousel Revolving Restaurant.

In the Xiyuan Hotel, 26th floor, 1 Sanlihe Lu, Xicheng District (southwest of the entrance to the Beijing Zoo). ☎ **010/6831-3388.** Reservations recommended on weekends. Set lunch 118RMB ($14); set dinner 138RMB ($17). AE, JCB, MC, V. Daily 11am–2:30pm and 6–10pm. ASIAN.

With the best view of Beijing and the Western Hills, this recently renovated revolving restaurant turns ever so slowly (taking about 2 hours for a complete revolution), giving you plenty of time to fully savor the view and the buffet. The table setting is formal, with white tablecloths, crystal, and blue padded chairs. The spread is mostly Asian, headlined by Thai, Malaysian, and Indonesian dishes, but with creations from Japan, Vietnam, India, Korea, and China. The head chef is from Penang, Malaysia. There's also a fresh salad bar, Western desserts, and an authentic German microbrew made on the premises. The poached salmon and the crab cakes are particularly worth sampling. This is a great spot to enjoy a fine evening in the western outreaches of the city, particularly when the city lights spread out to the east, although a night of fog (or smog) can be a romantic background as well.

✪ Fangshan Restaurant.

Inside Beihai Park on the northern shore of Beihai Island, Xicheng District. ☎ **010/6401-1879.** Main courses 150–250RMB ($18–$30). AE, JCB, MC, V. Daily 11am–1:30pm and 5–7pm. BEIJING IMPERIAL.

Beijing's first imperial restaurant, opened before the Revolution (1949), Fangshan serves dishes dating from the Qing Dynasty's reign in the Forbidden City. The setting couldn't be more appropriate: a courthouse mansion looking out on the long covered

The Food of the People:
Nostalgia for the Bad Old Days

As unlikely as it seems to anyone who has read about or especially lived through the horrific, chaotic days of the Cultural Revolution (1966–1976), when China shut down and fed upon itself, its Mao-inspired Red Guards ransacking the nation's intellectual and cultural heritage, there's a certain nostalgia for the simpler days of the Chairman Mao dynasty. If you want to see what the people ate before the economic reforms launched China into the modern world in the 1980s and 1990s, a few "novelty" restaurants now create that milieu and serve sanitized versions of the harsh and simple fare of the people. The food tends to be quite salty, with such items as fried dough (*su hung cai*), vinegary cucumber sticks, and "Earth's Three Freshnesses" (*disanxian*), which are potatoes, eggplants, and green peppers mixed and fried together. The Cultural Revolution cafes are run-down, plain storefronts or courtyard houses with cement and brick walls and floors, benches and tables, and Mao posters and memorabilia for decorations. They are interesting re-creations of Communist China's recent past and favorites of many foreign visitors:

Sunflower Village Food Street Restaurant, 51 Wanquanhe Lu, Haidian District (☎ 010/6256-2967), on the way to the Summer Palace, has red painted rooms and clay dishes and bowls. Lunch and dinner (from 10am to 2pm and 4:30 to 9pm) cost about 100RMB ($10).

Heitudi (Black Earth) Restaurant, 9 Heplingli Dong Dajie, Chaoyang Northeast (east of the Lama Temple near the northeast corner of the Second Ring Road; ☎ 010/6427-1415), also serves Red Guard lunches and dinners (from 11am to 2pm and 5 to 11pm), has an English-language menu, and is noted for its walls where locals, including many Chinese leaders and celebrities, pin notes seeking to regain contact with comrades lost in the bad old days.

Recall Past Sufferings and Contemplate the Present Happiness Restaurant (Yiku Sitian Dazayuan Fanzhuang), 17 Pichai Hutong, Xicheng District (1 mile west of the Forbidden City in an alley off City Xidan Bei Dajie; ☎ 010/6602-2640), is a courtyard restaurant with tree leaves and fried black ants on its menu of the bitter Past and chicken and mushrooms on its menu of the sweet Present. Most items are $1 to $3 and can be shared, making this an inexpensive meal. This place is mainly of interest to tourists (overseas Chinese and Western), as it gives a strong hint of what and where the previous generation of Beijingers ate.

corridor along the northern shores of an imperial pleasure park, a stone's throw from an old temple and its white dagoba. The staff has donned Forbidden City dress, and the dining room is decorated in red, gold, and yellow with imperial motifs and wooden carvings. This is a bit of a tourist trap, but the set lunches, at 100RMB ($12.50) and 150RMB ($18.75), give a good sampling of what's meant by imperial cuisine. Small steamed pastries, peas from the wok, and roast duck and chicken are the standard fare of the hearty, plain food of North China. More flavorful are the bean curd cakes, the spicy squid soup, and the duck baked in a walnut batter. One of the more expensive royal treats is the steamed lake fish (*tian xiang bao yu*), a challenge for the chopsticks at 250RMB ($30). This is one of the prime stops for tourists looking for a taste of China's past glories.

Sichuan Fandian.

In Prince Gong Mansion (Gongwangfu), 14 Liuyin Jie, Xicheng District (north of Beihai Lake). ☎ **010/6615-6924.** Reservations recommended on weekends. Main courses 100–150RMB ($12.50–$18). AE, JCB, MC, V. Daily 11am–2pm and 5–9pm. SICHUAN.

Located in an old courtyard mansion amid a scholar's gardens in one of Beijing's major tourist sites, the Sichuan is synonymous with good Sichuan dishes. The decor is classical Qing Dynasty, and the friendly staff knows some English, since this is a popular stop for tour groups, foreign travelers, and expatriates. This was the capital's most famous Sichuan restaurant at its former location (the estate of Yuan Shikai, President of the Republic of China, 1912–16), but with native Sichuanese Deng Xiaoping no longer China's supreme ruler, the restaurant was removed in favor of the new exclusive China Club. Its new site here, in the home of a court Mandarin who served under Emperor Qianlong, is still elegant. Beyond the set menus, choices include such Sichuan classics as long noodles (*dan dan mian*), soft tofu soup (*mala douhua*), pork and vegetables over a sizzling rice cake (*guoba roupian*), tea-drenched duck smoked in camphor wood (*zhangcha yazi*), and a numbing plate of chili-infused bean curd chunks (*mapo doufu*).

MODERATE

✪ Shamiana.

In the Holiday Inn Downtown, 98 Beilishi Lu, Xicheng District (1 block northwest of the intersection of Fuchengmen and the Second Ring Road and the Fuchengmen subway station). ☎ **010/6833-8822,** ext. 7107. Reservations recommended on weekends. Main courses 80–150RMB ($10–$18). AE, DC, JCB, MC, V. Daily 11:30am–2:30pm and 6–10:30pm. INDIAN.

Beijing's premier Indian restaurant imports both its chef and its fresh ingredients from India. The decor is bright and fresh, with wood-paneled walls and Indian motifs. In the evenings, it is a busy place with live music and dancers. The set menus (starting at 80RMB/$10) change often, but include such popular items as the vegetable samosa (crunchy fried pastries), chicken or lamb curry, cottage cheese in tomato gravy, bread with carrom seed (*ajwaini naan*), chickpea flour in yogurt gravy (*kadhi*), plain rice (*chawal*), mango chutney, and rice pudding (*phirni*). Vegetable dishes, such as spinach and homemade cottage cheese with garlic and cumin (*saag paneer*), can be a main course or split as a side dish. The Tandoori Murgh is a good choice from the grill (leg and breast of chicken) at 45RMB ($5.65), and the clear mutton soup (*nosh jehangiri*) is a house specialty. Shamiana also produces one of the best snacks in Beijing, its minced lamb in a deep-fried triangular crust (*kheema patti samosa*), and at dinner you can partake of an entire plate of mixed kebabs for 112RMB ($13.75). There's no better spot in town for Indian dining.

INEXPENSIVE

Beijing Express.

In the Beijing New Century Hotel, 6 Shoudu Tiyuan Nan Lu, Xicheng District (southwest of the Beijing Zoo). ☎ **010/6849-2001.** Main courses 20–50RMB ($2.50–$6). AE, DC, JCB, MC, V. Daily 11:30am–2:30pm and 5:30–9:30pm. BEIJING.

Why go to McDonald's when Beijing has its own quick cuisine? This is Beijing fast food served with flair in a comfortable, modern setting at reasonable prices. The polished wood floors, carved block chairs, decorative roof tiles, Chinese lanterns, and new food stalls give a suggestion of the cuisine's origins: the streets of Beijing. Snacks, priced from 6 to 10RMB (75¢ to $1.25) include pancakes filled with vegetables, fried pork buns (*jiaozi*), rice cakes, and spring rolls. Noodles (from 12 to 21RMB/$1.50 to $2.65) feature shredded pork, Korean vegetables, or sliced eel in soup. Cold dishes run a similarly priced gamut from salty duck to deep-fried scorpions. Hot dishes include deep-fried chicken with chilies on a skewer to sautéed kale with chopped garlic.

Exploring Beijing 6

Beijing is packed with sights, ancient and modern, and it is China's most popular city for tourists, the majority of them from China itself. If your time is quite short, it is wise to book a day tour of the highlights through your hotel's tour desk, since getting around on your own, even via taxi or the subway, can be time-consuming at first. The city is flat, but the blocks are extremely long and what looks like a 10-minute walk on the map can turn into a much longer march. If time allows, however, it is certainly worthwhile to explore parts of the city on foot or by bicycle, immersing yourself in a place both familiar and alien. (See the next chapter, "Beijing Strolls," for four recommended walking tours.) Again, your hotel staff can tell you how to reach some of the best sights.

Beijing's most famous attraction, the **Great Wall,** is well out of the city. It and the **Qing Tombs,** the **Ming Tombs,** the **Western Hills,** and several other sites require excursions from Beijing, and they are covered in chapter 10, "The Great Wall & Other Side Trips from Beijing." The many treasures of the city itself—its temples, historic houses, museums, and parks—are described in this chapter, with a special focus on Beijing's four top attractions: **Tiananmen Square,** the **Forbidden City,** the **Temple of Heaven,** and the **Summer Palace.**

HOW TO SEE BEIJING

There are three basic ways to see the sights: by organized tour, by hired car, and on your own. The organized tours offered at hotel tour desks give quick, superficial views of major sights in the company of English-speaking guides. They usually start at about 240RMB ($30) for a half-day tour, 480RMB ($60) or more for a full-day tour that includes lunch. This is a good way to cover ground in a hurry, with a minimum of hassles. **China International Travel Service (CITS),** with headquarters at 28 Jianguomenwai Dajie, Chaoyang District (☎ 010/6515-8566), can arrange private group tours with a guide and transportation at a much higher fee. CITS maintains convenient branches in most hotels.

A second option is to hire a car for the day through your hotel to take you to as many sights as you can fit in. There's no guide, but the car waits, and you can take your time to see the sights at your own pace. This is an expensive option, costing from 800 to

Beijing Attractions

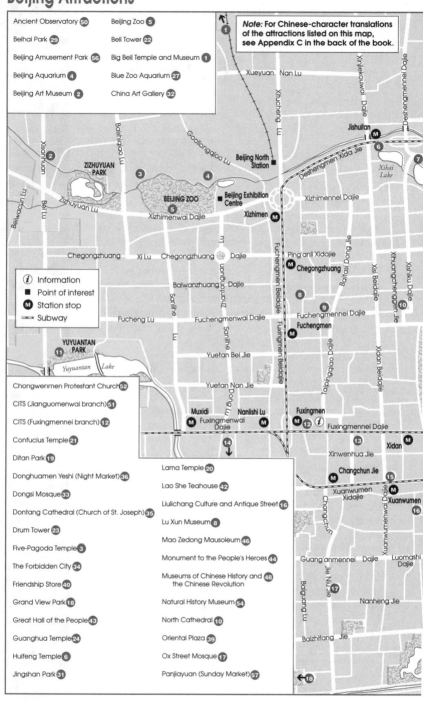

Ancient Observatory 50	Beijing Zoo 5
Beihai Park 29	Bell Tower 22
Beijing Amusement Park 56	Big Bell Temple and Museum 1
Beijing Aquarium 4	Blue Zoo Aquarium 27
Beijing Art Museum 2	China Art Gallery 32

Note: For Chinese-character translations of the attractions listed on this map, see Appendix C in the back of the book.

Xueyuan Nan Lu
Xinjiekouwai Dajie
Deshengmennei Dajie

Xitucheng Lu

Jishuitan M
6
7

Gaoliangqiao Lu

Beijing North Station

Deshengmen Xida Jie
Xihai Lake

Xisanhuan
2
Baishiqiao Lu

ZIZHUYUAN PARK
3
4
Xizhimennei Dajie

Beiwa Lu
Bei Lu
zizhuyuan Lu

BEIJING ZOO
5
Xizhimenwai Dajie

Beijing Exhibition Centre
Xizhimen M

Chegongzhuang Xi Lu   Chegongzhuang Dajie
Ping'anli Xidajie
Baitasi Dong Jie
Xihuangchenggen Jie
Xishiku Dajie

Chegongzhuang M

Baiwanzhuang Dajie
8

Fucheng Lu
Sanlihe
Zhanlanguan Dajie
Fuchengmenwai Dajie
9
Fuchengmennei Dajie
Xidan Beidajie

Fuchengmen
M

(i) Information
■ Point of interest
M Station stop
⇢ Subway

YUYUANTAN PARK
11
Yuyuantan Lake
Sanlihe Lu
Yuetan Bei Jie

Taipingqiao Dajie

Yuetan Nan Jie

Chongwenmen Protestant Church 52
CITS (Jianguomenwai branch) 51
CITS (Fuxingmennei branch) 12
Confucius Temple 21
Ditan Park 19
Donghuamen Yeshi (Night Market) 36
Dongsi Mosque 33
Dontang Cathedral (Church of St. Joseph) 35
Drum Tower 23
Five-Pagoda Temple 3
The Forbidden City 34
Friendship Store 40
Grand View Park 18
Great Hall of the People 43
Guanghua Temple 24
Huifeng Temple 6
Jingshan Park 31

Muxidi M   Nanlishi Lu M
Fuxingmenwai Dajie

Fuxingmen
M 12 (i) Fuxingmennei Dajie

13
Xidan M

14

Xinwenhua Jie
Changchun Jie M
15
Xuanwumen Xidajie
Xuanwumen M
16

Changchun Jie
Xuanwumennei Dajie

Lama Temple 20
Lao She Teahouse 42
Liulichang Culture and Antique Street 16
Lu Xun Museum 8
Mao Zedong Mausoleum 46
Monument to the People's Heroes 44
Museums of Chinese History and 48
    the Chinese Revolution
Natural History Museum 54
North Cathedral 10
Oriental Plaza 39
Ox Street Mosque 17
Panjiayuan (Sunday Market) 57

Guang'anmennei Dajie
Luomashi Dajie

17
Jie Niu Jie
Nanheng Jie

Baiguang Lu

Baizhifang Jie

← 18

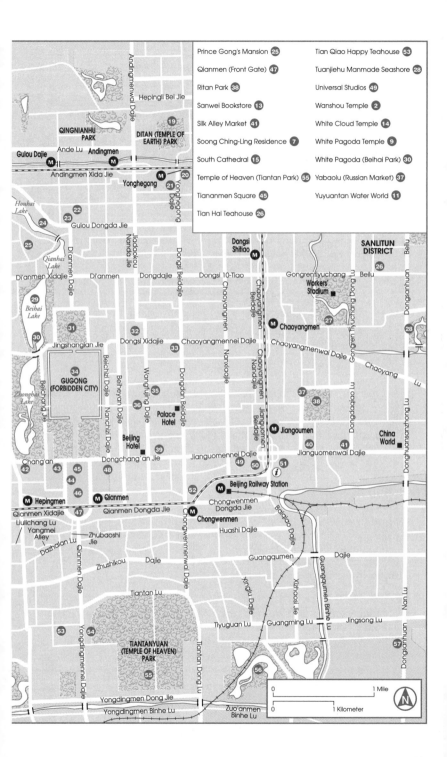

Prince Gong's Mansion 25
Qianmen (Front Gate) 47
Ritan Park 38
Sanwei Bookstore 13
Silk Alley Market 41
Soong Ching-Ling Residence 7
South Cathedral 15
Temple of Heaven (Tiantan Park) 55
Tiananmen Square 45
Tian Hai Teahouse 26

Tian Qiao Happy Teahouse 53
Tuanjiehu Manmade Seashore 28
Universal Studios 49
Wanshou Temple 2
White Cloud Temple 14
White Pagoda Temple 9
White Pagoda (Beihai Park) 30
Yabaolu (Russian Market) 37
Yuyuantan Water World 11

QINGNIANHU PARK
Hepingli Bei Jie
DITAN (TEMPLE OF EARTH) PARK
Ande Lu Andingmen
Gulou Dajie
Andingmen Xida Jie
Yonghegong
Houhai Lake
Gulou Dongda Jie
Qianhai Lake
Di'anmen Xidajie Di'anmen
Dongdajie
Dongsi Shitiao
Dongsi 10-Tiao
SANLITUN DISTRICT
Beilu
Beilu
Gongrentiyuchang Beilu
Workers' Stadium
Beihai Lake
Dongsi Xidajie
Dongsi Xidajie
Chaoyangmennei Dajie
Chaoyangmen
Chaoyangmenwai Dajie
Chaoyang Lu
Jingshangian Jie
GUGONG (FORBIDDEN CITY)
Zhonghai Lake
Palace Hotel
Beijing Hotel
China World
Jiangoumen
Jianguomenwai Dajie
Chang'an
Dongchang'an Jie
Jianguomennei Dajie
Hepingmen Qianmen
Beijing Railway Station
Qianmen Xidajie Qianmen Dongda Jie
Chongwenmen Dongda Jie
Chongwenmen
Liulichang Lu
Yangmei Alley
Zhubaoshi Jie
Dazhalan Lu
Qianmen Dajie
Zhushikou Dajie
Huashi Dajie
Guangqumen
Guangqumen Binhe Lu
Tiantan Lu
TIANTANYUAN (TEMPLE OF HEAVEN) PARK
Tiyuguan Lu Guangming Lu
Jingsong Lu
Yongdingmennei Dajie
Tiantan Dong Lu
Yongdingmen Dong Jie
Zuo'anmen Binhe Lu
Yongdingmen Binhe Lu

0   1 Mile
0   1 Kilometer

Impressions

Of all the great cities of the world none can rival Peking for the regularity and harmony of its plan. . . . Thus in Peking there are always walls within walls, moat within moat, and gates—pierced by great boulevards—leading to still further gates. . . . All the citizens of Peking, Chinese or foreign, are conscious of the city's majesty; the sheer breadth of the setting enhances composure and lends dignity to everyday manners.
—George N. Kates, *The Years That Were Fat, Peking: 1933–1940*

1,200RMB ($100 to $150) to hire a driver and car—it's cheaper if you hire a taxi for the day yourself on the streets.

The last option is to strike out on your own with a map and a plan, using taxis, the subway, a rented bicycle, and your own two feet. This allows you to see the sights at your own pace at relatively little expense, but you do have to make your own arrangements and pay your own entrance fees.

Suggested Itineraries

The top attraction, the **Great Wall,** isn't in Beijing but about 2 hours away, so a group tour there is almost mandatory. Most day tours stop for an hour or so at the Great Wall and swing by one or two of Beijing's other top attractions, with a stop for lunch along the way.

If You Have 1 Day

Spend your only day in the capital playing tourist, booking a tour to the **Great Wall** through your hotel. This is the one sight you shouldn't miss, and it will use most of the daylight hours. If you have extra time or if you want to skip a walk on the wall, have an early breakfast in your hotel and take a taxi to the **Temple of Heaven,** where you can survey its main attractions in an hour. Take another quick taxi ride north to **Tiananmen Square.** You can traverse the world's largest square in 20 minutes, with glances at Mao's Mausoleum, the Great Hall of the People, and the Monument to the People's Heroes. Cross Chang'an Avenue, pass under the Gate of Heavenly Peace, and proceed into the vast **Forbidden City.** You'll emerge at the northern moat around lunchtime. Grab yet another taxi for the **Summer Palace,** relax, have lunch there, and then stroll its Long Corridor. Grab another taxi to take you downtown, where you still have time to walk up and down Beijing's number-one shopping street, **Wangfujing,** before a late dinner. Treat yourself to Beijing duck. You won't have trouble sleeping.

If You Have 2 Days

Spend your first day taking excursions to the **Great Wall** and the **Summer Palace,** and finish up with a real Beijing dinner at the Sihexuan Restaurant in the Jinglun Hotel. The next day, concentrate on city-center attractions: **Tiananmen Square,** the **Forbidden City,** and the **Temple of Heaven.** Two days should give you time to take in **Silk Alley** and the **Friendship Store** for shopping and the chance to visit Beijing's most popular religious site, the **Lama Temple.**

If You Have 3 Days

Three days is the minimum to do much Beijing sight-seeing. It requires 2 days just to take in the top sites listed in the 1- and 2-day itineraries. On the third day, take a stroll on the historic antique avenue of **Liulichang** (see Walking Tour 1 in the next chapter, "Beijing Strolls") and, if you're here on a Sunday, start very early with a visit to the **Dirt Market (Panjiayuan).** It's worthwhile to book a **Hutong** tour of the Back Lakes area in the afternoon or to explore the area yourself on a rented bicycle. If there's a sunset, don't miss it from the top of the **Ancient Observatory.**

If You Have 4 or More Days

This will give you time to take a look at most of Beijing's best attractions, although a week would be better. You'll be able to sift through all the big sights and begin to explore those that are off the beaten track. Return to Tiananmen Square to tour Mao's Mausoleum, the Great Hall of the People, and the Museum of Chinese History. From the north gate of the Forbidden City, strike out for the views from Jingshan Hill and Beihai Park. Plan to visit some ancient temples, poke around the Soong Ching-Ling Residence and Rear Lakes neighborhood, enjoy lunch or late-night fun in the Sanlitun district, browse the shops and new department stores on Wangfujing Dajie, and poke through some of the open-air markets around town. Don't be afraid to make a walking or biking tour on your own. If there's time left over, book an excursion to one of the less-visited sections of the Great Wall, to the Western Hills, or to the Qing Tombs. Actually, even a week isn't enough time to do more than take a glance at everything worth seeing in the capital, but it will give you a broad picture of China old and new.

1 The Heart of Red China: Tiananmen Square (Tian'anmen Guangchang)

This is the world's largest public square, the size of 90 football fields (covering 99 acres), with standing room for 300,000 people. It is the heart of Beijing and of the Chinese nation. The square received a face-lift over the winter of 1998–99; its old paving blocks were replaced with granite stepping stones, laid just in time to celebrate the 50th anniversary of the founding of the People's Republic of China on October 1, 1949. Chairman Mao Zedong stood that day on the Gate of Heavenly Peace at the entrance to the Forbidden City, across Chang'an Avenue from the square, and announced the founding of a new China to the masses. Mao's portrait now hangs from that reviewing stand, where a new generation of leaders gathers every October 1 to face the citizens of China. Tiananmen Square has served as China's open-air forum through much of the 20th century, the scene of both historic ceremonies and protest demonstrations. It is best known to the outside world (via live international television coverage) as the arena for the democracy demonstrations that culminated in the crackdown on June 4, 1989. When foreigners stroll across Tiananmen Square, as most visitors do at least once, it is the specter of that event that still seems to haunt the stony expanses and its monuments.

Tiananmen Square stands on the central north-south axis of the old imperial city. In fact, there was no square here during the time of the emperors, only a wide boulevard, the Imperial Way, lined with state offices. The Imperial Way ran from the Gate of Heavenly Peace south to **Qianmen (Front Gate),** which still stands guard at the southern end of Tiananmen Square. Qianmen was one of the nine great gates of Beijing's city walls, which were removed in 1958. The Imperial Way was the southern axis of the city, stretching from the Forbidden City all the way to the Temple of Heaven. Qianmen, which dates back nearly 500 years,

A Man & a Tank

The photo of a man standing alone on Chang'an Avenue in Beijing at the height of the Tiananmen democracy protests in 1989 with his hand lifted to prevent a tank's advance is an indelible image, recognized worldwide. But what became of the man? The lone protestor was quickly identified as Wang Weilin, and reports at the time had him arrested, executed, or killed during the siege of Tiananmen Square. However, President Jiang Zemin reportedly said in 1990 that no one named Wang Weilin had been arrested or killed during the turmoil, and a computerized search by police, which turned up 400 men named Wang Weilin, placed none of them in central Beijing at the time. The widespread feeling is that he disappeared into the underground and remains undiscovered, at large, whereabouts and true identity unknown. He remains the most mysterious figure of modern history, one of only two Chinese who made *Time* magazine's list of the major figures of the 20th century—the other being Chairman Mao.

remains a city landmark. Its northern passage is known as the Main Gate and its southern passage is the Arrow Tower. Just beyond the square stands the world's largest KFC.

Today, Tiananmen Square contains fresh monuments to the new city. On the square itself are the Monument to the People's Heroes and the Mao Zedong Mausoleum. To the west is the Great Hall of the People and on the east flank are the Museum of Chinese History and the Museum of the Chinese Revolution. Each site is open to the public. The square itself is open daily from dawn to dusk. At twilight each day, there is a ceremonial lowering of the Chinese flag by a detachment of the People's Liberation Army, a popular photo opportunity among visitors. Those contraptions that look like video cameras on the speaker poles encompassing the square are just what you suppose—surveillance devices to record what happens in China's most sensitive and venerated public forum.

The **Museum of Chinese History** and the **Museum of the Chinese Revolution** on the east side of Tiananmen Square are described in the "Museums & Mansions" section later in this chapter.

✪ Mao Zedong Mausoleum (Mao Zhuxi Jinian Bei).
On the south side of Tiananmen Square. Free admission. Mon–Sat 8:30–11:30am; Mon, Wed, Fri 2–4pm. Subway: Qianmen.

Mao has received more than 5 million visitors a year since this memorial opened in 1977, a year after his death. Check your cameras and handbags at the kiosk on the east side and join the lines forming in front of the north entrance. You'll be quickly ushered into the northern reception hall, where a large white marble statue of a seated Mao awaits, then into the central chamber where the Great Helmsman lies in state in his crystal sarcophagus. He has a rather ghoulish patina. Onlookers maintain complete silence for a few seconds before they are ushered out. The poem inscribed in gold in the south hall on your way out is by Mao, who left behind hundreds of poems in public places (rather as some of the old emperors did). Upstairs there's a commemorative hall to three of Mao's political cohorts (Zhou Enlai, Liu Shaoqi, and Zhu De), but it's not worth viewing (a lame attempt to counterweight Mao's importance). Obviously, the Mao memorabilia for sale on the way out of the mausoleum is overpriced. Shop in the markets for such prizes.

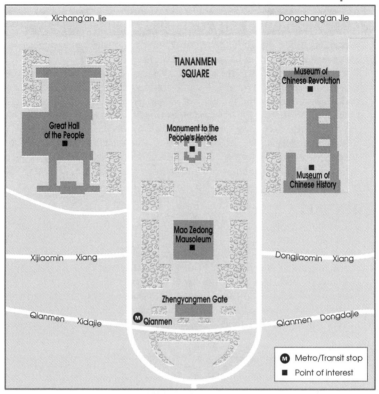

Monument to the People's Heroes (Renmin Yingxiong Jinian Bei).
Southwest section of Tiananmen Square.

This 124-foot granite obelisk, erected in 1958, is carved with tableaus of revolutionary martyrdom and victory, from a popular uprising in 1851 to the Communist Revolution of 1949. It most recently became the combat post of the young democracy protestors during the 1989 occupation of Tiananmen Square. On the front of this cenotaph, in Mao's calligraphy, is an inscription: THE PEOPLE'S HEROES ARE IMMORTAL. Until the recent renovation of the square, locals said they could still see bloodstains and bullet impressions from 1989 in the stone stairway.

Great Hall of the People (Renmin Dahui Tang).
West side of Tiananmen Square. ☎ **010/6309-6156.** Admission 35RMB ($4.25). Daily 8:30am–2pm.

Whenever the National People's Congress is not in session, the Great Hall is usually open for tours (it's worth it to have your hotel desk check ahead). The hall is immense, more than half a mile long, and the main auditorium, with the great big red star on the ceiling (outlined by 500 light bulbs), seats 10,000 and is in fact called the 10,000 People Hall (*Wanren Dalitang*). The chief interest in seeing China's legislative center from the inside is the decorative elements that make up its 32 ostentatious reception rooms (each done in the style and motif of a separate province, autonomous region, or municipality). The scale of the banquet and assembly rooms is also impressive, especially since this whole complex was a patriotic rush job, taking just 10 months to complete (opening in 1959).

2 The Forbidden City (Palace Museum)

Westerners call it the Forbidden City (Zijin Cheng), the Chinese prefer Palace Museum (Gu Gong), but by any name it is simply the most magnificent Imperial Palace in China, perhaps in the world. It is vast, its courtyards and palaces covering an area the size of 166 football fields (183 acres), dwarfing Tiananmen Square. This ancient royal city, stuck in the heart of the modern city of Beijing like a life-sized time capsule, is nearly a half-mile wide (east to west) and more than a half-mile long (north to south). Its palaces, pavilions, and halls are divided into 9,000 rooms, and the whole complex is enclosed in thick walls over 30 feet tall and by a moat 170 feet across. Twenty-four emperors and empresses of the Ming and Qing (Manchu) dynasties made this their home and held court here across a span of 5 centuries. The first of the emperors to reside in the Forbidden City moved inside in 1421.

ESSENTIALS

The Forbidden City, located on Chang'an Avenue (☎ **010/6513-2255,** ext. 615) is open daily from 8:30am to 5pm, but the ticket window closes at 3:30pm. Admission is 30RMB ($3.75) or 55RMB ($9) for a ticket that also includes admissions to special displays in side halls. The main entrance is via the Gate of Heavenly Peace (Tiananmen), the massive archway with Chairman Mao's portrait on it facing Tiananmen Square to the south. But the ticket booth is many blocks to the north at another massive gate (*Wumen* or Meridian Gate) in an open area also known as the east entrance to the Forbidden City. The ticket window is to the right (east) of Meridian Gate.

SEEING THE HIGHLIGHTS

There are five main segments of the Forbidden City from south to north. In order, they are (1) the entrance gates, (2) the outer court, (3) the eastern exhibit halls, (4) the inner court, and (5) the imperial gardens.

From the Gate of Heavenly Peace, walk north along the great central axis of old China. At Wumen, the Meridian Gate, buy a ticket and enter the outer court of the Forbidden City, which contains the three great ceremonial halls and their wide courtyards. The three great halls are laid out one after the other on a central meridian. You then arrive at the inner court of the Forbidden City, which consists of the palaces and halls that served as royal residences. The pavilions on the east side of the inner court now house special exhibits of the imperial treasures. At the northern end of the Forbidden City are the imperial gardens and a Daoist shrine. It usually takes from 90 minutes (on an organized tour) to 4 hours (lingering on your own) to make the procession through the Forbidden City

THE ENTRANCE GATES

GATE OF HEAVENLY PEACE (TIANANMEN)   Used as a reviewing stand by government officials, Tiananmen Gate is now open to the public. The entrance to the gate is inside, to the west. Admission is 30RMB ($3.75), which gains you access to the upper portion of the gate. There's not much reason to pay this admission charge, however, unless you want a panoramic view or a picture of Tiananmen Square. To reach the Forbidden City ticket booths, pass under the gate and keep walking north. The long corridor between the Gate of Heavenly Peace and the entrance to the Forbidden City at Meridian Gate to the north was once used for staging troops. It now contains food and souvenir stands, a yard for commercial photographers who pose tourists in imperial costumes (east side), and a sideshow

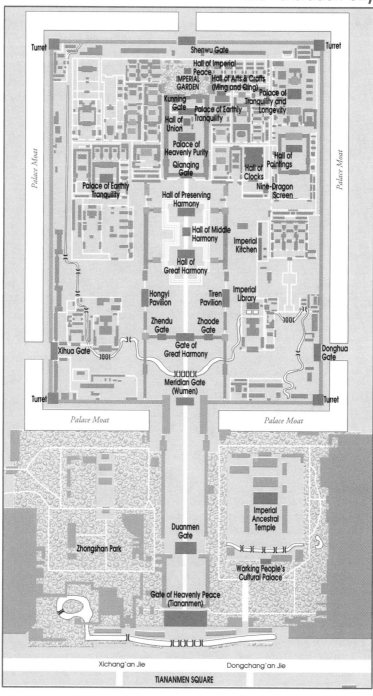

The Forbidden City

Turret

Shenwu Gate

Hall of Imperial Peace

IMPERIAL GARDEN

Hall of Arts & Crafts (Ming and Qing)

Palace of Tranquility and Longevity

Kunning Gate

Palace of Earthly Tranquility

Hall of Union

Palace of Heavenly Purity

Qianqing Gate

Palace of Earthly Tranquility

Hall of Clocks

Hall of Paintings

Nine-Dragon Screen

Hall of Preserving Harmony

Hall of Middle Harmony

Imperial Kitchen

Hall of Great Harmony

Hongyi Pavilion

Tiren Pavilion

Imperial Library

Zhendu Gate

Zhaode Gate

Gate of Great Harmony

Xihua Gate

Donghua Gate

Meridian Gate (Wumen)

Turret

Turret

Palace Moat

Palace Moat

Palace Moat

Palace Moat

Imperial Ancestral Temple

Duanmen Gate

Zhongshan Park

Working People's Cultural Palace

Gate of Heavenly Peace (Tiananmen)

Xichang'an Jie

Dongchang'an Jie

TIANANMEN SQUARE

With 007 as My Guide

If you want to rent a portable audio tape (acoustiguide) that describes the major features as you walk through the Forbidden City, buy your admission ticket at the ticket booth, and then go in the entrance marked AUDIO just to the right of the main south entrance (Meridian Gate). The audio rental is 30RMB ($3.75), but you are required to leave your passport or driver's license as a security deposit. The only option is to leave another form of ID *plus* 400RMB ($50) in cash. Actor Roger Moore (James Bond in the movies) narrates the tape, and a start/stop button on the player enables you to control the narrative. The acoustiguide is an excellent aid for first-time visitors, as it offers some help in navigating the labyrinth and gives commentary for each site as you reach it.

(west side) where two female mummies (entombed in A.D. 1274 and 1482) are on display (admission 4RMB/50¢).

MERIDIAN GATE (WUMEN)   This gate is the proper southern entrance to the Forbidden City's inner court. The ticket booth and audio rental hall are here. The gate was built in 1420 and renovated in 1647 and 1801. The emperors reviewed their armies here. Also called the Five Phoenix Tower, this gate had separate entrances (on the left) for court officials and (on the right) for the imperial family.

GATE OF GREAT HARMONY (TAI HE DIAN)   Immediately inside the Meridian Gate entrance is a wide courtyard with five marble bridges spanning the Golden River. The Gate of Great Harmony, erected in 1420 and rebuilt after a fire in 1889, stands on the central axis to the north. This is where the emperor listened to reports from his ministers.

THE OUTER COURT

HALL OF GREAT HARMONY (TAI HE DIAN)   Through the Gate of Great Harmony is a stunningly vast courtyard, flanked by closed halls on both sides, that leads to the first great ceremonial hall, Tai He Dian, popularly known as the Hall of the Imperial Throne. From this throne the emperor marked New Years, important birthdays, and other grand occasions. There are gorgeous carved columns within this pavilion, which was the tallest edifice in Beijing for centuries.

HALL OF MIDDLE HARMONY (ZHONG HE DIAN)   The second great hall of the outer court, Zhong He Dian, built in 1420 and rebuilt in 1627, was where the emperor received ministers of the imperial rites before he performed official ceremonies. There is a smaller throne here.

HALL OF PRESERVING HARMONY (BAO HE DIAN)   The final outer court hall was the site under the Qing emperors for the Palace examinations that selected the nation's best students for the civil service. It also was the site of imperial banquets.

THE EASTERN EXHIBITION HALLS

✪ HALL OF CLOCKS   The royal collection of timepieces is in the Hall of Worshipping Ancestors (Feng Xian Dian), which requires a detour to the east (right) before entering the inner court. Follow the signs. There's a separate admission charge (5RMB/60¢), unless you carry the all-inclusive admission ticket. You must also pay a 2RMB (25¢) charge for plastic slippers that pull over your shoes. The slippers are designed to preserve the marble floors, but these overshoes quickly disintegrate. The collection of watches and clocks is fascinating. Most of the foreign timepieces here came from England and Europe in the 18th century.

NINE DRAGON SCREEN (JIU LONG BI)   Southeast of the clock museum is a courtyard with this much-prized mosaic, fashioned in 1773, of shining ceramic tiles, 96 feet wide and nearly 12 feet high.

HALL OF JEWELRY   Northeast of the Hall of Clocks is a second collection, housed in the Palace of Tranquility and Longevity (Ning Shou Gong) complex. If you don't have an all-inclusive ticket, the separate admission charge is 5RMB (60¢); the protective slippers are required. Within these eastern halls running northward is an extensive collection of ornaments, gold figurines, ceremonial plates, jewelry, royal robes, and jades. The fabled Empress Dowager of the final dynasty celebrated her 70th birthday (1904) in one of these halls and received the wives of foreign envoys in 1903 in another (Yang Xing Dian), where her throne can still be seen. Through the Belvedere of Flowing Music (Changyinge), a three-tiered theater supported by Empress Dowager Cixi, is Zhen Fei Well, where the Empress Dowager was alleged to have drowned her nephew's favorite concubine. In the far northeast section of the Forbidden City is Qianlong Garden, a tranquil rockery where the Qing emperor enjoyed drinking games.

THE INNER COURT

GATE OF HEAVENLY PURITY (QIAN QING MEN)   Resuming course on the main north-south axis after detouring to the eastern exhibition halls, this gate marks the entrance to the inner court of the Forbidden City, where only the emperor, his family, his concubines, and the palace eunuchs (who numbered 1,500 at the end of the final dynasty) could enter. The view of golden roof upon golden roof is breathtaking here.

PALACE OF HEAVENLY PURITY (QIAN QING GONG)   The first palace of the inner court is where emperors up to the time of Kangxi in the 18th century lived.

HALL OF UNION (JIAO TAI DIAN)   This residence contains the throne of the empress.

PALACE OF EARTHLY TRANQUILITY (KUN NING GONG)   Bedchamber of a Ming Dynasty empress, this is where Qing Emperor Kangxi was married and where China's last emperor, Puyi, married as a child in 1922.

THE IMPERIAL GARDENS

Near the northern gate is an elaborate garden of fantastic rockeries and pavilions, Yu Hua Yuan, which was created during the Ming Dynasty. Many of its cypress trees are ancient. There are several kiosks nearby selling refreshments and snacks. The northern exit is through the gate behind the last large structure, the Hall of Imperial Peace (Jin An Dian), a shrine to the God of Fire, Xuanwu, although you are free to walk back to the southern gate (against the human tide).

3 The Summer Palace (Yi He Yuan)

China's grand imperial garden has been the site of imperial palaces for 8 centuries, but its present outlines were created under Emperor Qianlong from 1749 to 1764. He enlarged both the pretty lake and the hills on its shore, adding numerous pavilions. In 1860, French and British troops destroyed most of the park. It was rebuilt by the Empress Dowager Cixi in 1886, but again leveled by foreign armies. What we see today is the Empress Dowager's second re-creation of a Summer Palace, completed in

---

Two Emperors & a Notorious Empress Dowager

Much of the surviving imperial legacy of Beijing has the imprint of three notable sovereigns who ruled during the Qing Dynasty (1644–1911). Emperor Kangxi (1711–1799) and his grandson Qianlong (1654–1722), two of the longest-reigning rulers in Chinese history, were responsible for maintaining and renovating the palaces of the Forbidden City as well as the royal parks and temples you see today. Empress Dowager Cixi (1835–1908), reviled as the power behind the throne who plotted and poisoned her way to power, is blamed for the decline of the final dynasty. Her treasures are scattered throughout Beijing, in the halls of the Forbidden City, in her massive tomb outside the city, and most of all at the Summer Palace, which she rebuilt during her reign.

1903. This became her summer retreat and increasingly her full-time residence. Once the site of her lavish birthday parties, the park remained a countryside version of the Forbidden Palace until it was declared a public park in 1924 and spruced up in 1949. It is the most beautiful of Beijing's parks—the lake, hills, and groves enhanced by Qing Dynasty pavilions all bear the Empress Dowager's imprint.

ESSENTIALS

The Summer Palace (known in Chinese as Yi He Yuan, or Garden for Cultivating Harmony; ☎ 010/6288-1144) is 7 miles northwest of Beijing in the suburb of Haidian, about a 45-minute taxi ride away (about 60RMB/$7.50 each way). There is no nearby subway stop. It's open daily from 7am to 6:30pm (or until sunset), and admission is 30RMB ($3.75). The main entrance is at the East Gate (Donggongmen). The least-crowded time to visit is in the morning, as early as possible. Allow 4 hours to tour the major sites on your own. Organized day tours include the Summer Palace as one stop on a larger itinerary, allowing for a brief visit of 1 to 2 hours.

EXPLORING THE SUMMER PALACE

This spacious park, about 700 acres, consists of **Kunming Lake** to the south and **Longevity Hill (Wanshou Shan)** to the north. Kunming Lake occupies most of the parklands. It's transected by several long dikes, creating smaller portions known as West Lake and South Lake. There are many beautiful bridges and islands in Kunming Lake. The north side of Longevity Hill has its own Back Lakes, but the most popular area for strolling is the south side of Longevity Hill along the northern shore of Kunming Lake. It is here that the Long Corridor links the pavilions, halls, and courtyards stretching from the East Gate of the Summer Palace to the Marble Boat on the western side of the park.

Organized tours usually allow time only for a stroll along the shore of Kunming Lake under the Long Corridor, a look at the Marble Boat, and sometimes a boat ride back to the East Gate. You'll get many striking views on such a tour, but you'll miss out on most of the other Qing Dynasty halls, pavilions, and sites.

✪ **LONG CORRIDOR (CHANG LANG)**   This covered wooden promenade runs about half a mile (2,550 feet) along the northern shore of Kunming Lake, from the Eastern Halls to the Marble Boat. Its crossbeams, ceiling roof panels, and pillars are painted with more than 10,000 scenes from Chinese geography, history, literature, and myth, making this a promenade into a picture encyclopedia of China. The paintings are crude but bright, and the Long Corridor is exceptionally

In case you want to be welcomed there.

We're here to see that you're always welcomed at establishments everywhere. That's why millions of people carry the American Express® Card – for peace of mind, confidence, and security, around the world or just around the corner.

do more

Cards

In case you're running low.

We're here to help with more than 190,000 Express Cash locations around the world. In order to enroll, just call American Express at 1 800 CASH-NOW before you start your vacation.

do more AMERICAN EXPRESS®

Express Cash

And in case you'd rather be safe than sorry.

We're here with American Express® Travelers Cheques. They're the safe way to carry money on your vacation, because if they're ever lost or stolen you can get a refund, practically anywhere or anytime. To find the nearest place to buy Travelers Cheques, call 1 800 495-1153. Another way we help you do more.

do more

Travelers Cheques

The Summer Palace

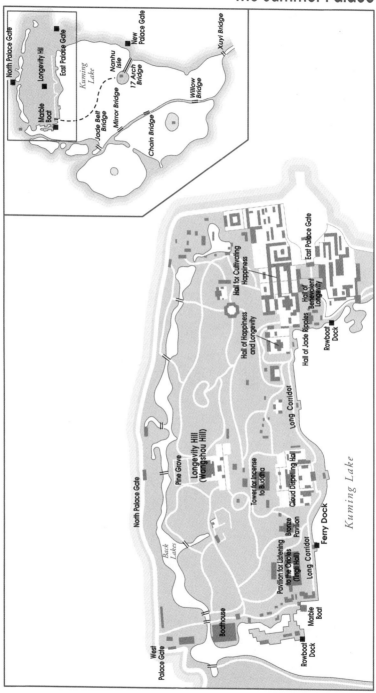

North Palace Gate
Longevity Hil
East Palace Gate
New Palace Gate
Xuyi Bridge
Nanhu Isle
17 Arch Bridge
Kuming Lake
Willow Bridge
Marble Boat
Jade Belt Bridge
Mirror Bridge
Chain Bridge

East Palace Gate
Hall for Cultivating Happiness
Hall of Benevolent Longevity
Hall of Jade Ripples
Hall of Happiness and Longevity
Rowboat Dock
Long Corridor
Pine Grove
Longevity Hill (Wangshou Hill)
Tower for Incense to Buddha
Cloud Dispelling Hall
North Palace Gate
Kuming Lake
Bronze Pavilion
Ferry Dock
Back Lakes
Pavilion for Listening to the Orioles (Tingli Hall)
Long Corridor
Boathouse
Marble Boat
West Palace Gate
Rowboat Dock

Tunnel of Love

The Long Corridor is such a lovely spot for a stroll that locals say any couple who enters at one end will emerge at the other engaged to be married.

charming. Built in 1750 (and rebuilt and restored many times since), the Long Corridor consists of 273 crossbeam sections and four pavilions that lead to cafes, boat docks, or sites on Longevity Hill.

HALL OF BENEVOLENT LONGEVITY (RENSHOU DIAN)   Located directly across the courtyard from the East Gate entrance, this hall is where the Empress Dowager Cixi and her nephew (who was appointed emperor, but placed under her protection) received members of the court. Cixi occupied the dragon throne.

HALL OF JADE RIPPLES (YULAN TANG)   This is the lakeside residence of the Empress Dowager's nephew, Emperor Guangxu, where he was kept from the throne, a prisoner of his aunt.

HALL FOR CULTIVATING HAPPINESS (YILE DIAN)   Ensconced on her gold lacquer throne, the Empress Dowager here enjoyed performances in her private three-stage theater, built for her 60th birthday. Now a theater museum, this hall contains some of Cixi's own garments, her perfumes, and the first car imported into China (a Mercedes-Benz).

HALL OF HAPPINESS AND LONGEVITY (LESHOU TANG)   This complex on the northeast tip of the lake was the Empress Dowager's private residence. Most of the furniture, the bed curtains, and the glass lamps (China's first electric lamps) are original. The Long Corridor begins here.

HALL OF DISPELLING CLOUDS (PAI YUN DIAN)   Located halfway along the Long Corridor on the foot of Longevity Hill, this hall served the Empress Dowager for her birthday parties and now contains some of the presents she received, including her most famous portrait, painted by Dutch artist Hubert Vos in 1905 for her 70th birthday.

PAVILION FOR LISTENING TO THE ORIOLES (TINGLI GUAN)   At the west end of the Long Corridor, this complex is now the location of an imperial restaurant.

✪ **MARBLE BOAT (BOAT OF PURITY AND EASE)**   Outfitted with paddlewheel, stained glass, and mirrors in 1893, the Marble Boat has become a symbol to Beijingers of the extravagance and cruelty of the Qing Dynasty. The funds that were to have shorn up the Chinese Navy went instead into a stone boat in Cixi's private pleasure garden, and China soon paid the price when Japan and other aggressors invaded. The story is probably not true, but it enhances the Empress Dowager's image as an imperial villain. The Marble Boat (118 feet long) can be photographed, but visitors are no longer allowed to board it.

SEVENTEEN-ARCH BRIDGE (SHIQI KONG QIAO)   This quintessential arched bridge, 492 feet long and fashioned of marble, connects South Lake Isle (Nanhu Dao) to the east shore. If time allows, it is quite pleasant to book a seat on a pleasure barge, sail across the lake to this bridge, and return to the main East Gate on foot. Even nicer is to rent a rowboat and row and drift at your leisure, perhaps enjoying a picnic on Kunming Lake with all the ancient beauty of Longevity Hill and its halls and pavilions as a poetic background.

4 The Temple of Heaven (Tiantan)

At the same time that Ming Emperor Yongle laid out and built the Forbidden City (1406–1420), he oversaw the construction of an enormous park and altar to heaven directly south of the palace. Each year on the winter solstice the emperor would lead a procession out of the Forbidden City across what is today Tiananmen Square southward down the Imperial Way to Tiantan, the Temple of Heaven, where he would perform rites and make sacrifices to the cosmos on behalf of China. Much of the architecture of these ancient rites survives in Tiantan Park (Tiantan Gongyuan), but what makes this park so singular among attractions in China is a single remarkable building, a magnificent tower known as the Hall of Prayer for Good Harvests (Qinian Dian).

If you are on an organized tour, you might have time to view only the Hall of Prayer, which is grand indeed, but Tiantan Park has several other architectural marvels. It's also a fine public park to poke around in for glimpses of how ordinary Beijingers enjoy themselves.

ESSENTIALS Temple of Heaven Park (Tiantan Gongyuan; ☎ 010/6702-2617), is open daily from 5am to 9:30pm in summer and from 8am to 5:30pm in winter. Tour buses and taxis favor the west entrance, since it is nearest Qianmen Dajie, the major thoroughfare to the city center. Admission is 30RMB ($3.75).

SEEING THE HIGHLIGHTS Located south of Tiananmen Square on the east side of Qianmen Dajie, Tiantan Park is rounded like heaven on the north and squared like the Earth to the south, following ancient Chinese cosmology. There are four entrances at the four cardinal points on the compass. The west entrance is used most often. The major halls and vaults all lie on a north-south axis roughly in the center of the park.

There are four important sights in the park:

✪ **Hall of Prayer for Good Harvests (Qinian Dian)** This circular wooden hall with its three soaring blue-tiled roofs, capped with a golden ball, has become an emblem of China's imperial architecture. The colors used inside and out—red, blue, green, and gold—are bold and rich. The entire edifice was constructed without a single nail, its pieces artfully fitted and snapped into place without cross beams. The 28 massive pillars support much of the load, particularly the four massive central columns, called the Dragon Well Pillars. The Hall of Prayer stands 125 feet high and 98 feet across. Here the emperors of China performed the ancient rites intended to bring the dynasty and the nation into harmony with the will and course of the heavens.

Unfortunately, there's little you can do here but stand and admire this great altar from the outside. Visitors are no longer allowed within, although you can still peek inside. This tower was finished in 1420 and remained in place until 1889, when lightning set it ablaze. What we see now is a meticulous reconstruction of the original. The tall, straight timbers used to rebuild were imported from Oregon by a U.S. shipping owner, Robert Dollar, although official Chinese sources claim the lumber is from Yunnan Province.

Circular Altar (Yuan Qiu) This three-tiered marble terrace is an open altar, built in 1530 and enlarged in 1749 by Emperor Qianlong. It is located at the southern end of the park. Bundles of silk were once burned here as gifts to heaven. The emperors communed with the cosmos from this platform, which is also said to

The Temple of Heaven

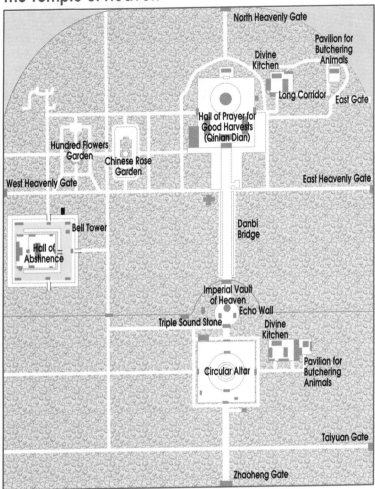

possess strange acoustical properties, magnifying the sound for the voices of orators who stand at its center (but diminishing it for their immediate audience).

Imperial Vault of Heaven (Huang Qiong Yu)   Straight south from the Hall of Prayer via the Bridge of Vermilion Stairs, this pavilion with the blue-tiled roof, a smaller version of the Hall of Prayer, was built of wood in 1530 to store ceremonial stone tablets. The vault is encircled by **Echo Wall.** On a quiet day, it is still possible to experience the remarkable acoustics, which work like a walkie-talkie, enabling two people to conduct a whispered conversation along the wall no matter how far apart they are. The three Echo Stones at the base of the main staircase are also fun to try. Clap your hands sharply while standing on the first stone and a single echo is returned; one clap on the second stone step produces two echoes, and a clap on the third step is echoed three times—or so says the tradition.

Hall of Abstinence (Zhai Gong)   At the west entrance, these halls and the Bell Tower are where the emperor cleansed himself by fasting before making his report and conducting the sacrifices to heaven. These days this hall is seldom visited, but nearby in the early mornings many locals gather to perform their morning exercises (tai ji quan) and students claim benches to read their books.

5 Temples, Mosques & Churches

Beijing's most popular Buddhist shrine is the **Lama Temple,** a must-see for most visitors. It is situated a few blocks from another major temple complex, the **Confucius Temple.** The most interesting Daoist place of worship is the less-touristy **White Cloud Temple (Bai Yun Guan).** The **White Dagoba** in Beihai Park, **Baita Temple,** and **Wuta Temple** near the zoo are also notable Buddhist complexes, well worth viewing, and there are several other Buddhist or Daoist temples off the beaten track (described below). Beijing also has active Christian churches and Islamic mosques that foreign visitors may attend or tour.

TEMPLES

Confucius Temple (Kong Miao).
13 Guozijian Jie, Dongcheng District. ☎ **010/6407-3593.** Admission 10RMB ($1.25). Tues–Sun 9am–5pm. The temple is west of the Lama Temple, across Yonghegong Dajie, on the old street with archways.

Built in 1306, the temple honors China's great philosopher and is a part of the Imperial College (Guozijian). It is China's second-largest Confucian shrine (behind the temple in Confucius' hometown, Qu Fu), and a quiet refuge from the crowded Lama Temple nearby. In the first courtyard are 198 steles (carved stone tablets) bearing the names of successful candidates in the national civil service examinations during the Yuan, Ming, and Qing dynasties. There are also many ancient trees, including a 700-year-old cypress in the main courtyard. The Hall of Great Achievements (Da Cheng Dian) stands at the north end of the complex, fronted by a statue of Confucius in the center and a group of 18th-century ceremonial stone drums on the right. Side halls sell antiques and inexpensive rubbings (about 50RMB/$6) of the steles. Running along the east wall is a museum of Beijing history, chronologically arranged, with signs in English, quite worth strolling. The grounds also contain the complete text of the Confucian Classics carved on 189 stone tablets, as well as the Sir Donald Sussman Center for Chinese Antiques, established in 1995. Qing Dynasty emperors once came to this temple to expound the teachings of Confucius, and students competed in the highest examinations for the title of Jinshi.

Five-Pagoda Temple (Wu Ta Si).
24 Wutasicun, Haidian District. ☎ **010/6217-3836.** Admission 3RMB (35¢). Daily 8:30am–4pm. Across the Nanchang River directly north of the Beijing Zoo, a 10-minute walk east of Baishiqiao Lu, a major street running north off Xizhimen Wai Dajie; it's also possible to reach the temple directly from Beijing Zoo via a bridge over the Nanchang River at the northwest zoo exit.

One of the most striking and unusual of Beijing's temples, the Five-Pagoda Temple is on the grounds of Zhenjue Temple and the Beijing Stone Engraving Art Museum, an outdoor collection of more than 500 fascinating stone carvings. The Five-Pagoda tower at the center consists of a square hall, its walls engraved with the niches of 1,000 Buddhas and topped by five magnificent pagodas (each about 25 feet high, built in 1473) that are more Indian than Chinese in style. For an extra 5RMB (60¢), you can climb the stairs into the central pagoda.

Guanghua Temple (Guanghua Si).

Xicheng District. Admission 5RMB (75¢). Daily 8am–5pm. On the southeast shore of Houhai Lake along Ya'er Hutong, 5 blocks west of the Drum Tower (see "Museums & Mansions," below).

This lovely little temple, the only one to survive on the eastern shores of the Back Lakes, is called the "Great Transformation" temple after a wandering monk who ate only half the rice he received from the people, with the other portion helping to pay for (being transformed into) this temple. The four engraved stone tablets (stele) in the main courtyard show great damage, probably by the marauding Red Guards during the Cultural Revolution (1966–76). There are just two small temples on the grounds, enshrining statues of the three Buddhas (past, present, and future), with painting of the 18 *lohans,* Buddha's semi-divine followers. The temple receives few tourists, but at least 20 monks are in residence here.

Huifeng Temple (Huifeng Si).

Xicheng District. Admission 50 mao (5¢). Daily 8am–8pm. On the island at the far northern tip of Xihai Lake, south side of the Second Ring Road, east of Jishuita subway station.

This temple is far off the beaten track, although its location could hardly be more picturesque: on a rocky island just offshore in the most western of the Back Lakes, with a view south over the water toward central Beijing. The rocky crag presents a short but steep climb to reach the temple on its summit. Formerly thought to be a site for worshipping Guanyin, the Goddess of Mercy, Huifeng today is not an active shrine, but its halls have been recently renovated with fresh brick, cement, and statuary. There is a small museum with astronomical charts, displays, and celestial instruments related to the Yuan Dynasty (1215–1368). The real draw is its romantic location, the island rockery, and the fine views.

✪ Lama Temple (Yong He Gong).

12 Yonghegong Dajie, Dongcheng District. ☎ **010/6404-3769.** Admission 15RMB ($1.85). Tues–Sun 9am–4pm. The temple entrance is on the east side of the street, a block south of the Yonghegong subway station.

The one temple everyone must see in Beijing is quite crowded except in the early morning and late afternoon, but it is a gorgeous complex and well worth investigating anytime. Built in 1694 as the residence for the prince who became Emperor Yongzheng, it was converted to a temple in 1744. Later, during the rule of Emperor Qianlong, it became the major center (outside Lhasa) of the dominant Yellow Hat sect of Tibetan Buddhism. Even today it has a strong hand in determining the next Dalai Lama, the "living Buddha," and about 200 monks, many from Mongolia, live, pray, and study here.

A long walkway leads to the temple gate, through which there is a courtyard with a bell tower, a drum tower, and a collection of 108 carved stone tablets. In the first five magnificent worship halls, there is a large statue of the future Buddha, Maitreya, also known as the laughing Buddha. In the courtyard beyond the first hall is a large copper cauldron, Beijing's oldest incense burner, dated 1747, and a pavilion containing an immense stone tablet bearing the words of Emperor Qianlong carved in Tibetan, Mongolian, Manchu, and Chinese.

The **Hall of Harmony,** crowded with prayer wheels, contains Buddhas of the past, present, and future flanked by the 18 *luohan* (disciples who have achieved transcendence but elected to return to Earth to help others). The Hall of Eternal Blessing is a few steps to the north.

In the fourth great hall, **Wheel of the Law (Falun Dian),** there is a 40-foot bronze statue of the founder of this sect (in the yellow hat). The Dalai Lama's throne is on the left. Here the monks pray and study on raised platforms equipped with electric brass reading lamps.

The final of the five central halls contains an immense image of the Buddha carved from a single Tibetan sandalwood tree. It is over 75 feet tall, with Buddha's head beaming out from the third floor above. This must have been an awesome showstopper in the past when monks and followers made pilgrimages here by the thousands.

Seldom pointed out by local tour guides in the Lama Temple are the displays of esoteric Buddhist figures in the side halls lining the east wall, particularly near the temple entrance. Many of these entangled Tantric figures (some life-sized, most smaller) are discreetly draped in scarves to conceal their true activities. This aspect of Tibetan Buddhism takes a Kama Sutra approach to matters of body and spirit, and the religious statuary in these side halls, while quite inventive, is not for the easily offended.

Wanshou Temple (Wanshou Si).

Xisanhuan Lu, Haidian District. ☎ **010/6841-3380.** Admission 10RMB ($1.25). Tues–Sun 9am–5:30pm. Located on the Changhe River, on the east side of the Third Ring Road West, 4 blocks from the Shangri-La Hotel.

The Wanshou Temple (Temple of Longevity), which dates from the Ming Dynasty (1577), is a lovely Buddhist complex of halls and pavilions that now houses the **Beijing Art Museum (Zhongguo Meishuguan,** discussed below under "Museums & Mansions"). It was renovated in 1761 by Qing Emperor Qianlong. The Empress Dowager Cixi stayed overnight here on her way to the Summer Palace aboard the royal barge from the Forbidden City. The entrance gate, capped by a painted carving of blue sky, clouds, and 100 red bats (signifying good fortune), leads to a courtyard with a drum tower on the left and a bell tower (with a small store) on the right, both built in 1577. The first central hall is devoted to the worship of the laughing Buddha and the four heavenly kings. The second shrine, the Precious Hall of the Buddha (Dayanshou), contains lovely statuary and is for the worship of the "Medicinal Buddha of the Pure Glazed World." A long courtyard leads to a large meditation hall (50 feet wide by 75 feet deep) that now serves as a gallery of modern paintings. Behind the meditation hall is a rock garden with three halls devoted to the divinities presiding over three sacred Chinese peaks (Mt. Wutai and Wenshu to the left, Mt. Emei and Puxian to the right, and Mt. Putuo and Guanyin, Goddess of Mercy, in the center). At the rear of the temple behind the rock garden are two pavilions built in 1761 (one housing a stone tablet recounting the rebuilding of this temple, signed by Emperor Qianlong in several languages), as well as two interesting arched gates, built under Qianlong in 1761, in a Western style reminiscent of the gates destroyed in 1860 at the Old Summer Palace.

✪ White Cloud Temple (Bai Yun Guan).

6 Baiyunguan Jie, Xuanwu District. ☎ **010/6346-3531.** Admission 8RMB ($1). Daily 8:30am–4:30pm. To reach the temple, head south down Baiyun Lu, a major market street, cross the city moat, and go east 1 block on Baiyunguan Jie.

Beijing's leading Daoist temple, and the most fascinating temple complex in the capital, this is a highly active place of worship among locals. The clouds of incense are thick inside. The Wind Containing Bridge in the first courtyard is surrounded with worshippers trying to hit the golden coin suspended from a large 17th-century copper bell with small modern coins, a feat ensuring good luck. Beyond the first hall, which enshrines the temple's god, Wang Shan, lies the Spring Hall for the Jade Emperor, a major Daoist deity. Inside you will see the faithful rubbing their hands over engravings and the golden feet of the statues (as these are gods of wealth). There are several similar shrines on the central axis (with signs on the stairways reading "DO NOT SPIT EVERYWHERE!"), which leads north to an unusual two-story hall dedicated to the Four Celestial Emperors. At the very rear (north) is a rockery (Cloud Gathering Garden), where you might see dozens of novice monks receiving training. The side halls on the west side are particularly intriguing, with shrines dedicated to solving eye problems, increasing fertility, ensuring wealth, getting a good job, passing exams, and guaranteeing good fortune and longevity (once you locate your place on the zodiac). At every stop, the crowds burn incense and touch the powerful deities, praying that their wishes be granted, a remarkable return to ancient Daoist beliefs. Festivals occur here on the 1st and 15th day of every lunar month—it's a great time to visit and mingle.

White Pagoda Temple (Bai Ta Si).
Xicheng District. ☎ **010/6616-0023.** Admission 10RMB ($1.25). Daily 9am–5pm. On north side of Fuchingmennei Dajie, a 10-minute walk east from Fuchingmen subway stop.

Newly renovated (1998), this temple features the largest Tibetan pagoda (usually called a *dagoba* or *stupa*) in China, built more than 700 years ago (1279) by order of Kublai Khan. The main gate and museum in the first courtyard are new. The museum contains Buddhist statuary and Emperor Qianlong's handcopied sutra (written in 1753, unearthed in 1978). The **Hall of the Great Enlightened Ones** to the north contains thousands of little Buddhas in glass cases, which are even set into the columns. There are two more beautifully renovated halls and then the White Pagoda itself, an immense structure 167 feet high.

MOSQUES & CHURCHES
In addition to the places listed below, there are many other cathedrals, churches, and places of worship in Beijing. For the locations and times of Catholic, Protestant, and Jewish services in Beijing, inquire at your hotel.

Chongwenmen Protestant Church (Chongwenmen Tang).
D2 Hougou Hutong, Chongwen District. ☎ **010/6524-2193.** Service: Sun 9:30am (in Chinese). Located northeast of Chongwenmen subway station, behind the Jinlang Hotel.

Methodists from the United States built the first church here in 1876. Razed during the Boxer Rebellion (1900), it was rebuilt in 1904. It was closed during the Cultural Revolution (1966–1976) and reopened in 1982. This church is now served by three ministers and attracts overflow crowds (2,500 worshippers) on Sundays. This church has been visited by the Archbishop of Canterbury (George Carey) and U.S. President Bill Clinton. The American evangelist Reverend Billy Graham has preached in this church on two occasions.

Ox Street Mosque (Niu Jie Qingzhen Shi).
88 Niu Jie, Xuanwu District. ☎ **010/6353-2564.** Admission 10RMB ($1.25). Daily 9am–sunset.

Spiritual center of Beijing's 200,000 Islamic followers, this is the capital's largest mosque, dating from A.D 996. Its main prayer hall (facing Mecca to the west) can hold 2,000 (non-Muslims are not permitted to enter). The courtyard is surrounded by a Tower for Viewing the Moon, a minaret (for calls to prayer), a hall of inscribed clay tablets, and the tombs of Muslim leaders from the Yuan Dynasty (1271–1368). Beijing's other mosque that welcomes foreign visitors is the **Dongsi Mosque**

(**Dongsi Qingzhen Si**), located at 13 Dongsi Nan Dajie, a short walk northeast from the Wangfujing shopping area.

South Cathedral (Nan Tang).

141 Qianmenxi Dajie, Xuanwu District. ☎ **010/6602-5221**. Services Mon–Fri 6am (Latin), 7am (Chinese); Sat 6:30am (Latin); Sun 6am and 7am (Latin), 8am (Chinese), 10am (English). Located 1 block east of the Xuanwumen subway stop on north side of the boulevard.

Beijing's main Catholic cathedral was built on the site of Jesuit missionary Matteo Ricci's house in 1650 and rebuilt for the last time in 1904. It is known in English as the Cathedral of the Immaculate Conception of the Blessed Virgin Mary, or Mary's Church, by expatriates who worship here. The cathedral is quite large and active, but not ornate (no stained glass). There is a "Holy Things Handicraft Department" selling small items at the southern gate and a pretty rock garden dedicated to the Virgin on the southwest corner.

Other major cathedrals in Beijing include the **North Cathedral (Bei Tang),** 33 Xishiku Dajie, Xicheng District, (☎ **010/6617-5198**), built in 1887, with services conducted in Chinese only, and **Dongtang Cathedral (Church of St. Joseph),** 74 Wangfujing Dajie (☎ **010/6524-0634**), an imposing structure now hidden away in the heart of the central shopping district, with Sunday services performed in Chinese and Latin.

6 Parks & Gardens

Beijing's parks are splendid places for a stroll. The best, such as Beihai, combine scenic beauty and people-watching with historic monuments, imperial courtyard restaurants, and Buddhist temples. All are particularly lively in the hours of dawn, when people gather for their morning exercises (ranging from the shadow-boxing forms of *tai ji quan* to ballroom dancing). All are gated, with a ticket booth charging a small admission at the entrance.

✪ Beihai Park (Beihai Gongyuan).

1 Wenjin Jie, Xicheng District. ☎ **010/6404-0610**. Admission 10RMB ($1.25). Daily 6am–8pm. South entrance is just northwest of the Forbidden City; east entrance is 2 blocks west of Jingshan Park.

Containing the city's largest lake and a landmark white pagoda, this is the capital's oldest imperial garden, with an 800-year history, although it wasn't opened to the public until 1925. It makes for a wonderful stroll. In the **Round City** (Tuan Cheng) at the south entrance is a massive jade bowl that was once the prized possession of Kublai Khan, and the Light Receiving Hall houses a 10-foot Buddha of white jade sent to Emperor Qianlong as a gift from Burma.

Qionghua Isle contains the most spectacular sights in Beihai, starting with the nicely maintained halls of the **Yongan Temple (Yongan Si)** and leading up Jade Hill to the White Pagoda. The island itself is constructed of the materials excavated to create Beihai Lake. The Tibetan-style **White Pagoda (Bai Ta),** 118 feet tall, dates from 1651; it commemorates a visit by the Dalai Lama and is believed to contain precious Lama relics. The views from the peak, across the lake and toward the Forbidden City, are dazzling. If you look due south, between Zhonghai Lake and the Forbidden City, you can see the compound where China's Communist government is sequestered. The northern shore of the islet is rimmed with a covered walkway with painted scenes in the fashion of the Long Corridor at the Summer Palace. The cluster of buildings here is known as the Hall of Rippling Waters (Yilantang) and is a former palace (as well as the site of an imperial restaurant, Fangshan; see review in chapter 5, "Dining").

The northwest shore is the site of a glazed-tile Nine Dragon Screen (1417), smaller than the one in the Forbidden City, and a botanical garden. The eastern shore contains halls and pavilions known as the "Gardens Within Gardens," where emperors and empresses once enjoyed the lakeshore. Today's commoners take to the waters in paddleboats and rowboats during the summer and on ice skates in the winter. Beihai Lake was drained and cleaned and its shoreline renovated in the late fall of 1998, making it an even more beautiful spot to tour. For a walking tour that includes sights in Beihai Park, see Walking Tour 3 in the next chapter, "Beijing Strolls."

Grand View Park (Daguan Yuan).

Guang'anmen Beibinhe Lu, Xuanwu District. Admission 15RMB ($1.85). Daily 8am–8pm. At the southwest corner of lower Second Ring Road and the city moat.

A newly built park, opened in 1986 on the site of the Imperial Vegetable Garden, Grand View is a reproduction of the classic family garden described in one of China's most famous novels, *The Dream of the Red Chamber,* an elaborate soap opera written by Beijing resident Cao Xueqin (1715–63). The park has already served as the set for a Hong Kong TV movie of the book. Complete with a central pond, bamboo lodges, pavilions, arched bridges, towers, and halls, Grand View is a faithful modern version of the classic Chinese garden. It's a pleasant diversion if you are in the neighborhood.

Jingshan Park (Jingshan Gongyuan).

Dongcheng District. Admission 5RMB (65¢). Daily 8am–8pm. Located directly across Jinshan Qian Jie from the north gate of the Forbidden City.

Also called **Meishan (Coal Hill),** this promontory overlooking the Forbidden City was created from the excavations of the imperial moat in 1420. According to the principle of *feng shui* (Chinese geomancy), this hill would protect the Forbidden City from the evil spirits swooping in from the north, but it was on this hill that the last Ming emperor, Chongzhen, hanged himself from a tree before the Manchu conquerors could arrive (from the north, of course). Today, Jingshan is a pretty park that requires a steep walk from the Beautiful View Tower (Qiwang Lou), an exhibition hall at the southern foot, to the viewing pavilion (Pavilion of Everlasting Spring, *wan chun ting*) on its middle summit. The view over the golden-tiled roofs of the immense Forbidden City and Tiananmen Square to the south is justifiably a celebrated one, but there are also superb vistas of the Drum and Bell towers and the Back Lakes to the north. The pavilion's balcony fills up with locals enjoying the view, while the old interior has been taken over by a souvenir and snack outlet.

Old Summer Palace (Yuan Ming Yuan).

Qinghua Xilu, Haidian District. ☎ 010/6255-1488. Admission 5RMB (65¢). Daily 6:30am–7pm. North of Beijing University, a short taxi ride east of the "new" Summer Palace.

China's largest imperial park when Qing Emperor Kangxi built it in the 18th century, Yuan Ming Yuan was smashed and burnt to the ground by French and British troops during the Second Opium War and never restored. It is today a haunting picnic spot, with a few ruins of its hundreds of original pavilions, gazebos, and goldfish ponds still visible. The most evocative remains of this Versailles of China are located in the **Garden of Eternal Spring (Changchun Yuan),** where the emperor oversaw the creation of European-style mazes, marble fountains, an aviary, and a concert chamber. The broken and fallen columns and arches of the Hall of Tranquility form an ideal setting for a picnic in the suburbs of Beijing, with a hint of Old Cathay.

Ritan Park (Ritan Gongyuan).
Ritan Lu, Chaoyang District. ☎ **010/6502-1743.** Admission 5RMB ($1.25). Daily 6:30am–8:30pm. Located 3 blocks north of the Friendship Store and Silk Alley (Jianguomenwai Dajie).

Like its more famous sister, the Temple of Heaven (Tiantan), the Temple of the Sun (Ritan) served as an altar for the emperor to conduct annual cosmic rites. Built in 1530, Ritan today is an exceptionally pleasant park in the heart of a tree-lined diplomatic quarter. To the northwest of the park are Russian restaurants and an outdoor market. The altar is on the southern summit of the park, where a new pavilion has been erected. High-rise buildings now surround the park, which gives it the feel of a small version of New York's Central Park. There is a pleasant rock garden and pond on the southwest side, where fishing poles can be rented (10RMB/$1.25) and the catch (mostly grass carp) is priced by weight; the park fishing fee is 10RMB ($1.25)

The other two imperial altars, also built in the early 16th century, are located in similar small city parks. **The Temple of the Earth Park (Ditan Gongyuan)** is north of the Lama Temple, just across the Second Ring Road North, and the **Temple of the Moon Park (Yuetan Gongyuan),** where stamp collectors swap and sell their wares, is just west of the Second Ring Road West. In the old days, these four altars encircled the city walls of Beijing and roughly corresponded to the four cardinal points of the compass.

7 Museums & Mansions

Many of Beijing's outstanding museums are housed in ancient temples, towers, and historic garden residences throughout the capital. The setting in many instances is one of the chief attractions. While the lighting and the displays are seldom state-of-the-art and English signage can be spotty or nonexistent in some cases, simply viewing the objects in these fine storehouses can be fascinating.

✪ Ancient Observatory (Guguan Xiang Tai).
2 Dongbiaobei Hutong, Chaoyang District. ☎ **010/6524-2202.** Admission 10RMB ($1.25). Wed–Sun 9–11:30am and 1–4:30pm. Located 1 block south of Jianguomenwai Dajie, on the west side of the Second Ring Road overpass, near the Jianguomen subway stop.

The Imperial Observatory has been here, atop the Jianguomen gate in the city wall, since 1442, even if it is now surrounded by expressways, skyscrapers, and the city's busiest avenue. Inside is a collection of some of the world's rarest astronomical instruments, most them originally fashioned by Jesuit missionaries who took up residence in Beijing in the 17th century and charmed the emperor with their scientific knowledge of the heavens. The observatory has a wonderful gold foil map of the stars as they were plotted in the Ming Dynasty and fine copies (for the most part) of the old instruments used to plot the heavens. On the roof, which offers superb views of the Forbidden City, are copies of the Jesuit-designed armillary sphere, bronze gnomons, and other large ornate bronze devices that the Son of Heaven depended on 3 centuries ago.

Beijing Art Museum (Zhongguo Meishuguan).
In the Wanshou Temple, Xisanhuan Lu, Haidian District. ☎ **010/6841-3380.** Admission 10RMB ($1.25). Tues–Sun 9am–5:30pm. On the Changhe River, east side of the Third Ring Road West, 4 blocks from the Shangri-La Hotel.

Beijing's newest art museum occupies the grounds of the **Wanshou Temple (Temple of Longevity),** a small Buddhist complex of Ming Dynasty halls and pavilions dating from 1577 (see "Temples, Mosques & Churches," above). The meditation hall (50 feet wide by 75 feet deep) in the center of the grounds serves as a gallery of modern oil paintings, with prices in the $2,000 range. The halls on the west side have displays of paintings, scrolls, textiles, ceramics, furniture, and artifacts from the Ming and Qing dynasties, as well as Japanese artworks created during the occupation of Manchuria in the 1930s and 1940s.

Big Bell Temple and Museum (Da Zhong Si).
31A Beisanhuan Xi Lu, Haidian District. ☎ **010/6255-0843** or 010/6255-0790. Admission 10RMB ($1.25). Daily 8:30am–4:30pm. On the north side of the Third Ring Road between Haidian Lu and Xizhimen Bei Dajie.

The temple, built in 1733, got its present name in 1743 when an enormous bronze bell, the largest in China, was brought here on ice sleds. It's thought that this Big Bell was cast in 1420 when Yongle, builder of the Forbidden City, was emperor. Weighing in at 46 tons and standing 23 feet high, it is displayed in its own tower in a rear courtyard. Emperor Qianlong lit incense and prayed for rain before it. For fun and good fortune, you can climb the spiral stairs to the top of tower and, like Buddhist pilgrims of old, cast coins into the bell's opening, which makes a pleasing sound. This ritual was once the major source of income for the temple monks. Before the temple reopened as the bell museum in 1985, it served as the Beijing No. 2 Food Factory.

Other halls in the former Juesheng (Awakening) Temple house 4,000 years of Chinese bells, including a set of stone chimes from the Warring States Period (475–221 B.C.) that visitors are invited to ring (for a small fee). Among the 700 or so relics are friendship bells from New Zealand and Italy and newly cast Chinese bells used to mark great occasions (such as the resumption of sovereignty over Hong Kong in 1997).

China Art Gallery (Zhongguo Meishuguan).
1 Wusi Dajie, Dongcheng District. ☎ **010/6401-9833.** Admission 15RMB ($1.85). Daily 9am–5pm. Entrance on north side of Wusi Dajie, 1 block west of intersection with Wangfujing Dajie.

Housed in a monumental Chinese-style edifice (built in 1959 and renovated in 1991), the 14 galleries of China's national gallery include traditional artworks as well as the work of emerging Chinese artists, some at work in studios here. Contemporary works can be purchased at the gift shop (west wing), as can woodcuts and traditional papercuts.

Drum Tower (Gulou).
At the corner of Gulou Dajie and Dianmenwai Dajie, Dongcheng District. Free admission. Daily 9am–4:30pm.

Beijing's original Drum Tower, which sounded the hours with the beating of drums, was built here by Kublai Khan in 1272 and rebuilt by the Ming rulers in 1420. It's worth climbing the 69 steps in the narrow stairwell for the view from the open balconies above. Only one of the 24 watch drums once in use has survived. Its cattle-skin head was slashed in 1900. What is said to be the world's largest drum (8.5 feet in diameter, constructed in 1990), is also on display, but the chief attraction is the view over the lakes and hutong neighborhoods of old Beijing. The **Bell Tower (Zhonglou)**, rebuilt in 1747, is just a few blocks from here directly north up an alley and affords similar views.

Lu Xun Museum (Lu Xun Bowuguan).
19 Gongmenkou Ertiao, Xicheng District. ☎ **010/6616-4169**, ext. 4080. Admission 1RMB (12¢). Tues–Sun 9am–4pm. Located 3 blocks north of Fuchengmennei Dajie and 4 blocks northeast of Fuchengmen subway station.

Heralded as China's greatest 20th-century writer, Lu Xun (1881–1936) is best known for *The True Story of Ah Q*. His museum contains letters, diaries, manuscripts, and even his clothing, as well as English translations of his work for sale.

✪ Museum of Chinese History (Zhongguo Lishi Bowuguan).

East side of Tiananmen Square, Chongwen District. ☎ **010/6512-9381**. Admission 5RMB (65¢). Tues–Sun 8:30am–3:30pm. Ticket booth is on first flight of stairs to the right (south).

This is China's largest collection of historical artifacts and complements the holdings in the Forbidden City. It's in the southern wing of the massive building that also houses the Museum of the Chinese Revolution (see below) and consists of two courtyard floors. The exhibits are arranged chronologically, starting on the ground floor and moving clockwise. The first gallery, "Primitive Society," has skeletons and pottery from the Stone Age site at Banpo. The "Slave Society" gallery has artifacts from the Xia and Shang dynasties (21–11 centuries B.C.). The "Feudal Society" gallery has shoes from the Warring States Period, two terra-cotta warriors and a horse from the Qin Dynasty, and an outstanding sampling of silks and pottery from the Tang Dynasty. On the second floor (four flights up) are many objects from the Qing (the last dynasty), concluding with two Western printing presses dated 1895. The displays grow more remarkable as you advance on the time line, although there are no signs in English. Many of China's true national treasures are stored here among the 300,000 relics. Cameras and handbags must be checked before entry.

Museum of the Chinese Revolution (Zhongguo Gemin Lishi Bowuguan).

East side of Tiananmen Square, Chongwen District. ☎ **010/6512-3355**. Admission 2RMB (25¢). Tues–Sun 8:30am–5pm.

The north wing of this massive building that also houses the Museum of Chinese History (see above) is not nearly as interesting as its sister museum. The exhibition of more than 100,000 items focuses on the history of the Chinese Communist Party from 1919 to 1949. The photographic record is interesting, and there are a few signs in English to help. Cameras and handbags must be checked before entry.

Natural History Museum (Ziran Bowuguan).

126 Tianqiaonan Dajie, Chongwen District. ☎ **010/6702-4431**. Admission 20RMB ($2.50). Tues–Sun 8:30am–5pm. Entrance north of the west gate to Temple of Heaven Park (Tiantan).

This spacious gallery contains some fine specimens of primitive man and of dinosaur skeletons and eggs excavated in China.

Prince Gong's Mansion (Gong Wang Fu).

17 Qianhai Xi Lu, Xicheng District. Admission 5RMB (65¢). Daily 9am–5pm. Located west of Qianhai Lake and east of Liuyin Jie.

Prince Gong's estate is Beijing's best-preserved example of how the upper class lived during the Qing Dynasty. It consists of 31 pavilions, halls, and residential buildings; nine courtyards; several arched bridges; large ponds with islands and swans; one immense rock garden in the classic style; and even its own private pagoda for gazing at the moon. Prince Gong's brother was China's emperor from 1851 to 1861, and Gong served as regent for the next emperor, along with Cixi, who would become the Empress Dowager. Gong's son, Puyi, became China's last emperor. Prince Gong moved into this palace estate in 1852, but its design originated more than a century earlier. The mansion has its own stage for outdoor performances of Peking Opera, as well as a teahouse open to hutong tour groups.

✪ Soong Ching-ling Residence (Song Qing Ling Guzhu).

46 Houhai Beiyan, Xicheng District. ☎ **010/6404-4205**. Admission 8RMB ($1). Daily 9am–4:30pm. Located on the northeast shore of Houhai Lake.

Wife of the founder of the Republic of China, Sun Yat-sen, and sister-in-law of Chiang Kai-shek, Soong Ching-ling lived her life as if in a Chinese opera played out at the highest levels. After the communists triumphed in 1949 and Chiang Kai-shek fled to Taiwan, Ching-ling stayed. Her sister, Soong Mei-ling, became famous in America as the great defender of Taiwan against Mao's China, while Soong Ching-ling, who supported the other side, served as vice-president of the People's Republic. Soong's Beijing residence has been preserved both as a family museum and as a fine example of a courtyard estate. Soong lived here from 1963 until her death in 1981. A large red sign in Chinese is all that identifies the entrance to her villa these days, but inside are many signs in English identifying not only objects in the museum, but the pavilions and plants that make up the impressive garden grounds. This was originally the garden of a Dr. Mingzhu, a scholar during the rein of Emperor Kangxi, and there are trees here he planted over 200 years ago. A fine view of the landscaping—with its winding lanes, pavilions, flowers, and pine trees girding a pond and stream fed by the Imperial Jade Spring—can be seen from the Fan Pavilion (Shan Ting). The Soong museum, housed in the large former residences, contains a chronology of her life in pictures, letters, newspaper articles, and memorabilia, such as a radio with a golden case (a gift from her brother, T.V. Soong) and X-ray equipment airlifted into China during World War II.

8 Hutongs & Siheyuans (Lanes & Courtyard Compounds)

Hutongs are the narrow, twisting, east-west lanes and alleyways of old Beijing, and much of the city's history during the Ming and Qing dynasties is preserved in their layout and colorful names. *Siheyuans* are the small courtyard dwellings behind the hutong walls. These rectangular complexes usually had an arched entry gate facing south and an outer courtyard with side halls surrounding an inner courtyard. In the old days, such a courtyard house would be owned by a single family with servants. In modern times, these siheyuan have often been divided up by many families. Roughly half of Beijing's population lives in some form of hutong, although these neighborhoods are rapidly disappearing under the bulldozer of urban renewal.

The Back Lakes area of Beijing (north of Beihai Park and the Forbidden City, on either side of Qianhai Lake) is the most popular area for touring the hutongs. The city's shortest hutong is **Yichi Dajie** (about 30 feet long) and the narrowest is on **Qianshi Hutong,** which squeezes down to just 15 inches. This area is full of pedicabs offering tours, although English-language communication and fare-bargaining can be problems when you're on your own—which is why Beijing's largest hutong tour company, ✪ **Beijing Hutong Tourist Agency,** 26 Dianmen Xilu, Xicheng District (☎ **010/6615-9097,** 010/6612-3236, or 010/6505-2288), has been so successful with its organized pedicab tours. A hutong tour is an essential Beijing experience.

The Beijing Hutong Tourist Agency employs a fleet of pedicabs (bicycle-driven rickshaws) holding one or two passengers each. One English-speaking guide leads the procession. Tours are offered daily from 9 to 11:30am and from 2 to 4:30pm. Tickets are 180RMB to 240RMB ($25 to $30). Most travelers purchase tickets the day before from the tour desk in their hotel. A hotel taxi to and from the rendezvous point is sometimes included in the service, but at about three times the cost of taking your own taxi, which is usually costs from 25RMB to 32RMB ($3 to $4). The ticket agent at your hotel will furnish directions to the departure point, which

The Last Hutong in China

The courtyard houses of old Beijing's narrow lanes (hutongs) are fast disappearing. "Given the city's bad traffic and residents' difficult living conditions," explained one senior city planner, "we have no choice but to renovate the old districts." Many, perhaps most, Beijingers agree. The question is how many of the present 2,600 hutongs will be preserved. In 1990, 260 hutongs with 2,000 *siheyuans* (courtyard dwellings) were placed in cultural protection zones. This means only 10% of Beijing's present old neighborhoods will survive long into the 21st century.

There are some signs of protest, however, including a rare sit-down demonstration by about 50 middle-aged and elderly residents who gathered at city government headquarters near Tiananmen Square in April 1998, because they did not want their homes demolished to make way for a new subway line. Nor did they want to be forced, as thousands have, into tall modern apartment complexes in the far suburbs.

One man much in the news recently, octogenarian Zhao Jingxin, has simply refused to budge from his 400-year-old courtyard house that stands on a hutong slated to become a shopping plaza. He ignored eviction notices and refused extravagant offers to evacuate (6 apartments for $190,000). All of his neighbors have given in and the demolishers are working nearby. Like a few others in Beijing, Zhao is arguing that Beijing should end the wholesale eradication of its historic architecture and begin preserving what's left. He argues that the government should exile the new commercial buildings to the suburbs instead of the old downtown residents, but this position has few converts in the boomtown that is modern Beijing.

is at the corner of Dianmenxi Lu and Shishahai Tixiao. Plan to arrive 20 to 30 minutes early.

The pedicabs with the red canopies snake through the alleys and streets, usually visiting such sights as the Drum Tower, the Shisha Lakes, and Guanghau Temple. The highlight is a walking tour of several hutongs and a chance to go inside a siheyuan, see its courtyard rooms, and talk with the family who lives there today. The tours usually end with a stroll and tea at Prince Gong's Mansion (see "Museums & Mansions" above), which is an immense, stately version of a courtyard house. The tours last about 4 hours and can include from 20 to 60 people.

The same company also offers extended 6-hour hutong tours that enable visitors to stay longer with the residents and enjoy a family meal with them. Groups of at least 10 visitors are required. I recommend the shorter 4-hour tour, though, as the longer tour can be boring, depending on the hutong family you chat with. The family meal you share with the hutong family can be unforgettable, but it can also be simply tedious.

9 Especially for Kids

In a country known for the emphasis it places on the family—and for the lengths to which a family will go to spoil its "only child"—attractions for children are commonplace. The following are some that could appeal particularly to younger foreign travelers in Beijing.

Beijing Amusement Park.
West entrance of Longtan Lake Park, 1 Zuoanmennei Dajie, Chongwen District. ☎ **010/ 6714-6909** or 010/6711-1155, ext. 221. Admission 35–50RMB ($4.25–$6). Mon–Fri 8:30am– 7pm; Sat–Sun 8am–7:30pm.

This old-fashioned (1970s) amusement park with Ferris wheel, water slide, looping roller coaster, and teacup rides has added an animal park, a go-cart track, and an IMAX theater.

Beijing Zoo (Beijing Dongwu Yuan).
Xizhimenwai Dajie, Xicheng District. ☎ **010/6831-4411.** Admission 10RMB ($1.25) adults; 3RMB (35¢) children. Daily 7:30am–5:30pm. Located 6 blocks west of the Xizhimen subway station.

Once a private garden estate, the Beijing Zoo was created here by Empress Dowager Cixi, who imported hundreds of exotic animals from Germany in the late 19th century. The main gate and many of the animal exhibition halls and outdoor pens seem to have changed little after a century. Most Western visitors abhor the conditions here, with its emphasis on cages for most of the 6,000 animals. The new Panda Garden, with its six adults and baby twins, is an improvement over the general facilities, with outdoor as well as indoor spaces.

Blue Zoo Aquarium.
At the south gate of the Worker's Stadium, Chaoyang District. ☎ **010/6591-3397** or 010/6591-3398, ext. 1177. Admission 75RMB ($9.25) adults; 50RMB ($6) children. Daily 9am–8pm.

Highlighted by a 100-yard-long underwater tunnel surrounded by baby sharks and piranhas, this water park has tanks, classrooms, and educational galleries and is a favorite among expatriate kids and their families.

Chinese Ethnic Culture Park.
At the southwest corner of the Fourth Ring Road and Beichen Lu, Chaoyang District. ☎ **010/6206-3640.** Admission 60RMB ($7.50). Daily 8am–7pm summer; 8:30am–5:30pm winter.

In this ethnic theme park, costumed representatives of China's 55 minorities re-enact their customs in reconstructed model houses and villages. Song and dance performances occur regularly on the grounds, and ethnic nationality food is served at small restaurants.

Dynasty Wax Works Palace.
Xiguan Traffic Circle, Changping County. ☎ **010/6974-8675.** Admission 60RMB ($7.50). Daily 9am–6pm. Located on the highway to the Ming Tombs and the Great Wall at Badaling.

Billed as the world's largest wax museum, this palace of effigies is home to the famous and infamous from the Chinese world.

Kaite Mini-Golf.
At the north entrance to Ritan Park, Chaoyang District. ☎ **010/6415-1047.** Admission 25RMB ($3). Daily 8am–10:30pm.

Arched bridges, walls, gates, pavilions, and other maddening obstacles—all in miniature—pose a pleasant challenge in the park.

Five Colours Earth Craft Center.
East Children's Palace, 10 Dongzhimen Nanlu, Dongcheng District. ☎ **010/6415-3839.** Admission 50RMB ($6) per hour. Daily 9am–6pm. On the Second Ring Road East, north of Poly Plaza, across from Dongsishitiao subway station.

The center features do-it-yourself arts and crafts in ceramics, plate-painting, paper-making, tie-dying, and embroidery. The instructors are Chinese, but directions are in English.

Fundazzle.
Gongrentiyuchang Lu, Chaoyang District. ☎ **010/6593-6193.** Admission 40RMB ($5) for 2 hours. Daily 9am–6pm.

Indoor playground with slides, a pool of balls, games, and a climbing wall—a place for kids to work off excess energy.

Lido Park.
Next to the Holiday Inn Lido Hotel, Jichang Lu and Jiangtai Lu, on the Airport Expressway, Chaoyang District. ☎ **010/6438-0882.** June–Sept daily 6am–11pm.

This large park offers plenty of summer arts and crafts classes for kids, rents fishing poles, and has outdoor swimming (30RMB/$3.75 for children under 17).

Putt-Putt Golf.
At the Beijing Dongdan Sports Center, 108 Chongwenmennei Dajie District. ☎ **010/ 6528-8495.** Admission 25RMB ($3). Daily 8am–10pm. Located north of Chongwenmen subway station at Dongdan Park.

Good, clean, all-American fun, favored by expatriate families.

Taipingyang Underwater World.
11 Xisanhuan Zhonglu, Haidian District. ☎ **010/6846-1172.** Admission 50RMB ($6.25). Daily 9am–9pm.

Penguins and sharks cavort as visitors watch from a conveyor belt.

Tuanjiehu Manmade Seashore.
Tuanjiehu Park (east side of Third Ring Road East), Chaoyang District. ☎ **010/6507-3603.** Admission to swim 20RMB ($2.50) adults; 15RMB ($1.90) children. Daily 7am–9pm June–Sept. Closed Oct–May.

The artificial beach is a great place for hot-weather swimming in the park pool. Admission to the park only is just 25¢.

Universal Studios.
In the basement of the Henderson Center, 18 Jianguomenwai Dajie, Chaoyang District. ☎ **010/6518-3404.** Admission 30RMB ($3.75) weekdays and 35RMB ($4.25) weekends adults; 25RMB ($3) weekdays and 30RMB ($3.75) weekends children. Mon–Fri noon–8pm; Sat–Sun 10am–8pm.

Special effects and behind-the-scene peeks at Hollywood moviemaking are presented with sets, scenes, and characters from *Waterworld* and *Jurassic Park.*

World Park (Shijie Gongyuan).
Fourth Ring Road South, Fengtai District. ☎ **010/6382-3344.** Admission Mon–Thurs 40RMB ($5); Fri–Sun 48RMB ($6). Daily 8:30am–5pm.

China's largest theme park (116 acres) and an extreme—but fun—curiosity, World Park consists of miniaturized reproductions of more than 100 of the world's great sites, skylines, monuments, and landmarks, from a 30-foot-tall Eiffel Tower to a 30-foot-tall Statue of Liberty to a 30-foot-tall Sphinx.

Yuyuantan Water World.
In Yuyuantan Park, Fourth Ring Road West, Haidian District. ☎ **010/6851-4447.** Admission 15RMB ($1.86). Daily 9am–6pm June–Aug. Closed Sept–May.

Beijing's largest water park has plenty of slides, sluices, and swimming pools and is next to the Soong Ching-Ling Children's Science Park and the Diaoyutai Guest House, where world leaders are put up.

10 Organized Tours

Most Beijing hotels have tour desks that can arrange a variety of half- and full-day tours for guests. These tour desks are often extensions of China International Travel Service (CITS), with offices at 28 Jianguomenwai Dajie (☎ **010/6515-8562**) and 103 Fuxingmennei Dajie (☎ **010/6601-1122**, ext. 705). CITS operates most of the English-language group tours in Beijing, even if you buy your ticket in your hotel. The only reason to go directly to the CITS office is to arrange a special tour, perhaps of sites not offered on the regular group tour list or for a private tour with guide, driver, and car.

The ordinary **group tours** are usually inexpensive and seldom have more than 20 people. An average day tour usually costs about 320RMB ($40) per person if there are at least four people signed up (tours can cost more or less, depending on sites visited and number of people in group). A typical full-day tour might consist of (1) the Great Wall and the Ming Tombs; (2) the Forbidden City, Tiananmen Square, and the Temple of Heaven; or (3) the Summer Palace, the Lama Temple, and the Panda Garden at the Beijing Zoo. Lunch is included. There are also regular group tours that focus on a traditional Beijing duck dinner. Hotel tour desks sometimes feature entertainment packages for an evening at the Beijing Opera or a dinner show with the acrobats, but they seldom include a guide or transportation to and from the hotel.

Group day tours are always rushed and quickly run past the highlights at each stop. At major sites, such as the Summer Palace, the Forbidden City, and the Temple of Heaven, group tour participants are shown only a fraction of what's there. A good guide can fill you in on the history and culture of each site, but there is usually no more than an hour to see each. Most of the commentary is given during the bus ride between sites. If you want additional commentary at a particular site, it's a good idea to stick close to the guide.

CITS and other private travel agents can arrange in-depth **specialized tours,** for example, to schools, colleges, and Children's Palaces; to less-visited sections of the Great Wall; to hutong neighborhoods; to art museums and galleries; to hospitals and clinics. These agencies can also set up overnight tours, with guides, to nearby cultural cities, such as Chengde, and can sometimes arrange outdoor and adventure tours for those interested in hiking, mountain climbing, or even bungee jumping. Specialized tours include an English-speaking guide, a driver, and a private car; the starting price for a full day's touring starts at around 1,200RMB ($150) per person (less for groups of three or more).

One proven private travel agency providing tours, tickets, and hotel reservations to international clients is **Sunshine Express,** Jing Ding Commercial Building, 2 Dongsanhuan Lu (Third Ring Road), Chaoyang District, Beijing 100020 (☎ **010/6586-8069;** fax 010/6586-8077; e-mail: sunpress@public.bta.net.cn).

11 Staying Active

Most visitors to Beijing do not come intending to pursue outdoor recreation or sports, but China's capital offers a surprisingly wide range of such activities. Hotels provide exercise equipment and limited court sports, routinely offering exercise machines, weights, aerobic and workout areas, swimming pools, locker rooms, and, less often, tennis and squash courts at little or no charge to their guests. It is possible to use the fitness facilities and courts of most hotels and private health clubs on a daily basis, too, even if you are not a guest (although the fees can be steep).

Michael Jordan in China

His Airness is worshipped by sports fans even in China, where he is known as *Fei Ren,* the Flying Man. When he retired in 1999, Michael Jordan made the front pages across the Middle Kingdom; the *Beijing Morning Post* mourned his departure as "touching the hearts of hundreds of millions." The Chinese admire Jordan for his athleticism and easygoing style. Air Jordan sneakers and Chicago Bulls caps and jerseys are still hot items; black market versions sell at street stalls from Kashgar to Beijing. Some 50 million Chinese play basketball regularly, 20 million in more than 1 million amateur leagues, and the NBA Game of the Week is broadcast on Saturdays by China Central Television (CCTV) across the nation.

Joggers in Beijing can always take to the early morning streets (before the crowds block them), but the large public parks are much nicer places for a run. No one bats an eye at runners these days; Beijing, after all, has its own international marathon every October.

Golf, bowling, and billiards have become the three most popular recreational sports in Beijing, pursued by well-to-do locals, foreign residents, and overseas visitors, but horseback riding, ice-skating, and traditional *tai ji quan* can also be enjoyed in the capital. Beijing even boasts paintball emporiums, shooting ranges, rock climbing walls, and China's first bungee jumping venue.

Spectator sports, on the other hand, are more limited and less to Western tastes, although professional basketball, inter-league soccer, and international badminton and volleyball matches draw large crowds in the capital.

ACTIVITIES FROM A TO Z

BOWLING   Bowling experienced a boom in China during the 1990s, when more than 15,000 alleys were built, many of them in Beijing. There are alleys in the **Holiday Inn Lido,** the **Capital Hotel,** the **Beijing International,** and other hotels (see chapter 4, "Accommodations." The **China World Hotel,** 1 Jianguomenwai Dajie (on the northwest corner of the intersection with the Third Ring Road East, Level B2; ☎ 010/6505-2266), has 12 lanes with special off-hour rates. Monday through Thursday the charge is 10RMB ($1.20) per lane from 11:30am to 2pm, 15RMB ($1.80) per lane from 2 to 7pm, and 25RMB ($3) per lane from 7pm to 1am; Friday through Sunday the charge is 20RMB ($2.40) from 11:30am to 7pm and 25RMB ($3) from 7pm to 1am; shoe rental is 5RMB (65¢).

GOLF (GAOERFU)   Greens fees at Beijing's handful of golf courses run from $80 to $100 on weekdays and from $100 to $150 on weekends. Caddies cost $10 to $20 and club rental $30 to $40. All courses require advance reservations; summer weekends are particularly crowded. The 18-hole **Beijing International Golf Club,** also known as the **Ming Tombs Golf Course,** northwest of Beijing in Changping County (☎ 010/6974-5678 or 010/6974-6388), is still the capital's top course. The **Beijing Country Golf Club,** northeast of Beijing on the airport road, Mapo Village, Shunyi County (☎ 010/6944-1005), has 36 holes. The **Beijing Grand Canal Golf Club,** on the Grand Canal in the Tongzhou District, east of Beijing (☎ 010/8958-3058), is a new 18-hole course with night golf. **Chaoyang Golf Club,** Tuanjiehu, Shangsilu, Chaoyang District (☎ 010/6500-1149), has just nine holes and a driving range,

Where to Learn Tai Chi (Tai Ji Quan)

The venerable and graceful "shadow-boxing" exercises that tens of thousands of Beijingers practice every morning before work can be learned at tai ji quan classes held in the Lido Club (Tuesday and Thursday from 9 to 10am) in the Holiday Inn Lido, Jichang Lu, Jiangtai Lu, Chaoyang District (☎ **010/6437-6688,** ext. 1603).

but is the closest course to Beijing. The **Huatang International Golf Club** (☎ **010/6159-3930**), located in the Sanhe Yanjiao Development Zone (15 miles from airport; there's a free shuttle bus from Traders Hotel), is opening Beijing's newest 18-hole championship course (designed by Graham Marsh).

HEALTH CLUBS   Some hotels offer day rates to outsiders. The **Gloria Plaza Hotel** has step machines, exercise bikes, treadmills, weights, an indoor pool, and locker rooms (120RMB/$15 per day). The **Great Wall Sheraton** has two outdoor tennis courts, locker rooms, exercise bikes, stair machines, rowing machines, Ping-Pong, and an indoor pool (150RMB/$19 per day). The **Holiday Inn Lido** has a gym, exercise machines, weights, and an indoor pool (120RMB/$15 per day). The **Kempinski Hotel** provides a weight room, lockers, machines, an indoor pool, an exercise area, and squash and tennis courts (200RMB/$25 per day). The **Shangri-La Hotel** has exercise machines, locker rooms, an indoor pool, Ping-Pong, aerobics, volleyball, basketball, bowling, squash courts (60RMB/$7.50 per hour), tennis courts (160RMB/$20 per hour); most facilities are located in a separate fitness building (150RMB/$19 per day). **Traders Hotel** has Nautilus equipment, step machines, treadmills, exercise bikes, and a locker room (100RMB/$12.50 per day).

HORSEBACK RIDING   The fitness center at the **Movenpick Hotel,** Xiao Tianzhu Village (near the airport), Shunyi County (☎ **010/6456-5588,** ext. 1217), can arrange a day's ride in the steep and scenic hills northeast of Beijing. Prices range from 160RMB to 200RMB ($20 to $25) per hour.

ICE-SKATING   Beijing has superb outdoor ice-skating in the winter at **Beihai Park** and the **Summer Palace** (with skate rental concessions on the shore). Indoor skating is available at the new (1998) **Ditan Ice Arena,** near the Ditan Park north gate, 14A Hepingli Zhongjie, Dongcheng District (☎ **010/6429-1618**), open daily from 9am to midnight. Admission is 25RMB ($3) per hour for adults, 15RMB ($1.90) for children. Beijing's newest skate rink is set to open in the new underground shopping center connecting **Traders Hotel** to **China World,** 1 Jianguomenwai Dajie, Chaoyang District.

ROCK CLIMBING   It costs only 15RMB ($1.80) per hour to climb the indoor walls at the **Qidagudu (Seven Ancient Cities) Climbing Club,** 183 Xuanwumen Dajie, Xuanwu District (☎ **010/6605-3563**), open daily from 10am to 9pm.

SPECTATOR SPORTS

The **Chinese National Basketball League (CNBL)** has been building a strong following across China since its inception in 1994. Each team is allowed to hire two

Go Fly a Kite

The Chinese have been flying their invention for over 2,000 years. The best places to buy and fly local kites are at the Summer Palace, Tiananmen Square, or in the parks, particularly Tiantan (Temple of Heaven).

foreign players (usually Americans). The **Beijing Ducks** play their home basketball games at Worker's Stadium, as does Beijing's popular **Guo An (National Guardians)** professional soccer team. Tickets for either home team can be purchased at the Worker's Stadium north gate or from **Li Sheng Selection,** 74A Wangfujing Dajie, Dongcheng District (☎ **010/6525-0581**), daily from 9am to 8:30pm. The soccer season runs from April through November, and the basketball season is November through April.

7

Beijing Strolls

Few world capitals are as frustrating, yet as fascinating, to walk as Beijing. The frustration comes first from the fact that much of the city is not meant for strolls: Although Beijing is flat, it is quite sprawling, and many of its long blocks are monotonous, ugly, and uninteresting. Yet there are fascinating walks, utterly unlike any found in the West. Some of these walks, however, are embedded with their own frustrations. Street signs are difficult to spot and interpret, addresses are omitted from buildings, and the sidewalks are not only crowded with other pedestrians, but with bicycle parking lots, construction sites, vendors and their carts, card players, laundry strung between doors and trees, and even a brazenly parked car or two. More than once you may find yourself walking in the streets and gutters just to get around these obstacles, yet it is just such obstacles that make a stroll through Beijing so fascinating. Crowded, dusty, odoriferous—these are city streets that still have character, streets where barbers with a chair, a water pan, and a straight razor line up at park entrances, where itinerant vendors from Tibet sell yak skulls, where even foot masseurs work the sidewalks.

Strolling Beijing is exhilarating, but also strangely tiring. Half a day's walk is usually plenty. You may return to your room feeling not so much exhausted as bruised—bruised by the polluted air and dust, the raw odors, the jarring sounds, the slamming crowds, and the grinding obstacle course. The strolls described in this chapter are the most fascinating and least grueling possible. Each of them also lends itself to bicycling. Renting a bike from your hotel is not necessarily the suicidal act it appears to be at first. Bike traffic is quite orderly in Beijing, the basic rule being that cars have the right of way even when they shouldn't, which is the basic rule of survival on foot as well. *Cars always have the right of way, even when you have a green light, so look both ways and always be prepared to yield.* Whether you walk or ride, adjust to the flow of Beijingers themselves. They know how and when to proceed across the intersections. Follow, don't lead, and slow down: Savor these walks through the capital of China.

Walking Tour 1
The Liulichang Antiques Street

Start: Intersection of Liulichang Xi Jie and Nanxinhua Jie (subway station: Hepingmen).

Finish: Qianmen Gate, south end of Tiananmen Square (subway station: Qianmen).

Time: 2 to 3 hours.

Best Time: Any weekday starting by 10am or 2:30pm.

Worst Times: Sundays are unbearably crowded, and Saturdays aren't much better. Avoid early mornings (before 10am) and from noon to 2pm (lunchtime). Most shops close at about 8:30pm. The Dazhalan neighborhood southwest of Tiananmen Square contains several of old Beijing's most historic streets. **Liulichang Street,** with a 500-year legacy dating back to the Ming Dynasty, was renovated in the 1980s to capture the look and atmosphere of Qing Dynasty Beijing with its finely decorated tile-roofed shop houses. Scholars and art connoisseurs frequented Liulichang in the old days. Now it is noted for its shops selling scrolls, rubbings, handmade paper, paintbrushes, ink sticks, jade carvings, and above all antiques. Liulichang runs about 6 blocks east and merges with **Dazhalan,** another old shopping street that has been converted into a cobblestoned pedestrian-only mall. Dazhalan terminates at **Zhubaoshi** Street, which runs north, parallel with Qianmen Dajie, into Qianmen (Front Gate) at Tiananmen Square. There are many pre-Revolutionary shops on Zhubaoshi and Dazhalan streets, including apothecaries selling traditional medicines. This stroll should give you the feel of Old Beijing's bustling commercial districts at a time when the emperor still ruled China from the nearby Forbidden City.

To begin, take a taxi or walk straight south from the Hepingmen subway station down Nanxinhua Jie to:

1. **Liulichang Culture Street West (Liulichang Xijie),** which presently occupies 3 blocks and is pushing ever westward. This end of Liulichang Jie (Glazed-Tile Factory Street) has plenty of tiny storefronts and vendors' stalls selling collectibles and art supplies, including the renowned:

2. **Rongbaozhai** (shop no. 19, north side, open daily from 9am to 6pm), the most prominent shop on the west section of Liulichang. It sells woodblock prints, copies of famous calligraphy, historic paintings (reproductions), and art supplies. It is one of Beijing's top art shops and well worth browsing. The shop at no. 34 (south side) carries old books, and the store next door (no. 36) has an interesting selection of Chinese musical instruments.

Backtrack to Nanxinhua Jie, where the tour began, cross it, and enter:

3. The **China Bookstore** (no. 57), which carries a hodgepodge of classical Chinese books and piles of foreign-language books on Chinese culture. It's a good place for book lovers to "get lost" in the stacks.

You've now crossed over to:

4. **Liulichang Culture Street East (Liulichang Dong Jie),** which runs for about a half mile. There are interesting old shops on either side, including:

5. **Jiguge** (nos. 132–136), which offers reproductions of famous Chinese paintings and scrolls, clay tomb figures, rubbings from stone tablets, and fine jade carvings. Jiguge also carries a wide range of Yixing teapots and teas, which you can sip at a table in its teahouse daily from 9am to 11pm.

6. **Zhongguo** (no. 115), selling antiquarian books.

7. **Wenshenzhai** (no. 92), once the chief supplier of fans and paper lanterns to the Forbidden City.

8. **Daiyuexuan** (no. 73), in the artist brush business for over 80 years.

Liulichang east ends at Yanshou Jie. Make a southward jog until you come to a gate and the start of a pedestrian-only cobbled street. This is:

9. **Dazhalan pedestrian shopping street (Dazhalan Jie,** also called Dashilan Jie). It is a bit more modern than Liulichang, but quite interesting. Relax and enjoy the window shopping.

    In the first block on the right side you'll come across, in order:

10. **Neiliansheng Shoe Store** (no. 34), established in 1853, and still the place to buy footwear.

11. **Tongrentang Traditional Medicine Shop** (no. 24), established in 1669, Beijing's most celebrated pharmacy.

    ☕ **TAKE A BREAK**   If you're ready for a rest, stop in for a cup of tea and a Chinese steamed pastry right next door to the traditional medicine store at the **Zhang Yi Yuan Tea Shop,** 22 Dazhalan Jie, open daily from 8am to 7pm.

    Just down the street is a real curiosity, the:

12. **Underground City.** At no. 18 Dazhalan Jie is an arrow pointing down to the Underground City, a vast labyrinth of tunnels built in the late 1950s as Beijing's underground air-raid shelter. It was built by hand. Take a peek. There are dozens of little shops and stands in the tunnel, as well an entire hotel.

    When you reemerge, you're nearly at the east end of Dazhalan. Don't miss its most famous store:

13. **Ruifuxiang Silk and Cotton Store,** established in 1893. It's on the north side. Within its gaudy marble entrance is a vast selection of silks and clothing. Once the prime outlet for Qing Dynasty royalty and rich merchants, it's open daily from 8:30am to 9:30pm.

    Next door is the:

14. **Qianmen Women's Clothing Store,** with suits, blouses, and a selection of wool and silk fabrics that can be custom-tailored. Open daily from 8:30am to 9pm.

    On the south side of the street is the:

15. **Liubiju Pickle Shop,** still going quite strong after 400 years.

    This marks the end of the Dazhalan pedestrian mall. Make an immediate left turn (north) up the side street known as:

16. **Zhubaoshi Jie,** which means "Jewelry Street." This street was the gateway to a major brothel and the theater district up until Liberation (1949). Today it is a major outdoor bazaar of stands and carts selling inexpensive clothing, collectibles, and edibles. (Although few tourists are made ill by the food here, I advise against partaking, as the quality is not up to the standards of hotels and restaurants.)

    Ahead looms:

17. **Qianmen (Front Gate).** North of the Zhubaoshi bazaar is the traffic arc that leads to the south end of Tiananmen Square. To the northeast you'll see the old Front Gate (Qianmen, officially known as Zhengyangmen), a towering remnant of the city wall, through which the emperors passed on their annual procession from the Forbidden City to the Temple of Heaven. You can ascend the tower at two points for excellent views of Tiananmen Square to the north and the Dazhalan District you've just strolled to the southwest. There's also a fine photographic exhibition of the streets and walls of old Beijing.

    ☕ **WINDING DOWN**   From Qianmen Gate you can go in any direction. The world's largest **KFC** is a block west on Qianmen Xi Dajie. A few blocks south, at 32 Qianmen Dajie (the old Imperial Way), is the city's most famous

Walking Tour—The Liulichang Antiques Street

1. Liulichang Culture Street West
2. Rongbaozhai
3. China Bookstore
4. Liulichang Culture Street East
5. Jiguge
6. Zhongguo
7. Wenshenzhai
8. Diayuexuan
9. Dazhalan pedestrian shopping street
10. Neiliansheng Shoe Store
11. Tongrentang Traditional Medicine Shop
12. Underground City
13. Ruifuxiang Silk and Cotton Store
14. Qianmen Women's Clothing Store
15. Liubiju Pickle Shop
16. Zhubaoshi Jie
17. Qianmen (Front Gate)

Beijing duck restaurant, **Quanjude Kaoyadian,** open daily from 10:30am to 1:30pm for lunch and 4:30 to 8:30pm for dinner, the perfect ending to a day on foot in old Beijing.

Walking Tour 2
Back Lakes Ramble

Start: Huifeng Temple, Xihai Lake (subway station: Jishuitan).
Finish: Prince Gong's Mansion.
Time: 4 to 6 hours.
Best Times: Sunday mornings (for the street markets), but any nice morning will do.
Worst Times: Mondays, when some of the museums and sites are closed. Don't start later than noon, in order to enjoy the lake scenery.

The three Back Lakes (Shi Sha Hai)—Xihai, Houhai, and Qianhai—were once the exclusive beachfront property of China's Qing Dynasty royalty, who alone could own and maintain houses here. The three Back Lakes were in turn connected to three lakes immediately to the south—Beihai, Zhonghai, and Nanhai—adjacent to the Forbidden City. Barges once used this string of lakes to transport grain from the Great Canal to the Imperial Court. Today, the Back Lakes neighborhoods teem with old Beijing's quickly disappearing, colorful *hutongs* (alleyways) and *siheyuans* (courtyard houses) (see "Hutongs & Siheyuans" in chapter 6, "Exploring Beijing"). The shores of these lakes are gorgeous in the summer and dazzling when frozen over in the winter, making them a prime spot for strolling and exploring by bicycle.

This Back Lakes ramble takes in the beautiful lakeshores, a seldom-visited island temple, one of the nine ancient gates to the city, the former residence of Soong Ching-ling (Song Qing Ling Guzhu), a Buddhist shrine, two exceptional outdoor markets, and the garden estate of a Qing Dynasty prince, with options along the way if you want to keep rambling.

Begin a few blocks east of the Jishuita subway station along the south side of the busy Second Ring Road at:

1. **Huifeng Temple (Hifeng Si),** on the northern tip of the northernmost of the Back Lakes, Xihai. This forgotten temple has recently been restored. Located on a steep, rocky islet, it's the ideal place to survey the lake scenery to the south.

   Resume walking east on the Second Ring Road until you spot the:

2. **Deshengmen Arrow Tower,** an impressive fragment of the city wall. The tow-ering gate and guardhouse (with archers' windows) of Deshengmen is one of Bei-jing's nine Ming gates. Cross over at the overpass to the tower where a courtyard house contains an ancient coin museum (Gudai Qianbi Zhanlanguan) open daily from 9am to 5pm (admission 4RMB/50¢). There's a coin and open-air antiques market here, too. Upstairs in the tower are exhibits on the history of Beijing's architecture and balcony views of the Back Lakes (open from Tuesday to Sunday 9am to 4pm).

   Cross the Second Ring Road directly south and follow:

3. **Deshengmen Street (Deshengmennei Dajie),** the main street leading to the bridge between the two northernmost Back Lakes. This is an interesting old street to stroll. Keep to the right where it soon branches off (Gulou Xi Dajie is the big street heading west). Deshengmen is a strictly Chinese street, with plenty

Walking Tour—Back Lakes Ramble

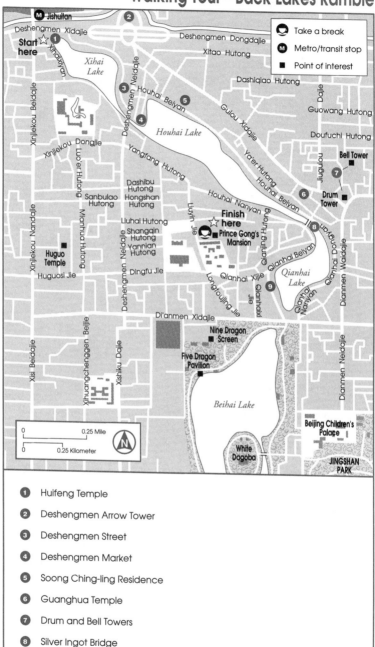

1. Huifeng Temple
2. Deshengmen Arrow Tower
3. Deshengmen Street
4. Deshengmen Market
5. Soong Ching-ling Residence
6. Guanghua Temple
7. Drum and Bell Towers
8. Silver Ingot Bridge
9. Lotus Flower Market

of local flavor. Cross to the east side and walk south to the bridge dividing Xihai Lake from Houhai Lake.

To your left is a fascinating outdoor market:

4. **Deshengmen Market,** which runs along both sides of the narrow passage between these two lakes and can be hopelessly crowded, particularly on a Sunday morning when the market is at its best. Fresh produce, spices, and meats are the main wares, but there's always an odd assortment here (including roving vendors hawking white toilet seats). Many of the vendors sell from cases or drums on the back of their bicycles. This is not a touristy market.

Work your way east, then north along the shore of Houhai Lake, heading toward:

5. **Soong Ching-ling Residence (Song Qing Ling Guzhu),** which is located a few blocks down the northeast shore of Houhai Lake at 46 Houhai Beiyan. There's no sign at the entrance in English, just a big red sign in Chinese. The grounds consist of a pretty classical garden and a museum filled with interesting photos and belongings of this legendary Soong sister, who married Sun Yat-sen and stayed in communist China while her sister married Chiang Kai-shek and fled to Taiwan. Ching-ling resided in this palatial estate from 1963 until her death in 1981. Open daily from 9am to 4:30pm; admission is 8RMB ($1) (see "Museums & Mansions," in chapter 6, "Exploring Beijing").

Continue south down the lakeshore to:

6. **Guanghua Temple (Guanghua Si),** a half-mile from the Soong estate. It is an active temple now, with monks in residence, and worth a brief tour.

At this point you can make an optional detour eastward to the:

7. **Drum and Bell Towers (Gulou and Zhonglou),** visible on the horizon and just a few blocks from Houhai Lake via a convoluted hutong (at the intersection of Gulou Dong Dajie and Dianmenwai Dajie). The Drum Tower (described in chapter 6) can be climbed. The Bell Tower is directly north, with the alley between enclosing an interesting market where you can buy street snacks from vendors (but be aware that hygiene and sanitation standards are dangerously low in the streets).

Retrace your path to the lakeshore and prepare to cross:

8. **Silver Ingot Bridge (Yin Ding Qiao),** which separates Houhai (Back Lake) from Qianhui (Front Lake). If the day is clear and you can see as far as the Western Hills, you will be enjoying one of the Eight Grand Views of Beijing, as enumerated by Emperor Qianlong in the 18th century. This white marble bridge has stood here for centuries, although the latest version is the work of modern masons (1984).

Cross the bridge and stick to the winding road along the west shore of Qianhui Lake until you come to the:

9. **Lotus Flower Market (Lianghua Shichang),** which is a lively market lying on the southwest shore of Qianhai Lake. This is also one of the prettiest areas in the Back Lakes region. There's shade under the willows, summer lotus near the lake shore, snack and souvenir vendors aplenty, and in the evenings a night market of hot foods (eat at your own risk; you probably won't get sick, but then again you might) and amateur opera singers.

☕ **WINDING DOWN**   Northwest of the Lotus Flower Market is **Prince Gong's Mansion (Gong Wang Fu),** 17 Qianhai Xi Lu, which is open daily 9am to 5pm. It's the most lavish of the courtyard houses in the Back Lakes region, and its pavilions and rockeries are a page out of imperial Beijing, as are the Back

Lakes themselves. Prince Gong's Mansion is described in chapter 6, and the lovely courtyard restaurant adjacent to it, the **Sichuan Fandian,** 14 Liuyin Jie, is reviewed in chapter 5, "Dining"—it's a fine place to conclude a Back Lakes ramble with a fiery lunch or dinner.

Walking Tour 3
The Imperial Parks, from Beihai to Jingshan

Start: Round City, south entrance of Beihai Park.
Finish: Prospect Hill, Jingshan Park.
Time: 3 to 4 hours.
Best Times: Weekday mornings or summer afternoons.
Worst Times: Weekends can be hideously crowded, particularly Sundays. If you do go on a weekend, go early.

Many visitors get only as near as the Forbidden City's northern gate to two of Beijing's loveliest parks, Beihai and Jingshan. It's a pity. If time allows for a half-day park stroll, these two are the prime candidates. Jingshan (Prospect Hill) Park, also called Meishan (Coal Hill), is literally at the back door of the Forbidden City; its present heights were created from the soil scooped out to create the imperial moat. It is a mountain park made by hand with a superb view of central Beijing.

Virtually next door to Jingshan Park is Beijing's most beautiful urban park, Beihai. Its lovely artificial lake is 8 centuries old and was the site of Kublai Khan's palace. Marco Polo walked its shores. Emperor Yongle, builder of the Forbidden City, enlarged Beihai, and the Qing Dynasty elaborated its beauty. Empress Dowager Cixi kept a garden on its shore for picnics. These days Beihai is a favorite of locals year-round.

Begin this walk at the south entrance to Beihai Park, within a block of the northwest corner of the Forbidden City, on the east side of the marble Rainbow Bridge that dates from the Ming Dynasty. Buy your Beihai Park admission ticket (10RMB/$1.25) at the booth northeast of the big bridge and enter the:

1. Round City (Tuan Cheng), the site of the barracks of the royal troops during the reign of the Khans. Here, in the Hall of Receiving Light (Cheng Guang Dian), is a large jade Buddha, a gift from Burma to Empress Dowager Cixi. In a pavilion in the courtyard is Beihai's oldest relic, an enormous Jade Jar (weighing more than 3 tons), thought to have been used by Kublai Khan himself.

Proceed northward through the large ornate gate (*pailou*) and cross the marble bridge to:

2. Hortensia Isle (Qiong Hua Dao), also known as Jade Isle. You'll see Beihai's famous landmark rising from the center of the island, the **White Dagoba (Bai Ta),** which can be explored on your return to the island after you circle the lake.

Bear right along the eastern shore of the island and walk north to the eastern entrance of Beihai Park. At the large ornate gate known as **Nirvana Pailou,** turn right, cross the bridge to the east, and then follow the path north to a cluster of buildings on the right known as:

3. Hao and Pu (Hao Pu Jian), built in 1757 by the emperor as a garden within a garden. The rockeries here are exquisite, as is the pond, pavilion, and seven-arched bridge at its center. Empress Dowager Cixi would come here to hear musical performances.

Pass the boat houses on the eastern lakeshore as you head another 400 yards to the:

4. **Studio of the Painted Boat (Hua Fang Zhai)**, also built by Qing Emperor Qianlong. The square stone pool here is lined with corridors where the French army bivouacked in its 1900 siege of Beijing.

   Proceed north past a large amusement park to the:

5. **Altar of Silkworms (Can Tan)**, an altar for performing rites to the Goddess of Silkworms. You have nearly reached the northeast tip of the lake.

   Cross the bridge and turn left, heading south along the northwest shore to the:

6. **Studio of the Serene Mind (Jing Xin Zhai)**, a beautiful garden where China's last emperor, Pu Yi, composed his memoirs. The halls, courtyards, pools, and rock gardens are quiet and relaxing.

   TAKE A BREAK   If you're ready for a rest, there's a teahouse in the **Room for Roasting Tea (Bei Cha Wu)**, at the eastern edge of the Studio of the Serene Mind complex.

   Return to the northwest lakeshore and follow it south to the:

7. **Hall of the Heavenly Kings (Tian Wang Dian)**, once a Ming-era studio for printing Buddhist sutras (collections of Buddhist holy writings).

   Behind Tian Wang Dian and to the east is the 83-foot-long:

8. **Nine Dragon Screens (Jiu Long Bi)**, decorated on both sides in colorful glazed-tile dragons and built by Emperor Qianlong as a wall to ward off evil spirits heading to Beihai Lake.

   Farther south along the western shore are the:

9. **Hall of Pleasant Snow (Kuai Xue Tang)** and the **Iron Spirit Screen (Tie Ying Bi)**, a dark rock slab carved on both sides with a mythological beast during the Yuan Dynasty.

   Pleasure boats depart from the docks near here (on the north side of the **Five Dragon Pavilions**) for the 5-minute voyage back to Hortensia Isle, but before you board, continue due east to inspect:

10. **Little Western Heaven (Xiao Xi Tian)**, a 1770 shrine to Guanyin, Goddess of Mercy. This square pagoda with a moat and four guard towers was restored in the 1980s, and it is magnificent, the largest pagoda complex of its kind in China.

    Return to the lakeshore and buy a boat ticket (departures every 30 minutes) for the trip to the:

11. **Fangshan Imperial Restaurant** in the complex of buildings known as the **Hall of Rippling Waters (Yi Lan Tang)**, on the north shore of the isle at the foot of the White Dagoba. Treat yourself to a set lunch or dinner at Fangshan, which was staffed by Forbidden City chefs when it first opened at Beihai in 1926 (see review in chapter 5).

    After a royal repast, set out to explore the delights of Hortensia Isle itself, turning left (west) under the north shore veranda to the tower at its western end, the:

12. **Pavilion of Shared Coolness (Fen Liang Ge)**. A stone path leads up the steep hill toward the White Dagoba, coming first to the:

13. **Plate for Gathering Dew (Cheng Lu Pan)**, a whimsical bronze statue of an old emperor gathering dew (thought to be an elixir of immortality).

    Higher up still is the:

14. **Tower for Reading the Classics (Yue Gu Lou)**, which contains nearly 500 specimens of ancient calligraphy carved on stone tablets.

Walking Tour—The Imperial Parks, from Beihai to Jingshan

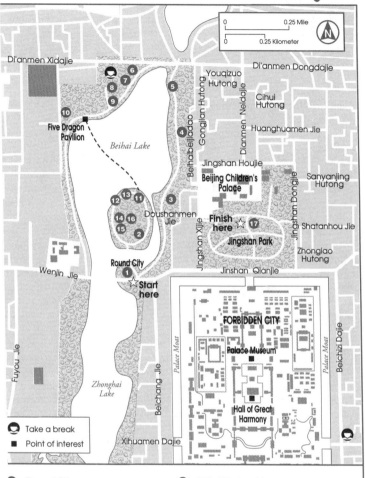

Take a break
■ **Point of interest**

1. Round City
2. Hortensia Isle
3. Hao and Pu
4. Studio of the Painted Boat
5. Altar of Silkworms
6. Studio of the Serene Mind
7. Hall of the Heavenly Kings
8. Nine Dragon Screens
9. Hall of Pleasant Snow and the Iron Spirit Screen
10. Little Western Heaven
11. Fangshan Imperial Restaurant/ Hall of Rippling Waters
12. Pavilion of Shared Coolness
13. Plate for Gathering Dew
14. Tower for Reading the Classics
15. Temple of Eternal Peace
16. White Dagoba
17. Pavilion of Eternal Spring

. . . I felt giddy, for there is nothing, not even Versailles, which evokes such a sense of majesty, of earthly power, of wealth, of pomp, as the imperial palaces of Beijing.
—Curzio Malaparte, *Viaggio in Russia e in Cina,* 1958

Turn to the south and enter the:

15. Temple of Eternal Peace (Yong An Si), a Lama Buddhist complex that has been nicely restored.

The temple courtyards lead due north to the summit, where you'll at last reach the:

16. White Dagoba (Bai Ta), the crowning glory of Beihai Park. Built in 1651 in honor of a visit by the Dalai Lama, it soars 118 feet above the man-made hilltop.

Retrace your steps southward or pick your way carefully northeastward down the maze of rock pillars. Your goal is the east entrance, where you can exit Beihai Park and walk across to the western entrance of Jingshan Hill and climb to the:

17. Pavilion of Eternal Spring (Wan Chung Ting), located on the central peak. Jingshan contains five peaks that look down on the Forbidden City (and shield it from evil spirits flying down from the north). Each peak once had a pavilion and a golden image of the Buddha, but the statues are gone and only this central pavilion is now favored for its extraordinary panoramas. Relax here after a day in the imperial parks, sit on the balcony ledge with the locals, buy a soda from the concessionaire in the pavilion (which still has its dazzling painted ceiling), and enjoy the famous view.

☕ **WINDING DOWN**   If you have any walking energy left, exit Jingshan Park to the south or east, skirt the northeast corner of the Forbidden City, and head south, following the moat down Beichzi Dajie to **The Courtyard** (95 Donghuamen Lu) for a fabulous dinner or a drink, taking in yet another exceptional view of the Forbidden City, this time from ground level. The Courtyard is reviewed in chapter 5.

Walking Tour 4
Wangfujing Shopping Circle

Start: Beijing Hotel.
Finish: Oriental Plaza.
Time: 2 to 4 hours.
Best Times: Weekday mornings or late afternoons
Worst Times: Weekends and evenings are jammed with shoppers. Lunchtime any day (from 11:30am to 2pm) is also crowded.

Wangfujing is the capital's number-one shopping street, but it is worth strolling even if you aren't interested in buying a single thing. The newest and literally the oldest human enterprises in China's capital are right along Wangfujing. All of commercial China seems to be encapsulated within a few crowded blocks, too, with old silk shops and open-air markets shoulder-to-shoulder with ultramodern shopping plazas. Situated just a few blocks east of the Forbidden City, Wangfujing was a favorite residential neighborhood of the rich and the royals during the Ming and

Walking Tour—Wangfujing Shopping Circle

Legend:
- ⊠ Post office
- ☕ Take a break
- ■ Point of interest

Map labels:
Wusi Dajie · Dongsi Xidajie · Chaoyangmen Neidajie · Cuihua Hutong · Dongsi Mosque · Dongchang Hutong · Capital Theatre · Qihelou Jie · Lishi Hutong · Daboge Hutong · Holiday Inn Crowne Plaza · Dengshikou Xijie · Dengshikou Dajie · FORBIDDEN CITY · Baishu Hutong · St. Joseph's Church · Ganyu Hutong · Ganmian Hutong · Xitangzi Hutong · Bank of China · Donghuamen Dajie · Dong'anmen Dajie · Jinyu Hutong · Chinese Children's Theatre · Calchang Hutong · Jixiang Theatre · Meridian Gate · Daruanfu Hutong · Datianshuijing Hutong · Waijiaobu Jie · Working People's Cultural Palace · Xizongbu Hutong · Taxi Station · Tiananmen Gate · Xiagongfu Jie · Start here · Finish here · Qingyi Theatre · Dongchang'an Jie · TIANANMEN SQUARE · Museum of Chinese Revolution & History · Zhengyi Lu · Taijichang Dajie

Street names (vertical): Beichizi Dajie · Beiheyan Dajie · Donghuangchengga Nanjie · Fujiang Hutong · Wangfujing Dajie · Dongsi Nandajie · Nanchizi Dajie · Pudusiki Xiang · Nanheyan Dajie · Chenguang Jie · Wangfujing Dajie · Dongdan Beidajie

Scale: 0 — .25 Mile · 0 — .25 Kilometer

1. Beijing Hotel
2. Wangfujing Department Store (no. 255)
3. Sun Dong An Plaza (no. 138)
4. Foreign Language Bookstore (no. 235)
5. Jeans West, Kodak, and China Silk Shop
6. China Art Gallery
7. Playboy, Lotteria, Red Taps, Patty, Bossina, and Billy
8. Jianhua Fur and Leather Store
9. Palace Hotel
10. Hutong markets
11. Stamp street and coin market
12. Capital Hospital
13. The Agricultural Bank of China shopping arcade
14. Oriental Plaza

Qing dynasties and was named for the well that supplied the mansions of ten Ming Dynasty princes here. By the end of the 19th century, it was beginning to attract resident foreigners as well, including an influential correspondent for the *London Times* named Morrison, which became the street's name for a time among Westerners. Tradesmen set up their shops on Wangfujing and the attached *hutongs* (alleys), but it was not until 1928 that Wangfujing was paved.

Wangfujing is not only paved these days, it's transformed. Much of the retail district outlined by Wangfujing and the parallel shopping street to the east, Dongdan, is being rapidly modernized. How long the small art galleries and brush stores, the optical shops and the silk stores, survive is anyone's guess.

Our walking tour is a circle—north up Wangfujing and south down Dongdan—beginning and ending in the historic Beijing Hotel on Chang'an Avenue. It takes in old and new shops, cafes, open-air markets, religious shrines, art galleries and museums, historic spots, and even archaeological sites, starting with the:

1. **Beijing Hotel (Beijing Fandian)**, which was opened as the Grand Hotel de Pekin in 1917 under French management. Enter at the east wing, on the Wangfujing Dajie, and wander through the lobby, from the old grand piano to the shopping arcades. Unfortunately, much of the middle section of the hotel was recently remodeled, but try to take a peek at the grand (very grand) old ballrooms at the top of the lobby staircases.

Outside, turn east and go up the first street on your left, Wangfujing Dajie. In the first block on your left (west side of the street), there used to be plenty of photo shops, but it is undergoing reconstruction and has no doubt been transformed.

With any luck, farther up the street you'll still find the landmark:

2. **Wangfujing Department Store** (no. 255). Aging, sprawling, and rumored to be on the verge of a face-lift, this was once Beijing's big-time department store. It's now a fascinating throwback to the 1970s and 1980s, chock-full of Chinese products for the Chinese consumer.

By way of abrupt contrast, at the next cross street (called Dong'anmen Dajie to the east, Jinyu Hutong to the west), head over to the other side of Wangfujing, and enter a 21st-century department store:

3. **Sun Dong An Plaza** (no. 138), Beijing's glitziest shopping plaza, where you can wander for hours among its seven levels and multiple atriums, complete with glass elevators and chrome escalators. Bossini, London Fog, Burberrys, Flying Scotsmen? They're all here, along with a Mickey Mouse logo store (Toonsland), a Nike store, a McDonalds, and an espresso bar named Boodles. (There's also a Bank of China branch on the first floor, open weekdays only.) The supermarket, electronics, and large appliances are in the basement, and deeper in the labyrinth are eight movie theaters.

Back out on the streets, convinced that Beijing has indeed caught up with the consuming nations of the West, cross back over to the west side of Wangfujing and head a half block north to the:

4. **Foreign Language Bookstore** (no. 235), located on the floor above **Dunkin' Donuts.** This is a must for anyone interested in books, since it houses Beijing's largest selection of English-language materials on several floors.

As you continue north, look across Wangfujing. You can catch sight of a massive Catholic Cathedral, St. Joseph's (Dongtang), which looks abandoned but holds masses every Sunday in Chinese and Latin. Meanwhile, on the west side of the street you pass:

5. **Jeans West, Kodak, China Silk Shop** (no. 133, quite small), and a tea shop at no. 119 with a nice selection of pots. This brings you to a second major intersection, **Dengshikou** street, with the Holiday Inn Crowne Plaza Hotel and the massive One World Department Store on opposite corners. It's time to:

☕ **TAKE A BREAK**   Wangfujing is filled with cafes and restaurants, inside and outside major hotels, but one bright new spot to pause is **Timeless Medley,** in the basement of the Tianlun Dynasty Hotel, 50 Wangfujing Dajie, open daily from 11am to 1am. Choose from more than 200 local snacks and enjoy the decor (famous Chinese movie scenes) in what's described as Beijing's first cafe to combine film and food culture.

In the final block of your stroll up Wangfujing, you'll pass some new Western-style cafes (Boulevard Bistro, Red Lion Restaurant) and two Beijing institutions (the very strange subterranean **Banpo Primitive Hot Pot Beer Hut,** 26 Wangfujing Dajie, and the **Capital Theater,** 22 Wangfujing Dajie, which sometimes stages Western dramas). At the big intersection with Wusi Dajie, visit the:

6. **China Art Gallery (Zhongguo Meishuguan),** 1 Wusi Dajie, which is the national art gallery of China and always worth a visit.

Dongdan Street runs parallel to Wangfujing on the east and offers plenty of shopping, too. Walk the long block from the China Art Gallery east to Dongsi Nan Dajie, turn right, and you'll be inundated with Beijing's latest in boutiques, bars, and bistros, including:

7. **Playboy, Lotteria, Red Taps, Patty, Bossina,** and **Billy.** These or their trendy replacements dominate the first block south down Dongdan. There are used bookstores on both sides of the Billy jeans shop (both carrying some titles in English).

Another long block down the street, on the northeast corner of Jinyu Hutong, is:

8. **Jianhua Fur and Leather Store.** Speaking of fashion, you might want to check out the latest in *qipao* fashions at **Mujianliao Chinese Clothing,** 46 Dongdan Bei Dajie. The *qipao* is the bright silk and satin dress with the slit up the side, a Manchu-inspired fashion that was the rage in 1920s China, banned in the politically correct Mao era, and now the basis for new fashions in the new China.

It's now high time to take a slight detour west on Jinyu Hutong to the luxurious:

9. **Palace Hotel,** 8 Jinyu Hutong, with a waterfall in the marble lobby (which looks like it was designed by Frank Lloyd Wright). The basement has the highest-end shopping in China, with the nation's first Armani, to go along with Cartier, Hermes, and others.

The lobby is a refreshing spot for tea or coffee before returning to Dongdan, which grows more interesting with the:

10. **Hutong markets** running east, with vendors selling collectibles and edibles from their carts or blankets spread out on the sidewalks. (Eat at your own risk here; the food in this market is not subject to stringent hygiene inspection.) The east side of Dongdan also features a row of six portable pay toilets and a wedding shop where brides and grooms are coifed and outfitted for a Western-style ceremony.

Back on the west side of the street there's a:

11. **Stamp street and coin market** in full swing on one hutong, next door to a tape and disc music store named **FUN.**

Of an entirely different nature is the entrance to the:

12. Capital Hospital (Peking Union Medical Hospital, *Xiehe Yiyuan*), with an emergency clinic for foreign patients on the sixth floor. Part of this medical complex is in the mansion of a Qing Dynasty prince, part in a modern high-rise. The hospital was founded in 1915 and underwritten for decades by American millionaire John D. Rockefeller.

The final commercial enterprise on Dongdan these days is:

13. The Agricultural Bank of China shopping arcade, with shopfronts for Red Taps (boasting "The Original Spirit of American Jeans") and a Hush Puppies outlet.

To close this shopping circle, head west to the Beijing Hotel on Chang'an Avenue or through the newest shopping plaza-cum-office complex (built in 1999 on the site of the short-lived "world's largest McDonald's"), the:

14. Oriental Plaza, where you can take a look at the archeological display in the basement. It was here, in the heart of the capital's retail center, that the oldest human settlement in Beijing was discovered, a result of the construction dig. Even 20,000 years ago, it seems, there were residents of Wangfujing, perhaps lured here by the shopping.

Shopping 8

Until the economic reforms took hold in China in the 1980s and kicked into high gear in the 1990s, Beijing could not be described as a shopper's city. Now it can at least offer an interesting variety of goods, from local and regional specialties to international luxuries. The focus of most travelers is on uniquely Chinese products, and they are now widely available at private as well as government-run department stores and shops, at sidewalk stalls as well as hotel kiosks, and in open-air free markets where bargaining and caution are the bywords. Shopping, in other words, has become fun in Beijing, after decades of dreary and monotonous retailing. The Chinese enjoy shopping immensely, and they are known as careful buyers and master sellers. Expect to find elbow-to-elbow shopping at some sites, and be prepared to head into the fray with your commercial wits sharpened. Language won't be a problem. English may be the world's second language, but shopping is universal.

1 The Shopping Scene

Western-style shopping malls are beginning to flex their muscles in Beijing, where they are replacing the traditional shopfronts, Chinese department stores, and alley markets. Even the new, privately run stores on major shopping streets tend to be versions of the boutiques and specialty outlets familiar to shoppers in the West. But there are still plenty of open-air markets and street vendors offering traditional arts and crafts, collectibles, and clothing, usually at prices far below those in the big plazas and modern stores. If you're looking for souvenirs or Chinese treasures, check out the prices and selection at hotel shops, the Friendship Store (see box below), and modern shopping malls first; then see what's available on the streets and at markets.

BEIJING'S BEST BUYS

Beijing is known for selection and low prices in **cashmeres** and **silks** (both off the bolt and in finished garments). Jewelry can also be a bargain, particularly jade and **freshwater pearls,** but bargaining and a critical eye are required.

One of the most popular gifts is a **chop** (also called a seal), which is a small, stone, custom-engraved stamp with your name (in English, Chinese, or both), used with an ink pad to print your ID on paper. Chops can be created the same day or overnight, sometimes even while you wait. Prices depend on the stone you select and the skill of the engraver. Among other popular crafts made in Beijing are **cloisonné, lacquerware, porcelains,** and **carved jade.** Prices vary considerably. The best rule is to find something you truly like, and then consider how much it is worth to you.

Artworks are also abundant, often in the form of a **hand-painted scroll** or a **rubbing** taken from a carved stone tablet. Again, buy what you truly like, since these works are priced across the spectrum, from 100RMB to 1,000RMB ($12.50 to $125) and up. Shop around.

The market in **antiques** is vast. A red wax seal must be attached to any item created between 1795 and 1949 that is taken out of China; older items cannot be exported. Many hotel shops and modern department stores will send purchases to your home, and the Friendship Store has a highly efficient shipping department.

Packaged **tea** is a good buy in Beijing, but **electronics** and other high-tech goods are not, although **small appliances** such as razors can be found in department stores for low prices.

Among **folk arts and crafts,** there are good buys in paper kites, hand-stitched embroideries (including sheets and pillowcases), teapots, bamboo items, fans, chopsticks, and decorative ornaments (excellent for small Christmas gifts). These items are often sold in markets and on the sidewalks by itinerant vendors.

Collectibles include Mao buttons and posters, old Chinese coins, small religious statues, old wood carvings, and painted plates—all priced lowest at markets and stands.

Furniture in traditional Chinese styles can be purchased or custom-ordered at several factories, and the prices are good, although shipping can add considerably to the bill.

THE ART OF BARGAINING

It helps to know the going prices for items you're interested in. The Friendship Store is worth scoping out with prices in mind, since it sets the standard price for most items. Also check the prices in hotel shops and at the new megamalls. This will give you a notion of the high-end price. Then see if you can beat the price elsewhere.

Street markets usually have the lowest prices. For example, at the Lido Market (see below) porcelain chopstick rests start at 5RMB (65¢), sandalwood fans at 10RMB ($1.25), silk shirts at 100RMB ($12.50), quilts at 150RMB ($18), and ecru tablecloths at 200RMB ($25).

Haggling is not done at government-run stores, most hotel stalls, or modern shops, but it is expected on the street and in small private stores. A good rule of thumb is to offer no more than half the quoted price and not to accept the first counteroffer. Try to reach a compromise. Walking away with a firm but polite "no" often brings about a more favorable price. Remember that locals are demon shoppers who scrutinize each potential purchase and exercise mountains of patience before making a buy.

Shopping Hours

Most stores are open daily from 8am to 8pm (even later in the summer). Weekends (especially Sundays) are the most hectic days to shop, since most Beijingers make their purchases then and thousands spend these days off window-shopping.

One note of caution: The open-air markets that line the entrances to major tourist sites generally charge extravagant prices and offer mass-produced kitsch of shoddy quality, including outright fakes. **Jade** is particularly difficult to evaluate and prone to being fake, so buy only what you like and don't pay much.

BEIJING'S TOP SHOPPING AREAS

Beijing's top shopping area is downtown on **Wangfujing** and **Dongdan** streets (described in chapter 7, "Beijing Strolls"), where the most modern and the most traditional modes of retailing commingle.

Equally popular among locals is **Xidan Street** running north from Chang'an Avenue. Xidan is located about a mile west of Tiananmen Square (near the Xidan subway stop). It's lined with clothing stalls, music stores, and a fascinating mall, the **Xidan Shopping Center,** a four-story emporium and department store. Two *hutongs* (alleyways) immediately south of this shopping center are filled with stalls, and across the street is yet another new shopping center (Xidan International Mansion) that includes a Pierre Cardin outlet. Xidan also has a branch of the Foreign Language Bookstore and will be the site of at least two new megamalls by the year 2000, including one called Times Square.

Another major shopping street is **Jianguomenwai Dajie,** several miles east of the Forbidden City, stretching from the China World Trade Center to the **Friendship Store** and **Silk Alley.** Many of Beijing's top international hotels are situated here as well. The Friendship Store is Beijing's number-one outlet for souvenir shoppers, while Silk Alley is the most popular open-air market among tourists.

A strong mix of modern malls, department stores, private storefronts, and open-air markets is located northeast of city center along the **Third Ring Road North** where the Hilton, Sheraton Great Wall, and Kempinski hotels are clustered. It is an easy walk from this sector of the Third Ring Road southwest to the adjoining **Sanlitun** neighborhood and **Gonrentiyuchang Beilu (Worker's Stadium Road North),** a street with an excellent assortment of small shops and big stores.

Last but not least is the **Liulichang/Dazhalan** culture street and pedestrian mall southwest of Tiananmen Square off Qianmen Dajie (see chapter 7), Beijing's best shopping district for antiques, arts and crafts, and traditional merchandise.

2 Markets & Bazaars

Beijing's most interesting shopping experiences are to be had in its street markets and alley bazaars. Curios, crafts, collectibles, antiques, jewelry, and coins are all here for those not afraid to bargain hard. Most of these markets are outdoor affairs where the vendors pitch their stalls and awnings on both sides of a narrow passageway (often a *hutong*), and customers squeeze their way through. Perhaps the most common items you'll find in the markets these days are not silk, souvenirs, or crafts, but designer-label clothing, much of it knockoffs (copies) with the upscale labels sewn in, although some items are factory seconds or overruns (sometimes smuggled out of legitimate brand-name factories and sold on the side). Many of the markets also sell fresh produce, seafood, spices, and other consumables to residents, along with snacks and drinks. These markets and bazaars are quite colorful and the prices can be low, but they are also attractive to pickpockets, so don't bring a purse or

One-Stop Gift Shopping at the Friendship Store

It's easier to shop for gifts, souvenirs, and Chinese treasures at the Friendship Store than anywhere else in Beijing. The merchandise is targeted at foreign travelers, the selection is good, and the prices (no bargaining allowed) are high enough to ensure quality, while generally lower than in the high-end hotel shops and megamalls. Start here to get an overview of what's available in Beijing at a fair price, shop the streets and malls, and then return to make those last-minute purchases.

Friendship stores began as outlets exclusively for foreigners in China (at one time, no local Chinese were allowed inside), but they now compete freely with department stores, shopping plazas, private stores, and street vendors. Beyond its wide selection, quality goods, and convenience, the Beijing Friendship Store has a foreign exchange counter and honors credit cards. It also has an overseas shipping department to handle those big purchases. One old-fashioned procedure remains: At most counters, the clerk hands you a slip for what you've decided to purchase. You must take the slip to a cashier in a nearby kiosk, pay there, and take your receipt back to the clerk to claim your merchandise (a system that keeps many people employed, it seems).

The ground floor sells sundry items, from Chinese musical instruments to home appliances. There are Chinese kites, papercuts, teas, medicines, watches, and porcelains. Near the back is a section devoted to English-language books, magazines, and international newspapers. To the east is a supermarket, carpet store, and Chinese furniture showroom. Escalators on the west wing lead to three more floors. The second floor has a large selection of clothing for adults and children (cottons, silks, brocades, and cashmeres). The third floor is crammed with gifts, including cloisonné, lacquerware, jade, silver, and freshwater pearls. The fourth floor handles artworks (scrolls and paintings), crafts (carved screens and opera masks), and antiques.

In other words, you can find most of the items that foreigners coming to China dream of buying. Even the entrance has a Western flair, flanked by Dairy Queen, Baskin Robbins, and Dunkin' Donuts. The **Beijing Friendship Store** (☎ 010/6500-3311), a frequent stop for group tours and hotel shuttle buses, is located at 17 Jianguomenwai Dajie, a 20- to 30-minute walk due west of the Forbidden City. It's open daily from 9am to 8:30pm.

wallet and keep all your valuables in a concealed pouch or money belt. And speaking of valuables, these market vendors are seldom, if ever, equipped to deal with credit cards. Cash is the sole means of exchange.

The most popular market is **Silk Alley,** while the most interesting is **Panjiayuan** (also known variously as the "Dirt Market," the "Sunday Market," or the "Ghost Market"), but there are many others worth browsing.

SILK ALLEY   Silk Alley Market (Xiushui Shichang), at Jianguomenwai Dajie and Xiushui Jie (the first alley west of Dongdaqiao Lu), is a half-mile east of the Friendship Store, in the Chaoyang District. The south entrance looks to be nothing more than a hole in the wall where a storefront might have once stood, but this is the gate to Beijing's most popular clothing market. Hawkers barking "CD-ROM!" stalk the sidewalk and driveway outside, selling bootlegged music and movie discs (of dubious quality). Squeeze in through the main gate and then press along either of the two main passageways for a look at hundreds of booths. There's not much silk in Silk

Alley these days, and the astonishingly low prices that once thrilled travelers are gone. The initial asking price seems to be about three times what it should be. There are good deals to be had here on "name-brand" sportswear, Gore-Tex jackets, silk apparel, fake Levi jeans, sweaters, and Nike-like footwear. Try them on—some of these items may be the real McCoy. Logo luggage and handbags abound, as do Timberland shirts and designer-label shirts and blouses. (I've had mixed luck here: poor-quality designer shirts for $10, but a good duffel bag for $5 and reasonably good faux silk ties for $1.25.) There's a fair amount of duplication among vendors, so keep browsing before you haggle. Silk Alley runs on for a few blocks due north, emptying out at the intersection of Xiushui Dong Jie and Xiushui Nan Jie near the embassies of Ireland, Bulgaria, and the United States in a pleasant diplomatic district.

✪ **PANJIAYUAN ANTIQUE AND CURIO MARKET** Also called the Sunday Market, the Dirt Market, and the Ghost Market, the Panjiayuan Market is well south of downtown on Huaweiqiaoxi Nan Dajie, inside the Third Ring Road (Dongsanhuan). The best time to go to this rough-and-tumble market (the only time, according to locals) is Sunday morning at dawn or shortly after. Panjiayuan is open all week, but it doesn't get rolling until the weekends, and early Sunday morning is the hot time to look and buy. As many as 120,000 shoppers visit here each Sunday. Taxis from downtown hotels take about 25 minutes to reach this market (25RMB/$3 each way). The attractions are ceramics, furniture, antiques, and the exotic, with an emphasis on collectibles, many of which seem to have been family heirlooms. The vendors are as interesting to watch as the wares. The market is surprisingly well organized, divided into aisles beneath flowing, brightly striped canopies. As many as 3,000 vendors gather here (paying 300RMB/$37 a month for space). The aisles are even numbered and labeled, rather haphazardly, in English. There's an aisle for "Jade," another for "Folk Secondhand," and one for "Brone[sic] Teapot." Scrolls are displayed on a side wall. Among the more massive items are rusty cannons, Mao posters, Tibetan costumes, Qing dynasty furniture, sewing machines, large Buddhist statues, and even upright pianos. There are food stands just outside the marble aisles and an air-conditioned building serving fast food, apparently intended for foreigners and named "House of Guests." (The food is safe to eat inside the restaurant, but not from the vendors outside.)

LIDO MARKET Located straight across from the main entrance to the Holiday Inn Lido on Jiangtai Lu, on the east side of the Airport Expressway, Chaoyang District, Lido Market is one of Beijing's newest markets, with lower prices than Silk Alley for similar merchandise. The market is entirely indoors, in a narrow, one-story white-tile building about 2 blocks long, next door to a tiny boutique with a big sign reading MYSTERY GARMENTS. More than 100 numbered stalls and adjacent tables line both sides of the long hall. There's a selection of designer-label sportswear, silk blouses and scarves, scrolls, swords, stuffed animals, luggage, coins, and bric-a-brac. Some of the vendors can be too eager, latching on to you as you pass. It lacks the color and atmosphere of Silk Alley, but the prices are reasonable.

Jackpots & Junk

In 1996, a farmer from Henan Province sold a piece of pottery at the Panjiayuan Sunday Market in Beijing for the hefty price of 800RMB ($100). This purchase turned out to be a Qing Dynasty antique appraised at 250,000RMB ($30,000). But be careful. Some vendors "age" newly minted porcelains by smearing them with clay and blackening the surface with smoke.

What You Need to Know About Knockoffs & Fakes

The customs services of many nations frown on the importation of knockoff goods. The U.S. Customs Service allows U.S. residents to return with one trademark-protected item of each type—that is, one counterfeit watch, one knockoff purse, one camera with a questionable trademark, and so on. For instance, you may not bring back a dozen "Polo" shirts as gifts for friends. Even if the brand name is legitimate, you are not a licensed importer. In addition, copyrighted products such as CD-ROMs and books must have been manufactured under the copyright owner's authorization; otherwise, tourists cannot import even one of these items—they are pirated. The U.S. Customs Service booklet *Know Before You Go* and the U.S. Customs Web site (www.customs. ustreas.gov) have further guidelines.

MORE MARKETS   Also known as the Russian Market, **Yabaolu Market** is on the northeast corner of Ritan Park on Ritan Lu, Chaoyang District. This outdoor market is near the Russian restaurants and for years has catered to Russian business travelers who shuttle back and forth across borders with furs, leather goods, wool coats, and other textiles in bulk.

Chaowai Flea Market, a few blocks north of Ritan Park on Chaowei Shichang Jie (northern extension of Ritan Lu), Chaoyang District, is popular with the foreign diplomatic corps on the weekends. Under the arching roof there's a wide selection of furniture, wood carvings, collectibles, and a few antiques in the back section.

Known for its vintage jewelry, pins, and curios, **Liangmaqiao Market,** opposite the Kempinski Hotel (1 block east of the Third Ring Road East, 49 Liangmaqiao Lu, Chaoyang District), is always worth a browse, since anything could turn up. The vendors can be pushy.

Houhai Market, east side of the Deshengmen Bridge between Xihai and Houhai lakes, on the northwest shore of Houhai Lake, Xicheng District, is jammed every Saturday and Sunday with itinerant vendors, some of whom display their wares from the back of their black one-speed bicycles. (See the Back Lakes stroll in chapter 7, "Beijing Strolls").

✪ **Hongqiao Market** (also called Chongwenmen Market or Farmers' Market), just northeast of the Temple of Heaven (Tiantan) near the park wall (north of Tiyuguan Lu), Chongwen District, is Beijing's best market for luggage and sundries. It's like an outdoor version of a department store. There's also an indoor section, in the five-story building with the sweeping tiled eaves, with an exceptional jewelry selection on the third floor, notable for its freshwater pearls (see box, "The Dos and Don'ts of Buying Pearls in China" in section 3). This is where visiting heads of state are often taken to do their pearl shopping.

The **Scroll Market** is 2 blocks north of the Chegongzhuang subway stop, just inside the Second Ring Road North, off Ping'anli Xi Dajie, Xicheng District. The scroll market sells painted scrolls and artworks at bargain-basement prices. There are $3 scrolls here, there are $10 scrolls here, but the better sort sell for $25 to $100, with some costing three times that. Artists here will do scrolls to your design (but it could take 10 days). This is also an inexpensive place to buy chops (ink stamps). As a bonus, the market has a large section devoted to goldfish (heaven for a photographer on a sunny day).

Beijing's best outdoor **Bird Market** (also known as the Guanyuan Market) is north of the Xizhimen subway stop, just inside (east of) the Second Ring Road West, Xicheng District. The delicate, ornate cages here are as pretty as the larks, orioles, and other songbirds. There are also singing crickets for sale (as well as cats, dogs, turtles, and mice). This streetside market is just one subway stop north of the Scroll and Goldfish Market at Chegongzhuang—just 10 minutes due south on foot—but because of urban renewal projects in this area, its location is subject to change.

Wicker furnishings from tables and chairs to baskets and screens are sold at the **Sanlitun Wicker Market,** on the west side of Sanlitun Lu, north off Gongrentiyuchang Beilu, Chaoyang District. There is also an extensive clothing market on Sanlitun Lu itself, in the midst of Beijing's number-one bar and cafe strip.

Beijing Curio City (☎ 010/6773-6018) is south of the Panjiayuan Market, on the west side of Huawei Bridge, Third Ring Road, Chaoyang District. Dealers who formerly worked at the nearby Jinsong Porcelain Market have moved indoors here, where there are four floors of jewelry (including diamonds and jade), old clocks, cloisonné, furniture, and porcelain, as well as curios and genuine antiques. This establishment gets its share of tour groups, meaning the prices start high, but bargaining is acceptable. This is a good place to check out the porcelains. Credit cards can be used and international shipping is provided. Curio City is open daily from 9:30am to 6:30pm.

3 Beijing Shopping from A to Z
ANTIQUES & CURIOS
The markets and bazaars (listed above) are a primary source of antiques and collectibles, as are hotel shops, but there are several private antique stores worth checking out.

Century Art Center.
On the west side of Ritan Park in Jufu Palace, Chaoyang District. ☎ **010/6502-1627.**

Specialists in handmade Tibetan cabinets, chests, carpets, and religious artifacts, Century Art Center is located in a courtyard house in the park. Many of the pieces here are genuine centuries-old antiques. The Tibetan chests are the most popular pieces, wooden boxes for storage decorated in cloth, yak leather, and religious paintings. Small chests start at 5,000RMB ($600), about a third of the overseas price. Carved cabinets start at 7,000RMB ($850). There is also a wide selection of well-restored Qing Dynasty scholar's studio furniture, including hand-carved chairs and lacquered screens. Open Tuesday to Sunday 10am to 5pm.

Guang Han Tang Beijing Classical Furniture Company.
East of the Third Ring Road and Jing Guang New World Center (Chaoyang Lu) on Qingnian Lu at Ganlu Yuan 3. ☎ **010/6557-4659.**

A large dealer in antique furniture and furnishings, Guang Han Tang has opened a second showroom in the Kempinski Hotel (Unit S. 108), ☎ **010/6465-1030.** Open daily 10am to 5pm.

Hua Yi Classical Furniture Company.
Showrooms at 89 Xiaodian Dongwei Lu and in Beijing Curio City, third floor, no. 69, off the Third Ring Road South, Chaoyang District. ☎ **010/6773-5909.**

This company specializes in restored furniture items from the late Qing Dynasty. Packaging and shipping available. Open daily 9am to 6pm.

The Dos & Don'ts of Buying Pearls in China

In the Chinese tradition, pearls are the gems of love. Ground into a powder, in fact, they are the essential ingredient in Nanzhung tablets, a Chinese aphrodisiac.

These days, China's oyster beds remain among the world's most fertile grounds for pearls, of both the saltwater and freshwater variety. On the third floor of the Hongqiao Market's shopping center, for example, there are more than a hundred stalls and counters featuring pearls of varying quality, color, and setting. These are cultured (farmed) pearls. Most are sold in 40-cm tassels. The only problem is how to determine quality and a fair price.

Saltwater pearls are usually more expensive than the freshwater gems, but in both cases the qualities to look for are roundness, luster, and size. The bigger, rounder, and shinier the pearl, the better (and the more expensive).

Fakes can be detected by nicking the surface of the pearl with a sharp blade (the color is uniform within and without); rubbing the pearl along your teeth (to feel or hear a grating sound, since a real pearl's surface is actually scored and minutely cratered); scraping the pearl on glass (pearls leave a mark); or passing the pearl through a flame (fakes turn black, but real pearls don't).

Try to pick a string of pearls that are of the same size, shape, and color. Here's a rough pricing guide, based on what's charged in the market:

10 to 20RMB ($1.25–$2.50) for a string of small rice-shaped pearls.
20 to 40RMB ($2.50–$5) for a string of larger pearls of mixed or low luster.
50 to 100RMB ($6.25–$12.50) for a string of larger pearls of different colors.

A string of very large, perfectly round pearls of the same color sells for considerably more, 10,000 to 20,000RMB ($125 to $250) and more. Tassels of odd-shaped pearls can also fetch higher prices, selling for 100 to 1,000RMB ($12.50 to $125).

U.S. President Bill Clinton stopped by a stall (#99) in the Hongqiao Market during a state visit in 1998 and established a benchmark for the shopper to go by, picking up ten strings for about 800RMB ($100). You should be able to do better if you bargain hard enough.

ART SUPPLIES

The **Liulichang Cultural Street** (see chapter 7) has many small shops selling traditional artist brushes, ink stones, paper, and other art supplies. The largest art store in Beijing, however, is on Wangfujing Dajie: **Gongyi Meishu Fuwubu,** 200 Wangfujing Dajie, Dongcheng District (☎ 010/6512-4160), open daily 8am to 6pm.

BOOKS

Hotel kiosks and shops are often the best place to find English-language guides to Beijing attractions and books about China, but there are several bookstores with decent selections.

China Bookstore.

57 Liulichang Xi Jie, Xuanwu District. ☎ **010/6303-5759.**

Located on the corner dividing east and west Liulichang Cultural streets, China Bookstore focuses on old Chinese books and used foreign publications. Open daily 9am to 6:30pm.

Mao's Little Red Disk

Chairman Mao Zedong has entered the computer age, and his Little Red Book, a compilation of his sayings that became the Bible for thousands of devout and fanatical Red Guard followers during the Cultural Revolution (1966–1976), has been released on CD-ROM. Along with 20 volumes of Mao's anti-Western political thought, the disk contains 120 film clips and 3,000 pictures from the Mao archives. So far, there have been no mass rallies of latter-day Red Guard nerds at Tiananmen Square waving their Little Red Disks with the downloaded sayings of the late Great Helmsman.

Foreign Language Bookstore.
235 Wangfujing Dajie, Dongcheng District. ☎ **010/6512-6922.**

Largest collection of English-language books and tapes in Beijing, starting on the second floor. Open daily 9am to 6pm.

✪ Friendship Store.
17 Jianguomenwai Dajie, Chaoyang District. ☎ **010/6500-3311.**

The collection of English-language books and magazines is in its own room at the back of the store on the first floor. Open daily 9am to 8:30pm.

Sanwei Bookstore.
60 Fuxingmennei Dajie, about 1 mile west of the Forbidden City on the south side of Chang'an Avenue, Xicheng District. ☎ **010/6601-3204.**

Upstairs is a traditional teahouse, downstairs a small bookstore with a few English-language titles and the friendliest staff in town. Open daily 9am to 10:30pm.

CARPETS

Check over carpets carefully, with an eye to faded colors. Colors should be bright and the threads fine. A 6-by-8-foot silk carpet, tightly woven (300 to 400 stitches/inch) can cost 50,000RMB ($6,000) or more.

Beijing Carpet Import and Export Corporation.
First floor of the Hong Kong Macau Center, Third Ring Road East, Dongsishitiao, Chaoyang District. ☎ **010/6523-5293.**

Excellent choice of styles. Most carpets are new Chinese creations, but there are some Persian designs and antique rugs. Open daily 7:30am to 11pm.

China Beijing Carpet Trade Center.
90 Weizikeng, Liangjiazhuang, Fengtai District. ☎ **010/6761-6018.**

One of China's biggest carpet stores, with thousands of handwoven carpets in all styles. Open daily 9:30am to 4:30pm.

Qianmen Carpet Factory.
Basement of Chongwen Cultural Palace, 44 Xingfu Dajie, Chongwen District. ☎ **010/6701-5079** or 010/6715-1687.

Selection of older northwestern Chinese and Tibetan carpets. Cleaning and repair services available. Open daily 9am to 8pm.

White Peacock Art World.
Bei Binhe Lu, Deshengmenwai Dong Dajie, Xicheng District. ☎ **010/6201-3008.**

Good selection of new carpets in silk and wool. Open daily 9am to 7:30pm.

CRAFTS

Beijing Arts and Crafts Factory.
5 Xinkang Jie, Xinjiekouwai Dajie, Xicheng District. ☎ **010/6201-2228.**

Good selection of local arts and crafts. Open daily 8am–6pm.

Huaxia Arts & Crafts Store.
Two locations: 12 Chongwenmennei Dajie, Chongwen District, and 293 Wangfujing Dajie, Dongcheng District (☎ **010/6501-5079** for both stores).

The main store on Chongwen has a superb collection of Beijing opera masks, costumes, and Chinese collectibles; the Wangfujing branch carries porcelains, folk art, and skilled handicrafts. Open daily 8:30am to 6pm.

Ji Gu Ge.
136 Liulichang Dong Jie, Hepingmenwai, Xuanwu District. ☎ **010/6301-2897.**

This venerable outlet, the best arts and crafts shop on historic Liulichang Culture Street, has fine reproductions of Chinese artwork. There is also a good selection of tea, scrolls, paintings, porcelain, and jewelry. Open daily 9am to 8pm.

White Peacock Art World.
Beibinhe Lu, Deshengmenwai Dajie, Haidian District. ☎ **010/6201-3008.**

Well known for its carpets, this store carries embroidered goods and a range of arts and crafts. Open daily 9am to 7:30pm.

DEPARTMENT STORES

Beijing's one-stop department stores are being eased aside by the onslaught of megamalls and shopping plazas (see "Malls & Shopping Plazas," below), but the single-owner department store is still worth a shopping visit, both the traditional Chinese variety (fast disappearing) and the new superstore format. This category includes the store that matters most to most tourists, despite all the advances in retailing: Beijing's original **Friendship Store.**

✪ Friendship Store.
17 Jianguomenwai Dajie, Chaoyang District. ☎ **010/6500-3311.**

For the foreign visitor to Beijing, this is the ultimate one-stop shop, containing a generous sampling of nearly everything worth hauling home: arts and crafts, jewelry, silk, books, souvenirs, antiques (see the box on the Friendship Store, in section 2). This should be your first and last shopping stop. Open daily 9am to 8:30pm.

Parkson.
101 Fuxingmennei Dajie, Xicheng District. ☎ **010/6601-3377.**

This ultramodern department store tower has high prices but superb clothing and fashions and an excellent arts and crafts department (fifth floor) that complements an in-house gallery called the National Treasures Exhibition Centre. Restaurants and a grocery are on the top floor. Open daily 9am to 9pm.

PriceSmart Membership Shopping.
Three locations: 54 Third Ring Road South, Chaoyang District, ☎ **010/6779-1113;** A18 Xueqing Lu, Haidian District, ☎ **010/6292-7011;** and Yuquan Lu at Fuxing Lu, Fengtai District, ☎ **010/6818-2211.**

This wildly successful, American-based, membership bulk-shopping warehouse opened in Beijing in 1997. Offering everything under the sun in massive quantities at a discount (from cleaning supplies to movie tapes), PriceSmart just keeps growing in lock step with China's Westward-leaning economy. Open daily 10am to 10pm.

Wangfujing Department Store.
255 Wangfujing Dajie, Dongcheng District. ☎ **010/6512-6677.**

A true-blue department store in the traditional mode, Beijing's leading Chinese emporium is considering a massive remodel. Too bad, because even without escalators, it's worth exploring, filled with goods the locals can actually afford to buy. The toy department on the first floor remains the best in Beijing, too. Open daily 8:30am to 8:30pm.

Xidan Shopping Center.
East side of Xidan Bei Dajie, Xicheng District.

Modern, Western-looking, but decidedly for the local Chinese shopper, this crowded and chaotic complex is stuffed with everything a department store should have, from food and toys in the basement to cosmetics and hearing aids on the first floor, with sports equipment, clothing, and appliances filling up three more floors. Open daily 9am to 8pm.

JEWELRY

Beijing Jewelry Import/Export Corporation.
44 Wangfujing Dajie, Dongcheng District. ☎ **010/6525-5380.**

Specializes in jade and pearls. Open daily 9am to 7pm.

Shard Box.
1 Ritan Bei Lu (corner of Jianguomenwai Dajie), Chaoyang District. ☎ **010/6500-3712.**

A good selection of silver and jade creations. Open daily 8:30am to 7:30pm.

MALLS & SHOPPING PLAZAS

Beijing's mammoth shopping plazas consist of scores of independent brand-name and designer-label outlets, most with international merchandise. They are known for their boutique shopping, high prices, restaurants, basement supermarkets, and entertainment (including fashion shows and exhibits).

China World Trade Center Shopping Center.
1 Jianguomenwai Dajie, Chaoyang District. ☎ **010/6505-2288.**

This three-level mall caters to foreign business travelers and expatriate families. Its outlets have been expanded recently by the opening of the underground shopping mall (complete with ice rink) that connects the China World Hotel with Traders Hotel 1 block north. The ground level of China World contains airline offices, shops, and cafes. Upstairs there's a Sparkice Internet Cafe. Downstairs is most of the shopping. Kerry's Beijing Fashion Center (Basement no. 127) is a department store featuring imported and domestic men's and women's clothing. Gourmet Corner (Basement no. 124) has been joined by China's first Starbucks coffee cafe. Wellcome Supermarket is crammed with imported edibles. A number of small Chinese arts and crafts outlets and aisle stalls are also set up for business here. Open daily 9am to 9pm.

COFCO Plaza.
8 Jianguomennei Dajie, Dongcheng District. ☎ **010/6526-6666.**

Facing outward and flanking the entrance to this megamall are a branch of the Hongkong and Shanghai Bank (open Monday to Friday 9am to 12:30pm and 1:30 to 5pm) and a McDonald's (open daily 7am to 11pm). Inside, expensive clothing stores dominate the four floors and three basements that orbit around a flashy central atrium. On the first floor, you can find a branch of the China Silk Shop and a florist; outlets for Crocodile, Christian Dior, and Benetton; Copy Max and a

Konika Photo Express (fast developing); and a store selling nothing but cowboy boots. Park 'N Shop supermarket (open daily from 8am to 10pm) is in Basement one; a large furniture store and a Baskin Robbins ice cream parlor are in Basement two; and a bowling alley (Haiba Bowling Club) is in the third basement. An underground walkway connects this mall to the north side of Chang'an Avenue. Open daily 9am to 9pm.

Full Link Plaza.
18 Chaoyangmenwai Dajie, Chaoyang District. ☎ **010/6588-1997.**

Opened in 1997, this spacious mall has four floors and two basements of shops and restaurants. The first floor includes a Watson's Drug Store and a Nautica outlet, and the second floor has Esprit and MacGregor outlets. There's a Kenny Roger's Roasters Restaurant on the fourth floor and a Park 'N Shop supermarket in the basement. Also in the basement is Tully's, the Seattle-based cafe and espresso bar that beat Starbucks to China. Open daily 9am to 9pm.

Lufthansa You Yi Shopping Center.
9 Third Ring Road East, Chaoyang District. ☎ **010/6435-4930.**

Located on the east side of the Third Ring Road and connected to the Kempinski Hotel, Lufthansa Center is the largest and most modern mall in northeast Beijing (site of a number of international chain luxury hotels). There's a department store in the thick of things, with a range of upscale specialty shops, boutiques, and restaurants on the ground floor and above. The basement has a busy supermarket. Open daily 9am to 8:30pm.

Palace Hotel Shopping Arcade.
Basement of the Palace Hotel, 8 Jingyu Hutong (1 block east off Wangfujing Dajie), Dongcheng District. ☎ **010/6512-8899.**

Shop the swank lobby and then take the escalator down behind the waterfall to Beijing's most upscale collection of designer-name outlets. To its fine international lineup (Gucci, LV, Baccarat), the Palace recently enlisted China's first Armani. Credit cards are accepted (and probably needed) here. Open daily 9am to 9pm.

Scitech Plaza.
22 Jianguomenwai Dajie, Chaoyang District. ☎ **010/6512-4488.**

Formerly known as CVIK Plaza, this mall is on the south side of Chang'an Avenue, a long block east of the Second Ring Road and the Jianguomen subway stop. There's a branch of the Friendship Store in the front, a supermarket in the second basement, European housewares in the basement, and plenty of cosmetics kiosks on the ground floor. Open daily 9am to 10pm.

✪ Sun Dong An Plaza.
138 Wangfujing Dajie, Dongcheng District. ☎ **010/6527-6688.**

Currently Beijing's grandest, most up-to-date megamall (built on the site of a humble farmers' market and small business arcade in the heart of Wangfujing), Sun Dong An is a series of galleries and atriums rising six flights, higher than any temple in the Forbidden City. Basement levels contain a supermarket, several department stores, and large appliances. Level 1 has cosmetics and camera outlets, Level 2 men's wear, Level 3 women's wear, Level 4 shoes and hats, Level 5 snacks (Chinese and Western), and Level 6 the restaurants. Among boutiques and brand-name outlets are Bossini, Burberry, Esprit, London Fog, and Nike. McDonald's and DeliFrance have restaurants on Level 2, and Bank of China has a branch on

Does Sex Sell in Beijing?

Beijing, like the rest of China, wears a puritanical face, despite a flourishing underground in prostitution and pornography (both punishable by death). The city is not besmirched by sex shops and adult entertainment districts, but some "sex health shops" are permitted. They haven't made much of an inroad into the newly free marketplace. In the Maizi Dian neighborhood (east of the Great Wall Sheraton Hotel), a few sex shops have sprung up, many run by Korean families. They turn out to be tame versions of their counterparts in the seedier districts of the West and are stocked with dry academic texts on sexual behavior and an assortment of traditional love potions. Taxi drivers know the way to these shops, which have lately been selling a Chinese counterpart to Viagra for the treatment of male impotency. Known in Beijing as *Weige,* or "Great Brother," these expensive pills (300RMB/$37 each) allegedly bolster the performance of "Little Brother." One of these shops has been displaying an unintentionally wishful sign in English reading: "Thank You For Your Coming," although few foreign shoppers seem to venture in.

Level 1 (open Monday to Friday 9am to noon and 1:30 to 5pm). Open daily 9am to 9pm.

Vantone New World Shopping Center.
2–8 Fuchengmenwai Dajie, Xicheng District. ☎ **010/6858-8256.**

Leased and managed by a U.S. firm (the first such enterprise in Beijing), this mall has a McDonald's on the northwest corner (intersection of Fuchengmennei Dajie and Beilishi Lu) and a subway entrance (Fuchengmen) on the northeast side. Inside are more than 100 specialty shops and boutiques. Open Monday through Friday 9am to 8:30pm and Sat through Sun 10am to 10pm.

MUSIC

Beijing Accordion & Piano School.
South side of Xi Chang'an Jie, between Xidan shopping street and Tonglingge Lu.

Take a peek (and a picture) of this one-of-a-kind Western musical instrument store with the piano in the window, right next door to Beijing's first heavy metal shop (at no. 16), with all the punk accessories and plenty of Bob Marley posters.

Hongsheng Musical Instruments.
225 Wangfujing Dajie, Dongcheng District. ☎ **010/6513-5190.**

Chinese musical instruments make fine gifts or souvenirs. Open daily 8:30am to 7pm.

Youdai Records.
78 Yude Hutong, Xinjekou, Xicheng District. ☎ **010/6618-1701.**

Beijing expatriates' favorite store for records, tapes, and discs. Modern Chinese and Western music. Open daily noon to 6pm.

SILK, EMBROIDERY & FABRIC

Baizhifang Embroidery Factory.
A44 Liren Jie, Xuanwu District. ☎ **010/6303-6577.**

Silk yardage and a good selection of embroidered tablecloths, sheets, and pillowcases. Open daily 8am to 5pm.

Qianmen Women's Clothing Store.
Dazhalan pedestrian street, west off Qianmen Dajie, Chongwen District.

Silk and wool yardage, custom tailoring, blouses, suits, and dresses. Open daily 8:30am to 9pm.

Ruifuxiang Silk and Cotton Store.
Dazhalan pedestrian street, west off Qianmen Dajie, Chongwen District.

Plenty of silk fabrics and ready-made clothing. Open daily 8:30am to 9:30pm.

Yuanlong Embroidery and Silk Store.
At the south entrance to the Temple of Heaven (Tiantan), 15 Yongdingmenwai, Chongwen District. ☎ **010/6511-4635.**

Largest selection of fabrics in silk, brocades, and wools. Tailoring and shipping services. Open daily 9am to 6:30pm.

SUPERMARKETS
Beijing's hotels might have a small shop with some Western snacks and bottled water, but for a broad range of familiar groceries, try one of the large-scale supermarkets listed here.

Holiday Inn Lido Supermarket.
In the Holiday Inn Lido, Jichang Lu, Jiangtai Lu, Chaoyang District. ☎ **010/6437-6688**, ext. 1541.

Excellent selection of imported foods and drinks, from potato chips to frozen dinners. Open daily 8:30am to 9pm.

Jenny Lou's.
Sanlitun Bei Lu, Chaoyang District. ☎ **010/6415-3244.**

A grocer popular with expatriates in the Sanlitun diplomatic compound, Jenny Lou's carries the best fresh and imported fruits and vegetables in Beijing. A second outlet is open on Gongrentiyuchang Bei Lu, near Worker's Stadium, and next door to an excellent Italian cheese store. Open daily 7am to 7pm.

Park 'N Shop.
Basement Level 2, Full Link Plaza, 18 Chaoyangmenwai Dajie, Chaoyang District. ☎ **6588-1908.**

Emphasis on Western imports (more than 1,000 items), including cheese and dairy products, wines, and soft drinks. Features an in-store Western-style bakery and delicatessen. Credit cards are accepted. Open daily 8:30am to 9:30pm. (There's also a Park 'N Shop in the basement of COFCO Plaza, 8 Jianguomennei Dajie, open daily from 8am to 10pm.)

Wellcome Market.
Basement Level 1, China World Trade Center, 1 Jianguomenwai Dajie, Chaoyang District. ☎ **010/6505-2288.**

Everything the Western heart yearns for in one convenient, very modern supermarket. Open daily 9am to 9pm.

TAILORS
While other cities in Asia offer more extensive tailoring of suits, shirts, blouses, and dresses, Beijing has several reliable and reasonably priced custom tailor shops. Some specialize in *qipao*, the high-necked silk dress with the side slit.

Cao Shi Fu Qipao Shop.

In a *hutong* (alley courtyard house) at 25 Shi Jie Hutong, off Dongsi Nan Dajie, Dongcheng District. ☎ **010/6526-4515.**

Mr. Cao Senlin has been making *qipao* for 6 decades. One dress takes him a month to complete. He does all the work in his small house.

Kanna Custom Clothing Specialty Store.

Across from China World Trade Center, 2 Jianguomenwai Dajie, Chaoyang District. ☎ **010/6594-8997.**

Hundreds of fabrics converted into clothing of your choice within 48 hours. Open daily 10am to 6pm.

Mujianliao Traditional Chinese Fashions.

Wangfujing shopping area, 46 Dongdan Bei Dajie, Dongcheng District. ☎ **010/6513-5205** or 010/6513-8694, ext. 17.

The main focus of this tailor and fabric shop is on women's dresses in Chinese styles, including *qipao*. Mujianliao also has a new branch in the Sun Dong An Plaza on Wangfujing Dajie. Open daily 8am to 6pm.

TEA

Bichun Tea Shop.

233 Wangfujing Dajie, Dongcheng District. ☎ **010/6525-4722.**

Nice assortment of classic teapots and packaged Chinese teas. Open daily 8:30am to 8:30pm.

✪ Jiguge Teahouse.

132–136 Liulichang Dong Jie, Xuanwu District. ☎ **010/6301-7849.**

Good selection of Yixing clay teapots, tea sets, and packaged Chinese teas. Open daily 9am to 11pm.

Qinglinchun Tea Shop.

9 Qianmen Dajie, Chongwen District. ☎ **010/6303-8512.**

Teas, teapots, and tea sets, all made in China, are on offer here. Open daily 8am to 8pm.

Xidan Tea Shop.

209 Xidan Bei Dajie, Xicheng District. ☎ **010/6605-7640.**

Features a small but select range of teaware and teas for sale. Open daily 8am to 8pm.

9 Beijing After Dark

Until the 1990s, Beijing offered its foreign visitors very few venues for nighttime entertainment. At sunset, the city closed down, and tourists were largely confined to their hotels, unless they were part of a group tour that had arranged an evening outing to the Beijing Opera. Recently, however, the possibilities for an evening on the town have multiplied. Beijing is still not in the same late-night league as Hong Kong or Tokyo, but once the sun sets on the Forbidden City and the shopping plazas, foreigners in China's capital do not have to tuck themselves in.

On the one hand, Beijing still offers large-scale performances of opera, acrobatics, and music by China's premier artists. And the performing arts are no longer confined to the capital's theaters. Teahouses have opened their doors to foreign visitors with presentations of opera excerpts, dance, music, acrobatics, and comedy in intimate, traditional surroundings.

On the other hand, Beijing has experienced an explosion of Western-style entertainment. The small cafe bars in Sanlitun and other districts that foreign residents frequent after hours are experiencing a boom. More than watering holes, these restaurants-by-day become music clubs by night, featuring live rock and jazz until the wee hours. There's even a Beijing branch of the Hard Rock Cafe. Discos are extremely popular, too, and like the cafe bars have become mixing bowls for locals and foreigners. Sports bars and small international cinemas are also sprouting up.

Beijing will not be mistaken for Paris, London, or New York after dark, but it isn't sleeping anymore either.

1 The Performing Arts

Beijing opera and acrobatics are the two most popular theatrical events, but puppetry, drama, and classical music (both Eastern and Western) are regularly featured in the capital's theaters, hotel auditoriums, and concert halls.

BEIJING OPERA

Nearly extinguished in the early 1990s, Beijing's most famous performing art, the traditional Beijing Opera, is thriving, thanks to a resurgence in popularity among locals and the funding of several theaters. Beijing Opera (*Jing Ju*) is derived from 8 centuries of

How to Find Out What's On & Get Tickets

Check the entertainment listings in *China Daily* or the English-language monthly papers such as *Beijing This Month, Welcome To Beijing, City Edition, Metro,* and *Beijing Beat.* Your hotel tour desk or concierge may be able to secure tickets; otherwise, you'll have to go to the ticket office yourself. Locations of theaters, concert halls, teahouses, cafes, bars, cinemas, and other entertainment sites are listed in this chapter.

touring song and dance troupes, but became institutionalized in its present form in the 1700s under the Qing Dynasty. The stylized singing, costuming, acrobatics, music, and choreography set Chinese opera quite apart from Western opera. It usually strikes foreigners as garish, screechy, and incomprehensible. It helps to know the plot (usually a historical drama with a tragic outcome), and English subtitles are sometimes provided. Songs are performed on a five-note scale (not the eight-note scale familiar in the West). Gongs, cymbals, and string and wind instruments punctuate (often jarringly) the action on the stage. Faces are painted with colors symbolizing qualities such as valor or villainy, and masks and costumes announce the performer's role in society, from emperor to peasant.

Most Beijing Opera these days consists of abridgements, lasting 2 hours or less (as opposed to 5 hours or more in the old days), and with the martial arts choreography, the spirited acrobatics, and the brilliant costumes, these performances can be a delight even to the unaccustomed, untrained eye. With the closure of Beijing's oldest and most venerated opera house, the Zhengyici Theater (see box below), the Liyuan Theater has become the leading opera house. Other opera houses include **Chang'an Grand Theater,** 7 Jianguomenwai Dajie, Chaoyang District, (☎ 010/ 6510-1309), with performances Friday and Saturday from 7:30 to 9:30pm, and tickets for 60 to 180RMB ($7.50 to $22.50); **Hu Guang Guild Hall,** 3 Hufangqiao, Xuanwu District (☎ 010/6351-8284), with performances nightly from 7:15 to 9pm, and tickets for 20 to 150RMB ($2.50 to $19); and **Grand View Garden Theater,** 12 Nancaiyun Jie, Xuanwu District (☎ 010/6351-9025), with performances nightly from 7:30 to 8:45pm, and tickets for 40 to 150RMB ($5 to $19).

Liyuan Theater.
In the Qianmen Hotel, 175 Yong'an Lu, Xuanwu District. ☎ 010/6301-6688, ext. 8860. Tickets 30–150RMB ($3.75–$19). Nightly performance 7:30–8:45pm.

The best bet for the foreign traveler, this theater puts on spirited Beijing opera abridgements from at least three operas performed by the Beijing Opera Troupe. Simultaneous translations into English are flashed on subtitle screens. The price levels reflect the quality of the seating and the range of snacks provided during the performance.

ACROBATICS

For 2,000 years the Chinese have been perfecting their acrobatic performances. These days the juggling, contortionism, unicycling, chair-stacking, and plate-spinning have entered the age of modern staging. The **Beijing Acrobatic Troupe** (also known as the Tianqiao Acrobatics Troupe) spends most of its year outside Beijing touring the stages of the world, but the groups left home are superb. Acrobatic shows receive surprisingly high marks from foreign visitors. Local acrobatic stages include the following:

The End of the Road for Beijing's Oldest Opera House

The leading venue in Beijing (in all of China) for traditional opera had long been the **Zhengyici Theater.** Originally a temple (built in 1620) and constructed entirely of wood, it had served as a theater since 1713. Closed after Liberation (1949), it was restored and reopened in 1994 by a wealthy patron, but competition from karaoke parlors, cinemas, discos, television, and videos doomed its existence once again, in October 1998. Beijing's Education Bureau now owns the old building, located at 220 Xiheyan Dajie in the Xuanwu District, and it plans to convert the theater into a community center where children can study traditional arts and culture.

Chaoyang Theater.
36 Dongsanhuan Beilu (Third Ring Road East), Chaoyang District. ☎ **010/6507-2421.** Tickets 80RMB ($10). Performances nightly 7:15–8:45pm.

Performances by the China Acrobatics Troupe or the Sichuan Acrobatic Troupe. Martial arts and magic are included in the varied program, but the tightrope walkers steal the show.

Poly Plaza International Theater.
Poly Plaza Hotel, 14 Dongzhimen Nan Dajie, Chaoyang District. ☎ **010/6500-1188,** ext. 5127 or 010/6608-4160. Tickets 50–500RMB ($6–$60). Performances nightly 7:15–9pm.

A Las Vegas–style acrobatics and magic show (titled "Chinese Soul") performed largely before tourists by the China Acrobatic Circus. Tickets are sold through hotel tour desks or at the Poly Plaza ticket office, with prices determined by seating and dining options (snacks to full dinners).

Wansheng Theater.
95 Tianqiao Market, Xuanwu District. ☎ **010/6303-7449.** Tickets 100–150RMB ($12.50–$19). Performances nightly 7:15–9pm.

Home of the renowned Beijing Acrobatic Troupe, the most artistic of the capital's performers.

PUPPETS
Puppet shows (*mu ou xi*) have been performed in China since the Han Dynasty (206 B.C.–A.D. 220). Shadow puppets, hand puppets, and string puppets (marionettes) all perform on an irregular basis, but they are sometimes featured in the variety shows at Beijing's teahouses (see "Teahouse Theater," below). Most theatrical performances, including weekend matinees, are held at the **China Puppet Art Theater,** A1 Anhuaxili (near Third Ring Road North), Chaoyang District (☎ **010/6424-3698** or 010/6425-4798), where the admission is 20 to 25RMB ($2.50–$3).

OTHER PERFORMING ARTS VENUES
Beijing is the site of major national and international music, drama, and dance performances nearly every day of the year. Many of these concerts are held in the **Beijing Concert Hall** or the **Poly Plaza International Theater.** The Beijing Philharmonic and the Central Ballet (China's premier dance company) perform frequently in Beijing when not on tour, and an increasing number of major orchestras, symphonies, ensembles, and soloists from abroad have put Beijing on their itineraries. The capital has also spawned the Beijing Symphony Orchestra, the

Beijing Chamber Quartet, the Beijing International Orchestra, and a number of ensembles playing traditional Chinese music.

The most important formal performance hall in China is the **Beijing Concert Hall,** Liubukou, 1 Beixinhuajie, Xuanwu District (☎ **010/6605-7006** or 010/6605-5812). Seating 1,000, it serves wine and sells CDs in the foyer. During a recent 2-week period, it presented a French pianist, the Hua Ying Women's Military Orchestra, the Beijing Chamber Ensemble, the Tibetan Lamas Ensemble, the China Singing and Dancing Ensemble, the Children's Philharmonic Orchestra, the Canadian True North Brass Group, and the Beijing Symphony Orchestra. Tickets for most performances are 30RMB to 120RMB ($3.50 to $15), with prices for local performers lower and prices for international stars (such as Yo Yo Ma, who played here) considerably higher.

Many of Beijing's top classical and traditional musicians perform in hotel lobbies and hotel restaurants on a regular basis. The **China World Hotel** hosts a 55-piece orchestra in its lobby every Sunday (from 4 to 6pm). The **Jianguo Hotel** has classical piano music nightly (6 to 9pm), and opera singers often turn up there at the Sunday brunch. The **Holiday Inn Crowne Plaza** holds small concerts in its Art Salon, and its lobby atrium is filled with song every evening.

2 Teahouse Theater

For centuries, China's teahouses were the chief gathering places for artists and mandarins, intellectuals and dilettantes, places of leisure where traditional culture and the performing arts were appreciated and sustained. They almost disappeared from modern China, but in Beijing, teahouses are undergoing a revival. The teahouses that offer theater are especially attractive to foreign visitors. They are the Chinese version of the Western dinner theater, offering snacks or full meals while presenting on intimate stages a spectrum of traditional performing arts: highlights from Beijing Opera, acrobatics, magic, crosstalk (standup) comedy, puppetry, singing, dancing, and music played on ancient instruments. There's no better place to enjoy a full banquet of Chinese performing arts.

Beijing Teahouse.
8 Changdian, Liulichang Jie, Xuanwu District. ☎ **010/6303-3846.** Free admission. Daily performances 2:30–4:30pm.

This teahouse, open for tea and snacks daily from 9am to 9pm, is noted for its traditional storytellers who perform every afternoon. It's an excellent place to take a break while shopping on Liulichang Culture Street.

✪ Lao She Teahouse.
Third floor, Dawancha Bldg., 3 Qianmenxi Dajie, Chongwen District. ☎ **010/6303-6830.** Admission 60–130RMB ($7.50–$16). Performances nightly 7:40–9:20pm.

Every night's entertainment is different, but expect a sampling of opera, traditional music, acrobatics, comedy, magic, and storytelling. The higher admission charges provide better seating (closer to the front) and more snacks.

Sanwei Bookstore.
60 Fuxingmennei Dajie, Xuanwu District. ☎ **010/6601-3204.** Admission 30RMB ($3.75). Performances Fri 9–11pm and Sat 8:30–10:30pm.

About 1 mile due west of the Forbidden City, on the south side of Chang'an Avenue, Sanwei is a bookstore on the first floor, a traditional teahouse decorated in dark carved woods upstairs. It offers a relaxed studio setting for taking in jazz by

A Night at the Movies

China limits the release of new Hollywood films to just ten a year, all dubbed into Mandarin. The leading import seems to be Hong Kong kung fu action films. Chinese directors produced some of the best films in the world during the 1980s and 1990s, but even some of these can't be shown in China. Non–Chinese-speaking visitors hungering for a night at the pictures do have some outlets these days. Perhaps the most interesting venue is **Cherry Lane Cinema,** Sino-Japanese Youth Exchange Center, International Conference Hall, 40 Liangmaqiao Lu (☎ **010/6522-4046**), about 1 mile east of the Lufthansa Center, off the Third Ring Road East. Cherry Lane screens contemporary Chinese films (with English subtitles) for foreign audiences. Screenings are usually held on alternate Fridays at 8pm; tickets are 50RMB ($6).

Some of Beijing's cafe/bars show foreign films (in English) in a video format on large (6-foot) screens. The **Keep In Touch Pub** (☎ **010/6462-5280**), located in a *hutong* (alleyway) across from the Kempinski Hotel off the Third Ring Road East, shows recent foreign video releases Wednesday nights at 8pm. It's usually a double feature, and admission is free.

local groups on Friday nights and classical Chinese music on Saturday nights over tea and Beijing snacks.

Tian Hai Teahouse.
On Sanlitun Lu, ½ block north of Gonrentiyuchang Bei Lu, Chaoyang District. ☎ **010/ 6416-5676.** Daily 10am–10pm.

A serene wooden and bamboo interior, a Qing Dynasty–attired waitstaff, and musical and operatic performances every Friday and Saturday evening re-create the quiet feel of an old teahouse tucked away down a hutong in Beijing's busiest bar strip. There's no admission charge, but you're expected to buy food and drinks.

✪ Tian Qiao Happy Teahouse.
A1 Beiweilu (no. 113 Tianqiao Market), Xuanwu District. ☎ **010/6304-0617.** Performances Tues–Sun 7–9pm.

The Happy Teahouse has all the atmosphere of a Qing Dynasty theater. Waiters are dressed in imperial costumes, and they never stop serving tea. The opera excerpts are quite energetic. Acrobatics, music, and comedy can be sampled from tables in front of the stage or the balcony above. Admission is 180RMB ($22.50) for a table and snacks, 330RMB ($40) for a Beijing duck dinner.

3 The Bar & Club Scene

Beijing today is undergoing an avalanche of bar openings, much of it centered on **Sanlitun,** a tree-lined neighborhood of foreign diplomatic compounds in the Chaoyang District northwest of the city center, between the Worker's Stadium and the Third Ring Road North. These small, privately owned cafe/bars serve Western cuisine by day and imported beer, wine, and spirits by night. They attract large numbers of foreign residents, diplomats, and students as well as young and mon-eyed Beijingers. In the summer, most of these cafe/bars have outdoor seating, pleasant places to while away the sunlit hours. In the evenings, most become meccas for after-dinner drinks and live music, particularly rock music.

The international hotels also have their own lounges and lobby bars that are popular with foreign travelers. Recently the city has added such Western venues as sports bars, jazz clubs, cinemas, and discos. There's no shortage of places for foreign travelers to relax and enjoy a drink or to dance into the wee hours. The surroundings are like those in the West, as are the cover charges and prices for drinks and snacks.

BARS IN THE SANLITUN & BEYOND

The liveliest and most compact nightlife district in Beijing is on Sanlitun Lu, officially designated as **Sanlitun Bar Street** (*Sanlitun Jiuba Jie*) in 1996. By the end of 1996, 25 bars had moved onto the street and its hutongs. A dozen more opened their doors the next year, and as the year 2000 approaches, the tally is over 60 and still expanding. Some of these cafe/bars barely lasted 6 months, but others have been at Sanlitun for years. The scene is always changing rapidly, making it an ideal place to stroll by day and barhop after the sun sets.

Currently, most of the bars and cafes are situated chock-a-block on the east side of Sanlitun Lu running north from the intersection at Gongrentiyuchang Bei Lu (west of the Third Ring Road East). **Annie's Café,** at the intersection of Sanlitun Nan Lu and Gongrentiyuchang Bei Lu (☎ 010/6594-2894), open daily from 11am to 2am (see restaurant review in chapter 5), is the southern anchor, adjacent to a kiosk labeled GOD CHOSEN TRAVEL SERVICE. Across the street is a green sign announcing (in English) the gateway to SANLITUN BAR STREET, where the sidewalk is strung with bright pennants and table umbrellas. Here the **Upside Down Club,** 54 Sanlitun Lu (☎ 010/6416-4191), stays open daily around the clock and has a good selection of coffees and espressos.

The first hutong to the east is the location of **Jazz Ya,** 18 Sanlitun Lu (☎ 010/6415-1227), open daily from 10:30am to 2am; it's a Japanese joint-venture that serves Western food and drink and plays moody jazz music. Farther up the street, the bars are interspersed with small boutiques, art galleries, and rattan furniture shops, but it's mostly bars with names like Jack and Jill's, Swing, and Skyline, an upscale bar that opens daily at 2pm and doesn't shut its doors until 6am the next morning.

The west side of Sanlitun Lu features a sidewalk clothing market with designer-label knockoffs, an alley of rattan furniture displays and stalls, and one of the best cafe bars in Beijing, the ✪ **Kebab Kafe** (☎ 010/6415-5812), near the bamboo market. It's open daily from 10:30am to 2am and is known for its fine German food, imported beers, Western desserts, and excellent patio drinking and dining in the summer (see restaurant review in chapter 5).

The north end of Sanlitun Lu contains foreign embassies and consulates, but cafes and bars are sprouting up here, too. Newly opened is the Fly Bar and Restaurant with its "Fly Menu" of Western lunch and dinner specials posted on a signboard outside, and nearby, next to a grocery, is the **Sentiment Bar** (☎ 010/6415-3691), which keeps rather respectable hours (daily 9am to 9pm). Along the southern shore of the Liangma River, 1 block west off Sanlitun Lu, is **Schiller's II,** 1 Sanlitun Bei Lu (☎ 010/6507-1331), a bar popular with local expatriates open daily from 5pm to 1am. If you follow the river east, you'll come to the Third Ring Road area, where more bars and late-night cafes are springing up between the Kempinski and Hilton hotels. This is also the location of Beijing's **Hard Rock Cafe** (see below).

If Sanlitun and the Third Ring Road don't do you in, there's now a barhopping street within easy walking distance west of Sanlitun on Gongrentiyuchang Bei Lu towards the Worker's Stadium: **Dongdaqiao Xie Jie.** This little street curves south and west, and it is bidding to become a Sanlitun South. Cafe bar names run the gamut from Home Station and Free Man to the Jungle Bar and Dirty Nellie's Irish Pub, but the best-known spots are the **Minder Cafe** (☎ 010/6500-6066), open daily from 11am to 2am with live music nightly except Monday, and **Hidden Tree** (see below). Dondaqiao Xie Jie connects to Beijing's original expatriate bar, the ever-popular **Frank's Place** (see below), directly across the street from the east entrance to Worker's Stadium—a most comfortable place to begin and end an extended barhop through Sanlitun.

Here's a list of some of the most popular late-night bars and cafes that foreigners (travelers and residents alike) frequent. Most are in the Sanlitun, Dongdaqiao Xie Jie, and Third Ring Road East areas described above.

✪ Frank's Place.
Across from the east entrance to Worker's Stadium, Gongrentiyuchang Dong Lu, Chaoyang District. ☎ **010/6507-2617.**

Founded in 1990 by Frank himself, this American bar and grill is Beijing's original expatriate hangout, comfortable as an old shoe, crowded and lively. The hamburgers, fries, and Philly cheese streaks, as well as the full dinners, are some of the best Western fare in the city. If home is North America, this is the place to come home to in Beijing. Frank's is open daily from 11:30am to 2am. Credit cards accepted.

Half and Half Cafe.
15 Sanlitun Nan Lu, Chaoyang District. ☎ **010/6416-6919.**

Tucked into an alley east of the frantic Sanlitun strip, this quiet little bar is a welcome retreat, with good beer, burgers, and fries. It's open daily 11am to 2am.

Hard Rock Cafe.
8 Dongsanhuan Bei Lu (Third Ring Road East), Chaoyang District. ☎ **010/6590-6688,** ext. 2571. Cover 100RMB ($12.50) after 10pm.

The music, live and loud, really kicks in at 10pm (as does the cover charge), except on Sundays. The American fast food is among the best served in China, and the beer and mixed drinks are fine, too, but quite expensive (up to $20 for some cocktails). The dance floor is always full. It's open Sunday to Thursday 11:30am to 2am, and Friday and Saturday 11:30am to 3am. Credit cards accepted.

✪ Henry J. Bean's.
West Wing, China World Trade Center, 1 Jianguomenwai Dajie, Chaoyang District. ☎ **010/ 6505-2266,** ext. 6334.

This is Beijing's best American-style bar and grill, with live dance bands most evenings (see restaurant review in chapter 5). It's open Sunday to Thursday from 11:30am to 1am and Friday and Saturday from 11:30am to 2:30am. Credit cards accepted.

Hidden Tree.
12 Dongdaqiao Xie Jie, Chaoyang District. ☎ **010/6509-3642.**

You'll get live music by local bands on weekends at the bar that started the rush to make Dongdaqiao Xie Jie the new Sanlitun Bar Street South. Good Mediterranean food, too, served late. Open daily 5pm to 3am. Credit cards accepted.

John Bull Pub.
44 Guanghua Lu, Chaoyang District. ☎ **010/6532-5905.**

This is Beijing's best English pub and English grub (see restaurant review chapter 5). Open Sunday to Wednesday 11am to 1am, Thursday from 11am to 1am, and Friday and Saturday 11am to 2pm. Credit cards accepted.

Keep in Touch.
Across from the Kempinski Hotel, Jiuxianqiao Donglu, Chaoyang District. ☎ **010/6462-5280.**

Here you'll find live rock music by local Chinese bands, an art gallery, and beer on tap for about $2 a glass. Open daily from 5pm to 1am.

Mexican Wave.
Dongdaqiao Lu, Chaoyang District. ☎ **010/6506-3961.**

This is one of Beijing's oldest expatriate hangouts, established in 1990 (see restaurant review in chapter 5). Open daily from 10am to 2am.

New Cafe Cafe.
Dongdaqiao Xie Jie, Chaoyang District. ☎ **010/6507-1331,** ext 5127.

This place attracts an upscale clientele, from diplomats to local artists. There's an outdoor patio and an indoor courtyard for dining on international cuisine (Italian and Japanese). It's open daily 11am to 2am.

Press Club Bar.
Beijing International Club Hotel, 21 Jianguomenwai Dajie, Chaoyang District. ☎ **010/6460-6688.**

The nearby Beijing International Club, renowned in days gone by as the meeting spot for foreign correspondents, inspired this elegant upscale creation, which seats just 55. Bookshelves with leather-bound tomes, a marble fireplace, a grand piano, leather armchairs, brocade sofas, and old prints and vintage photos of Beijing pundits and press correspondents line the long bar. During the daily happy hour (from 6 to 8pm), waiters in white jackets serve complimentary hors d'oeuvres from silver platters. Open daily from 4:30pm to midnight. Credit cards accepted.

Richmond Brewery.
46 Dongdan Bei Dajie, Dongcheng District. ☎ **010/6512-9497.**

Live rock music most nights by local bands, with microbrews on tap. It's located downtown, 1 block east of Wangfujing, and open daily from 10am to 2am.

San Francisco Brewing Company.
West Wing, Asia Jinjiang Hotel, 8 Xinzhong Xi Jie, Gongrentiyuchang Bei Lu, Chaoyang District. ☎ **010/6500-7788,** ext. 7156.

This big bar has American food from the grill and microbrews on tap, Cuban cigars, and weekend videos shown on a 6-foot screen. Open daily from 11am to 11pm. Credit cards accepted.

T.G.I. Friday's.
19 Dongsanhuan Bei Lu (Third Ring Road East), Chaoyang District. ☎ **010/6595-1380.** Daily 11am–midnight.

This American chain (see restaurant review in chapter 5) is open daily from 11am to midnight. Credit cards are accepted.

Trader's Bar.
28 Dongdan Bei Dajie, Dongcheng District. ☎ **010/6523-3929.**

This two-story cafe/bar has rock music nightly by local bands. It's located downtown, 1 block east of Wangfujing, and is open daily from 11am to 2am.

Zum Fass.
10 Sanlitun Bei Xiao Jie, Chaoyang District. ☎ **010/6462-9666.**

Swiss food, darts, and occasional live music. Open daily from 11am to 2am.

SPORTS BARS

Grandstand Sports Bar.
Holiday Inn Lido, Jichang Lu, Jiang Tai Lu, Chaoyang District. ☎ **010/6437-6688.**

Here you'll find sports posters and all-sports TV, located above the Freezer Disco. Open Sunday to Wednesday 5pm to 2am and Thursday to Saturday 5 to 10pm.

Pit Stop.
Harbour Plaza Hotel, 8 Jiang Tai Xi Lu, Chaoyang District. ☎ **010/6436-2288,** ext 2617.

American snacks from the open grill, a dance floor, and plenty of satellite TV monitors with the latest sports broadcasts—what more could you ask for? The bar has a Formula-One racing theme. From 9am to midnight, it's all-you-can-drink for 120RMB ($15). Open Sunday to Thursday from 4pm to 1am, and Friday and Saturday from 4pm to 2am.

Sports City Cafe.
Second floor, Gloria Plaza Hotel, 2 Jianguomennei Dajie. ☎ **010/6515-8855.**

This is Beijing's biggest and brightest new sports bar, with half-court basketball, darts, putting green, billiards, sports video games, large TV screens, a cigar room, and a dance floor. Open daily from 7pm to 1am.

JAZZ CLUBS

✪ Aria.
Levels 2–3, China World Hotel, 1 Jianguomenwai Dajie, Chaoyang District. ☎ **010/ 6505-2266.** No cover.

Live jazz by local and international soloists and groups is performed nightly at the piano bar in Beijing's plushest wine bar and grill. Open daily 11am to midnight.

CD Cafe Jazz Club.
South of the Agriculture Exhibition Hall, Dongsanhuan (Third Ring Road East), Chaoyang District. ☎ **010/6501-8877,** ext 3032. Cover 20RMB ($2.50).

Here you'll find live jazz every weekend, starting at 9:30pm, blues bands on Sundays at 9:30pm, and solo performers Monday through Thursday from 8pm to midnight. Open daily from 11am to 2am.

Sanwei Bookstore.
West of the Forbidden City on south side of Chang'an Avenue, 60 Fuxingmenwai Dajie, Xicheng District. ☎ **010/6601-3204.** Cover 30RMB ($3.75).

Live local jazz is performed upstairs in this traditional teahouse every Friday night at 7:30pm. Open daily from 9:30am to 10:30pm.

Shadow Cafe.
Attached to Club-X Disco, 31 Kexueyuan Nan Lu, Haidian District. ☎ **010/6261-8587.** No cover.

Head here for live local jazz and improvisations Saturday nights from 9pm to 1am. Open daily from 8:30pm to 2am.

DANCE CLUBS

Club Banana.
Fifth floor, Sea Sky Shopping Center, 12 Chaoyangmennei Dajie, Chaoyang District. ☎ **010/ 6599-3351.** Cover 50RMB ($6) Sun–Thurs; free for foreigners Fri–Sat.

Once an exclusive nightclub with an MTV room and a dress code, this is now an anything-goes disco with plenty of seating. Open daily from 8:30pm to 1:30am.

The Sexual Underground

A sexual as well as an economic revolution may be sweeping China these days, but the gay and lesbian scene is still far underground, even in "liberal" Beijing. Gay bars do pop up now and then, only to be closed. It's all right for people of the same sex to walk down the street hand in hand—many Chinese friends do so—but embracing or kissing is not acceptable. China's puritanical approach to sexual expression will probably strike many homosexuals from the West as naive rather than barbaric, since anti-gay policies seldom surface and rarely, if ever, afflict foreign visitors, at least overtly.

On another sexually forbidden front, it is worth noting that at least one bar in the quiet southern end of the Sanlitun bar district, the **Golden Eye Pub** on Sanlitun Nan Lu (☎ **010/6509-3267**), has been recently staging what it bills as transvestite stage shows. Moreover, Beijing's best-known transsexual, Jin Xing, who owns a Sanlitun cafe/bar herself (called the **Half Moon** in press reports, but otherwise unidentified), has been quoted on several occasions by foreign reporters. The former army colonel and men's dance champion, known for her flashy gowns and shiny nail polish, claims that the Clinton scandals would have never been an issue in China. At the same time, she admits that her own love life after a sex-change operation could be better. "I'm too much for Chinese men," she concludes. "But I'm able to lead a normal life in Beijing. No discrimination."

Freezer Disco Club.
Holiday Inn Lido, Jichang Lu, Jiang Tai Lu, Chaoyang District. ☎ **010/6437-6688,** ext 1414. No cover.

Chill out in this spacious, dark, loud joint, complete with a bar, a stage with live bands, a sunken dance floor, and plenty of table seating. Open Sunday to Wednesday from 5pm to 2am, and Thursday to Saturday from 5 to 10pm.

✪ Hot Spot.
South of the Jingguang New World Hotel, Third Ring Road East, Chaoyang District. ☎ **010/6501-9955.** No cover for foreigners.

Currently the hottest spot in Beijing for a disco evening, Hot Spot is inside the grounds of the People's Liberation Army (PLA), and PLA soldiers in uniform are on hand to greet customers. The stage and cage shows are provocative by Beijing standards. Break dancing, hip-hop, and rap are performed on stage, while the scantily clad cage dancers rise and fall overhead as they dance in their metal cages. This is a favorite of foreigners and locals alike, some who dance all night, some who come only to drink and stare. Open nightly from 8pm to 2am.

NASA.
2 Xitucheng Lu, Haidian District. ☎ **010/6203-2906.** No cover for foreigners.

A long-standing institution in Beijing, NASA has a largely military theme, with an army jeep serving as the bar and a helicopter suspended from the balcony. It's a favorite of the university crowd, both local and foreign. Open Sunday to Thursday from 9pm to 1am, and Friday and Saturday from 9pm to 2am.

Nightman Disco.
West side of International Exhibition Center, 2 Xibahe Nanli, Chaoyang District. ☎ **010/6466-2562.** No cover for foreigners with ID.

This cavernous club surrounded by large screens broadcasting music videos is one of Beijing's older discos, but it's still going strong. Open nightly from 9pm to 2am.

Poachers Inn the Park.
West gate of Tuanjiehu Park, east side of Third Ring Road East, Chaoyang District. ☎ **010/6500-8390** or 010/6532-3063. Cover 50RMB ($6).

Ensconced inside a Chinese-style mansion within a classic Chinese garden, Poachers consists of Smugglers Bar, an English-style pub, and a disco dance floor with stone walls and floor. In the summer months, the dance and music sometimes move outdoors onto the more inviting Island Park stage. Open daily from 3pm to 3am, or later.

The Great Wall & Other Side Trips from Beijing

The Great Wall is the number-one site in the Beijing vicinity—the number-one site in all of China—and it should not be missed. Four other places near Beijing are worth an excursion, too: the legendary Western Hills, the famous archaeological site of Peking Man, and the tombs of the Ming and Qing dynasty emperors. From Beijing, each of these treasures requires just a day trip, but it can add up to a long day. Most travelers book a group tour with an English-speaking guide to smooth the way. The main drawback to such an arrangement is that you have but a short time to explore the site, often 2 hours or less. Alternatives are to hire a driver and car yourself, with the assistance of your hotel concierge, or to use public buses (the cheapest, but most grueling, way to make the trips). Whatever means you choose, seeing these ancient remains outside Beijing is well worth a day's journey.

1 The Great Wall

The Chinese call it *Wan Li Chang Cheng,* the "Long Wall of Ten-Thousand Li," there being three *li* to the mile. Actually, the Great Wall is even longer than its poetic name claims, measuring about 6,200 miles from east to west, counting all its serpentine sections. The wall's origins date back at least to the 5th century B.C., when the rival kingdoms of the Warring States Period (453–221 B.C.) built defensive ramparts against their enemies. The First Emperor of unified China, Qin Shi Huang Di, fortified the barriers in the 3rd century B.C. Over a 10-year period, 300,000 conscripted laborers, many of them slaves, knit the walls into a continuous rampart to protect the western frontier. New sections extended the wall east to the Yellow Sea.

The Great Wall was constantly repositioned along new routes as successive dynasties rose and fell. In the year A.D. 607, more than a million workers toiled on this line of defense, but soon after the Great Wall was abandoned. The Mongols eventually broke through from the north and established the Yuan Dynasty (A.D. 1271–1368), making Beijing their capital. Their successors, the emperors of the Ming Dynasty (A.D. 1368–1644), set in motion the last great phase of wall building, which created the Great Wall as we see it today north of Beijing.

Side Trips from Beijing

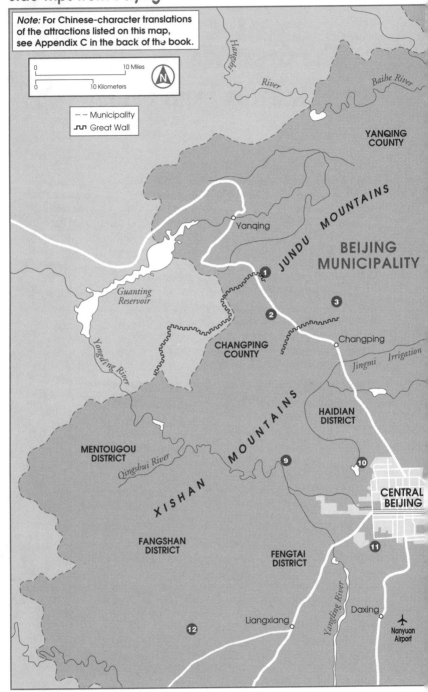

Note: For Chinese-character translations of the attractions listed on this map, see Appendix C in the back of the book.

0   10 Miles

0   10 Kilometers

– – Municipality

Great Wall

YANQING COUNTY

Hanguin River

Baihe River

Yanqing

JUNDU MOUNTAINS

BEIJING MUNICIPALITY

Guanting Reservoir

Yongding River

CHANGPING COUNTY

Changping

Jingmi Irrigation

HAIDIAN DISTRICT

MENTOUGOU DISTRICT

Qingshui River

XISHAN MOUNTAINS

CENTRAL BEIJING

FANGSHAN DISTRICT

FENGTAI DISTRICT

Liangxiang

Yongding River

Daxing

Nanyuan Airport

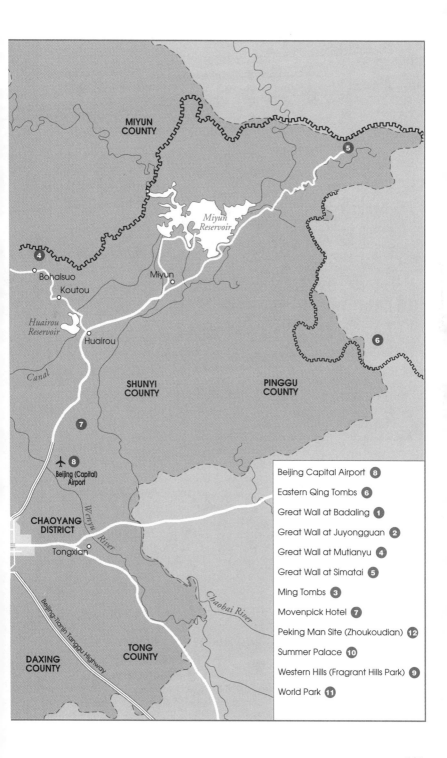

MIYUN COUNTY

Miyun Reservoir

Bohaisuo
Koutou
Miyun

Huairou Reservoir

Huairou

Canal

SHUNYI COUNTY

PINGGU COUNTY

Chaobai River

Beijing (Capital) Airport

CHAOYANG DISTRICT

Tongxian

Wenyu River

Beijing-Tianjin Tanggu Highway

DAXING COUNTY

TONG COUNTY

Beijing Capital Airport **8**

Eastern Qing Tombs **6**

Great Wall at Badaling **1**

Great Wall at Juyongguan **2**

Great Wall at Mutianyu **4**

Great Wall at Simatai **5**

Ming Tombs **3**

Movenpick Hotel **7**

Peking Man Site (Zhoukoudian) **12**

Summer Palace **10**

Western Hills (Fragrant Hills Park) **9**

World Park **11**

To think that these walls, built in apparently inaccessible places, as though to balance the Milky Way in the sky, a walled walk over the mountain tops, are the work of men, makes it seem like a dream.
—Comte de Beauvoir, *Voyage Autour du Monde*, 1867

Today, the Great Wall can be visited most easily at four dramatic points near Beijing: **Badaling, Mutianyu, Simatai,** and **Juyongguan.** All are appealing. Badaling is where most tourists walk on the Great Wall. Mutianyu is a fine alternative, beautifully restored and less crowded. Simatai is a wild, nearly unrestored segment, farther from Beijing and, consequently, far less inundated with tour buses. Juyongguan is the newest section to be opened to tourists and the nearest to Beijing. All four sections are 300 to 500 years old, dating from the Ming Dynasty, and all four are beautiful sections of the Great Wall, coiling up and down impossibly steep terrain. They are fitting representatives of the greatest wall ever built by man—what one 19th-century traveler called a "fantastic serpent of stone."

THE GREAT WALL AT BADALING
42 miles NW of Beijing

Almost everyone who pays a call on the Great Wall, from heads of state to adventurers crossing China with backpacks, visits Badaling. This is a grand section of the wall, set in a steep, forested mountain range. Here the wall, its stairs, and the magnificent watchtowers were carefully restored, beginning in 1957. While many a traveler pooh-poohs Badaling as a deplorable tourist trap, crowded beyond all endurance, it disappoints few travelers. It may be crowded, but so is China, especially at its top sites.

Construction of this Ming Dynasty section of the Great Wall began in 1368 and continued for almost 200 years. Built of stone, the wall averages 24 feet in height, is 21 feet wide at its base, and 18 feet wide on top. The interior is a mixture of tamped soil and rubble. The sides are covered in stone, the top in layers of brick. In fact, the bricks we associate with building the Great Wall weren't introduced until the Ming builders set to work here, northwest of Beijing.

The wall at Badaling has been restored to reflect its Ming Dynasty grandeur. Gateway arches and watchtowers run the length of the wall, which served as a highway through the mountains. Five horses could ride abreast, drawing carriages. Today, the main parking lot and squares, filled with vendors, are reflections of China's modern economic boom.

ESSENTIALS
VISITOR INFORMATION   The Great Wall at Badaling (☎ **010/6912-1308**), is open daily from 6am to 6:30pm (until 10pm on summer weekends). Admission is 30RMB ($3.75). The cable car is 100RMB ($12.50) round-trip.

GETTING THERE   **China International Travel Service (CITS),** with headquarters at 28 Jianguomenwai Dajie, Chaoyang District (☎ **010/6515-8566**), arranges guided tours to the Great Wall at Badaling. CITS maintains convenient branches in most hotels. Group tours to the Great Wall at Badaling leave from various hotels at 8:30am daily and cost about 400RMB ($50) per person, including lunch and stops at the Ming Tombs, souvenir stores, and other regional sites. Time on the wall itself is usually limited to less than 2 hours.

To hire a driver, car, and guide for the day costs about 1,200RMB ($150) total. To hire just a car and driver costs about 800RMB ($100). The cost to hire a taxi on your own from the street for the day depends on your powers of negotiation, but it should cost less than 400RMB ($50).

A new expressway connects Beijing to the Great Wall at Badaling. Tour buses make the trip in about 90 minutes, unless the expressway is clogged with other buses or there's been an accident (which is not uncommon). Government-sponsored tour buses (the green no. 1 buses) make the run every 20 minutes in the morning, beginning at 6am and leaving from in front of Qianmen Gate (at the south end of Tiananmen Square) for 8RMB ($1) each way. Other buses depart from the Beijing Railway Station southeast of Tiananmen Square (bus no. 2); from Dondaqiao, near the Silk Alley Market (bus no. 3); from the Beijing Zoo (bus no. 4); and from Qianmen Xi Dajie, west of Tiananmen Square (bus no. 5).

The train from Beijing to Hohhot stops near the Badaling section of the wall at Qinglongqiao West train station. The rail journey (train no. 527) takes about 3 hours from Beijing's Yongdingmen train station, departing at 9:40am (one-way fare 20RMB/$2.50). There are many other trains as well. The Qinglongqiao West train station is near the southern end of Badaling. In the winter, when the Great Wall at Badaling is dusted with snow, a train trip from Beijing is a delight. There are almost no tourists on the wall, the sun is bright, and the mountain peaks and guard towers are gorgeous.

EXPLORING THE WALL

A long stairway runs up to the wall. You can head northeast or southwest and walk a mile or so in either direction. The incredible steepness of the Great Wall and the high rise of its stairs always astound visitors. Walking up to the highest watchtower is often enough to exhaust a visitor thoroughly, especially on a hot day. There's no reason to hurry. The scenery is splendid. The two-story watchtowers, consisting of a guardroom below and an observation house above, are fine places to recuperate.

If you walk along the southwest section of the wall about two-thirds of a mile, you'll come to an unrenovated spine of the wall that has a much more primitive feel. Few tourists venture out this far. The stairs are crumbling and the sides of the wall are broken, exposing the earthen filling.

If you choose to walk Badaling in the other direction, you'll come to a terminal for the Great Wall cable car that takes you down to another parking lot. Beyond the cable car, the Great Wall also reverts to its former ruins, and you are again free to explore the wall as it was centuries ago.

The way back down the wall where you came in requires a steep descent down high stairs. Some travelers walk back down facing backward. The modern handrails help. At the bottom of the wall is a "Great Mall" of endless souvenir stands, a movie

Great Wall Travel Tips

To avoid the thickest crowds, visit the Great Wall at Badaling and Mutianyu on weekdays rather than weekends, and early in the morning if possible. Early spring and late fall are the most pleasant time to go; June through September is high tourist season. If you're visiting the Great Wall on a guided tour that includes lunch, you'll dine at one of the restaurants catering to foreigner groups with set Chinese lunches. The Great Wall at Badaling even has a branch of Kentucky Fried Chicken. If you're on your own for food, it's best to pack a lunch in Beijing and enjoy it on the wall.

Impressions

To me, the least agreeable aspect of present-day China is the rampant entrepreneurism that lines the path of every notable sight, from the Great Wall down, with frantically aggressive vendors. The tend to vend the same things—bottled water, silk scarves, chiming "healthy balls," carved jade, used and discarded copies of the once sacred Little Red Book—for prices that, translated out of yuan, amount to little enough, but the clamor of beseechment drives all thought of purchase from the head of any but the most hardened souvenir hunters.
— John Updike, "Back from China," *The New Yorker,* December 7–14, 1998

---

hall, and cafes. Prices are exceptionally high for trinkets, crafts, and "I Climbed the Great Wall" T-shirts, even when you bargain like mad.

THE GREAT WALL AT MUTIANYU
55 miles NE of Beijing

The Great Wall at Badaling proved so popular that authorities restored a second section of the wall in 1986, at Mutianyu. Mutianyu was supposed to relieve the overcrowding at Badaling, particularly on weekends. The ploy has not completely succeeded, but Mutianyu is often less busy than Badaling. Its setting is more rough and rugged than that at Badaling, even if it now has summer traffic jams of its own.

ESSENTIALS

VISITOR INFORMATION   The Great Wall at Mutianyu (☎ **010/6964-2022**) is open daily from 6:30am to 6pm (until 10pm in the summer). Admission is 30RMB ($3.75). The cable car is 100RMB ($12.50) round-trip. For the same price as the cable car, there is a new **rollertrain** that winds up and down the hillsides along the wall for about two-thirds of a mile, reaching speeds of 20 m.p.h.

GETTING THERE   **China International Travel Service (CITS),** with headquarters at 28 Jianguomenwai Dajie (☎ **010/6515-8566**), arranges guided tours to the Great Wall at Mutianyu. CITS maintains convenient branches in most hotels. Group tours to the Great Wall at Mutianyu leave at noon on Tuesdays, Thursdays, and Saturdays from various hotels and cost about 220RMB ($27) per person. These tours usually make stops at a pearl factory or similar outlet on the way and include tours of other sites in Beijing, leaving less than 2 hours on the wall itself.

If you are not on a tour, you can catch a minibus to Mutianyu in front of the Great Hall of the People in Tiananmen Square. A kiosk sells tickets (10RMB/$1.25 each way) the day before. Morning departure times vary, so check ahead. There is no train service to Mutianyu.

To hire a driver, car, and guide for the day costs about 1,200RMB ($150) total. To hire just a car and driver costs about 800RMB ($100). The cost to hire a taxi on your own from the street for the day depends on your powers of negotiation, but it should cost less than 400RMB ($50).

EXPLORING THE WALL

The mile-long segment of the Great Wall of Mutianyu was among the first built during the Ming Dynasty, beginning over 500 years ago. As at Badaling, a long stairway leads up to the wall. The hike can take up to 20 minutes, so you might want to use the nearby cable car. If you turn right at the top of the entrance, you can walk the ramparts for over half a mile. At the end is a barrier; visitors are not permitted to venture beyond this point. All you can do is contemplate the wall in ruins, which gives you an excellent idea of what most of the Great Wall, even those sections built just a few hundred rather than a few thousand years ago, looks like now.

If you turn left after reaching the wall, there are several steep and scenic guard towers ahead. The view of the undulating wall and forested mountains is stunning. There's also a cable car station here, which is the kindest way back down (for your knees and thighs). The vendors who line the path at the base of Mutianyu are friendly, but persistent. They will probably remember you. The prices on souvenirs tend to drop dramatically as you descend.

THE GREAT WALL AT SIMATAI
77 miles NE of Beijing

The Great Wall at Simatai is quiet, remote, and virtually unreconstructed. Locals proclaim it the most dangerous section of the Great Wall. Since it is largely unrestored, it does indeed have difficult and dangerous passages to hike. Fortification aficionados consider Simatai the most beautiful section of the Great Wall. It is beautiful, but its main aesthetic attraction is its state of ruin. This is how the Great Wall really looks 500 years after the Ming constructed it. Simatai is also a paradise for hikers and hill walkers, with its dramatic natural scenery, the contours of the sharp peaks heightened by the outline of the Great Wall, and its crumbling watchtowers.

The Chengde highway to Simatai is smooth, the countryside green. At Miyun Reservoir, the terrain gets steeper. The roadside is clotted with fishing families selling their catch, enormous reservoir trout, many 3 feet long, sheathed in plastic and suspended on posts like lanterns. At Gubeikou, 70 miles northeast of Beijing, a country lane winds 7 more miles through the foothills to Simatai Village and the entrance to the wall. The town at the base is tiny. The main street leading to the wall has a few beef noodle cafes, souvenir shops, and vendor shelters stocked with T-shirts and Great Wall tablecloths, but this is a mere minnow pond of sellers compared to the ocean of hawkers flooding the gates to Badaling and Mutianyu. Towering high over the village is the formidable outline of the Great Wall at Simatai, slithering like a dragon's back over a series of sharp, clipped peaks.

ESSENTIALS
VISITOR INFORMATION   The Great Wall at Simatai (☎ **010/6993-1095**), is open daily from 8am to 5pm (until 10pm in the summer). Admission is 20RMB ($2.50). The cable car is 60RMB ($7.50) round-trip.

Simatai is far less crowded than other sections of the Great Wall near Beijing.

Food stands at the base sell simple dishes for about $2 a plate. You can also pack a lunch in Beijing and enjoy it on the wall.

GETTING THERE   **China International Travel Service (CITS),** with headquarters at 28 Jianguomenwai Dajie (☎ **010/6515-8566**), can arrange private guided tours with a driver and an English-speaking guide to the Great Wall at Simatai. The cost for a solo traveler is about 1,200RMB ($150). CITS maintains convenient branches in most hotels.

You can also hire a taxi, without a guide, for about 400RMB ($50); book a minibus (100RMB/$12.50 round-trip) at the tourist office in the **Jinghua Hotel,** Nansanhuan Xi Lu (☎ **010/6722-2211**); or catch the public bus that leaves the Dongzhimen bus station in Beijing at 7am and arrives at Simatai 3 or 4 hours later (a cheap but rough alternative).

EXPLORING THE WALL

Beyond the village is a half-mile walk up to the first stairway and watchtower. The sandy path rises and skirts the small Simatai Reservoir, where in the heat of summer tourists from Beijing board pleasure boats for a sail along the Great Wall. But from the water, the wall remains high and remote. The reservoir lies in a deep crease dividing two sections of the wall—Simatai to the east, Jinshanling to the west.

Ascending the stairs to the first watchtower at Simatai is a matter of pounding a few hundred stone steps, the treads of this staircase often just half as deep as an average foot length. The climb is a struggle, but the view from the first of the ascending towers, taken through open cannon archways, is magnificent: endless mountain chains to the deserted north; watchtowers crowning the ridgelines east and west; and the reservoir, village, and farmlands far below, rolling southward toward Beijing.

This first portion of the Great Wall at Simatai has been restored, as have virtually all the walkways and towers tourists see along Badaling and Mutianyu, but from here on at Simatai, the wall has been left to crumble. The grand stairways disappear. The pathway becomes a ledge of rock and sand along the outside of the rising wall, narrowing to sheer drop-offs. Sometimes there are no footholds at all. Shedding its stair treads over the centuries, the wall is as treacherous to scale as a waterslide of gravel.

The wall bricks, each with its own stamped number, date from the Ming Dynasty. Many of the bricks have fallen away, exposing the original earthen core with which the large work gangs fortified the mountain peaks. From the towers on the wall, signals of fire and smoke once alerted those inside the wall to impending invasions from outside.

At Simatai you can still see the results of the Ming Dynasty building program in high relief. The toll taken by 5 centuries of weather and civilization is substantial, but far from complete. Simatai survives as a wild run of ruins, its main outline intact, stretching from peak to chiseled peak on ridges sometimes pitched to 70-degree inclines. Best of all for the traveler, Simatai is as peaceful as it is untouched, and as beautiful as the mountains it dances across. There are 14 watchtowers at Simatai, stationed at quarter-mile intervals and strung across the peaks until the wall dissolves into scattered bricks, piles of sand, and fragments of bone from the workers buried within the wall.

Coming down Simatai is more daunting than going up. Locals recount stories of visitors who have broken into tears during the descent, unnerved by the steepness, the lack of stairs, and the unstable footings. Some come down the stairless top of the wall backward, on all fours. The name "Simatai" shares the same sounds in Chinese as the words "Dead Horse Platform," a reference to a horse that fell in a famous battle fought beneath the wall here. So far, no tourists have added their names to this venerable tradition.

In fact, there is a safer way to scale Simatai. East of the entrance is a gondola. Visitors can hop a ride part way up and climb a new, safer set of steep stairs to the 2,624-foot-high eighth tower on the wall. From here, on a clear evening, you can see the lights of Beijing.

WHERE TO STAY

Adventurous travelers might want to stay overnight at the rustic accommodations provided by **Simatai Village** (☎ **010/6903-1221**), a compound with cabins and dormitories. The cabins, which sleep up to four people, come with clean private

The "Newest" Section of the Great Wall

In 1998, China opened another section of the Great Wall to tourists at **Juyong-guan.** Juyongguan lies 36 miles northwest of Beijing, making it the closest point to the capital for a view of the wall. There, a 2.5-mile section was renovated under a 5-year program costing $14 million. Juyongguan is the site of one of the Great Wall's most famous mountain passes, and the massive guard towers there are quite impressive, as is the wall itself, which undulates over the peaks and ridges of the Taihang Mountains. Several of the many temples and gardens at the pass have also been restored.

Juyongguan (meaning the "Tower That Bestrides the Road") was erected in A.D. 1345, predating the Ming Dynasty. It is famous for its Buddhist bas-relief carvings and the inscriptions in six languages (Chinese, Uighur, Tangut, Mongolian, Tibetan, and Sanskrit).

At present, there are no regularly scheduled group tours to Juyongguan, but it is only 6 miles southeast of the Great Wall at Badaling, on the same main highway, so check with hotel tour desks and CITS when you arrive. In the meantime, adventurous travelers rely on the slow but cheap tourist buses that depart for Badaling from five Beijing locations every morning at 8:30am (Tourist Bus no. 1 from Qianmen, the gate at the southern end of Tiananmen Square; no. 2 from the Beijing Railway Station southeast of Tiananmen; no. 3 from Dondaqiao, near the Silk Alley Market; no. 4 from the Beijing Zoo; and no. 5 from Qianmen Xi Dajie, west of Tiananmen Square).

bathrooms (toilet and hot-water shower) and rent for 606RMB ($75) a day. Four-person dormitory rooms cost 96RMB ($12) per person. The compound boasts its own restaurant and snack bar.

2 The Western Hills (Fragrant Hills Park)

17 miles NW of Beijing

The Western Hills (Xi Shan) have been a refuge from the summer heat for China's rulers since the Liao Dynasty (A.D. 907–1125), when the first imperial villas appeared on these shady slopes. Under Qing emperor Qianlong in the 18th century, the mountainside retreat became the site of a formal park, with temples, pavilions, 28 officially designated scenic locations, and an exotic wildlife park stocked with white deer. This portion of the Western Hills, now the destination of ordinary Beijingers desiring to escape the city heat, is known as **Fragrant Hills Park (Xiangshan Gongyuan).** The Fragrant Hills, which encompasses 4,000 acres, has been a public park since 1957. The highlight for most park-goers, particularly in the late autumn when the leaves of the Huanglu smoke tree are changing color, is to hike the trail or ride the chair lift to the summit of Fragrant Hills, known as Incense Burner Hill.

ESSENTIALS

Fragrant Hills Park (☎ **010/6259-1155**) is open daily from 8am until 5pm (until sunset in the summer). It is sometimes included on CITS group tours offered through hotels. The park is just 6 miles from the Summer Palace. From downtown, taxis can reach the Fragrant Hills in about 1 hour at a cost of around 80RMB ($10) one-way. Bus no. 360 from the Beijing Zoo and bus no. 333 from the Summer Palace also serve Fragrant Hills; the fare is 2RMB (25¢). Admission is just 3RMB (35¢). The chair lift to the summit of Incense Burner Peak costs 30RMB ($3.75) each way.

EXPLORING THE AREA

There's plenty to see in the Western Hills. A mile east of the north gate to Fragrant Hills Park is the **Temple of the Sleeping Buddha (Wo Fo Si).** Its most famous attraction is a lacquered, reclining statue of Buddha about to enter Nirvana. The figure's age is in some dispute (some think it dates back as far as A.D. 1321), but its length is easily fixed, stretching the tape to 16 feet (5 meters). The enormous shoes displayed in the flanking cases are gifts presented to the Buddha by devout worshippers, perhaps even some Qing Dynasty emperors. The temple is open daily from 8am to 4:30pm; admission is a modest 2RMB (25¢).

Just inside the northern gate to the Fragrant Hills Park (immediately to the right and north across the bridge) is the **Temple of the Azure Clouds (Bi Yun Si)** (☎ 010/6259-1205). This large complex climbs the hillside, courtyard by courtyard, hall by hall, crowned by the Diamond Throne Pagoda, built in the style of India's *stupas* (dome-shaped monuments containing holy relics) in the late 18th century and decorated with well-restored Buddhist sculptures. The **Diamond Throne Pagoda (Jinggang Baozuo Ta),** built in 1748, consists of a white marble pagoda 115 feet (35 meters) tall and a cluster of four lesser pagodas and two *dagobas* (bulb-shaped towers). The most interesting display is in the Luohan Hall, where 508 lifelike, lively, and sometimes gruesomely surreal gilded statues of Buddha's disciples are glumly displayed in dusty glass cases. The middle hall of the complex memorializes Sun Yat-sen, founder of the Chinese Republic, who lay in state in this temple complex until his body was moved to Nanjing. His steel and crystal coffin, a gift from Russia, is still on view, and his hat and coat were left behind, sealed up in the Diamond Throne Pagoda. The temple is open daily from 7:30am to 4:30pm; admission is 10RMB ($1.25).

The ticket office for the chair lift to the summit of the Fragrant Hills is also just inside the northern entrance. This is the park's top attraction, affording marvelous panoramic views of the forested hills. The summit is called ۞ **Incense Burner Peak (Xiang Lu Feng)** because of the enormous incense burner–shaped dual rock formation on its crown. Open daily from 8am to 5pm, the two-person chair lifts take about 20 minutes to make the ascent through the 20 numbered stations to the top (elevation 1,827 feet/557 meters). Fuzzy recorded music accompanies every chairlift passenger from cable tower to cable tower. On the right as you ascend you can see the Temple of Azure Clouds and its lovely pagoda. On the left, you'll see Spectacles Lake (*Yanjing Hu*), two lakes joined by a bridge that resemble a pair of eyeglasses. Farther away, you'll see a 16th-century garden, the Pavilion of Introspection (*Jian Xin Zhai*), with a moon-shaped pool. Near by are the remains of a lama temple (Zhao Miao) and its seven-story pagoda (Liu Li Ta), noted for its glazed tiles and bronze bells dangling from the eaves. You can take a closer look at these sites on foot after you descend.

The peak is a spacious one, with pavilions, courtyards, vendors, and a plethora of paths leading up and down more peaks in every direction. To the east, you can see the Summer Palace. During the prime season in the Fragrant Hills—late October to early November, when the leaves change to a sizzling red in the autumn—the peak is full of young couples and families, lured by the romance conferred by the foliage and advertised by classical poets since the Tang Dynasty. Young women and girls all seem to wear wristbands and headbands of fresh flowers. The fall foliage is a nice change from the drab urban landscapes, but don't expect it to be quite as luxuriant in the Fragrant Hills as it is in New England and northeast Canada.

The chair lift makes for a quick, scenic descent, but the most healthful way down from the peak is a 45- to 60-minute walk on the zigzagging path, which consists of more than 2,000 steps. The path is known as *Guijianchou,* "Even the Devil Is Scared," but it is far from tortuous or dangerous. If you keep to the right as you descend, you'll end up at a road that leads north (a left turn) to the **Fragrant Hills Hotel,** designed by I. M. Pei, the renowned American architect. A blend of Western and Chinese as well as ancient and modern styles, the hotel and the grounds invite strolling. The hotel also serves the best food in the park (Western and Chinese); its restaurants accept credit cards. From the hotel you can walk back to the north entrance, taking in the temples, pagodas, and gardens you spotted from above.

3 Museum of Peking Man

31 miles SW of Beijing

A team of archaeologists excavating a site known as **Dragon Bone Hill (Long Gu Shan),** near the village of Zhoukoudian, made one of the great discoveries in modern paleontology on December 2, 1929, when they turned up the skull of a new human ancestor, Peking Man (*Homo erectus pekinensis*). This and other remains of Peking Man, who is thought to have lived here as long as ago as 690,000 years, means that man's closest ancestor probably evolved in Asia. The cave where Peking Man dwelt measures 460 feet wide by 130 feet deep. Up the north-facing hillside researchers located a second cave, the Upper Cave, where Stone Age Man dwelt a mere 20,000 to 50,000 years ago. The Upper Cave yielded the remains of eight people, their stone tools, bone ornaments, and a sewing needle. The much older Peking Man cave yielded six complete skulls, nine skull fragments, and 152 teeth, the remains of as many as 40 cave dwellers, as well as evidence of the use of fire and stone tools. Following an intensive period of excavation from 1927 to 1937, almost all these fossils disappeared en route to America for safekeeping during the war, apparently pilfered along the way (some say by the Japanese, some say by the Taiwanese, and some say by American archaeologists or collectors).

ESSENTIALS

Located at Zhoukoudian Village, Fangshan District, **Peking Man Museum** (☎ **010/6930-1272**), is open daily from 8:30am to 4:30pm. Admission is 20RMB ($2.50). If you want to visit in the company of an English-speaking guide, which I recommend, contact your hotel concierge or **China International Travel Service (CITS),** 28 Jianguomenwai Dajie (☎ **010/6515-8566**).

EXPLORING THE AREA

For those with a keen interest in archaeology or paleontology, the **Peking Man Museum** at Zhoukoudian is an absolute must, but for most tourists it is not a highlight. The museum, rebuilt in 1972, houses the remains of Peking Man's cave on one side and an Exhibition Hall on the other. The educational displays in the Exhibition Hall are ponderous, there's not much information in English, and the fossils and relics aren't terribly impressive, either, consisting largely of plaster molds of the missing skulls, prehistoric animal bones, some stone tools, and statues of Peking Man. There are trails to the excavation sites (which are numbered) and to the upper and lower caves on Dragon Bone Hill, so named because local peasants had been digging up the bone fragments of prehistoric man for years, thinking they were the bones of ancient dragons.

4 The Ming Tombs

31 miles NW of Beijing

Of the 16 emperors who ruled China during the Ming Dynasty (A.D. 1368–1644), 13 are buried in elaborate complexes in the valley of the Ming Tombs north of Beijing. Tomb construction began here in 1409 and continued for 2 centuries. A red gate at the only entrance sealed off the valley, and guards were posted to keep out the people. No one, not even the emperor, could ride a horse on these grounds. The same emperor, Yongle, who oversaw the construction of the Forbidden City, chose the site of this huge cemetery. The tombs reflect a similar conception of imperial architecture, consisting of walls, gates, courtyards, stairways, and elaborate pavilions with yellow tile roofs (yellow being the color of emperors). The actual burial chamber (a tumulus) is underground. The emperor, his wife, and his favored concubines were the only people buried there, along with enough royal treasure to stuff a small museum. Yongle's two Ming Dynasty successors are entombed in Nanjing, and the seventh Ming emperor chose to be buried nearer Beijing (on Jinshan Hill). Otherwise, this is Ming China's ultimate old boy's club (afterlife branch).

The entrance to the Ming Tombs, a long and celebrated Spirit Way, is lined with statues of guardian animals and officials. The tombs are dispersed around the edges of a box canyon. Three of the tombs have been restored (Ding Ling, Chang Ling, and Zhao Ling). The rest can be visited, but not entered. The 10 unrestored tombs are among the favorite summer picnic spots of resident foreigners in Beijing. This "Forbidden Valley" of dead kings covers about 15 square miles.

ESSENTIALS

The Ming Tombs (known in Chinese as *Shisan Ling,* the "Thirteen Tombs"), in Changping County (☎ 010/6976-1424), are open daily from 8am to 5:30pm. Admission, collected at the Spirit Way entrance to the tombs, is 16RMB ($2). Admission to each restored tomb is an additional 30RMB ($2.75). Many group tours to the Great Wall at Badaling (see above) stop here. Check with your hotel about group tours or contact **China International Travel Service (CITS),** 28 Jianguomenwai Dajie (☎ 010/6515-8566). If you want to visit on your own, you can hire a taxi or take any of the special Tourist Buses that stop here on the way to the Great Wall. These buses depart Beijing every morning starting at about 8:30am (Tourist Bus no. 1 from Qianmen, the gate at the southern end of Tiananmen Square; bus no. 2 from the Beijing Railway Station southeast of Tiananmen; bus no. 3 from Dondaqiao, near the Silk Alley Market; bus no. 4 from the Beijing Zoo; and bus no. 5 from Qianmen Xi Dajie, west of Tiananmen Square).

The Ming Tombs are at their most charming along the Spirit Way entrance and off the beaten track on the grounds of the unrestored tombs. The restored tombs, where tour groups are funneled by their leaders, are largely uninspiring, dank, and usually too crowded to enjoy. In fact, the Ming Tombs are so unpopular with foreign tourists that they are now more often than not excluded from the group itinerary. A more impressive cemetery of kings is the Eastern Qing Tombs (see below).

EXPLORING THE AREA

The ✪ **Spirit Way (Shen Dao),** the formal entrance to the Ming Tombs that funeral processions from the Forbidden City would have trod over, extends almost

4 miles from the entrance gate to the first restored tomb. The five-arched marble entrance gate, 95 feet wide, was carved in 1540. A second passageway, the **Great Red Gate (Da Hong Men),** served as the old entrance to the valley, its middle door opened only to admit an emperor about to be entombed. The next relic is a carved stone tablet (stele) dating from 1426, with an inscription added by Qing Emperor Qianlong 3 centuries later. It is followed by the most famous site at the Ming Tombs, the **Avenue of the Stone Animals.** Most royal tombs have such an avenue of sculptures, but none as impressive as the Ming Tombs. There are 12 pairs of animals, including elephants, lions, and mythological beasts, and six pairs of court and military officials. It is worth walking this portion of the entrance, as the old sculptures, some dating from A.D. 1435, are a delight.

The tombs lie at the end of the Spirit Way, which passes through the **Dragon Phoenix Gate (Long Feng Men)**—said to separate the living from the dead—and across the **Shisanling (13 Tombs) Reservoir.** The largest and best preserved of the tombs is straight ahead: **Chang Ling,** the tomb of Emperor Yongle, the third Ming ruler, who presided over China from 1403 to 1424 and created the Forbidden Palace and Temple of Heaven. He is buried with his wife, Empress Xu. Aboveground, the complex is like a miniature Forbidden City, with gates, courtyards, and halls mounted on tiers of marble terraces. Slabs engraved with dragons and phoenixes divide the stairways. The yellow-tiled roof of the massive **Hall of Eminent Favors (Ling En Dian)** is supported by scores of sandalwood columns, transported from distant Yunnan Province in the 15th century. The hall now contains a gallery of treasures extracted from another Ming tomb (the Ding Ling tomb), including armor and imperial gowns. The **Soul Tower,** containing a stone tablet and marble altar, is behind the Hall of Eminent Favors in the third courtyard. Then comes the underground burial palace, surrounded by the 1,640-foot-long circular **Precious Wall (Bao Cheng).** Unfortunately, archaeologists have not yet figured out how to safely enter the tomb below. There are 16 satellite graves at Emperor Yongle's tomb, one for each of his concubines, who are said to have been buried alive.

To enter a Ming Dynasty underground burial vault, visitors must line up at **Ding Ling,** the tomb of the 13th Ming Emperor, Wanli, his wife Empress Xiaoduan, and his number-one concubine Xiaojing. Wanli ruled from 1573 to 1620. He had been overseeing the construction of his Underground Palace from the age of 22. When it was completed, he threw a party in the funeral vault, where he was buried 30 years later. Ding Ling was the first imperial tomb ever officially excavated in China, opening in 1958. The 13,000-square-foot Underground Palace, a marble vault divided into five chambers, lies 88 feet below ground. The stairway down is cold and claustrophobic. Each carved archway once contained an ingenuous system of "self-acting stones" that fell into place as locks the first time the door was closed, sealing in the dead.

Ding Ling still contains the white marble throne of the emperor and the large porcelain jars outfitted with sesame oil and wicks to burn eternally underground. In the Burial Chamber are three red coffins—the emperor's in the middle, flanked by those of his wife and concubine. There are also 23 wooden chests filled with jewelry, costumes, cups, silk, jade belts, and gold chopsticks—about 3,000 precious objects, many now on display at the Chang Ling tomb. It was in this emperor's casket that researchers made a rare discovery, a winged crown of gold mesh with coiling dragons and a pearl, the only imperial crown ever excavated in China.

5 The Eastern Qing Tombs

78 miles NE of Beijing

The eastern tombs of the Qing Dynasty (A.D. 1644–1911) far surpass in splendor and majesty their more famous predecessors, the Ming Tombs, but they are seldom visited, owing to their relative remoteness from Beijing. The tombs form a countryside version of the Forbidden City, and are nearly as elaborate. Tastefully restored, this imperial city is vast, grand, and uncrowded.

The Eastern Qing Tombs (**Dong Qing Ling**) are the final resting place of the three rulers who did the most to preserve the historic treasures of Beijing that you see today. Emperor Kangxi (1654–1722), his grandson Emperor Qianlong (1711–1799), and Empress Dowager Cixi (1835–1908), whose lives spanned that of China's last dynasty, are all buried in splendid underground palaces at this site. Also interred in the same royal cemetery, which extends over a mountain valley 21 miles wide, is Emperor Shun Zhi (1638–1661), founder of the Qing Dynasty. While on a hunting trip, he came upon this valley and reserved it for the imperial burial ground. It would become China's largest dynastic cemetery, entombing 5 emperors, 15 empresses, more than 100 concubines, princes, and princesses, and even Emperor Kangxi's teacher. Tomb construction began in 1661 and required 274 years to finish, not ending until the last imperial concubine was interred in 1935, 24 years after the Qing Dynasty itself ended. Altogether, five tombs were built for emperors, four for empresses, five for concubines, and one for a princess. A total of 161 members of the royal family and court were buried here.

The layout of the Eastern Qing Tombs is orderly and traditional, and follows the outlines of the Forbidden City, since this was to be the Imperial Palace of the Afterlife. A long Sacred Way leads to the tomb of the first Qing emperor, and secondary Sacred Ways branch off to the tombs of succeeding emperors. Leading to the first Qing emperor's tomb is a series of gates, courtyards, bridges, and halls. The tomb, at the northern end of the complex, is covered with a circular mound of raised earth (a tumulus). A raised pedestal and tower called a "Square City" fronts this "Precious Citadel." In Chinese cosmology, a square represents the Earth, and a circle the Heavens. The burial chamber beneath the mound, the "Underground Palace," is usually a full palace, built of stone, divided into vaults, and filled with imperial treasures for enjoyment in the next world. At the Eastern Qing Tombs, two of the "Underground Palaces" are open: Emperor Qianlong's and Empress Dowager Cixi's, hers being perhaps the most lavish burial chamber ever built in China.

ESSENTIALS

The Eastern Qing Tombs are a 4-hour drive northeast of Beijing, 47 miles beyond the Beijing Capital Airport, just across the municipal border at the town of Malanyu in Zunhua County, Heibei Province. The most practical way to get there is by hiring a private car or taxi from your hotel or arranging for a special tour with an English-speaking guide and car through **China International Travel Service (CITS),** 28 Jianguomenwai Dajie (☎ **010/6515-8566**). The tombs are open daily from 8:30am to 4:30pm; admission is 35RMB ($4.25). CITS has an office here and can provide English-speaking guides if you arrive independently. The **Qingdong Tombs Guest House** (☎ **0315/694-4061**) is within walking distance and provides barely acceptable overnight accommodations starting at 240RMB ($30) for a double with private bathroom and no amenities.

Location, Location, Location!

Why did the Qing Emperors decide to be buried so far from their home, the Forbidden City in Beijing, when the only way to reach their remote cemetery grounds was by horseback or on foot? In a word, the reason was location. The site of the Eastern Qing Tombs possessed unparalleled, irresistible *feng shui*. By ancient tradition, geomancers were always consulted to determine where best to locate a new building or monument. The chosen ground should have protective natural elements to screen off the threat of evil forces both from the front and the rear. The mountain ranges in this remote valley formed perfect protective screens, blocking the northward flow of evil. A peak to the south would protect the dead from the wind, and hills to the east and west stood guard. Twin rivers embraced the cemetery as well. Although *feng shui* failed to detour grave robbers, many Chinese to this day consider the Eastern Qing Tombs to be in a cosmically fortified location. Locals point out that floods, droughts, and other natural disasters have never visited these tombs in recorded history. Even the 1976 earthquake that leveled Tangshan, 60 miles away, and killed 250,000 in a single blow caused no damage to the tombs. Moreover, it is said that at the Eastern Qing Tombs the rain falls precisely 72 times each year, no more and no less, even in years of severe drought—a phenomenon worthy of the Chinese X-Files.

EXPLORING THE AREA

Running north for 3 miles, the **Sacred Way** is lined with 18 pairs of stone sculptures, splendid renderings of lions, elephants, horses, camels, and unicorns, as well as army generals and court advisors. The path, which royal funeral processions would have followed after the long journey from Beijing, ends at the oldest tomb, **Xiao Ling,** where Shunzhi, first emperor of the Qing Dynasty, is buried. The grounds are vast, encompassing 28 clusters of buildings, but the tomb itself is not open. To the east, about a third of mile away, is **Dong Xiao Ling,** a tomb complex built for Emperor Shunzhi's wife (Empress Xiaohui Zhang) and his 28 concubines.

Jing Ling, the tomb of Emperor Kangxi, also has not been excavated, but it is worth visiting for its magnificent halls. Kangxi's tomb has its own Spirit Way, lined with five pairs of stone sculptures, which curves along a riverbank. This tomb, southeast of the first Qing emperor's tomb, is reached by crossing the 350-foot-long **Five-Arch Bridge,** the grandest of the many stone bridges in the Eastern Qing cemetery. Among the treasures in the sacrificial halls is Emperor Kangxi's ceremonial Dragon Throne.

✪ **Yu Ling,** the tomb of Emperor Qianlong, the longest ruling monarch in Chinese history, has been excavated, and the elaborate Underground Palace is open to visitors. Located 177 feet below ground and consisting of nine elaborately decorated vaults, this palace is divided by a series of marble doors 10 feet thick. The burial chamber contains the sarcophagi of the emperor and five of his consorts. Qianlong also built round earthen mounds at the rear of this complex to entomb his imperial concubines.

✪ **Ding Dong Ling,** the tomb of Empress Dowager Cixi, while not as large as that of Emperor Qianlong, is even more lavish. Her tomb has also been excavated and is open to visitors. Inside the sacrificial hall (Long En Dian) above her Underground Palace, there is today a life-sized waxwork diorama showing the Empress

Dowager as the Goddess of Mercy (*Guanyin*) in a Buddhist robe, crown, and beads, attended by a young woman and her favorite court eunuch. In the underground burial chamber, Cixi's sarcophagus is still in place. She was entombed in it, within a wooden double coffin painted with lacquer and gold powder. In 1928, the warlord Sun Dianying opened this tomb, plundered its treasures, and removed the Empress Dowager's corpse. The body was later retrieved and placed back in the tomb, but most of the imperial treasures buried with the Empress Dowager—including 25,000 pearls, 200 pieces of jade, 80 gems, and a pearl burial quilt 7 inches thick—disappeared with the looters. Nevertheless, many of Cixi's treasures have been rescued and are on display in two galleries at her tomb, including her summer robe, jewels, enamels, and carved ivories. Even the pictures decorating the walls of the pavilions and Underground Palace are lavish, each colored in gold foil, a process using some 300 pounds of the precious metal.

Appendix A: Beijing in Depth

1 Beijing Today

Many a traveler's first impression of Beijing is of a flat, sprawling metropolis, steeped in smog and dust and devoid of Chinese architecture, a city being systematically ripped apart at the seams by an endless procession of construction teams intent on turning an ugly Stalinesque city into a characterless Western-style capital. In fact, Beijing is not among the world's most beautiful capitals, but it is one of the world's most interesting, dynamic, and culturally enriched cities.

Statistics tell one story of modern Beijing, starting with its population: Over 11 million occupy the metropolitan area, including 7 million living within the city limits. This makes Beijing a bit smaller than Shanghai, but the capital still ranks as the 12th largest city in the world. Of Beijing's millions, over 100,000 are foreign-born, many of whom reside in the capital as diplomats, teachers, students, or employees of overseas companies. For foreign residents, Beijing can be brutally expensive. In a recent survey of the 20 most expensive cities in the world in which to live and do business, Beijing ranked third, far ahead of London, Geneva, and New York City.

While Beijing has overnight millionaires, high-ranking politicians, and many of the nation's top academic minds, ordinary Beijingers must be counted as residents of a developing rather than a developed nation. Living space, a slim 140 square feet per person, has not increased appreciably in years, and there is a severe shortage of adequate housing. Per capita income in the capital is barely above $100 a month. Thousands of Beijingers scrimp by on less than the official minimum wage (set at just above 1 U.S. dollar per day), holding either menial jobs or no jobs at all. Beggars congregate at tourist sites, temples, and avenues where visitors are likely to appear (as do postcard and souvenir hawkers). The unemployed, who arrive illegally in Beijing from the countryside in the hope of a better life, can be seen sleeping under bridges. Some find jobs. As many as 100,000 women from the rural areas now work in Beijing as maids (officially called "home helpers").

Nevertheless, Beijing has a definite air of prosperity, and deservedly so after a decade of double-digit economic growth. While 67% of Beijingers commute to work on bikes and 25% by bus, a surprising 17% are rich enough to go to work by car or taxi. And Beijing, the city of the bicycle, is rapidly becoming the city of the automobile. Up to eight million bikes clog the streets of the capital, but cars now number well over one million. The car population has been growing at a steady but dramatic rate of 15% yearly. At the same time, the capacity of the roads has risen no more than 0.4% annually, and there are only enough parking places for one in four Beijing cars and trucks. These figures explain a number of sights travelers invariably see in the streets these days: cars using the bicycle lanes; cars parked on sidewalks (making it almost as slow to walk as to drive); cars turning around by driving on the wrong side of the road; and crosstown taxis requiring over an hour to cover a few miles.

Numbers tell only one story, however. The real flesh and blood tale of Beijing today concerns the pull of two polar opposites: progress and preservation. The future and the past, the modern and the ancient, could not stand in starker contrast than in present-day Beijing. In a frenzy to rebuild itself as a modern capital worthy of a powerful new China in the 21st century, Beijing is a city altering its face as each day passes. Construction sites, smog, traffic jams, and shopping plazas are likely to form more immediate and lasting impressions than hutongs and parks, lakes and temples, or even the grand edifices of the Forbidden City and the Great Wall.

Material progress comes first these days, meaning that preserving the past is one of Beijing's most difficult challenges, especially since many locals view the past with little sentimentality. As narrow lanes and tile-roofed courtyard houses disappear in the wake of new housing projects and expanded road systems, many Beijingers dwell on the necessity of change and the benefits of progress. And the benefits are real enough in this crowded city, where only a few are wealthy and everyday amenities do not begin to match those of Western capitals.

Fortunately, the pendulum is always swinging in Beijing—now back toward preservation. The capital, after all, is China's most visited city precisely because it has a past worth seeing. Wisely, then, on the eve of the millennium (and the 50th anniversary of the founding of the People's Republic), Beijing responded by launching a concerted program of cleanup and restoration. Parkland lakes are to be scoured, waterways are to be banked in stone, many of the city's temples and pagodas are to be refurbished, and Tiananmen Square's humble cement blocks are to be replaced one by one with stately granite. A more direct highway now connects Beijing to the Great Wall, and more sections of the Great Wall have been opened to receive the overflow of visitors.

As Beijing preserves and beautifies its past, it is also rapidly upgrading its tourist services and facilities, which have not always been faultless. Scores of Beijing hotels have now achieved international standards of service. Independent restaurants and bars catering to Westerners are proliferating. Even the nightlife is no longer a joke, with teahouses making a comeback and bars and discos going strong. English-speaking guides can be hired easily for any tourist site. There are Internet cafes and espresso bars, plenty of McDonald's, and even a Hard Rock Cafe. Western fast food, Western brands, Western stores, and Western necessities are widely available—strong hints that Beijing is becoming an international as well as a Chinese capital.

One of modern Beijing's most publicized plagues is its air pollution. Headlines in the West have declared that the air in Beijing is five times filthier than the air in Los Angeles, and that breathing in Beijing for a day is equal to smoking three packs of unfiltered cigarettes. Indeed, some days the pollution is quite visible, and the city, along with the surrounding mountain ranges, is wrapped in a dark, soupy shroud. On the other hand, many a day, particularly in late autumn, is blessed with brilliant blue skies. Moreover, the government is moving on several fronts to reduce the level of the two chief pollutants: coal (for heating and industry) and petroleum (for vehicles). Beijing was the first major city in China to phase out leaded fuel. New cars must be fitted with catalytic converters. Buses that chug up and down Chang'an Avenue, the main east-west thoroughfare through the heart of the city, must now be fueled with natural gas, and police conduct spot checks of tailpipe emissions.

2 Beijing History 101

FROM PEKING MAN TO THE MING DYNASTY

The remains of Beijing's oldest residents, the skulls of **"Peking Man,"** date back as far as 500,000 years, although the caves where China's *homo erectus* once dwelled actually lie more than 30 miles southwest of the city, at Zhoukoudian, where the Peking Man museum is a popular attraction. No evidence of prehistoric settlement in the capital surfaced until 1996, when construction workers unearthed a Stone Age site 20,000 years old just a mile from the Forbidden City.

Historic records first mention a fiefdom existing within modern Beijing's city limits at the beginning of the Western Zhou Dynasty (1100–771 B.C.), but Beijing did not become a major Chinese city until almost 2,000 years later after the Tang Dynasty collapsed. The **Liao Dynasty** (A.D. 916–1125), made up of Khitan invaders from the north, controlled northern China and made Beijing for the first time a regional, if not a national, capital. The Liao was succeeded by the **Jin Dynasty**, which built a new capital on Beijing's outskirts. In turn, **Genghis Khan** and the Mongols overran the Jin rulers, leveling the imperial city. **Kublai Khan** eventually built his own capital, with his imperial palace situated on the shores of Beijing's Beihai Lake, in A.D. 1279, initiating the **Yuan Dynasty** (A.D. 1279–1368). For the first time, Beijing was the capital of a unified China, and it was this city, then known as Khanbaliq or Dadu (Great Capital), that **Marco Polo** visited in the late 13th century.

When the Yuan Dynasty fell to the all-conquering **Ming Dynasty** (A.D. 1368–1644), the imperial capital at Beijing was again razed, rebuilt, and renamed. While almost nothing of the three earlier dynasties that ruled from Beijing remains today, much of the Ming Dynasty capital has survived in glorious condition. **Emperor Yongle** renamed the capital Beijing (Northern

Dateline

- **500,000 B.C.** "Peking Man" occupies caves near present-day Beijing.
- **20,000 B.C.** Early man establishes settlements in what is today downtown Beijing, hunting buffalo and elephants.
- **A.D. 916–1125** The Liao Dynasty establishes its northern capital, Yanjing, at Beijing.
- **1153** The Jin Dynasty establishes its capital, Zhongdu, at Beijing.
- **1275** Marco Polo visits Beijing and later writes the first Western account of the capital.
- **1279–1368** The Yuan Dynasty establishes its capital, Khanbaliq, at Beijing.
- **1402** The Ming Dynasty moves its capital to Beijing and begins building the Forbidden City.
- **1601–1610** Jesuit Father Matteo Ricci lives in Beijing as court mathematician and astronomer. He makes few converts, but sends detailed descriptions of China to Europe.
- **1644–1911** The Qing (Manchu) Dynasty inherits the capital, builds the Summer Palace, extends the Great Wall, and refurbishes the temples and parks.
- **1860** French and English armies reduce the Summer Palace to ruins during the Second Opium War.

continues

- **1900**   Foreigners in Beijing are attacked during the Boxer Rebellion.
- **1903**   The Empress Dowager, Cixi, restores the Summer Palace.
- **1911**   The Qing Dynasty ends and the Republic of China is formed.
- **1919**   Students and others protest China's weakness in the "May Fourth Movement" on Tiananmen Square.
- **1923**   The "last emperor" is evicted from the Forbidden City.
- **1928**   Chiang Kai-shek makes Beijing the capital of the Republic of China.
- **1937–1946**   The Japanese occupy Beijing.
- **1949**   Mao Zedong proclaims the creation of the People's Republic of China.
- **1958–1959**   Tiananmen Square is expanded, the Great Hall of the People is built, the city walls are destroyed, and China's first subway begins to operate in Beijing.
- **1966–1976**   Beijing is effectively closed to foreign visitors during the turmoil of the Cultural Revolution, as many temples and historic sites are damaged by Red Guards.
- **1972**   U.S. President Richard Nixon visits Beijing and the Great Wall, signaling a reopening of China to the West.
- **1976**   Thousands mass on Tiananmen Square to protest the excesses of the Cultural Revolution.
- **1976–1978**   After the death of Chairman Mao and the arrest of the Gang of Four, Deng Xiaoping launches a program of economic reform.

continues

Capital) in A.D. 1403, finished the Forbidden City in 1421, and erected the Drum Tower, the Bell Tower, and the magnificent Temple of Heaven—all of which still grace Beijing. The Ming also saw to the restoration and lengthening of the **Great Wall** near the capital in a futile attempt to keep their dynasty safe from yet more invaders.

THE LAST EMPEROR

The Ming emperors did manage to rule China from the Forbidden City for most of 3 centuries, but the **Manchus,** yet another northern tribe, finally toppled them. The Manchus formed the **Qing Dynasty** (1644–1911), but happily, for a change, did not tear down the old capital and build a new one. As a result, Beijing has been able to preserve many of the imperial monuments and treasures of China dating back over the past 500 years.

The Qing rulers expanded Beijing's *hutong* (alleyway) neighborhoods of gray tile-roofed courtyard houses and undertook building the **Summer Palace** in 1750. The two great emperors of the time, **Kangxi** and his grandson **Qianlong,** each ruled 58 years, and had an enormous impact on Beijing's shape and appearance that lasts to this day. Many items from their royal collections of art and artifacts are still on display in the Forbidden City.

By the 19th century, the Qing Dynasty was waning and Western nations were exacting concessions from China, including the right to live in the capital itself. Foreign delegations, businesses, traders, and missionaries carved out their own special domain in Beijing, known as the **Foreign Legation Quarter,** south of the Forbidden City. In 1900, a native rebel group known as the Brotherhood of Righteous Fists, or **the Boxers,** entered Beijing. As the Qing court stood by, they laid siege to this foreign stronghold for 55 days. Eight Western nations struck back, even setting fire to the Summer Palace. The last of the Qing Dynasty's most powerful rulers, **Cixi,** the Empress Dowager, was blamed for Beijing's humiliation. She rebuilt the Summer Palace as we see it today, but she could not maintain her dynasty's "Mandate of Heaven." The **Republic of China,** founded by **Sun Yat-sen,** toppled the last official imperial dynasty in 1911, and in 1923, the last emperor, **Puyi,** was evicted from the Forbidden City.

In 1928, the **Guomintang Party,** led by **Chiang Kai-shek,** seized Beijing, and made it the capital of the Republic of China, but Japan would soon invade. In 1937, after a valiant battle at the Marco Polo Bridge, Beijing fell and Japan occupied the city until 1945.

With Japan's defeat in World War II, the ruling Guomintang Party and the revolutionary Chinese Communist Party, led by Mao Zedong (who had once worked as a library assistant in Beijing), resumed a civil war that had been brewing for several decades. The communist forces soon triumphed, the Guomintang survivors fled to Taiwan (establishing the Republic of China there), and a new era in China's long history unfolded.

THE CULT OF CHAIRMAN MAO

Chairman Mao Zedong proclaimed the People's Republic of China in Beijing on October 1, 1949. Under Chairman Mao, Beijing received another face-lift. Tiananmen Square was enlarged, the Great Hall of the People was erected, and the Great Wall was opened to tourists. An underground subway system was constructed along the path of the old city wall. Much of the new architecture that took shape in Beijing from 1950 to 1980 bore the stamp of Russia's "socialist realism" school—which translated into large, ugly cement boxes and wide concrete avenues.

Under Chairman Mao, the capital and all of China were rebuilt politically, culturally, and spiritually. The old social ills were removed (prostitution, gambling, and drug addiction disappeared from the streets) and the economy was reorganized along egalitarian and socialist lines, with communes in the countryside and structured work units in the cities, but China remained poor, if more self-sufficient. Beijing and the nation were racked by a series of disastrous political campaigns, beginning with the **Anti-Rightest Movement** (1957), which brought persecution of capitalists and Westward-leaning intellectuals, and the **Great Leap Forward** (1958 to 1960), an attempt to mobilize the populace to create an industrialized society overnight that ended in mass starvation.

These and other political movements culminated in the **Cultural Revolution** (1966 to 1976), in which Chairman Mao's youthful followers, known as the Red Guard, held mass rallies on Tiananmen Square and elsewhere, swore their fervent devotion to Mao and his doctrine of extreme

- **1979** The Democracy Wall Movement ends with arrest of "dissidents" who wrote wall posters in Beijing criticizing Mao and the Cultural Revolution.
- **1978** World's largest KFC (Kentucky Fried Chicken) fast-food outlet opens near Tiananmen Square.
- **1989** Students leading massive pro-democracy demonstrations occupy Tiananmen Square before a forcible eviction, June 3 and 4.
- **1989** Beijing's first successful independent Western bar and grill, Frank's Place, opens its doors.
- **1992** McDonald's opens its first Beijing outlet on Wangfujing Street.
- **1992** The annual Beijing International Jazz Festival debuts.
- **1994** First Internet server in China established at the Chinese Academy of Science in Beijing.
- **1994** Beijing hosts the United Nations' Conference on Women. Beijing's mayor, Chen Xitong, is indicted for official corruption.
- **1997** Beijingers line the streets for the funeral of Deng Xiaoping, who is succeeded as paramount leader by Zhang Zemin.
- **1998** Puccini's *Turandot* is staged in the Forbidden City, while bicycles are banned for the first time on a downtown Beijing street.
- **1998** China celebrates the Golden Anniversary of the founding of the People's Republic (1949–1999) on a newly renovated Tiananmen Square.
- **1998** The fifth official Chinese census since 1953 is launched in Beijing.

and constant revolution, and went on a prolonged rampage, destroying cultural landmarks, closing China's schools, and holding political trials. The whole country was torn apart in the ensuing chaos, many lost their lives or were sent to the countryside for "reeducation" in the doctrines of Mao, and China was sealed off from the outside world.

With Chairman Mao's death in 1976 and the return from disgrace of **Deng Xiaoping**, an economically liberal leader, yet another reversal and a new era began. Beijing was the site of the **Democracy Wall Movement** of 1979, when at the bidding of Deng, the people were encouraged to create wall posters that were critical of political leaders and policies. Deng soon reversed himself as the Democracy Wall Movement blossomed into calls for greater democracy. Eventually similar protests erupted in a far more threatening form in Beijing, with the occupation of **Tiananmen Square** in 1989, and again Deng ousted the pro-democracy opposition. Deng's liberalization was largely economic rather than political. In the late 1980s through the 1990s, the economy of Beijing and much of China underwent an unprecedented boom, and foreign investment, assistance, and tourism reached new heights. What remained of Beijing's cultural and historical legacy was finally protected and enhanced, as modernization altered the post-Revolutionary landscape of the 1950s and 1960s.

3 Chinese Ways & Manners

East is East and West is West, as the old adage goes—but in Beijing the two often meet, mingle, and occasionally collide. As visitors to China and guests of Beijing, travelers should be aware of differing customs and make adjustments accordingly. Of course, as Beijing modernizes, traditional ways are disappearing. Many Beijingers are worldly enough to have been exposed to Western behaviors. English-speaking tour guides, for example, have set answers to "embarrassing" questions that visitors sometimes ask. Uncomfortable topics include China's handling of political dissidents, the status of Tibet and Taiwan, restrictions on the media, abortion, prison labor, and the Tiananmen Square massacre—although many younger Beijingers seem eager to tackle these topics head-on. The problem is that visitors can put their hosts—who may have government jobs—on the hot seat by asking them politically sensitive questions. Feel free to ask the locals about anything—income, children, living conditions, sports, and so on—but remember that even in China's political capital, politics is still taboo, so avoid entering into protracted arguments over political issues.

Recently the government mandated a 5-day workweek. Most Chinese now work Monday through Friday. The workday begins about 9am, sometimes later, which enables thousands of Beijingers to do their morning exercises. The parks fill up with locals performing traditional *tai chi* or *chi gong,* and sometimes even Western ballroom dancing. No one seems to mind being watched, and foreigners sometimes join in, but it is the most quiet and private time of the day. Lunch comes at the noon hour, although most shops no longer close down for afternoon siestas. Dinner is fairly early, usually around 6pm, followed by time spent at home with the family. Saturday and especially Sunday are spent in shopping and enjoying the family in the parks and other attractions.

This typical weekly schedule overlooks a fundamental difference in viewpoints between East and West. The Chinese tend to view the individual as part of greater wholes—of the family, foremost; of the workplace; and of the nation. The group has more power than the individual, and it must be consulted before

In social settings, the Chinese often take great pains to preserve "face," which involves maintaining self-respect while deferring important decisions to those of higher rank within a group. To "lose face" is to suffer embarrassment before others. To be criticized roughly by a visitor, for example, or to be asked to do something that is impossible puts a Chinese person in a dangerous position. "Saving face" is achieved by compromising or sometimes by ignoring a problem altogether. Many Chinese go to extremes to avoid settling a dispute or handling a complaint, since any loss of face could reflect badly on their family and China, as well as on themselves.

What visitors need to do when making requests or issuing complaints in Beijing, then, is to control their tempers, avoid assigning personal blame, seek compromise when possible, and practice patience. A polite approach has a better chance of succeeding than does an aggressive, brutally frank, or simply angry outburst. In a nation renowned for the size and inertia of its bureaucracy, some things are slow to be done, and some things are never done at all. It often helps to ask a person to relay your complaint or demand to a superior, remembering that a response may not be immediate.

decisions are made. In practical terms, this translates into a respect for hierarchies. Those of higher rank within any organization, be it a family or a business, hold the power over others and decide what those of lower rank may do. The individual often has far less autonomy and power in Chinese society than in Western societies—even when it comes to apparently insignificant matters.

In the days of dynasties and eunuchs, China's tiny upper class practiced a number of elaborate courtesies that have all but disappeared from the modern People's Republic. Beijingers are not formal, nor do they have a set of enigmatic social rules that exclude outsiders. The Chinese do not bow (as the Japanese do), and they do not remove their shoes upon entering a house. Beijingers tend to be frank, and they do not as a rule thank others for favors, except by later actions. They shake hands but seldom embrace or kiss in public. They joke, but they do not speak loudly, and they seldom brag about their own accomplishments. Until recently, spitting in public and smoking whenever and wherever one pleased were common habits, but in recent years in Beijing, spitting has become unacceptable and smoking in many public areas has become unlawful.

Beijingers are quite inquisitive and direct, asking some questions that are perfectly acceptable in China, if not in the West. Questions from Beijingers you have just met can include details about your salary and the number of children in your family. You can answer such queries as you see fit, vaguely if you wish.

Among ancient customs that do endure in modern Beijing are the respect for age, which is synonymous with wisdom and stature; the respect for higher education; and the respect for family matters, of more importance than those of work, politics, or world affairs. Among new customs, perhaps the most ubiquitous is an exaggerated respect for money: The millionaire now seems more respected than the scholar, a reversal of 2,000 years of Confucian thought.

While women are equal to men by law and by Communist dogma, they are often considered as they once were in traditional Chinese society: second best to men. Many couples still prefer male children, who alone continue the family line, to females. Even among foreigners, men are often treated with slightly more respect than women, although modern education and the influx of Western ideas have begun to erode such prejudices.

A few other differences in customs are worth noting. The Chinese give their family names first, followed by their personal names, in the reverse order of most Western societies, and it is perfectly proper to refer to Chinese by their last names. Some Beijingers use English first names that they have either chosen or received at school. Despite Beijingers' fascination with the latest Western fashions, it is still advisable for Westerners to dress conservatively and to wear less jewelry than usual, if for no other reason than to avoid broadcasting their wealth to shopkeepers, vendors, touts, and pickpockets. Finally, before snapping a close-up photo of a fascinating Chinese face, ask permission, by pantomime if necessary. Many Beijingers do not want their photographs taken, although they usually give in when asked permission to take a picture of their children—whom the Chinese find as adorable as foreigners do.

4 Beijing in Print & on the Silver Screen

RECOMMENDED BOOKS

Two of the best introductions to modern Beijing (and to modern China) are by former *New York Times* bureau chiefs stationed in the capital. *China: Alive in the Bitter Sea* (1982), Fox Butterfield's classic account of Beijing in the aftermath of the Cultural Revolution, should be compared to the more optimistic vision of *China Wakes: The Struggle for the Soul of a Rising Power,* by Nicholas Kristof and Sheryl Wudunn, written a scant 12 years later. These journalists seem to have covered completely different cities.

Old Beijing comes alive in a number of engrossing memoirs, including *Twilight in the Forbidden City* by Reginald F. Johnston (the Englishman who served as tutor to the last emperor, Puyi, in the Forbidden City, from 1919 to 1924); *Old Madam Yin: A Memoir of Peking Life, 1926–1938* by Ida Pruitt, which gives a Chinese woman's view of life in the capital; and *The Years That Were Fat* by George N. Kates, who immersed herself in the romantic life of Old Peking from 1933 to 1940. More recent events in Beijing are the focus of *The Private Life of Chairman Mao,* a sensational memoir by Li Zhisui, the Great Helmsman's personal physician, and *Legacies: A Chinese Mosaic,* in which Bette Bao Lord weaves together stories of the Cultural Revolution, accounts of diplomatic life in Beijing from 1985 to 1989, and her experiences at Tiananmen Square.

Two engrossing page-turners by Sterling Seagrave paint unforgettable portraits of two of Beijing's most notable personalities: *The Soong Dynasty* is a biography of the Soong sisters, whose lives were intimately entwined with those of Sun Yat-sen and Chiang Kai-Shek. In *Dragon Lady: The Life and Legend of the Last Empress of China,* the myth of the Empress Dowager Cixi as China's Lady Macbeth is convincingly debunked, as is the popular version of the events known as the Boxer Rebellion. The more common but thoroughly Western version of the "Siege of Peking" during the Boxer Rebellion in 1900 is found in *55 Days at Peking* (1963), filled with heroes (Charlton Heston), heroines (Ava Gardner), and histrionics.

RECOMMENDED FILMS

Two of the best films both set and actually filmed in Beijing concern the fall from grace of an opera singer on one hand and an emperor on the other. The world of Beijing opera is rendered with shattering effect in the film *Farewell,*

My Concubine, starring China's best known actress, Gong Li, and directed by Chen Kaige, who has helped place China on the world map of modern cinema. An epic film version of China's last dynasty, filmed on location in the Forbidden City, is Bernardo Bertolucci's *The Last Emperor.* A "director's cut" of this 1987 Oscar-winning film was released in 1998; the extended version runs 219 minutes—well worth an evening's viewing before visiting Beijing. Or, if you are in a grim mood, rent *The Gate of Heavenly Peace,* a controversial but gripping documentary of the Tiananmen Square massacre.

Appendix B:
The Chinese Language

Speaking no Chinese is hardly an obstacle in Beijing these days, particularly if you stick to big hotels, guided tours, Friendship Stores, tourist sites, and restaurants catering to foreigners. But once visitors venture out on their own, hailing taxis, shopping local stores, buying admission tickets, getting lost on the streets, or ordering at an out-of-the-way restaurant, then speaking English—no matter how loudly or clearly—isn't always enough. There are, however, measures a smart traveler can take when confronted with the baffling mysteries of the Chinese language, whether spoken or written.

The Chinese language is ancient, complex, and quite alien to those who know only the languages of the West. In Beijing, nearly everyone speaks the official dialect, called *putonghua* or Mandarin Chinese. This is also the dialect that students throughout China learn to speak in school (where students are now taught English, too, although seldom thoroughly). Beijing natives, about two-thirds of the capital's population, actually prefer to speak the language of the streets, *Beijinghua,* which is a harsher version of standard Chinese. In the capital, at least, if you speak Mandarin, you are understood—but there's the rub, because even the rudiments of Mandarin can be difficult for those grounded in English or European languages. The four tones used in pronouncing each syllable of Mandarin (each generally equivalent to a word or written Chinese character) are crucial to making yourself understood. Chinese is rife with homonyms—words that sound alike except for the tone.

Nevertheless, if travelers have time beforehand, it is fairly easy to learn a handful of useful basic spoken phrases. Correct pronunciation can be learned as you go about in Beijing through careful listening. Since few travelers have time to take a Chinese language course before visiting China, a **Mandarin phrase book,** especially one that has the words and phrases printed in Chinese characters, is essential. The written language is universal in China, regardless of local dialects.

In addition to a phrase book, an essential traveler's companion is a **trilingual map** (in English, Chinese characters, and pinyin) of Beijing. If the map contains Chinese script in addition to English, helpful strangers in the street can consult it and point a wandering traveler in the right direction. Street signs, where they exist, can also be useful if they contain *pinyin* as well as Chinese characters. **Pinyin** is the official transcription of Chinese into an alphabetical form. For example, a sign reading *Tiantanyuan* means Temple of Heaven Park. Street signs often have the name of the street in pinyin followed by the transcription of one of the words for street (such as *dajie*).

It's in the Cards

Another help for travelers who don't speak Chinese are small cards offered at most hotels that have the name of the hotel and the name of your destination printed in Chinese characters. You can show the card to your taxi driver or to others along the way. These cards make getting to and returning from a site, restaurant, or shop quite easy.

The written form of Chinese is even more difficult to learn than the spoken form, since it does not use an alphabetical system. Students must memorize the meaning (and pronunciation) of thousands of written characters, a time-consuming challenge even for native speakers. Travelers must rely again on phrase books, bilingual maps, and hotel staff to unravel these enigmatic signs, although many visitors quickly learn to recognize some of the simpler and more common characters as they travel. It can be particularly useful to be able to recognize the difference between the symbols for male and female when approaching an otherwise unlabeled public toilet.

Probably the most common question asked of travelers in Beijing is "Ni shi cong nar lai de?" or "Where are you from?" The answer is "Wo shi Meiguo lai da" if you're from America. *Meiguo* means America, so if you're from another country, use it instead: *Aodaliya* means Australia, *Jianada* means Canada, *Yingguo* means England, *Faguo* means France, *Deguo* means Germany, *Helan* means Holland, *Aierlan* means Ireland, and *Riben* means Japan. China, by the way, is *Zhongguo* in Chinese.

Even if your pronunciation is poor at first, it's worth making an attempt. Beijingers are not only amused, but impressed, when foreigners make a stab at using Chinese, the language they regard as supreme.

The Chinese Language

English	Pinyin	Chinese
BEIJING	**Beijing**	北京
Ancient Observatory	Guguanxiangtai	古观象台
Chairman Mao Mausoleum	Mao Zhuxi Jiniantang	毛主席纪念堂
Forbidden City	Gugong	故宫
Lama Temple	Yonghegong	雍和宫
Old Summer Palace	Yuanmingyuan	圆明园
Summer Palace	Yiheyuan	颐和园
Temple of Heaven	Tiantan Gongyuan	天坛公园
Tiananmen Square	Tiananmen Guangchang	天安门广场

English	Pinyin	Chinese

Useful Phrases

English	Pinyin	Chinese
Hello	Ni hao	你好
How are you?	Ni hao ma?	你好吗？
Good	Hen hao	很好
Bad	Bu hao	不好
I don't want	Wo bu yao	我不要
Good bye	Zai jian	再见
Thank you	Xie xie	谢谢
Yes	Dui	对
No	Bu dui	不对
How's it going?	Ni chi le ma?	你吃了吗？
When?	Shenme shihou?	什么时候？
Excuse me, I'm sorry	Dui bu qi	对不起
How much does it cost?	Duoshao qian?	多少钱？
Too expensive	Tai guile	太贵了
It's broken	Huaile	坏了
May I take a look?	Wo neng bu neng kan yi kan?	我能不能看一看？
Do you speak English?	Ni shuo Yingwen ma?	你说英文吗？
What's your name?	Ni gui xing?	你贵姓？
My name is ____	Wo xing ____	我姓 ____
I'm lost	Wo milu le	我迷路了
I don't smoke	Wo bu chouyan	我不抽烟
I'm ill	Wo shengbing le	我生病了
Bill please!	Qing jiezhang!	请结帐！
I am vegetarian	Wo shi chisude	我是吃素的
Can I take a photograph?	Wo keyi zhao ge xiang ma?	我可以照个相吗？
I can't speak Chinese	Wo buhui shuo Zhongwen	我不会说中文
I don't understand	Wo ting bu dong	我听不懂
It doesn't matter	Mei guanxi	没关系
No problem	Mei wenti	没问题
Where are you from?	Ni shi cong nar lai de?	你是从哪来的？
I am from	Wo shi cong ____ lai de	我是从 ____ 来的
America	Meiguo	美国
Australia	Aodaliya	澳大利亚

English	Pinyin	Chinese
Canada	Jianada	加拿大
England	Yingguo	英国
France	Faguo	法国
Germany	Deguo	德国
Holland	Helan	荷兰
Ireland	Aierlan	爱尔兰
Japan	Riben	日本
Do you have a ____?	Ni you mei you ____?	你有没有 ____？
Do you know ____?	Ni zhi bu zhidao? ____	你知不知道__？
What do you call this?	Zhe jiao shenme?	这叫什么？
I want to go to ____	Wo xiang qu ____	我想去 ____
Where is ____?	____ zai nar?	____ 在哪儿？
I want ____	Wo yao ____	我要 ____
Airport	feji chang	飞机场
Bank	yinhang	银行
Beer	pijiu	啤酒
Bicycle	zixingche	自行车
Boiled water	kai shui	开水
Bus	gonggong qiche	公共汽车
Bus station	qiche zong zhan	汽车总站
Chinese "dollar" or renminbi	yuan or kuai	元，块
CITS	lüxingshe	旅行社
Credit card	xinyong ka	信用卡
Hot water	re shui	热水
Hotel	binguan, dajiudian, fandian	宾馆，大酒店，饭店
Map	ditu	地图
Mineral water	kuangquanshui	矿泉水
Passport	huzhao	护照
Police!	Jingcha!	警察！
Restaurant	fanguan	饭馆
Soft drink	qishui	汽水
Taxi	chuzu qiche	出租汽车
Telephone	dianhua	电话
Toilet	cesuo	厕所
Toilet paper	weisheng zhi	卫生纸
Train	huoche	火车
Train station	huoche zhan	火车站

English	Pinyin	Chinese
Zero	ling	零
One	yi	一
Two	er	二
Three	san	三
Four	si	四
Five	wu	五
Six	liu	六
Seven	qi	七
Eight	ba	八
Nine	jiu	九
Ten	shi	十
Eleven	shi yi	十一
Twelve	shi er	十二
Fifteen	shi wu	十五
Twenty	er shi	二十
Twenty-one	er shi yi (and so on)	二十一
Thirty	san shi	三十
Thirty-one	san shi yi (and so on)	三十一
One hundred	yi bai	一百
Two hundred	er bai	二百
Three hundred	san bai	三百
Four hundred	si bai	四百
One thousand	yi qian	一千
Two thousand	er qian	二千

Days of the Week

Sunday	Xingqitian	星期天
Monday	Xingqiyi	星期一
Tuesday	Xingqier	星期二
Wednesday	Xingqisan	星期三
Thursday	Xingqisi	星期四
Friday	Xingqiwu	星期五
Saturday	Xingqiliu	星期六
Yesterday	zuotian	昨天
Today	jintian	今天
Tomorrow	mingtian	明天

Appendix C: Chinese Translations— Accommodations, Dining & Attractions

Below are Chinese translations of the establishments and attractions listed on the "Beijing Accommodations" map in chapter 4, the "Beijing Dining" map in chapter 5, the "Beijing Attractions" map in chapter 6, and the "Side Trips from Beijing" map in chapter 10.

BEIJING ACCOMMODATIONS
See map on pp. 52-53

Beijing Continental Grand Hotel
五洲大酒店

Beijing Hilton Hotel
希尔顿酒店

Beijing Hotel
北京饭店

Beijing International Club Hotel
北京国际俱乐部饭店

Beijing International Hotel
国际饭店

Beijing New Century Hotel
新世纪饭店

Beijing Song He Hotel
松鹤大酒店

Capital Hotel
首都宾馆

China World Hotel
中国大饭店

China Travel Service Tower
中旅大厦

Exhibition Centre Hotel
北展饭店

Friendship Hotel
友谊宾馆

Gloria Plaza Hotel
凯莱酒店

Grand Hotel
贵宾楼饭店

Grand View Garden Hotel
北京大观园酒店

Great Wall Sheraton
长城饭店

Harbour Plaza
北京海逸酒店

Holiday Inn Crowne Plaza
皇冠假日饭店

Holiday Inn Downtown
金都假日饭店

Holiday Inn Lido
丽都饭店

Hotel New Otani Chang Fu Gong
长富宫饭店

Jianguo Hotel
建国饭店

Jing Guang New World Hotel
京广新世界饭店

Jinghua Hotel
京华饭店

Jinglun Hotel
京伦饭店

Kempinski Hotel
凯宾斯基酒店

Kerry Centre Hotel
嘉里中心饭店

Kunlun Hotel
昆仑饭店

Landmark Hotel
亮马河饭店

New World Courtyard Beijing
新世界万怡

The Palace Hotel
王府饭店

Peace Hotel
和平宾馆

Prime Hotel
华侨大厦

Qiaoyuan Hotel
侨园饭店

Radisson SAS Hotel
北京皇家大酒店

Scitech Hotel
赛特饭店

Shangri-La Beijing Hotel
香格里拉饭店

Swissotel
港澳中心

Tianlun Dynasty Hotel
天伦王朝饭店

Traders Hotel Beijing
国贸饭店

Wangfujing Grand Hotel
王府井大饭店

Xiyuan Hotel
西苑饭店

BEIJING DINING
See map on pp. 82-83.

American Chili's Grill
旗利餐厅

Annie's Cafe
阿密咖啡

Aria
(in the China World Hotel)
（中国大饭店内）

Ashanti
阿仙蒂餐厅

Baikal
贝加尔西餐厅

Bavaria Bierstube
巴巴利亚德餐

Beijing Express
(in the Beijing New Century Hotel)
（新世纪饭店内）

Berena's
柏瑞娜

Bleu Marine
兰玛利

Borom Piman
泰国餐厅

Cafe Renaissance
(in the Jing Guang New World
Hotel)
（京广新世界饭店内）

Carousel Revolving Restaurant
(in the Xiyuan Hotel)
（西苑饭店内）

The Courtyard
四合院

Danieli's
(in the Beijing International Club
Hotel)
（北京国际俱乐部饭店内）

Fangshan Imperial
仿膳饭店

Fortune Garden
越秀厅

Four Seasons
四季厅

Gold Cat Jiaozi City
金猫饺子城

Gongdelin
功德林素菜馆

Gourmet Corner
(in the China World Trade Center)
(中国国际贸易中心内)

Green Tian Shi
绿色天食

Haagen-Dazs
哈根达斯

Hard Rock Cafe
硬石餐厅

Henry J. Bean's
(in the China World Trade Center)
(中国国际贸易中心内)

Hong Kong Food City
香港美食城

Jinghua Shiyuan
京华食苑

Jinyang Fanzhuang
晋阳饭庄

John Bull Pub
尊龙酒吧

Johnny's Coffee
真的咖啡

Justine's
建国西餐厅

Kebab Kafe
连衣餐厅

Lao Shanghai
老上海

Laxen Oxen
北欧扒房

Li Family
厉家菜

Louisiana
路易斯安娜

Metro Cafe
意大利咖啡店

Mexican Wave
墨西哥风味餐厅

Nadaman
滩万

Nishimura
(in the Shangri-La Beijing Hotel)
西村
(香格里拉饭店内)

Omar Khayyam
味美佳餐厅/澳马克亚姆餐厅

Paulaner Brauhaus
普拉那啤酒坊

Plaza Grill
(in the Holiday Inn Crowne Plaza)
(皇冠假日饭店内)

Quanjude Hepingmen
和平门全聚德烤鸭店

Quanjude Kaoyadian
全聚德烤鸭店

Red Basil
紫天椒泰式餐厅

Ritan Park
日坛饭庄

Roma Ristorante
罗马西餐厅

Sampan
(in the Gloria Plaza Hotel)
(凯莱饭店内)

San Si Lang
三四郎餐厅

Schlotzsky's Deli
斯乐斯基餐厅

Shamiana
香味朗印度餐厅

Shanghai Cuisine
上海菜

Shanghai Moon
夜上海

Sichuan Fandian
四川饭店

Sihexuan
四合轩

Spageddie's
时得利餐厅

Summer Palace
颐和园

Texan Bar & Grill
德克萨斯扒房

T.G.I. Fridays
星期五餐厅

Trattoria La Gondola
(in the Kempinski Hotel)
北京燕莎中心

Uncle Afanti
阿凡提大叔

Windows on the World
世界之窗

Yihe Yaju
义和雅居

BEIJING ATTRACTIONS
See map on pp. 108-9.

Ancient Observatory
古观象台

Beihai Park
北海公园

Beijing Amusement Park
北京游乐园

Beijing Art Museum
北京艺术博物馆

Beijing Zoo
北京动物园

Bell Tower
钟楼

Big Bell Temple and Museum
大钟寺古钟博物馆

Blue Zoo Aquarium
富国海底世界

China Art Gallery
中国美术馆

Chongwenmen Protestant Church
崇文门基督教堂

CITS (Jianguomenwai branch)
中国国际旅行社（建国门外分社）

CITS (Fuxingmennei branch)
中国国际旅行社总社

Confucius Park
孔庙

Ditan Park
地坛公园

Donghuamen Yeshi (Night Market)
东华门夜市

Dongsi Mosque
东四清真寺

Drum Tower
鼓楼

East Cathedral
(Church of St. Joseph)
东堂（圣约瑟夫教堂）

Five-Pagoda Temple
五塔寺

The Forbidden City
紫禁城

Friendship Store
友谊商店

Grand View Park
大观园

Great Hall of the People
人民大会堂

Guanghua Temple
广化寺

Huifeng Temple
汇丰祠

Jingshan Park
景山公园

Lama Temple
雍和宫

Lao She Teahouse
老舍茶馆

Liulichang Culture and Antique
Street
琉璃厂文化街

Lu Xun Museum
鲁迅博物馆

Mao Zedong Mausoleum
毛主席纪念堂

Monument to the People's Heroes
人民英雄纪念碑

Museums of Chinese History and
the Chinese Revolution
中国历史博物馆/中国革命博物馆

Natural History Museum
自然历史博物馆

North Cathedral
西什库教堂（北堂）

Oriental Plaza
东方广场

Ox Street Mosque
牛街礼拜寺

Panjiayuan (Sunday Market)
潘家园周日市场

Prince Gong's Mansion
恭王府

Qianmen (Front Gate)
前门

Ritan Park
日坛公园

Sanwei Bookstore
三味书屋

Silk Alley Market
秀水东街市场

Soong Qing-Ling Residence
宋庆龄故居

South Cathedral
西什库教堂（南堂）

Temple of Heaven (Tiantan Park)
天坛公园

Tiananmen Square
天安门广场

Tian Hai Teahouse
天海茶屋

Tian Qiao Happy Teahouse
天桥乐茶园

Tuanjiehu Manmade Seashore
团结潮人造海滩

Universal Studios
环球影城

Wanshou Temple
万寿寺

White Cloud Temple
白云寺

White Pagoda Temple
白塔寺

White Pagoda (Beihai Park)
白塔（北海公园）

Yabaolu (Russian Market)
雅宝路（俄罗斯市场）

Yuyuantan Water World
玉渊潭水上公园

SIDE TRIPS FROM BEIJING

See map on pp. 182-83.

Beijing Capital Airport
首都国际机场

Eastern Qing Tombs
清东陵

Great Wall at Badaling
八达岭长城

Great Wall at Juyongguan
居庸关长城

Great Wall at Mutianyu
幕田峪长城

Great Wall at Simatai
司马台长城

Ming Tombs
明十三陵

Movenpick Hotel
国都茂盛宾饭店

Peking Man Site (Zhoukoudian)
周口店猿人遗址

Summer Palace
颐和园

Western Hills (Fragrant Hills Park)
香山公园

World Park
世界公园

Chinese Translations

Index

See also Accommodations and Restaurant indexes, below.

ACCOMMODATIONS

RESTAURANTS

FROMMER'S® COMPLETE TRAVEL GUIDES

Alaska
Amsterdam
Arizona
Atlanta
Australia
Austria
Bahamas
Barcelona, Madrid & Seville
Beijing
Belgium, Holland & Luxembourg
Bermuda
Boston
Budapest & the Best of Hungary
California
Canada
Cancún, Cozumel &
the Yucatán
Cape Cod, Nantucket & Martha's Vineyard
Caribbean
Caribbean Cruises & Ports of Call
Caribbean Ports of Call
Carolinas & Georgia
Chicago
China
Colorado
Costa Rica
Denmark
Denver, Boulder & Colorado Springs
England
Europe
Florida
France
Germany
Greece
Greek Islands
Hawaii
Hong Kong
Honolulu, Waikiki & Oahu
Ireland
Israel
Italy
Jamaica & Barbados
Japan
Las Vegas
London
Los Angeles
Maryland & Delaware
Maui
Mexico
Miami & the Keys

Montana & Wyoming
Montréal & Québec City
Munich & the Bavarian Alps
Nashville & Memphis
Nepal
New England
New Mexico
New Orleans
New York City
Nova Scotia, New Brunswick &
Prince Edward Island
Oregon
Paris
Philadelphia & the
Amish Country
Portugal
Prague & the Best of the Czech Republic
Provence & the Riviera
Puerto Rico
Rome
San Antonio & Austin
San Diego
San Francisco
Santa Fe, Taos &
Albuquerque
Scandinavia
Scotland
Seattle & Portland
Singapore & Malaysia
South Africa
Southeast Asia
South Pacific
Spain
Sweden
Switzerland
Thailand
Tokyo
Toronto
Tuscany & Umbria
USA
Utah
Vancouver & Victoria
Vermont, New Hampshire
& Maine
Vienna & the Danube Valley
Virgin Islands
Virginia
Walt Disney World & Orlando
Washington, D.C.
Washington State

FROMMER'S® DOLLAR-A-DAY GUIDES

Australia from $50 a Day
California from $60 a Day
Caribbean from $70 a Day
England from $70 a Day
Europe from $60 a Day
Florida from $60 a Day

Hawaii from $70 a Day
Ireland from $50 a Day
Israel from $45 a Day
Italy from $70 a Day
London from $85 a Day
New York from $80 a Day

New Zealand from $50 a Day
Paris from $85 a Day
San Francisco from $60 a Day
Washington, D.C.,
  from $60 a Day

FROMMER'S® PORTABLE GUIDES

Acapulco, Ixtapa & Zihu-
  atanejo
Alaska Cruises & Ports of Call
Bahamas
Baja & Los Cabos
Berlin
California Wine Country
Charleston & Savannah
Chicago

Dublin
Hawaii: The Big Island
Las Vegas
London
Maine Coast
Maui
New Orleans
New York City
Paris

Puerto Vallarta, Manzanillo
  & Guadalajara
San Diego
San Francisco
Sydney
Tampa & St. Petersburg
Venice
Washington, D.C.

FROMMER'S® NATIONAL PARK GUIDES

Family Vacations in the
  National Parks
Grand Canyon

National Parks of the American West
Rocky Mountain

Yellowstone & Grand Teton
Yosemite & Sequoia/
  Kings Canyon
Zion & Bryce Canyon

FROMMER'S® GREAT OUTDOOR GUIDES

New England
Northern California

Southern California & Baja
Washington & Oregon

FROMMER'S® MEMORABLE WALKS

Chicago
London

New York
Paris

San Francisco
Washington D.C.

FROMMER'S® IRREVERENT GUIDES

Amsterdam
Boston
Chicago
Las Vegas

London
Los Angeles
Manhattan

New Orleans
Paris
San Francisco

Seattle & Portland
Vancouver
Walt Disney World
Washington, D.C.

FROMMER'S® BEST-LOVED DRIVING TOURS

America
Britain
California

Florida
France
Germany

Ireland
Italy
New England

Scotland
Spain
Western Europe

WHEREVER YOU TRAVEL, *H*ELP IS NEVER FAR AWAY.

From planning your trip to providing travel assistance along the way, American Express® Travel Service Offices are always there to help you do more.

Beijing

China International Travel Service (R)
Rm. 417/F Cits Bldg.
103 Fuxingmennei Ave.
(86) 1066071575

do more AMERICAN EXPRESS
Travel
www.americanexpress.com/travel

American Express Travel Service Offices are found in central locations throughout Beijing.